Every Child a Wanted Child

every child
a wanted child

Clarence James Gamble, M.D.

and his Work in the

Birth Control Movement

DOONE AND GREER WILLIAMS

EDITED BY Emily P. Flint

Distributed by Harvard University Press for
The Francis A. Countway Library of Medicine
Boston : 1978

The Countway Library Associates
Historical Publication Number 4

Library of Congress Catalog Number: 77-90104
ISBN 0-674-27025-8

Contents

Foreword

My father's interest in birth control began in 1924 when he first met Dr. Robert L. Dickinson, the leading physician in the field of contraception, who urged him to "take up the work." From the earliest days that I can remember, his professional life was devoted exclusively to "The Great Cause." He believed that there was no way a physician could do more for the health and happiness of women, and, in fact, of all people, than by making it possible to plan and space children.

The goals of his birth control work were three-fold: to make birth control services available to all people; to persuade leaders that birth control, or family planning as we call it today, should be part of every health system; and to develop safe, simple and inexpensive contraceptives.

My childhood recollections of my father's work in the United States is hazy. I remember warmly some of the wonderful people he worked with—Margaret Sanger, Robert Dickinson, Edna McKinnon and Phyllis Page, to name but a few. I recall his joy when things went well and his disappointment when opportunities, as he perceived them, were lost. Though my understanding of the substance of his work was limited, I clearly remember his burning desire to make it possible for every child to be a wanted child.

In 1953, upon my discharge from the Army, it was my privilege to become a partner in his work, sometimes closely associated, sometimes only by telephone, by mail or through the occasional visit. Though we did not always agree on the best way to approach problems or the best use of the resources available, I always had the satisfaction of knowing we shared the same goals. I was with him on his first and last international trips. The story of his first, his 1952–53 visit to Japan, India, and other countries in Asia is told in the text. In 1966 when he visited me in Nigeria, his dedication, his joys and his disappointments were once again demonstrated. Though civil strife was breaking out he insisted on making what might have been a dangerous drive to attend a population conference in Ibadan. On his return to Lagos, he persuaded the Minister of Health, a gynecologist, to let him help introduce family planning into the Lagos Maternity Hospital where there were 30,000 deliveries annually. It would have been a step many years ahead of its time in Africa. The next morning the Army moved to quell the unrest. Following a quick and peaceful coup, the civilian cabinet was dissolved and the Minister was no longer in office.

The Pathfinder Fund was established by my father in 1957, and following his death in 1966, has continued to carry on his work. In the eleven years since his death a greater understanding of the relationship between the health and happiness of families and appropriate child-spacing, coupled with a growing concern with respect to the imbalance between the world's population and its resources, stimulated popular interest in birth control. Increased sums of money, from both the public and private sectors, became available for family planning programs. These greater resources have made it possible for Pathfinder, along with other organizations concerned with population issues, to grow substantially. The Pathfinder Fund, now located in Chestnut Hill, Massachusetts, a Boston suburb, became a public foundation in 1970. Today it has a headquarters staff of 25, five overseas offices, and an annual budget of $4,000,000, drawing its funds from private philanthropy and an annual grant from the United States Government under the Foreign Assistance Act. I was elected its full-time Executive Director in 1971, shortly after my return from Nigeria.

My father might not recognize the field of family planning today. So much has changed. In most countries it is no longer a question of *whether* to offer family planning services but *how* to do it so that as many people as possible can be reached effectively and efficiently. Increasing numbers of people are concerned about population size and growth. It may not be enough for every child to be a wanted child. The tradition for many people has been to *want* many children, but unless the average couple has only two children continued population growth may preclude successful economic development and make impossible an improved quality of life, both in the United States and in other countries. Unless people, women in particular, can achieve happiness in ways other than having many children, excessive birth rates may well continue to be the norm. Women must be able to find fulfillment and satisfaction in roles other than being mothers of large families.

The Pathfinder Fund also has changed—in response to the changing needs. Though must of our work still promotes the availability of birth control services, our goals have become broader. We assist programs that help leaders understand the consequences of excessive rates of population growth so they can subsequently develop policies which directly or indirectly may lead to lower birth rates. Pathfinder's Women's Programs Division has been set up to stimulate those changes in the status and role of women that will eventually lead to a wider range of roles as alternatives to the exclusively maternal, a process which is underway but hardly complete in the United States and which has barely begun in many countries.

The full extent of my father's work will never be known, but the writing of "Every Child a Wanted Child" has enabled even those closest to him to learn a great deal more. Thanks are due to many people for making it possible. My mother discussed the possibility of the book with her children shortly after his death. Without her initiative and persistence it never would have been written. Emily Flint encouraged, guided and assisted the family from the time the biography was a mere gleam in our collective eye through the final printing. She has been most generous with the use of her professional time in editing the book. Greer and Doone Williams, after talking to many people, reading much of my father's voluminous correspondence, and doing a great deal of research, have brought to life a man they never met. Richard Wolfe, Curator of Rare Books and Manuscripts at Harvard Medical School's Countway Library, has not only made it possible for my father's papers and those of other birth control pioneers to be in the Library, but has also been instrumental in the book's publication. Finally, great thanks are due to all those who, having been a part of my father's life, gave so generously of their time in talking to Greer and Doone Williams so that the whole could be put together from many parts.

Richard B. Gamble
Chestnut Hill, Massachusetts
September 1977

Introduction

The contributions of Dr. Clarence James Gamble to population planning were essentially twofold: (1) As a missionary "spreading the good news" of family planning and often the first to "get something started" in many parts of the world. (2) As a tireless experimentalist in search of a good contraceptive that the poor could afford to use. In sum, his objective was to show men and women the means of making conscious choices in determining the outcome of the sex act. In five trips around the world, Dr. Gamble missed no opportunity to make contraception both medically respectable and a dinner-table topic, accepting the risk that he might offend people, as he sometimes did.

Dr. Gamble was unusual in a number of ways. Born rich, he had the rare opportunity to answer for himself the question that so many dreamers ask themselves: "What would you do if you had a million dollars?" Recipient of his first million on his twenty-first birthday, and later many more as an heir to a fraction of the Procter & Gamble Company billions, Clarence Gamble invested himself and a substantial portion of his wealth in birth control.

Money, plus the natural endowments and scholastic aptitude of a man who graduated first in his class at Princeton (1914) and second in his class at Harvard Medical School (1920), gave Clarence Gamble security and independence. This position vis-a-vis life offered distinct advantages and some unsuspected disadvantages. He shared, as befitting his generation, in the local-boy-makes-good syndrome, but, being denied self-generated earning power as a measure of success, he had more than the average man's difficulty in fulfilling the universal human need for the validation of one's work by society. He felt deeply that the privileges of education and wealth should be put to use to help those less privileged. The rendering of such service was to him a genuine obligation, as is witnessed to by the career choices and life styles of all five of his children. Not having to meet the challenge of economic survival, he looked on life as a different kind of contest: he continually followed a pattern of seeking risks and setting up obstacles to be overcome. They were sometimes needless hazards and he did not always overcome them, but he seemed compelled to test himself, he was often frustrated, yet he never stopped trying.

A conventional Republican and expert in the conservation and management of his own estate, he expressed little discontent with his country's economic system or political philosophy. Nevertheless, in his career as a physician and birth controller he was constantly at odds with the Establishment; perhaps he harbored a compulsion to defy authority figures, but it would be equally valid to speculate that, being able to afford it, he was in a unique position to pursue the course he thought best. Since this course was almost always the shortest and most direct distance between two points, he was anathema to the ponderous processes and ritualisms of organizations.

He did his own thing at some cost, although a cost he concealed in his intense desire for privacy. While Dr. Gamble achieved somewhat better than average life expectancy for white American males (he died at the age of seventy-two), he underwent an astounding variety of illnesses and injuries, requiring hospitalization some two dozen times. He suffered seven fractures and countless infections. A peptic ulcer gnawed at his duodenum for thirty years; angina pectoris clutched at his chest for twenty; leukemia bested him in his last two.

As an advocate of family planning, through the wise choice of Sarah Merry Bradley as his wife, he made his five children a model of a "real family"; friends not only of the parents but also of the children often marveled at the Gambles of Milton. Dr. Gamble's family was his island. Home was both a stage on which he was the leading man and an audience that he entertained with good news and amusing accounts of his many sorties against an often unfriendly and uncomprehending world.

Acquaintances viewed Clarence Gamble as a "frail person." Five feet seven inches in height and normally weighing one hundred thirty-five pounds, he had two striking features; his brown eyes, as sharp and bright as a fox's, and a characteristic smile, sunny when he was a boy but, as a Korean doctor remarked, a "not so big one" in his later years. His classmates at Occidental Academy in Pasadena called him "Percy bright eyes." His brown hair turned to gray in his early forties; he wore a small mustache, glasses, and, in later life, a hearing aid.

Sarah Gamble and the children loyally defended him against his many critics, but the world of birth controllers saw him as a sharply two-sided personality, impulsively generous and kind in support of activities that he regarded as important but independent toward all else. He was frequently—and on occasion outrageously—unsympathetic, unperceptive, and unaccommodating to the other fellow's viewpoint—a characteristic, however, pandemic among his fellow birth controllers. He dealt with national and international birth control organizations for thirty-seven years (1929–1966), but he never was an organization man and never understood the dynamics of organizational process; he was locked in conflict with their officers, who complained that he nagged and pestered them to distraction. Superficially polite and even-tempered, although sometimes angry and tense, he tended to be abrasive and inarticulate in his efforts to develop warm, human relationships with these strangers. His family and close friends knew he had a sense of humor and saw his joy in his children, his shy warmth and thoughtfulness for those he loved. In early life he was afraid that others loved his money rather than himself. If it struck some of his colleagues in birth control that he did not care what they thought of him, they may have been wrong; from time to time, he asked Sarah why they disliked him. The fact that he did not understand, of course, suggested why. He chided his colleagues with putting the needs of organizations before the needs of women—especially the poor women they purportedly existed to serve.

Yet, when Clarence Gamble left the battlefield, the leaders whom he provoked and irritated came around to his ideas and modes of action sooner or later—sometimes much later. Perhaps this is a hallmark of a true pioneer. In the principles that he preached, he was less the originator than the applicator. He was quick to act. In the introduction of birth control in out-of-the-way places and the staging of field trials of contraceptive techniques, he often moved ahead of the large, respectable birth control organizations, not only in his early testing of spermicidal jellies and condoms but in his acceptance of new methods—oral contraceptive pills and intrauterine devices (IUD's). In the course of time he became totally obsessed with what he called "the Great Cause" and "my monomania." When he found himself at cross-purposes with natural allies who shared his commitment, he rationalized the difficulty by pointing out: "Birth controllers, being nonconformists, don't get along well with one another."

Overshadowing this truth was the larger fact that the pioneers of birth control did not get on well with any Establishment—the Church, government, police, business and industry, medical profession, foundations, or universities. In this realm, Dr. Gamble had touched all the right bases—family, fortune, religion, and education—but then deliberately chose an unpopular career. Ironically, when the public and indeed the world had embraced the Great Cause and he asked, in small ways, to be recognized for his knowledge and experience rather than his money, birth control organizations denied him recognition and he remained unpopular with them to the end. Yet he had both recognition and respect from the two figures of greatest importance in the movement, Margaret Sanger and Dr. Robert Latou Dickinson.

Among laymen, Margaret Sanger (1879–1966) is the one family planner who is universally remembered. Several biographies have been written about this dynamic, attractive, timeless heroine who introduced the term "birth control" and the slogan, "Every child a wanted child." Mrs. Sanger began in New York City as a nurse, a feminist, and a Socialist. She challenged the Irish Catholic policemen who came to close the birth control clinics that she opened and to put her in jail for writing and lecturing on contraceptive methods.

Among physicians in family planning, the leading figure of the early part of the century was Dr. Robert Latou Dickinson (1861–1950), a New York gynecologist and the first American sexologist. Dickinson quietly accepted the disdain of his profession in his efforts to convince it of the need for medical interest, research, and training in contraception, the only approved method then being the vaginal diaphragm of rubber laced with spermicidal jelly. The prudent general practitioner, in contrast, avoided any show of concern about sex in his women patients and would not think of examining the vagina for the repair and healing of nature's insults, lest fathers or husbands accuse him of concupiscent designs. Dickinson held that social condemnation of the possibility that the female, too, might find pleasure in sex was the predominant cause of mental strains and social maladjustments in women. He attacked the belief that it was a wife's duty to submit to her husband's lust whenever the man willed. This gentle scholar had an aphoristic way of writing, as when he said, "Birth control is simply self-control under various aliases."

Dr. Gamble became interested in the subject of conjugal relations, including contraception, in anticipation of his marriage in 1924. It struck him as logical that a young man going into a new field should read up on it. This interest led him to Dr. Dickinson, who advised him to plan and space his children, and made an effort to recruit him into the Great Cause: "Young men like you, who are also independent, ought to take up the work." The average practitioner dependent on community good will for his patients and his income feared to risk unpopularity. Drs. Stuart and Emily Mudd of Philadelphia, who became longtime friends of the Gambles, accelerated his interest when in 1929 they invited Clarence to head a maternal health group in Philadelphia and help them develop birth control clinics.

Both Mrs. Sanger and Dr. Dickinson took Dr. Gamble's side in his conflicts with birth control organizations, well knowing that pioneers may be seen by even their own kind as social misfits or troublemakers. They came to consider Gamble a kindred spirit and an important worker in their field. Dickinson ranked Clarence Gamble second only to Margaret Sanger as an initiator of programs, although some leaders of organizations did not agree. These organizations included the American Birth Control League, Birth Control Federation of America, Planned Parenthood Federation of America, International Planned Parenthood Federation, Population Reference Bureau, and the Population Council, a rather imposing list surely confirming the fact that Gamble was not a good joiner. Indeed, he accepted most encounters with organizations as occasions for insistence that they do things differently—that is, *his* way. He had in abundance convictions and the courage of his convictions; but he was inept in explaining the reasons for his convictions, or perhaps he simply felt it was a waste of time.

He won the acceptance of a small, select in-group as a private philanthropist, a lone prospector, and *agent provocateur* in the search for a good contraceptive and health and happiness for all the mothers in the world, as he liked to say. This makes him not only a subject for off-beat biographic scrutiny but also an appropriate vehicle for study of the birth control movement as medical social history.

Not destined to be hailed as a leader of men or even a defender of motherhood, Clarence Gamble saw it as his task to set an example for the organizational Goliaths. In the face of their insults and rebuffs, he remained cheerful, optimistic, and persevering, sometimes secretly hurt but always coming back for more. No David ever felt more challenged. In this role, he found his *joie de vivre.*

part 1   young man in search of himself

1 Boyhood Through Princeton

The most unusual fact about Clarence Gamble was that he was born rich and at no time in life had to work for a living. He hated this distinction, but he bore it bravely, his private cross. His grandfather, James (1803–1891), was cofounder of the fabulously profitable Procter & Gamble Company in Cincinnati; his father, David, as secretary-treasurer, was the last of the Gambles to play an operating role in the company. His mother, Mary Huggins, was the daughter of a poorly paid Presbyterian minister. Clarence was close to his parents and often expressed his gratitude to them.

From the start, Gamble saw that his good fortune set him apart from his peers. Much later, a young anthropologist who was a staff member of Dr. Gamble's Pathfinder Fund, shrewdly observed: "He was not comfortable with money."

This discomfort was made bearable by his commitment to philanthropy. In his boyhood first in Cincinnati and then Pasadena, Clarence Gamble was raised in the tradition of Christian charity and modesty. His parents taught him to despise

conspicuous consumption. The Gambles gave to religion, education, and hospitals, and especially to Christian foreign missions,
in those days a fashionable charity among wealthy Protestants
still confident they could save the world. One condition of David
Gamble's gift to his son was that he not expend capital. Another
was that he allocate ten percent of his income to charity. Clarence pursued this instruction faithfully, increasing the amount to
30 percent when the exemption from taxable income eventually
rose to that level, and even beyond. In a letter to his children, the
year before he died, Gamble reviewed his and his two brothers'
management of their estate with some pride but two regrets: ". . .
As Father had trained us, we reinvested, trying to select the
companies whose products people would want more and more in
the future. We'd probably have done better if we'd put all the
surplus into P & G, but it seemed better to diversify somewhat.
. . . We've used the funds for the good of others, though not as
much as we should have."

Satisfied on the whole, as he indicated, Gamble nevertheless
was not altogether pleased with his philanthropic acumen:

> . . . It seemed better, since I was in the medical research field, not to
> make contributions to the department in which I was working. This gave
> the comfort of feeling that I wasn't included in the program just because
> of expected gifts or made assistant professor for that reason, but I'm sorry
> now that I didn't invest in medical research. More could have been
> accomplished than was by my own efforts, and I could have stood the
> doubts as to the reason for my inclusion. If I were doing it again—
> As you know, the birth control field seemed neglected and in need of
> financial support, and I've explored that field to learn the best ways to
> make our funds effective. We've accomplished a remarkable amount, and
> a remarkable amount per dollar spent—though I wish I'd had the courage
> to invest and expand more energetically.

The regrets of a man whose distinction was that he had more
daring than most hint at a logical source of his discomfort with
money. He was jealous of it, for it competed with his sense of
personal worth. During college and medical school, where he

came by his reputation for brilliance honestly, ambitious mothers with daughters in the marriage market looked him over as a suitable candidate. This was one reason, he said, why he drove a model-T Ford, so people wouldn't think he was rich. Following marriage, he sometimes took his family on cabin-class boat trips to Europe, and he insisted on flying economy class, in the Gambles' frequent trips abroad. Likewise, when he made a long-distance telephone call, he laid down a stop watch beside the phone.

His denial of wealth also explains, somewhat perversely, his carefully nurtured reputation among birth controllers as a fierce penny-pincher. He wanted to be generous and habitually was, in a broad, humanitarian way, but no one should think he had money to throw around. There were innumerable anecdotes about his parsimony. Two will suffice here.

For a cab ride in New York City with one of his most effective field workers, Edith Gates, the fare came to ninety-five cents. Gamble handed the driver a dollar and, when offered the nickel in change, waved it aside. The driver tossed the nickel at him, saying, "Brother, you need it worse than I do." Gamble stiffly picked up the coin and retorted, "If you don't know the value of a nickel, I do."

He repeatedly embarrassed others with such demonstrations. On another occasion—a birth control conference in Puerto Rico—he pulled up a chair to a table in the hotel dining room where four of the delegates were having a continental breakfast. It consisted of fruit juice, sweet roll, and coffee for seventy-five cents. Gamble told the waiter that he would have the juice and roll, but no coffee. When later presented with a check for seventy-five cents, Gamble asked the cost of a cup of coffee. Informed it was fifteen cents, he laid down sixty cents. The waiter protested that the continental breakfast was priced as a unit. Gamble said he would not pay for the coffee because he did not have it. The waiter persisted, and Gamble said: "Call the manager." The manager came and smoothed over the situation by accepting the sixty cents.

CJG, aged four

One basis for his tension about wealth may have been, as he once revealed to Dr. Yoshio Koya of Japan, the feeling that the money was not his. It was his father's, he said. It became the son's responsibility to use it wisely and to transmit it to his heirs, as his father did to him. This was perhaps his oblique way of reacting to the credo that, in the land of opportunity, self-respect is supposed to derive from ambition, talent, and hard work. Gamble was sensitive on this point, as when he told the International Planned Parenthood Federation, "I have more to give than money." This feeling explains why Clarence Gamble looked upon unearned wealth as a handicap and wished to hide it.

CJG, aged seven

Parents

Clarence Gamble was born on January 10, 1894, in Avondale, a suburb of Cincinnati, Ohio, in a massive Victorian, red-brick, three-story house with a circular tower at one corner and an assortment of ornamental knobs and tall chimneys on the roof.

David and Mary Gamble had four children: Cecil Huggins Gamble (1884–1956), Elizabeth Gamble (1886–1890), Sidney David Gamble (1890–1968), Clarence James Gamble (1894–1966).

Clarence, as his mother said, was a "surprise baby," born when she was thirty-nine and his father forty-seven. His brothers were ten and four years ahead of him. Surrounded by this amount of maturity, stability, attention, and example, Clarence did not lack for mental and physical stimulation. A photograph taken when he was a year and half old showed him in a full-length white dress with lace collar and sailor hat, but by three he had progressed to a Buster Brown suit and high button shoes. His curls were long and golden, his brown eyes shining, and his smile a winning one. That smile was always there in the album photos of his youth.

What was remarkable about Clarence Gamble's evolving character, in view of his rebel streak as an adult, was how closely it conformed with the attitudes, traits, and habits of his father and mother. In the stock-breeding sense, he conformed, in an almost perfect blend.

From the volume of correspondence during Clarence's college years—normally, he wrote alternate letters to his mother and father every three or four days—it was evident that he was in continuous touch with both parents. The influence of his father is easily discernible from other evidence and can be at least partially categorized as a strong sense of financial responsibility and accountability; a commitment to Christian charity and benevolence; a love of travel; a technical and mechanistic, rather than humanistic or political, approach to human affairs; and an unexpected but unfailing, and sometimes mischievous, sense of humor.

As an early example of his own humor, Clarence when he was going on nine gave his mother a ball of twine for Christmas with the note: "I hope this will aid you in strengthening the ties between you and your husband." Such impishness pursued him throughout his life.

David Gamble wrote Clarence regularly when they were apart. Sometimes his letters sounded stiff and formal and were signed "Sincerely, D. B. Gamble." But on other occasions they were warm and chatty and signed "With a heart full of love. Father." Usually, they gave some evidence of his passion for bookkeeping. For example, when Clarence was in medical school in Boston his father wrote from Pasadena, "I took the $.85 that was in silver in

your pocket and will give you credit for same." He also listed
what Clarence owed him, so:

Expressage books	$4.87
Watch crystals	1.00
Postage	.29
	$6.16
Cash from pocket	.85
	$5.31

Both father and mother gave Clarence a deep sense of family,
later imparted to his own children. Like the racing pigeons that
interested him as a boy and again as an adult, he homed well, and
yet from early on he showed tendencies toward wilfulness, an
insistence on going his own way, on standing apart or above the
rest of the world. His mother once said of her three boys: "When
you asked Cecil to do something, he would storm and fuss and
then do it. When you asked Sidney, he would be perfectly sweet
and do it. When you asked Clarence, he would be perfectly sweet
and not do it."

A miscellany of old report cards from Miss Sattler's School in
1903 in Cincinnati, when Clarence was nine, revealed him as a
precocious child. He carried ten to twelve subjects, including
something called *sloyd* (manual training). The two top grades, 9's
and 10's, predominated. In 1905 and 1906, when he was eleven
and twelve, he attended the eighth and ninth grades at the University School in Cincinnati well ahead of those of his own age
group and still knocking off 95's and 100's, mainly, with a few
80's. He was consistently best in arithmetic, algebra, and
geometry; he had some ups and downs in English and French. Art
and manual training did not challenge him.

David and Mary Gamble fell easily into the habit of fleeing
some part of each Cincinnati winter to Florida or California, as
well as traveling in Europe and the Orient at other times. Clarence wrote: "We became so fascinated with the charms of
California and Pasadena, in particular, that we decided to locate
there permanently and, in consequence, I came to enter the Occi-

dental Academy in the middle of my third year of the high school course."

These were good years. He was active, even hyperactive, as the clean-cut, all-American boy who had everything. He moved freely among his own social group, with both boys and girls, and enjoyed himself with his peers; yet it was at this same time that he showed his first signs of being different from, or detached from, other people.

There was a physical basis for this singularity, inasmuch as Clarence was both younger and smaller than boys with whom he associated, first in Occidental Academy and then for one year in Occidental College, only a few miles from home. He was sixteen when he graduated from high school (1910); the following fall, he entered college. On his seventeenth birthday, January 10, 1911, he wrote in his diary:

Sixteen is passed. I don't know whether I'm glad or sorry. It's been a good year and I don't know but I'd like to go over it again. I wish however that the others in the college were a little younger. Found out today that James has been taken into Owl. It didn't seem too bad when it was only Walton, but now I'm the only one of the three that's not in it. I don't see why it is that Franny and that lot consider me so inferior. Probably it's principally because I'm younger.

He put a good deal in his diary about dating and about joy rides, as he called them, in one of the family's two electric cars, usually his Aunt Julia's (his mother's sister); often he would drive her to one destination or another and then go for a spin until it was time to pick her up.

He was particularly delighted with his first typewriter, and with it gave evidence of a lifelong passion for counting things, as well as for setting up challenges to be overcome. Writing letters for Aunt Julia, he did 366 words in ten minutes, he noted. "The word meter is working well. I wrote 4108 words altogether today, 8730 in eight days."

For a time, he was interested in track and kept careful account in his diary of his time in the mile-run—usually a few seconds over five minutes. His athletic career was aborted by a period of sickness with recurrent fever and rest in bed during the winter, capped by this note: "Went . . . to see Dr. Babcock. He examined my heart and told me what he thought of it. No more track work, he says. I had planned to go up Mt. Wilson tomorrow, but he said it wouldn't be a good plan after being sick."

Clarence was an avid student of astronomy. He built his own telescope, grinding and polishing the lens himself. Professor Allen permitted him to use the college telescope, and from time to time he went out to see Mr. Pease at the Mt. Wilson Observatory. He was occasionally called on to lecture to the Astronomical Society at college on such subjects as "The Heavens in January."

Clarence showed a potential literary bent in his teen-age compositions, some of which from 1909 and 1910 were bound and preserved in their original state. He dashed off some amusing bits of fiction, displaying a vivid imagination, some humor, and an exceedingly practical turn of mind.

In perhaps his first expression of opinion about a demographic question, a 300-word essay on "The Immigration Problem," Clarence took a four-square stance in favor of an open-door policy for Europeans. "Shall we who are fortunate enough to be descended from those who came here earlier declare that no more shall come to enjoy our privileges?" he asked. With proper regulation and distribution of population, he discounted the problems of overcrowding, slums, cheap labor, or importation of contagious diseases, holding, "the average European is able and willing to work for his living and work hard if necessary. . . . Their labor is greatly needed."

At Occidental Academy, as in Cincinnati, Clarence maintained his usual grades of A or B in his majors, including Latin and German as well as mathematics and science (where he always got A's). In his freshman year in Occidental College, when a classmate lost his physics book, Clarence said, "Here take mine. I won't need it." He was right. He never cracked the book. Yet he and his friend, Walton Brown, topped the class and, as reported in the local newspaper in June 1911, "Each made the highest record

ever made by a freshman in the history of Occidental." They had
flawless records of seven A's.

Princeton

Both of Clarence's brothers had gone to Princeton University. In
the fall of 1911, now a sophomore and two years ahead of his age
group, Clarence followed in their steps. Away from home for the
first time, Clarence abandoned his diary and chronicled his progress in frequent letters to "Dear Father" or "Dear Mother," typing
them and keeping carbon copies. His letters were filled with
chatter about trips into New York—about parties, dates, dances,
theater, opera, symphony, ice skating, skate-sailing, canoeing,
football games, bicycling.

As his letters showed, extracurricular activities occupied much
of his time and effort in his junior year. He was learning to play
the flute. But a freshman flutist, "who is quite a wonder," had
him topped for the Triangle orchestra. Clarence tried out for the
Orphic Order, but he found himself out-fluted again. He tried to
make Glee Club and Mandolin Club without success. He sold ads
for the *Tiger*, competing for the positon of circulation manager,
but without much luck. He aspired for a position on the rifle club,
but his score was too low. He also was regularly losing at tennis,
he reported.

Clarence's senior year at Princeton was an all-around success.
Again he was turned down for Mandolin Club, Glee Club, and
Choir, causing him to report: "Apparently I am cut out for nothing but a student." His flute also let him down in another try-out
for Orphic Order. Then his luck changed. The orchestra had an
opening for a piccolo player and no takers; it was suggested he try
out for that position. He rushed to New York and bought a
second-hand piccolo for thirty dollars and soon was playing this
instrument well enough to take his place in the orchestra, although he found the high notes and quick passages a bit of a
strain.

That was in October. In early December, he telegraphed a night letter with the big news. He had made Triangle by agreeing to play "not my flute and not my piccolo—not even my mandolin—but my new instrument, the bass viol." It was a big jump. The orchestra had two flutists better than he, but it also had two bass viols and only one player. The bass viol was available; one did not have to buy it. Clarence got an instruction book and some pointers from the other players and practiced for eighteen hours. He asked the orchestra leader if he would like to hear him play. He did so. The orchestra manager told the leader that they could not take an extra bass fiddle on tour unless it was absolutely necessary. So the decision was "very sorry."

Clarence, nevertheless, had another string to his bow. He was a camera buff and had taken pictures that were published in *Pictorial Review*. He received assignments to take action photographs of the Tiger football team for a Princeton publication, *Pic*. The editor of *Pic* now said he wanted a staff photographer to go along with the tour—a two-week series of eight concerts beginning in New York and ending in Chicago during the Christmas holidays. The orchestra manager informed the editor that the only problem of taking an extra man was the cost. *Pic* did not wish to pay for the trip either. So Clarence wired home for money. "No, I don't exactly like the idea of so-to-speak buying my position in the show, but I certainly think I have earned it." His parents agreed.

His overlapping interests in the camera and music posed a curious situation when he had to photograph the Orphic Order, in which he played the piccolo. He set his camera for a delayed-action exposure and then ran to take his place in the orchestra before the flash went off.

In January 1914, Clarence made the rifle team for the first time. He was now shooting as high as 187 out of a possible 200. He shot in seven of ten rifle meets, winning highest score in one.

The youth, now in high gear, was interested in compasses and barometers and trying to bring off aerial photography from a kite (this did not pan out).

Clarence entered his final exams with his Phi Beta Kappa Key in hand and finished *magna cum laude*. Biology, the only subject he had not favored and which he took for the first time in his final semester, was the only examination that gave him trouble. In his last two years at Princeton, his usual course and term grades were 1's. He dropped to 2 twice, and slipped as low as 3 only in Biology.

After Clarence's graduation in June 1914, his father wrote and asked the Princeton registrar to refresh his mind on how his three sons had stood in their class. Cecil ranked thirty-eighth in a class of 163 A.B.'s. Sidney ranked first in a class of 96 Litt B.'s. Clarence ranked first in a class of 102 Litt. B.'s. Although he now said he was a little sorry that he had stayed with the class of 1914, where the competition in extracurricular activities was so tough, Clarence had given his classmates age and weight and still had shown that he could hold his own.

chapter 2   *A Millionaire at Twenty-One*

One way of bringing your life into harmony with the world around you is to focus attention on an object as far distant from human behavior as possible, such as the movement of celestial bodies in relation to the earth. Corporate management did not attract Clarence Gamble, although he had no hangup about property ownership and the profit motive as sources of progress. Cecil became interested in business. Sidney turned to economics and sociology. Clarence had thought he would become an astronomer. He appeared well suited to a career that would focus his attention on the physical universe. The opportunity was ideal for a person already living in Pasadena, for the California Institute of Technology and the Mount Wilson Observatory were close at hand.

The world around him was an optimistic one, but in trouble; before the summer of 1914 was over, the great powers of Europe would be engulfed in World War I. In the United States, industry was involved in a bitter contest of capital and labor, of wealth and poverty. In 1913, the Sixteenth Amendment authorizing the first federal income tax had come into being. As 1914 began, Henry Ford was solving his labor problem by introducing a five-dollar, eight-hour work day (his auto workers previously had been paid $2.40 for nine hours). The Gambles were Republicans, but the Democrats were in power in Washington and some were doing what they could to bring the rugged individualism of American capitalism and Yankee imperialism in world trade under control. They were also doing their best to preserve American neutrality in the world armament race.

One source of conflict between capital and labor was immigration. Many Republican farmers and industrialists had favored the importation of working people from Asia and Europe as a source of cheap labor, although some Republicans opposed importation of foreigners, fearing dilution of old Anglo-Saxon stock. Theodore Roosevelt had charged that Americans were committing "race suicide" through the failure of favored classes to reproduce themselves. Organized labor demanded that immigration be restricted and, beginning with the Chinese exclusion law of 1882, social-minded politicians increasingly rejected as capitalist propaganda the noble proposition that the United States should be "the asylum of the oppressed of all nations." No one talked then in terms of population explosion, but rather of too many of the "wrong people," meaning those who were, because of language, custom, and political background, easy to exploit as workers perhaps but difficult to assimilate in the American way of life, where, it was said, every deserving man could work his way up the ladder. In 1912 and for the next five years, Congress worked to pass over Presidential veto a law closing immigration to illiterate Europeans; anarchists, prostitutes, and defectives had been barred earlier (Congress finally succeeded in 1917).

David Gamble, in his association with missionaries, who often came to visit in the Gamble house in Pasadena, had some interest in the immigration problem. If Christianity was to find a welcome in China, for instance, should not Chinese find a welcome in America?

Frankly, all Clarence really wanted to do when he finished college, he said, was enjoy a good loaf, probably at Harbor Point, Michigan, on Little Traverse Bay, where the Gambles had summer vacation roots extending back to the Cincinnati years. David Gamble, who believed in giving a boy as much freedom as he could handle, objected. He thought it time his son took a job. Clarence was twenty and never had worked.

The father also had an idea where Clarence could get a job, at least for the summer. The state of California had established a Commission on Immigrants and Housing to provide free help to foreigners who had been "wronged, abused, or defrauded." The Commission was started with private contributions, while awaiting a regular appropriation. Mr. Gamble had friends on the Commission and himself contributed.

Clarence went to work for the Commission as a case investigator in San Francisco in July 1914, at five dollars a week. By September, when Clarence had decided to stay on, the director wrote Mr. Gamble that Clarence was worth more than he received: "I am not trying to please you when I say he is exceptional in his efficiency in our work." However, the Commission's resources were scanty, and it had been forced to drop several staff members while awaiting its appropriation. "Till then could you help us out by contributing his salary?" And so it worked out that David Gamble, who already was paying Clarence's living expenses in San Francisco, now paid his son's salary. This rose to twenty dollars a week by the time his job ended, in July 1915. Clarence was unaware of the arrangement until much later; it gave him cause to lament to his own sons that the only time in his whole life he had a paying job his father put up the money.

It was nonetheless a fine year for Clarence Gamble, for a number of reasons. He thoroughly enjoyed the work. His letters home regularly reported "my latest detective job." He traced a baggage man who had cheated an immigrant by charging her $1.25 for the delivery of a trunk; the man had accepted the money and then hired an honest company to deliver the trunk for 50 cents. He investigated a report from neighbors of an Italian woman whose husband had beaten her and given her a black eye and meanwhile loafed on the money she earned in a cracker factory. She had three small boys and was afraid to do anything against her husband for fear he would kill her.

Land and home development frauds by real estate speculators were the most common complaint. The Tobin Park Development Company was doing direct mail advertising of lots and homes in a suburb of San Francisco. Clarence found it was an hour's train ride and an hour's walk to get to the property, which proved to be nothing but gullies and brush. The promoters hired him as an agent, placing him in an excellent position to testify against them when they were charged with mail fraud.

It was while he was in San Francisco that Clarence Gamble made up his mind to become a physician. As he later told his son, Dr. Walter Gamble, "I went to see a doctor about a sore throat and he talked me into becoming a doctor."

Clarence's mother had heard of Dr. Philip King Brown. When Clarence suffered a recurrence of his tonsilitis—he had been advised to have his tonsils out at various times but always had been too busy—he sought out Dr. Brown in his office at 350 Post Street. Dr. Brown sent Clarence back to his light-housekeeping room to rest and recover. The tonsils became worse and Clarence sought the doctor again in two days. Dr. Brown was out, so Clarence walked across the street, to St. Francis Hospital, and obtained admission, taking a larger corner room while waiting for the doctor to come. Dr. Brown enjoyed relating the anecdote later: his concern that an immigration worker making five dollars a week was in one of the most expensive rooms in the hospital for four days. Later, Mr. and Mrs. Gamble came up from Pasadena to see how Clarence was getting along, and "she in discussing his future intimated that he might not have to struggle very hard for his livelihood. I felt much better about the hospital bill."

Thenceforth, Clarence spent a good bit of time with Dr. Brown and the Brown family. Dr. Brown's sister was Dr. Adelaide Brown, who, like other rare woman physicians of those days, practiced obstetrics, gynecology, and pediatrics, and was interested in birth control. Until now, Clarence had shown little interest in either medicine or birth control.

Dr. Brown, a graduate of Harvard Medical School (1893), was a busy enthusiastic general practitioner with staff appointments in six hospitals. As his son, Dr. Cabot Brown, recollected, he "specialized in heart disease, stomach ulcers, and pulmonary diseases." He was one of the founders of the Arequipa Sanatarium for Wage-Earning Women with Chest Diseases in Marin County, a then new institution offering room, board, and medical care for one dollar a day, or $1.50 including nursing care. Dr. Brown took Clarence along with his two sons, some years younger, on outings combined with his professional rounds across the Bay and Clarence was a frequent dinner guest at the Browns. In one letter in September 1914, Clarence wrote his mother: "I am having a wonderful time with Dr. Brown. . . . I had some good chances for talks with him on subjects many and varied, and it surely was interesting: medicine, sociology, criminology, scenery, hunting, and pedagogy."

Clarence Gamble said nothing of his decision to study medicine in any letters home that have been found. At some point, it became obvious that to do so he would have to return to college for graduate study in the basic sciences of medicine.

Before then, however, an event befell him that, while not altogether unexpected, set him apart from most people, medical and lay. On Clarence's twenty-first birthday, January 10, 1915, David Gamble sat down in his den, put a sheet of note paper, [8½ by 5½ inches], in his typewriter with the purple ribbon and wrote:

Dear Clarence:

In honor of your arrival at man's estate your mother and I give you stock as per enclosed list. We hope that you will be able to make good use of the income. We have one request to make in connection therewith, that is you contribute at least one-tenth of the income to the church and other benevolences.

Lovingly, Father.

The stocks listed were equal to a round million dollars in value. Thus, in a few words, a father disposed of a son's need to work for a living for the rest of his life. Thus, too, David Gamble, imposed on Clarence, together with the blessings and responsibilities of riches, a handicap of a kind that he could not overcome—a kind of self-consciousness that would drive him to great, sometimes ridiculous, lengths to avoid the appearance of wealth, a feeling of need to be himself rather than simply a Procter & Gamble heir.

As his notebooks show, his concern about his inheritance was deep and immediate. Gamble's youthful diaries, like his letters to his mother and father, were mainly in a chatty vein, a casual account of the day's or week's events, usually written just before he went to bed at night, usually on the typewriter but occasionally in longhand. While his letters to his father and mother reflected an easy, comfortable relationship with them, and certainly exceeded the minimum standards of duty and respect, he seldom revealed his inner thoughts, attitudes, or aspirations. Not surprisingly, he had inhibitions about what he could tell his mother or father, as any young man would, but apparently there were many things he could not even tell his diary, at least not in plain English. Frequently, when he referred to a girl whom he had met and perhaps dated, and occasionally in reference to a male acquaintance, his comments submerged in an elaborate secret code, the key to which has not turned up in his memorabilia. One might guess that this was his way of handling intimate or derogatory opinion and gossip, although there is reason to believe he was at the same time exercising his fondness for mental gymnastics.

On a few occasions, however, he revealed himself in short soliloquies. One of these concerned his father's gift. From the way he wrote, several months after it happened, it would appear, as in his occasional use of code, that he imagined himself writing for an audience.

"I am a scientist and a millionaire," he wrote in this undated revelation. "I am glad to be a scientist but I know I would be happier were I not a millionaire. Many of you who read this even

though you are not numbered among the scientists will sym-
pathize with the first statement, but all of you, unless perchance
you possess a million, will laugh at the second. So intimately has
the desire for wealth been woven into the textile of modern
education that money never seems undesirable. Only when it
stands in the name of another can riches seem 'tainted.' To those
who have never owned a million dollars such a sum would seem
the answer to all wishes, the satisfaction of all desires. There was
a time when I should have agreed with them, but now I have a
million dollars—and I know.

"Perhaps it was the suddenness with which it descended on me
that made it seem most astounding.

"I was educated as most other sons of the so-called middle class
are educated. I went to a high school filled with children of those
with moderate means. I was sent to a college where the sons of
the very rich mingle on equal terms with those who earn their
way. I was taught that only by education and steady application
could I hope to attain all that a large bank account would furnish.
After graduation I found a job, one that gave me $85 a month and
enough of the unusual and unexpected to use all the brain power I
possessed. And then after a year there descended upon me the
million dollars.

"Up to that time my life was relatively simple—education that
had been planned for me, a moderate amount of thinking such as
no college man can escape, followed by work much like that to
which any of my classmates might look forward. But with the
advent of my fortune there were forced on me almost numberless
problems which demand instant consideration, immediate solution. If you think they were simple, just sit down with paper and
pencil and decide exactly what you would do with a million
dollars and the income that it would bring. I decided immediately
that I would not spend the million itself, but would content
myself with disposing of the dividends which it brought. This I
calculated might amount to $60,000 a year. But this amount
seemed so incomprehensible that I immediately reduced it to the
amount per day, roughly $160. This was in terms in which I was

accustomed to think, less than two months' wages. I visualized a
new suit, a set of Stevenson, a theater party with front row seats,
half a dozen of the other things that I had been saving for a few
paydays hence and the $160 was figuratively spent. Then I started
on the second day—a month's rent and some new furniture
finished that. The third day was more difficult, but an automobile
cancelled the next seven spaces in the calendar. Then I realize in
real earnest that my whole life must be completely reorganized to
meet this new and astounding condition.

"The most important change that was born in upon my com-
prehension at first was the complete freedom which money
brought. Hitherto work had been my creed, moderate in amount,
to be sure, but continuous, constructive, aiming always to make
myself more valuable to possible employers, to fit myself to earn
a greater share of the desirable things of life. But now all this must
end, for by no flight of imagination could I conceive of attaining a
salary that would compare with what I was already receiving. And
on the road even to moderate heights lay many dreary hours.
Besides I already had more than I could well spend, why struggle
and wear myself out for more? Why indeed? So I resigned my $85
a month and tasted the joys of release from daily round of office
work. 772."

The "772" was the number of words he had typed. It would take
more than a million dollars to make Clarence Gamble forget his
word-counting habit.

The arrival of responsibility—to look after his money—left him
moody at times. Since he was planning to go back to Princeton in
the fall for graduate studies, he would have to give up his job
anyway, but the decision was made for him. The Commission in
1915 had opened an office in Los Angeles and put him in charge
but, as the director wrote him, decided to close it at the end of
June. As a matter of fact, the Commission also was closing its San
Francisco office, through lack of public support of its work.
Nevertheless, Clarence chose to share personally in its failure.
"Apparently I haven't made a sufficient success of the office here
to satisfy them," he wrote to his father, who was in the East.

Back in Princeton

Margaret Sanger's name was much in the newspapers at the time
Clarence Gamble returned to Princeton in the fall of 1915 to take
his Master of Arts degree in the biological sciences. Anthony
Comstock (1844–1915), leader of the New York Society for the
Suppression of Vice and promoter of the so-called Comstock Law
passed by Congress in 1873 prohibiting as "obscene, lewd, and
lascivious" the dissemination of contraceptive information and
devices, was trying unsuccessfully at the time to send Mrs. Sanger
to prison for mailing a militant newspaper, *Woman Rebel*, containing various inflammatory articles such as "A Defense of As-
sassination." Among Mrs. Sanger's minor violations of the law
was distribution of a small pamphlet, *Family Limitation*, devoted
to contraceptive techniques. The United States Attorney dropped
charges against her following Comstock's timely death. Clarence
Gamble was not by nature a hero worshiper but even if he were
aware of Mrs. Sanger's crusade, it would be understandable that
he said nothing of her in his letters to his parents. Whatever the
case, she was blazing a trail that he would eventually follow but
with no publicity and, fortunately, in his time little risk of going
to jail, as she did in 1916 when she opened the first American
birth control clinic in Brooklyn.

During the course of these events, Clarence Gamble was dissecting the brain of the sand shark, the intestine of the pill bug,
and the muscles and bones of the cat, playing his flute—including
solo parts—in the Orphic Order orchestra, continually driving
and repairing "my pet"—his second-hand Model T Ford—and
otherwise preparing for a career as a physician.

He was, objectively, extremely fortunate to be in Princeton
Graduate School and able to study under some of the great
teachers in the life sciences, particularly Edwin Grant Conklin,
professor of biology, and E. Newton Harvey, professor of physiology. Under Conklin, he took cytology, the science of living cell
structure and function; under Harvey, physiology, the collective
functions of these cells as part of living organisms. Harvey, Clar-

ence sized up as a "reasonably good professor." About Conklin, he had some reservations, possibily because he had been a minister and tended to talk in a highly formalized and inspirational manner. Conklin assigned Clarence the problem of determining the function of the secondary nucleus in the one-celled paramecium, meaning that he had to grow these barely visible creatures and then dissect them with a glass needle under a microscope.

It was in graduate school that Gamble met Stuart Mudd, also a premedical student. They became close friends, Mudd being one of a few who knew Clarence as "Jim," which Clarence preferred. Mudd was serious-minded, hard-working, and enthusiastic about his teachers and also, he said, about Gamble's integrity and brilliance, particularly in the hard sciences. As professor of microbiology emeritus at the University of Pennsylvania, after Dr. Gamble's death, Dr. Mudd recalled that they not only took the regular premedical courses, including organic chemistry and comparative anatomy, as well as cytology and physiology, but:

We both took a course called Loomis's physics in the Engineering School. This was one semester in *heat* and one in *electricity* and *magnetism.* Jim did not bother to buy a text book; instead he studied mine the night before each examination. I worked hard on the course. At the end, Jim stood first, I second, and all the engineering students followed behind.

Mudd became interested in birth control, as a field of interest outside of his own specialty, before Gamble did. "I think I helped influence Clarence a little bit, and we talked together for fifty years about birth control matters .... I do remember—you never can tell whether something is purely coincidental and means nothing or whether it means something—but once in a Princeton University store, I remember Jim was sort of not sure what he was going to do next and I said, 'Look, this birth control business is terribly important. It is something you could really go to town on.' Now whether this had anything to do with it or not, I don't know."

Mudd was clear in the sources of his own interest in birth control. Conklin's influence was one root; the other was that, just after he graduated from Harvard Medical School, in 1920, he heard Margaret Sanger lecture: "I was a romantic young man. I was impressed by her experience."

He felt certain that Conklin laid the intellectual foundation for Gamble's interest in the quality and quantity problems of human life. Conklin, who was, along with Thomas Hunt Morgan, a leading American student of human evolution in those days, in 1915 published the first of several editions of his book, *Heredity and Environment in the Development of Man.*

Conklin's ideas influenced Clarence Gamble in the years to come. But we find no indication from him that Conklin's exposition on eugenics turned his head. In fact, at the end of May 1916, he noted: "Had a 'final exam' with Conklin this morning which consisted of showing him my laboratory drawings. In his most finished after-dinner-speech manner he told me that my work had been most satisfactory and even went so far as to call me Clarence. It's too bad he can't unbend a little more and begin earlier in the year." Clarence had finished his physiology work more than two months before and turned in his thesis. Without looking at the paper, Harvey told him it was excellent and that he had passed the examination.

It had been a good year, a mixture of some hard work and much fun. He had traveled all over the East in his Ford; as he wrote his father, "I've had such fun in so many different ways with the little auto—it's so nice to have the money to own and run it. In fact of the things that money will buy there isn't a thing that I've wanted and haven't had, thanks to you."

He had two setbacks. His tonsils had troubled him, and during Christmas vacation in Cincinnati and Chicago, a doctor had advised him to have them out by the following summer and meanwhile use a disinfecting spray.

"Then, too, I've found that in vacation I exploded a bomb under one of my nicest brownstone air castles and it's hard to keep from stumbling over the ruins every time I turn around." This, in a letter to his mother, was an oblique reference to a disappointment in love; a young lady named Ethel Dummer had not reciprocated.

3 Harvard and Then . . . ?

Clarence Gamble had leaned toward Harvard Medical School ever since he met its San Francisco alumnus, Dr. Philip Brown, but he kept his options open almost to the last minute. He went to Boston and talked to some of Harvard's famed physicians and medical scientists, including Walter Cannon, Harvey Cushing, and Richard Cabot. Gamble audited some of the classes, and noted the schedule: lectures and lab work from 9 to 1 o'clock and from 2 to 6 daily. "It looks like a rather strenuous life," he wrote his father. He had done some casual comparison shopping and collected the following possibly biased opinions of medical schools. Johns Hopkins was "past its zenith" and its graduates were "stuck up." Columbia was too heavy on the practical side. Harvard emphasized the theoretical too much but was a good place to do research.

In June 1916, only three months before the opening of the fall term, Gamble mailed his application to the registrar. Compared to modern times, the process was ridiculously simple. The application form consisted of a single sheet of paper and elicited only the most routine information—name, address, birthday, parents' names, schooling, degrees. There were no MCAT (Medical College Admission Test) requirement, no character references, no personal interview, and no essay on why the applicant wished to study medicine. A transcript of college and graduate school courses and grades was required; in Gamble's case his scholastic honors and two degrees spoke for themselves. The words *magna cum laude* melted the hardest academic heart. It had been only in the previous decade that Harvard Medical School had sought to limit its enrollment to college graduates with courses in physics and chemistry, but, for lack of sufficient qualified candidates, it sometimes admitted likely young men with three years of college, an agreeable personality, and stable family background. A Phi Beta Kappa key itself was virtually enough to open the door, and candidates not born in Boston were becoming increasingly attractive to a medical school then in transition from a local to a national institution. The question of financial means did not arise, at least officially, but it is certain that Dr. Brown, Clarence's sponsor, told Dr. Richard Cabot and others, as Mrs. Gamble had told him, that Clarence would never want for anything money would buy.

Then and in the next four years there was every outward indication that Clarence James Gamble, Class of 1920, was one of the most nonchalant young men ever admitted to Harvard medicine. A mere listing of his active interests in medical school, in addition to study, provided confirmation. His classmates noted (and those who survive still remember) his enthusiasm for his automobile, typewriter, dictaphone, other electrical gadgets, playing the stock market, leading a Boy Scout troop, aiding poor boys who had dropped out in continuing their public schooling, working with a club for ex-alcoholics, outdoor sports of all kinds, going to parties and dances, running the affairs of the Nu Sigma Nu Fraternity, attending church every Sunday morning, and writing affectionate letters to his parents every three or four days.

True to the tradition of medical education, which insists on beginning with the dead and working backward toward life and health, his first letter, on September 28, 1916, began with the dissection of a cadaver. "We were introduced to our new friends and had the enjoyable job of giving them a shave." Clarence and his teammate, John Woolredge, were assigned to dissect the back. After one nauseous week, Woolredge decided that he did not want to be a doctor after all, and transferred to the Business School. "So I had my corpse all to myself," wrote Clarence. Soon, however, two other students, "who had a poor subject" were assigned to work with him. Later on, they went on to the skull, "a terribly complicated thing to learn." Clarence almost immediately devised a teaching aid, a bookholder, "like the one in papa's den," so that he and his teammate could look at the book and memorize the parts while dissecting them.

Clarence felt the strain soon enough. "I seem to feel loss of sleep more than I should." On October 1, he went to Dr. Cabot at Massachusetts General Hospital for a physical examination, and also had a specialist look into his throat, which still bothered him although he'd had his tonsils out. There was "nothing very wrong." In late October, his parents came to see him, inspecting his boarding house and his meals, to be sure he was comfortably situated. By December, nonetheless, he was exhausted and back in his pattern, during these fatigue states, of sleeping twelve hours a night. He referred to this recurrent need, which pursued him throughout life, as "the sleeping sickness."

Harvard Medical School was then experimenting with a new, concentrated curriculum, generally offering the student one subject at a time for a period of weeks or months with morning laboratory work and afternoon lectures related to the pertinent textbook. The student saw little or nothing of live patients during the first year and a half, moving on from gross and microscopic anatomy to physiology and then pathology before entering the hospital to examine and care for patients. Clarence managed to humanize his first year to some extent by working with the social service department of the Boston Psychopathic Hospital as a supervisor of students who volunteered to drum up attendance in a men's club for "reformed drunkards" who met once a month.

These were heroic days in medicine, but Clarence Gamble was not much awed by persons in positions of power. His comments to his parents on some of Harvard's most famous physicians— Walter Cannon, the physiologist; Harvey Cushing, the brain surgeon, and Henry Christian, the internist—were less inspiring than what one usually reads in biographies of great doctors. He was sparing of his friend and mentor, Dr. Richard Cabot, however.

Cabot, chief of staff of Massachusetts General Hospital and later Harvard professor of social ethics, was one of America's leading medical humanists and clinical diagnosticians in the days when it was easier to show the patient personal concern than to effect a cure. He became famous both as the father of medical social work and of the Clinico-Pathological Conference (CPC). In the CPC, a hospital teaching device now employed throughout the world, a leading clinician—originally it was Cabot—reads the case history, examination, and laboratory tests records of a patient unknown to him and makes his diagnosis of the disease before assembled colleagues and students. Others present may disagree and make a different diagnosis. The hospital pathologist, who knows the final diagnosis—often from autopsy findings— reveals it at the climax of the conference. The exercise is an exciting one because it frequently involves a puzzling case and the clinician voluntarily puts himself on the spot, right or wrong. Cabot taught a course in physical diagnosis through this case-history method and, in the process, revealed another unusual talent—he learned and remembered the name of every member of the class.

Clarence Gamble, as a first-year student, often dined with Dr. and Mrs. Cabot and deepened, as well as complicated, this friendship by attempting to teach Mrs. Cabot how to drive his Model T. He stepped on her foot numerous times, in order to apply the brakes hard enough to save his car.

Invited with the Cabots to dine at the Cushings, Clarence was unusually enthusiastic about "a most thrilling visit to Olympus."

He wrote: "Cushing has a wonderful memory and a most interesting way of telling things, but he doesn't work over the raw material nearly as much as does Dr. Cabot. Cushing is the scientist and antiquarian while Cabot is interested in the psychological, social side—he thinks of the broken families, Cushing of the broken skulls."

More typical were Gamble's comments on Walter Cannon, who it generally has been acknowledged twice deserved the Nobel Prize but never won it. "They say that Cannon is not to do the lecturing this year, which was, the second-year men tell us, a cause for rejoicing." Again: "We had a most abominable lecture from Cannon, mostly ah's, but he is going to let one of the other men do most of it." The other lecturer turned out to be Dr. Cecil Drinker. "The physiologist who is lecturing in place of Cannon sounds like an elocutionist doing a take-off on a high school orator—language, gestures, delivery, and all. He has a keen appreciation of the history of science and has spent most of the time so far showing us pictures of the wigs worn by the men who invented physiology."

Gamble conceded Cannon would be "a nice man to work with," and got started with him on a research problem in his second semester. Cannon a few years before had done his fundamental work on the sympathetic nervous system and had demonstrated the role of hormones, such as adrenalin, in mobilizing the emotions of anger and fear—the fight-flight defense mechanism. Now the question he put to Gamble and other students was: Do such emotions produce chemical changes in red blood corpuscles? They tried dogs, cats, rats, and chickens and encountered fantastic problems, beginning with the not-so-simple matter of drawing a blood sample. By March, Clarence was "about ready" to assure his father that "there is no effect on a dog from his excitement in barking at a cat." No effect on his blood, anyway. In the end, however, the experiments left the question in a fairly confused state.

In April 1917, the United States entered World War I and the Harvard Hospital Unit, including Cabot, Cushing, and Cannon, soon left for France. "The medical school is most pacific," wrote Clarence. "All of us have been advised to keep on with our training and not get into things until men with training such as we have are absolutely necessary." Eventually, medical students were inducted into the Medical Enlisted Reserve Corps and assigned to continue their medical training, at the disposition of the Army Surgeon General. In 1918 Clarence made an effort to obtain leave to go to France as a civilian worker in the Y.M.C.A. for six months, but the Surgeon General's Office turned him down. As he said to his father, "I'd rather like to get over there for a while to see what the big show is like."

Clarence's letters were not often introspective, but one to his mother on February 25, 1917, dealt with a basic characteristic of his personality—his shyness with strangers and general inclination to be non-communicative:

One of the things that I've been learning this winter is the coordinated use of brain and tongue—and it seems terribly hard some times, and I'm afraid practice is still sadly needed. And yet somehow it goes better now than it used to. Perhaps it's because I'm more with people my own age. In college, being with fellows most of whom were a couple of years older, my mistakes were so frequent and obvious that it rather discouraged any wandering from the beaten path without careful scouting expeditions. But now that I know the character of the enemy somewhat better it's easier to feel my way, to guess ahead of time what will be interesting and how it should be deployed. And with greater knowledge has come somewhat greater freedom and more experiment. The most discouraging part of it is, though, that there seem to be so many times when my head goes back on me entirely and it's all I can do to hear what's being said to me without having a gray matter left over for considering the necessary answer. Sometimes it's hard work that does it. After a ten-hour day—yes, there are times when I've done that much, though not often—about all I can do is to crawl into bed. But too often there just ain't no reason, which is discouraging.

The fall of 1917 and the beginning of his second year found young Gamble, now going on twenty-four years old, much better adjusted. During the summer, a Pasadena doctor had found Clarence's blood sugar to be high, but a Harvard check-up by a leading

authority on diabetes, Dr. Elliott P. Joslin, showed it to be lower
or, as Gamble pointed out with true skepticism, perhaps the
methods of measurement were different.

In October, he drew up a will and, as he wrote his father, had
some difficulty figuring things out. "I don't know just what to do
with my post mortem millions. What would you suggest? I suppose it might be a good plan to let them do something in the
medical line in case I shouldn't be allowed to do it myself." Like
his father, he made the new federal income tax law required
reading; charwitable gifts up to fifteen percent were exempt.

By January, he reported, "Our work is getting a little more
interesting now as we get into a little hospital work," but "We're
getting a disgustingly large amount of memorizing—all of
anatomy to learn over again in the next month, and doses and
formulas and solubilities and actions of drugs—important, I suppose, but such a mechanical sort of studying—fit for a Chinese
scholar."

In May 1918, he succumbed to a common childhood disease,
measles, but bounced back in good shape and soon was piling his
Boy Scouts in his Ford and taking them on an overnight hike. He
had become a scoutmaster during the winter.

The fall of 1918 was distinguished by two events of vast human
consequence, the end of World War I and the worldwide sweep of
a virulent influenza that, teaming with pneumonia, produced the
worst pestilence civilization ever had known; it completely
dwarfed the war in the number of young adult lives that it took.
The total incidence in the United States alone was an estimated
20,000,000 cases—twenty percent of the population—with a
mortality of 850,000.

Boston, Harvard, and Clarence Gamble accepted the flu pandemic a good deal more calmly than they did the Armistice. In the
third year, the students began behaving like doctors, and Clarence
was busy with his required series of obstetrical cases; he delivered
thirteen babies in eight days among charity patients seen at
home.

His operating base for this work, done under the general supervision but not in the presence of a house officer, was the Boston

City Hospital. "Influenza . . . increased the normal amount of business considerably and there were only two and a half of us on the job instead of the usual four—so for the first three nights I averaged three hours sleep. The two cases on which I was supposed to get my instruction were abnormal and speedy, and the doc was too busy to do more than give me the usual little pamphlet before I went alone on a third. And just as I was wondering whatnell I ought to do, in comes a classmate assigned to me for some of his instruction—and the very first thing he said is 'Is this your first case?' right in front of the patient. (My) reply was to yawn and say, 'Yes, I've been lucky; could sleep later this A.M.'"

A few days after taking a test vaccine against influenza—made to protect against a bacillus rather than the actual cause, a virus, as it was eventually established—Gamble came down with the disease in mid-October. "I had quite an easy time of it with my taste of influenza. Temperature climbed most discouragingly half a degree each night up to 102 and then down the next day to normal. Four days later they let me out of the hospital." He made a quick and complete recovery and wrote, in summary: "We came very near losing one of our class and a number had the flu, but I think all have escaped so far." At the height of the epidemic, the Medical School was closed for a week.

Through the year, Gamble and his ninety classmates moved from one clinical field to the next—obstetrics, dermatology, pediatrics, surgery, psychiatry. "The work this year is rather discouraging in one way—there is so much that you ought to learn all at once," he wrote his mother. "In the clinical work you rub up against most every sort of problem and time after time you have to say 'I don't know.'"

Before Christmas, he learned that in his grades for the first two years, he was tied with two others for third place in the class. This entitled him to wear the Alpha Omega Alpha insignia, the medical equivalent of Phi Beta Kappa.

In January 1919, Gamble became an anesthetist as quickly as he had become an obstetrician. Students were assigned to the Free Hospital for Women to "do the etherizing" in rotation, one morning every two weeks. The first day, "I was warned not to give too little ether and let the patient interfere with the operating, so I kept dosing her with quite a bit of it and was told once or twice that I had gone too far the other way. The amount of instruction I got was certainly a minimum—but I didn't suffocate any of my four patients."

Meanwhile he was looking ahead. On one occasion, he wrote his father: "I cannot tell you how much it means to have the income that you've given me, and to be assured of it permanently. . . . In comparison with that of those around me it is quite appalling. And it will make my researching so much more fascinating. I can do the brain work and turn over the drudgery to someone else—and if only I have the brains can accomplish several lifetimes of work in the years ahead of me. And I'm beginning to believe that I have you and Mother to thank for a share of cerebral ability."

For his fourth year, 1919–1920, all the chiefs were back from France. Gamble began in the fall with ward rounds and diagnostic work-ups at the Peter Bent Brigham Hospital. His first examination of a ward patient evoked the most common disappointment in clinical medicine—an unexciting case. "It wasn't . . . very interesting . . . just a cold and bronchitis."

But his cases became more interesting and his history-taking lengthier:

My last patient was an English woman who acquired dysentery six years ago in Mexico. After a year or so there and in Los Angeles in which she nearly killed herself with medicine, she went to the Mayo's clinic and was most thoroughly pawed over, but not much of anything done. Then in Brazil they decided that it was another type of trouble entirely and gave her numberless injections of serum. Her husband was assassinated there, and now she's planning to settle down in California with her two children of 8 and 9. Fortunately she seems to have something to live on, and even her last six years haven't destroyed her faith in the virtues of medicine.

Another, the seventh child in a family of 14, had been married nine years, when coming back from a month away from home she found her husband had acquired syphilis—but she found it out too late. She was treated until her teeth began to get loose, but not nearly enough for now (nine years later) she can hardly walk and can tell where her feet are only by looking at them. And from her recent experience she now knows that her father died of the same disease, having taken it from using a glass that had been used by a boarder, a man who took medicine "on the sly." And before he died her father had seven years of blindness.

The third was a little dried up laundress who had been at work since she was nine years old—had learned to be an expert weaver, until her eyes gave out, and had done house work and laundrying ever since. And the habit of work is so strong that she's positively miserable just because of the inaction and wants to go back to the laundry with a temperature of 101.

Yesterday I saw them do a blood transfusion for an old Italian lady who is failing fast. It isn't quite the spectacular affairs that the papers make of it, but the effects are wonderful enough—for a few days. And then the same mysterious poison destroys ali the extra red cells and she's just as badly off as before.

In this same letter, September 28, 1919, Gamble took a jaundiced look at one of Harvard's medical teacher saints—Dr. Henry Christian, Johns Hopkins trained and Hersey professor of theory and practice of physic at the Brigham:

Dr. Christian has been conducting ward rounds for the last couple of days. He's the head of the hospital and the man who gave us most of our medical lectures last year. It gives one a little more intimate view of him—and I'm not impressed. His mind is of the ponderous type that makes a learned impression because of all the miscellaneous facts it can hold, stories of unusual cases, rare exceptions, geographical data on Mexico, names of leading scientists in Japan, percentages of people dying of starvation in India—but he made a most absurd statement on the physics of blood flow in the arteries. I'm afraid it's a statistical rather than a well-grounded, working, scientific knowledge. They say he's very nice to work with and to know, but I don't think my enthusiasm for working under him is increasing, or that I would look to him for much scientific inspiration.

I spent the sunset time out canoeing last night—it was very beautiful. A tree or two had begun to turn, just enough to give a touch of color, and there was a crisp suggestion of fall in the air. And my flute and a book were good company.

Here, in two paragraphs, Clarence perhaps revealed as much about Gamble as he did about Christian—his lack of awe, almost arrogance, toward academic authority figures, but, most of all, his continuously renewing love of the outdoors and of music.

Actually, he was thoroughly enjoying his hospital experience; only a week or so later, he remarked "My work at the Brigham has made me like the scientific end of it more than ever." He showed relish in reporting his latest clinical experiences:

Yesterday I did my first lumbar puncture—a great privilege for a mere medical student. It seemed as though the needle were going to come out the other side as I pushed it in and in. I was quite lucky with it, hitting the spot (in the lower spine) at the second poke. Then we gave my syphilitic patient a new type of intra-spinous treatment. . . . It was quite an interesting process. . . .

My latest patient is an asthmatic Jewess of 60 summers, who is most sensitive. Even the blood pressure machine makes her say "oi, doctor, it hurts, I cant stand it." And testing her knee jerks brought such protests that the whole ward began to giggle.

One teacher at the Brigham whom Gamble had no reservation about was Dr. Francis Peabody, then an assistant professor, a Harvard man who had trained at Johns Hopkins and the Rockefeller Institute for Medical Research. He was admired by faculty and students alike and is still remembered for his much-quoted words: "One of the essential qualities of the clinician is interest in humanity, for the secret of the care of the patient is in caring for the patient." Of him, Gamble wrote: "There is one man at the Brigham, Dr. Peabody, who really tries to do some teaching on his ward rounds in the morning, so I don't want to miss him."

Meanwhile he began a series of talks with Dr. Cabot at M.G.H. about "my idea." This was to develop an electrical stethoscope so that heart sounds could be amplified and heard not only by the physician holding the stethoscope to the chest but by a roomful of students and, through this device, to record the characteristic sound of the heart in health and disease on phonograph records so that they could be played any time. The possibility had occurred to him in 1919 as the result of talking to a friend (probably Frank Boice) who had worked during the war on problems of submarine detection. The friend told him of the invention of the radio vacuum tube for the magnification of sound waves electrically. Cabot told Gamble that such an invention would be a valuable teaching aid; in fact, he, like others, had experimented in this direction, but without success. He had been told that from an engineering standpoint, it wasn't possible to transmit such low-pitched sounds. Gamble decided he would discuss the problem with Western Electric Company engineers.

Although Gamble as yet had not had the opportunity of training under Cabot, his bias was easily recognized: "He's very much interested in his third-year teaching, and is trying some new things on the class. They seem to like him a lot. Some of those who have gone before say that he leaves them with the idea that things medical can be clearly classified, and that they spend most of their fourth year unlearning this impression, but his method of probabilities strikes me as much more productive than Christian's of exceptions."

As 1920 began, Gamble completed his hospital examinations and, as was customary then, made his bid for a hospital appointment as intern. The only place he wanted to go was Massachusetts General, to train on the West Medical Service under Cabot. He was confident that he could obtain the appointment, but indicated the Brigham as a second choice. When his M.G.H. appointment came through, however, he was not wholly satisfied. He wrote:

Discussion over the hospital appointments has been very warm, and when I consider my running mates I don't feel a bit proud of getting the job. So far as we have been able to figure out there wasn't one of the men appointed (myself included) who didn't get it through some special friendship or pull. Scholarship, intelligence, and practical ability seem to have counted for nothing. . . . I wish I dared tell Dr. Cabot some of the things that the class is saying of his appointments.

But Gamble did not dare, and it was just as well. He graduated from Harvard Medical School second in his class, so that he was hardly in position to say that favoritism outweighed scholarship in his case.

The last semester of his fourth year left Clarence with ample time for his extra-curricular activities. He took his hospital examinations in January and his general examinations in June, some oral and some written, and completed his required thesis, a 119-page sanitary survey of the City of Pasadena, which he had worked on at home the summer before. As usual in his examinations, he was "cool as a cucumber," in the words of Cabot. Clarence Gamble loved a contest.

A Busy Young Man

In medical school, Clarence managed to reduce his role as an automobile mechanic by buying a new Ford at the beginning of each school year and, when possible, selling it in the spring. At one point, he had two Model T's on hand. His Fords took him all over New England and enabled him to introduce ski-joring behind an automobile to the Boston winter scene. His fraternity brothers and he had many spills but survived speeds of twenty-five miles an hour over the snowy streets. The greatest difficulty was learning to turn a corner on eight-foot skis as well as the Ford did. Gamble was never long away from sports—ice-skating, skate-sailing, canoeing, sailing, swimming. Each winter, he and friends took their snowshoes and packs and climbed Mount Washington, a 6,288-foot-high mountain in New Hampshire where inexperienced winter climbers occasionally lose their lives.

Throughout his medical school days, Gamble maintained an account with Slattery & Co., New York investment securities brokers, and was an active trader although in relatively small amounts, usually in the hundreds and rarely involving more than a few thousand dollars. His major holdings were in a trust account managed by his father and brother, Cecil. Clarence was not hesitant about giving his father advice on the stock market. In 1918, he wrote: "And for something a little more speculative General Motors—it's a new company and somewhat unstable, but it has the Buick, Cadillac, Olds and Oakland. With the pleasure cars that peace will make more and more profitable it ought to do well."

At one point, Gamble tried to entice a classmate, Dr. Russell Wood of New Bedford, into the stock market, offering him several thousand dollars to play with and the opportunity to keep all the profits. Gamble also gave or loaned money to three or more students who needed financial aid to stay in medical school. Wood, who was making his way on a modest allowance, would not accept the responsibility. "If I lost, I should have to pay it back," he said. Clarence's theory was that it would give his friend some business and financial experience—something everyone could profit from.

Gamble tried to do somewhat the same thing with his program for the "needy and industrious boys of Boston." This was David Gamble's idea. In 1918, he offered to finance his son in this work. "The idea," as Clarence described it in a letter to a friend, "is to take some boy with a reasonable amount of brains who is about to drop out of school because he or his family lack sufficient funds and keep him at the books another year. The way I'm going to do it is to pay a weekly 'wage' below the market price for his work (to make sure that he is interested enough to make it worthwhile) and by requiring weekly or monthly reports to supervise what he is doing with his time more or less."

He hired a social worker to investigate likely boys who had been in trade or commerce school but had dropped out to help support their families. He began with five boys and increased to ten. Gamble paid a boy $6 a week, $4.50 to the mother for board and room and $1.50 to the boy for carfare and incidentals. He asked for a weekly accounting to give the boy experience in bookkeeping, and paid by check and asked the boy to start a savings account to give him experience with banks. He also gave the boys odd jobs to do around the fraternity house, which Gamble, as its president, was trying to lift out of the red where others had left it.

At first, Clarence termed his program, "good fun," but a month later mused that it "takes quite a bit of time." By January 1919, he was planning to give "my proteges" psychological tests so that he might better understand their aptitudes and prospects. Most of the ten were doing well under the plan, but one wanted to resign because of a sore back—his father didn't believe in hospitals—and another was failing in school—his father was a drunkard. As he explained to his own father, Clarence had to keep his youngsters going with a minimum of effort, because of his studies, but he did surrender to his own passion for counting things: "This week I'm starting a new proposition with them—having them report as to how they spend all twenty-four hours of every day. And then I'm going to get them to put it onto a chart, each square representing ten minutes, each sheet a week. They'll learn something, and I can see at a glance how they spend their time—each occupation such as sleeping, toilet, meals, school is to be a different color."

When Gamble got the psychological test scores on his boys, he was surprised. Those he thought least bright in some instances were above those he thought more intelligent. He was inclined to think his own judgment was better than the psychologists', but may have mistaken obedience for intelligence.

Meanwhile Gamble's friend, Stuart Mudd, transferred from Washington University to Harvard Medical School in 1918 and came to live at the fraternity house. Gamble now succumbed to his fondness for practical jokes when Mudd complained that he had been deprived of electrical education by his friend handling all of that part of their collaborative work.

Dr. Mudd speculated: "I had done some research in summers and I was writing it up. Jim thought I should become a leader of a Boy Scout troop. I thought doing well in Harvard Medical School and writing up research was all I could manage. Jim had a certain stubbornness about him. He wouldn't take no on this kind of thing. So he took an ingenious method of plaguing me. I was in a little room not much bigger than this table and I had one light over my desk. I found that when I was studying, suddenly the damned light would go off. About the time I could get up to do something about it, the light would go on again."

What was happening was simple to understand only if one knew electricity and Clarence Gamble. He had installed a slow blinker in the wiring leading to the study lamp, a device based on the phenomenon that the electricity heats a bimetal strip and opens the circuit until it cools again. Mudd was serious-minded, preoccupied, and did not realize that anyone might be playing a joke on him. Clarence let everyone, including fraternity brothers, housekeeper, and his parents in Pasadena in on it.

Mudd never figured the thing out until Gamble revealed it to him at a fraternity banquet. This was not the end of it either. Clarence rigged up an electric shocking machine by connecting electric wires to the springs in the living room sofa. "I would sit down and be playing bridge," said Mudd, "and I would get a terrible shock. Gamble would go on playing bridge as if nothing had happened. He had it rigged so he could press a button with his foot and activate the shocking device." Years later the Gamble sons, thoroughly educated in electrical matters by their father, carried the shocking device to school with dramatic results. The headmaster wrote on Dick's report card, "You would be amazed to know how your son keeps his masters moving."

Dr. Edward P. Churchill, a classmate, attempting to evaluate Gamble, said: "In summary, I would say Clarence had a wide circle of acquaintances but not friends. He wasn't sensitive to what other people were feeling."

There can be no doubt about the wide circle of acquaintances. The wealthy of those days, as of any day, appeared to be constantly on the move and then, probably much more than now, expected to stay at one another's homes as they traveled about the country. Overnight and weekend guests provided splendid excuses for dinner parties and dances. Clarence Gamble kept a notebook containing names and addresses of scores of people in Cincinnati, New York, Boston, Chicago, Pasadena, and elsewhere, together with notations about them, frequently in code. Of one young man, he said "recently married a woman old enough to be his mother." Of a young lady named Dorothy: "Beauty prize for those I met in Cin. About my height—well developed but not fat and pretty. Attractive otherwise too— though perhaps lacking a good head. Would like to know her better. Will be married by 1917." If he met "Blondy" Dinsmore at the Princeton-Yale game or Leslie Gates at the Smith College prom, he made a note of it.

There can be little question that Clarence took an intense, if somewhat detached, interest in the question of marriage. He saw debutantes for what they were, creatures bred, reared, trained, and groomed for entry in the matrimonial race and compelled by their mothers to show themselves on occasions, usually dances, when young men of equal or superior class—at any rate, unmarried—might be on hand to look them over and even dance with them. Clarence, as he noted, felt sorry for them. But he kept his own voluminous list of young ladies and their credentials, and also kept clippings of their engagement and wedding announcements, ticking them off as it were.

There is evidence that he still had "Happy" Dummer in mind, although she seemed to have made it clear that, while she considered him a good friend and welcome guest in her home, she was not in love with him.

In an undated bit of soliloquy, Gamble wrote: "'And they lived happily ever afterward.' Was there ever a greater fraud perpetrated on a gullible yet willing public. . . . They want to believe that such things do happen and they are willing to pay their dollar thirty-five cents net only for the happiest of endings. And yet in real life it doesn't work. The heroine doesn't always elude the villain and marry the handsome and upright hero. By the hard school of experience have I learned it, and as a warning for those that may follow, a warning that I know will pass unheeded, I want to record here the sad disillusionment that I have suffered."

From now on, he seemed to be saying, nothing but reality. He was a doctor of medicine, at the age of twenty-six.

Massachusetts General Hospital

Gamble served an eighteen-month internship at Massachusetts General Hospital under Dr. Richard Cabot. Interns were called "house pupils," or "pups" for short. The services, or wards, were divided into medicine and surgery, and sub-divided into male and female patients. There were no formal resident training programs specifically designed to train specialists. From this training, the young doctor emerged as a general practitioner, general surgeon, or "physician and surgeon," as his license described him. If he wanted to specialize, or to teach and do research, he then attached himself as an assistant to a senior man who served as his preceptor. By and large, the brighter and wealthier remained in clinical training longer, whereas the less intellectual and poorer opened an office as a solo practitioner as soon as possible after graduating.

M.G.H., incorporated in 1811 and affiliated with Harvard, was a pace-setter among American teaching hospitals, a continuously growing institution with hundreds of beds. During the period that Gamble knew it, the Hospital was largely concentrated in the old Bullfinch Building, near the Charles River, and organized into East and West Medical Services and East and West Surgical Services, each containing large wards of twenty-five to thirty beds plus a few single and double rooms for the very sick. In each of these services, from four to six interns began working every two or three months and so established a well-defined pecking order in which each man supervised the work of the man immediately below him. The sub-pups and pups were at the bottom of the hierarchy, the junior and senior house pupils in the middle level, and above them was the visiting physician, who was the chief of service, and high in the institutional clouds were the chief of medicine and chief of staff.

The appearance of any of these godlike figures making rounds among the patients on the wards was a momentous occasion, akin in spirit to the sultan's procession through the streets of Bagdad. But it was the pups who did the hard work: medical charity care in the out-patient department; routine blood, urine, and feces tests in the laboratory; case histories, physical examinations, tentative diagnoses, recommended treatment, and follow-up on the wards. The junior and senior interns made the day-to-day decisions, all of them subject, of course, to the review and final judgment of the visiting physician. The system was ideal for teaching the delegation of authority from the top down and the acceptance of responsibility from the bottom up.

Gamble, as pup, started work at 8:30 a.m. He finished in the later afternoon or evening when everything that had to be done for the old and new patients was done. Sleeping in his hospital quarters, he was still on call at night when the ward nurse decided a patient needed a physician.

A main characteristic of Dr. Cabot's service was personal concern for the patient. Few professors, of course, admit personal indifference to the patient's feelings, but their technical interest in the patient's disease and enthusiasm for instructing their students, plus personal egocentricity, are so strong that they often will discuss a patient with students as if the patient were not there, or, if they gave him any thought, often assume he is enjoying the discussion of his case as much as the teacher. Having detected this tendency in himself and recognized the need to check it, lest he say or do things or teach others to say or do things that would injure the patient or aggravate the disease, Dr. Cabot spoke out strongly against "the pedagogic enthusiasm of medical teachers," and warned his overeager students "not to overwork the patient."

One of his favorite examples was the demonstration of a "floating kidney" in a woman patient:

> When the student's hands are made to move in a particular way on the surface of the patient's body, the moveable kidney may be made to shoot out from between the hands as an orange seed can be swiftly squeezed between one's fingers. Now when this pleasant little trick is successfully performed by the physician—while the students look on—the physician's face is apt to assume an expression like that of a sportsman who sees game in the thicket. He may say nothing at all, but the patient is sure to see that he is interested and to feel that something has happened inside her. . . .

> Such a demonstration does harm because in the majority of cases the moveable kidney is a perfectly normal thing . . . not needing any treatment. The physician's duty . . . is to *keep it dark*. . . . When the patient sees that the doctor and students are keenly interested in this phenomenon—and especially if she hears the awful words "floating kidney"—she begins to have pains and other symptoms in that part of the body and soon develops a full-grown neurosis which it may take years or months to break up.

With this sensitivity to suggestibility, it was apparent that Cabot taught an internal medicine that rubbed shoulders with psychiatry. It would now be called psychosomatic medicine, as it dealt with the impact of emotions on organic function, but also would encompass iatrogenic, or doctor-induced, disease. In this way of teaching he differed markedly from some of his M.G.H. colleagues who were more prone to visualize the human body as a machine.

No account has come to light providing Gamble's critical thoughts about his clinical teacher. Little remains of his correspondence with his parents during this period, from December 1920 to June 1922. This could be because he employed a secretary and himself no longer filed carbon copies in his trusty, 5 by 8, Moore's Loose Leaf Binders. However, the preoccupations of internship would be sufficient to explain a shortage of letters home. Also, it was about this time that he began mailing dictaphone cylinders home. That he did communicate was evident in a few replies from his father which were preserved. In April 1921, for example, David Gamble wrote:

> We do hope that you will not have so much strenuous work in the future. You certainly should not, and if you find that it is affecting your health my advice to you would be to go to Dr. Cabot and tell him that you will have to surrender your position rather than to break down under it.

In May, the father wrote:

> I am glad that your nervewracking experience is over and hope that you can now skin thru with less work. You certainly have had your share of hard work. I do not suppose that your successor will trouble himself to do as much as you did.

Dr. Joseph Stokes, who became professor of pediatrics at the University of Pennsylvania, was an intern on the West Medical Service at the same time Gamble was there, but two pups ahead of him. His recollection was that Gamble was "a real gadgeteer," and "not much interested in the little ordinary things." Indeed, he was "a little careless about blood counts and things like that." He would work awfully hard in certain areas," but "had tangents he went off on." And, "he tended to become exhausted . . . and would sleep for twelve hours straight. Nobody knew where he was. He would be off sleeping. He often disappeared.

"He was a fellow, though, that everybody liked, although he was by no means a hale fellow well met," Stokes continued. "He was just so interested in doing things by himself, he wouldn't think of the little amenities of personal contact. One of the things I noticed about him was that when he was talking, for instance, he tended to look not directly at you, as though he had a whole realm of things he was thinking of and put only part of his time on what you were saying . . . as though he was occupied . . . like a chess player who plays eighteen or twenty games and wins them all."

In the absence of letters, Gamble left something of human interest, a collection of thirty poems characterizing some of the people whom he knew at M.G.H.; these, like his notebook soliloquies, demonstrate both his own sensitivities and a capacity for empathy. In June 1922, as his internship was coming to an end, he sent them to his mother, explaining "'These silhouettes were begun in days when I had to fill every spare cerebral minute with something other than patients and deaths and diseases . . . . Since then, I've added others . . . just to tell you of those with whom I've worked. . . . And I wish that you might have been here to meet the models who have unsuspectingly posed for them." His characters included doctors, interns, nurses, patients, and orderlies. They reveal a warm and sympathetic nature, a side of his personality that he was too shy to show openly. One about a patient dying of cancer, indicated how deeply he thought about the responsibilities of a doctor.

Adub Noomia

Slow as the march of a continental glacier,
And as irresistible
Was the growth of his malignant tumor
Deep within his chest,
Reaching ever for an unreleasable grasp
Upon his trachea.

There was little outward sign,
A lump that raised his collar just a bit,
A deadened sound on tapping
Where some of his lung should have been,
But the invisible ray that sees all things
Told of the coming catastrophe
In monosyllabic words,
Saying "Some day death by choking."
We told him nothing of the future
But we knew,
And we watched and waited powerless.
We gave him the magic of radium,
And the foot of the glacier melted a little
As under a summer sun.
But winter returned and the growth pushed onward,
Expanding as it went,
And ever his stomach protested
The use of the powerful ray,
As the early Pilgrims protested
The progress of science, calling it witchcraft,
Or the many cults of nature healers
Curse the life-saving power
Of vaccination.
We gave him added days,
But they were days of discomfort
And only postponed the evil time
Of suffocation.
One morning on my rounds he told me
His arm was swollen—then I knew
The growth had choked a vein.
That meant an inch, and it would choke his breathing,
And still I waited, powerless.
Another week, and he complained,
"Doctor, It's hard to swallow."
That meant his gullet—half an inch
And he would drown—on land.
    His windpipe warned and gave before the onslaught,
Then lodged against a bone, the end had come.
Hour after hour he coughed and fought for breath,
Ever the whistling in his throat grew shriller,
He lost his voice, his face grew blue

And livid as a walking ghost, or as a man
Full frozen and half thawed.
Each time I passed his bed, he stretched out a hand
Of silent pleading, and his eyes were wide
With the fear of ghastly death.
He could not speak, but ever motioned with his lips
"Please, Doctor. Please."
And ever as his throat grew tighter
The throttling grip of death.
    And then I knew myself a coward,
Crippled by the fear of laws and rules and precedents,
Held fast by the primeval tribal superstition
That human life is sacred.
One short note in the order book,
For five small grains of an alkaloid
And he would sleep in peace,
The sleep that is forever.
And yet I could not write. "Why not?" you ask.
Because I feared what "they" would say.
"A fatal dose! Is that the way you treat your patients?"
"What will you do to us?
Who are you, an intern, to say that death
Is inevitable and should come early.
Who knows that he might not have lived
For many happy years?"
And what would they say of Health Hall,
That allowed such a thing to be?
I could not reinforce my cowardice
By permission from those above me,
For how could they consent
To murder?
And so I failed, and by my failure
Gave to a fellow being two needless days of agony.
With much of the juice of the poppy I eased his pain,
So that he felt not that, but his eyes
Told me ever that deep in his brain
There was terror, and anguish of mind,
Fear of the unknown beyond, fear
Of the last, hard-fought-for
Breath.
For those two long days I cursed
My weakness, scarcely breathed myself,

Until at last the torture ended,
At last the outworn muscles relaxed,
The face turned inky black
The heart beat slower,
And slower
And stopped.

In medical school, Clarence Gamble had fixed his mind on
doing medical research. In fact, he purchased a lot across the
street from Pasadena Hospital—his father was president of the
board—with the idea of building a private laboratory there when
he had completed his training. Midway through his internship,
however, the human side of medicine—helping sick people—
exerted some pull on him, as indicated by a letter from his father
advising him "to get some information from your friend Dr.
Cabot or some others as to how it is best to start if you go into
general practice."

In January 1922, Clarence wrote his father of a long talk with
Dr. Cecil Drinker (whose lecture style he had despised in first-
year physiology). He now recognized Drinker as "the most promising of the younger researchers in the medical school," and "the
man who had done more original work in recent years than
anyone else there." Drinker was a visiting physician at M.G.H. "I
told him rather frankly of my interest and financial status."

Drinker quickly retracked Gamble's interest into research. He
did not feel Gamble could do first-class work in Pasadena and, in
any event, the most interesting opportunities lay in the Eastern
medical centers. He advised Gamble to begin with a two-year
apprenticeship in methods of medical research. He suggested that
the bulk of this time be spent working with Dr. A. N. Richards, a
physiological chemist who had done some fascinating studies of
the liver at Rockefeller Institute and was now professor of pharmacology at the University of Pennsylvania. Richards was conducting physiological studies of the heart and kidneys and "producing more original work than anyone else in medical fields at
present."

Because of Gamble's financial independence, it should not be difficult to arrange an appointment under Richards. For the immediate future, it was desirable for him to get away from Boston and "meet new points of view, and work at a place where the path would not be made too easy." When he was ready, he might return to work under the direction of Dr. Francis Peabody, who was planning to establish a research department at the Boston City Hospital (Thorndike Memorial Laboratory).

It was most important that he work under the guidance of an older man. As for institutional attitudes toward a man who would do research without asking for a salary, Drinker said, "Boston was peculiarly used to such an arrangement, as there are already many financially independent men working in the medical school. They are promoted exclusively on the basis of their output." Accepting a teaching assignment also was important "by way of advertising, especially in the hope that some of those who might elect courses under me would be interested enough and perhaps convinced of the quality of my leadership enough to want to work under my direction."

"Don't think that this means that I have decided to do just what he outlines," wrote Clarence, not willing to appear dependent on someone else's judgment, but "Do you know of anyone who might like to buy a good lot accessible to the hospital?"

With Drinker's recommendation, arrangement of an appointment with Richards in Philadelphia was simple enough. It was agreed that when Gamble had finished his internship and taken a summer vacation he would become an instructor in the department of pharmacology in September.

chapter 4   Exhaustion and Renewal

Clarence Gamble had a tendency to greet every vacation period and escape from the routine of work somewhat in the manner of a shot out of a cannon. The one thing, more than anything else, that drew him and Zenos Miller together was their love of adventure. This love cost Miller his life and, in the opinion of some medical colleagues, damaged Gamble's future in research. Their planned adventure was a trip from Boston to Pasadena in Gamble's airplane in July 1922. Following the first aerial combat in World War I, flying had seized the imagination of American youth. Quite a number of young aviators had lost their lives. Experienced pilots usually had been in crash landings.

Gamble gave his account of their accident, in a thin, black book written by friends *In Memory of Zenos Ramsey Miller*. They had met in 1920 when Clarence went back for a Princeton reunion. Miller was finishing his premedical work, preparatory to going to Harvard. Round-faced, red-headed, much admired, "Ze" was on his way to becoming a legend.

Born in China, the son of a poor missionary, a daring athlete, he had returned to the United States for his education, first at Wooster College in Ohio. He entered Princeton in 1916, but almost immediately joined the National Guard and the following summer transferred to the Aviation Corps in Canada. A hard-luck flyer, he broke both arms in training when a propellor struck him. He crashed twice in France; the second crash occurred behind German lines, leaving him a prisoner of war until Armistice came. But he was also a member of a select group of fifty American aces, with the Distinguished Service Cross, five Huns, and the Croix de Guerre with Palm to his credit.

Gamble was secretive about his benefactions, but friends said that Zenos Miller was one of those he was putting through medical school. Entering Harvard in 1920, Miller, never distinguished as a scholar, made many friends. Dr. Francis Peabody said that Zenos was "by far the most promising man in the entire medical school."

Miller flew a Nieuport 28 fighter plane during the war. He hadn't piloted an airplane for three years when, in the spring of 1922, he and Gamble planned to try a transcontinental trip. Clarence then was twenty-eight years old and Zenos, twenty-seven. The young men bought a second-hand S.V. Ansaldi biplane with an Isotta Fraschini motor, at Mineola, Long Island, through an agent who offered to act as flying instructor.

"I joined Zenos on July 3rd," Gamble wrote, "and from then until the 21st we worked continuously on the plane. During the trial flight it had heated excessively, so we were forced to install additional radiator surface. Then there was continual trouble with spark plugs. . . . As our agent had disappeared when he had received his payment we were forced to find another instructor. . . . Under his direction Zenos spent much time practicing starting and landing the plane. . . .

"Finally, on Friday, the 21st, with our compass installed as the last addition, we were ready for the trial trip to Boston, our first venture away from the mechanic. The trip went smoothly, and we circled over Boston and the Medical School, then westward to the field at Framingham."

Landing at the field, they were the envy of other pilots who shared their eagerness for transcontinental flight. Zenos's brother, Ralph, was also there on July 22.

"We were leaving for New York again about noon, and the question came up of taking Ralph Miller with us," Gamble wrote. "He had never flown before, and we felt that he would enjoy the trip. Having seen the ship perform with three aboard, I felt no hesitation, though I asked Zenos if he thought it were too great a risk to have two members of the family in the same plane. 'A little, perhaps, but nothing's going to happen anyway,' he said. So . . . the three of us climbed aboard and were ready to start.

"Just then one of the aviators ran up and said that one of the planes had had a forced landing, with a stalled engine, to the eastward. He didn't know just where and wanted us to see if the pilot needed any immediate attention. We agreed to return to tell them the exact position if the plane were injured, but were merely to cross the field and wave to them if the pilot was unhurt. We found the aviator on the edge of a smooth field beside his machine talking to a farmer, so we circled back, dipped low over the field and waved to the group of aviators and mechanics. The next thing I remember was looking up at one of the nurses in the hospital.

"Those who were on the ground tell us that we tipped as one would expect us to tip for a turn that we were making, but that something seemed to carry us too far over. Consequently we slipped down nearer to the ground. Zenos, they said, obviously did what was necessary, and got us levelled out—but we were so low that we struck the top of a tree and plunged into the edge of a swamp. With the shock of the impact Zenos fell forward fracturing his skull against the instrument board, losing consciousness instantly. One leg was pinned under the machine in such a way that those who came to rescue us could not take him out immediately. While they were struggling to do so, he breathed for perhaps an hour, but did not regain any trace of consciousness. And he died as peacefully as medical experience has shown me that patients with such injuries always do die.

"However much I do regret the loss of his friendship for myself and the many others who loved him, and the loss of all that he would have done for the world, I can feel no regret for what he went through in his going. For I tasted practically what he did, and I minded it not in the least. . . . And before that was all the pleasure that youth and adventure alone can give. . . . It is only the family and the friends who suffer."

Ralph Miller was injured, but less seriously.

Gamble was taken to Massachusetts General Hospital, where he had just finished eighteen months' training as a doctor and now returned as a patient in critical condition. When he regained consciousness, he saw the chief brain surgeon of M.G.H. gazing down on him and wanted to say, "Don't do anything to me if it's going to make me a vegetable," but it was too much trouble to speak. He suffered a broken nose, possible skull fracture, and broken collarbone, arm, and leg on his left side.

David and Mary Gamble, who only a month before the accident were rejoicing that Clarence had finished his internship without breaking down, wrote a few days after the accident: "We were greatly relieved to hear that you were not killed as first reported." Cecil, his older brother, came up from Cincinnati to look after him. Two weeks later, their father was doing his best to cheer up Clarence in a letter: "We have a paper from Iowa giving a fine account of Mr. Zenos Miller in the war and feel that you certainly had an experienced pilot."

Clarence's recovery was slow. During the first weeks of his convalescence he required a great deal of sedation—opiates and bromides—against pain and discomfort. It was nearly a month before he could write a letter to his parents. He then was able to sit up in a wheelchair, amusing himself by wheeling along the hospital corridors and spreading rumors among his many nurse and intern acquaintances to see how long it took for his words to come back to him in exaggerated or distorted form. In September, he still was unable to walk, but was well enough to make the train trip home to Pasadena. The head injury damaged his power to concentrate and left him with another reverse of his normal character—it was exquisitely difficult for him to come to any decision; even the selection of a necktie to wear was an agonizing process. He found it difficult to get to sleep; suffered some mental depression and irritability, but not as much as expected, and "was especially lucky in escaping headaches," of which he had none. He enjoyed the winter with his mother and father, but found "the excitement of sunrise and sunset doesn't quite fill the whole day." He used the occasion to grow a small mustache, took over his aging father's business correspondence, and "I climbed a mountain again."

Warning his parents that he expected to have trouble with his health, Gamble in early March 1923 felt strong enough to face the world. He headed east, visiting friends in Phoenix, Chicago, Cincinnati, and Boston, impelled, he told his mother, by a desire to see what a girl whom he had met in Boston was doing and to get started in his research job in Philadelphia.

Dr. Mixter, his physician at M.G.H., thought he was doing surprisingly well and advised him to work, but not too hard. "I still have difficulties with such intricacies as packing," he wrote, and "even gossip is too much effort."

The Electrical Stethoscope

Visiting the Western Electric Company in New York, Gamble got some good news. Since he had first talked to Dr. Cabot in 1920 about an electrical stethoscope that through multiple outlets would enable medical students to hear the chest sounds their teacher was explaining, Gamble had visited the Western Electric laboratories from time to time. The engineers there were interested in the problem, but equipment that could isolate and amplify heart and lung sounds fell short of what was required. Now, thanks to the invention of the radio vacuum-tube, H.C. Snook had designed an amplifier that appeared to meet specifications. He used vacuum tubes for three stages of amplification, and soon added a fourth. Gamble informed Cabot and got busy making arrangements for the first demonstration of the electrical stethoscope at M.G.H. As he later wrote: "My part in the electrical end of the game has been small, but in the whole thing I feel that it's quite large."

Late in April 1923, he began work in the Laboratory of Pharmacology at the University of Pennsylvania. "My boss, Dr. Richards, is the possessor of a good cerebrum for research and of a personality that is a delight for those about him," he wrote. Gamble's first assignment was to help others in the department work out a new method of measuring blood flow through a dog's kidney. However, making arrangements for the shipment and delivery of amplifying equipment to Boston and its installation in the Hospital, with the assistance of Delbert E. Replogle, an engineering student from Massachusetts Institute of Technology, kept him away from Philadelphia much of the time. Among other things, he had to arrange with Cabot to supply the patients who had the heart murmurs to be amplified.

From the Harvard Club on June 4, Gamble wrote an enthusiastic letter to Dr. Richards: "The debut of the electrical machine occurred this morning, and seemed most successful. Dr. Cabot had a series of cardiac murmurs for his seventy-five graduate students to listen to and so successfully did the amplifier transmit the murmurs that the class voted unanimously to spend the whole morning with it and not to attempt to review the patients by the usual stethoscope method. In the group of twenty cardiacs there was only one murmur—and that a very faint one—that Dr. Cabot was able to hear by the old method, but failed to get electrically."

The demonstration took place in the Ether Dome amphitheater of M.G.H. Cabot asked Gamble to make the introductory remarks about the instrument's development. The patient's bed was placed by a cabinet containing amplifier, batteries, and controls. Cabot moved a bell-shaped microphone about the chest to detect heart sounds. These traveled as electric waves through wires to the amplifier and then back over one circuit to the physician's stethoscope, at the same time going out over wires to the students' stethoscopes, pressed against receivers in their laps or on the arms of study chairs; their posture was one of intent listening, some with their eyes closed. As Gamble wrote, "They sit around the amphitheater like owls at a prayer meeting."

A friend of the Cabot family told Gamble that the success of the demonstration saved the day for Dr. Cabot because in the afternoon he flunked an examination for an automobile driver's license. Gamble promptly gave the doctor two more driving lessons. Cabot already had expressed himself as in Gamble's debt. Gamble and Replogle had given Cabot a small radio set the previous Christmas. "You have converted us to the Ford and now the radio," Cabot wrote. "I wonder what your next victory will be?"

Cabot, delighted with the results, made the electrical stethoscope a part of his June course in physical diagnosis. Meanwhile, Gamble assembled background information and wrote a preliminary article for Cabot's signature, entitled "A Multiple Electrical Stethoscope for Teaching Purposes." The article recalled Cabot's earlier, unsuccessful efforts beginning in 1904 and others' attempts "to find some device whereby both instructor and student might hear exactly the same chest sounds at the same time." It reported: "I have seen my aim accomplished. As the result of three years of experimentation, an electrical apparatus has been perfected whereby the heart and lung sounds can be perfectly reproduced and distributed—certainly to seventy-five students simultaneously, and presumably to a much larger number."

The American Medical Association promptly published the article in its *Journal* for July 28, 1923. The published article said the equipment was designed and loaned by the Western Electric engineering department, but made no mention of Gamble or Replogle. Gamble had left the determination of credit to his former chief, but had fully expected to receive recognition. When Gamble pointed out the omission, Cabot said it was an oversight and in the reprint of the article added a paragraph noting that the suggestion that such apparatus might be adapted to classroom work came from Gamble and many of the details were worked out by Replogle.

This incident became the source of ill feelings. The contest for recognition and credit in medical science is an old one, at Harvard as elsewhere, and perhaps was more of a problem fifty years ago under a more authoritarian academic system than at present. Some head professors were meticulous about bestowing due credit on their juniors, but others proceeded complacently on the assumption that full credit for any innovation under their supervision belonged to them.

Gamble and Replogle now jointly signed an article on the multiple electrical stethoscope describing the apparatus, a three-stage electrical amplifier, and published it in the *Journal* of the A.M.A. for February 2, 1924. This article, of course, referred back to Cabot's article. Once primary credit is established, even the original ghost writer cannot erase it.

In June 1924, Gamble delivered a report on the electrical stethoscope and demonstrated it to five hundred doctors at the annual meeting of the American Medical Association, using cases studied at the University of Pennsylvania Hospital in the service of Dr. Alfred Stengel, physician in chief, as well as patients at Presbyterian Hospital in New York who had lent their heart murmurs in the production of phonograph records.

The instrument captured the fancy of the press, particularly after Bell Laboratories introduced loudspeaker transmission involving amplification of ten billion times normal. For the next two years, one could read headlines such as TEST MAKES HEART ROAR LIKE WILD SEA, AMPLIFIED HEART BEATS RUMBLE LIKE THUNDER, HEART BEATS HEARD LIKE TRAIN'S ROAR, and HEART BEATS SOUND LIKE CANNON'S RUMBLE. Even an unborn baby's heart could be made to sound like a drum.

Gamble raised the question of whose name should come first when the Columbia Phonograph Company prepared in late 1925 to produce a set of records for sale to the medical profession. It was to be called "Cabot-Gamble Cardiac Diagnosis Records." The name of Cabot was famous in medicine, and had promotional value. Primary credit was quite satisfactory to Cabot, of course, but Gamble was irked at Cabot's failure to credit him in the first place and, furthermore, being a man of some independence, felt no necessity to be politic about the question. The Company indicated it would do anything of which Dr. Cabot approved.

Clarence kept his mother informed of the conflict virtually blow by blow. For example, on January 10, 1926, he wrote her about his latest work on the phonograph records and added: "When I was in Boston, I suggested to Dr. Cabot that, considering the relative amount of work put onto them, they ought to be published as the records of Dr. Gamble and Dr. Cabot. He didn't agree to this at all, saying that he had had the idea before I ever discussed it with him and that his ears and experiences were necessary. We finally agreed to prepare statements of our relative parts in the work, and submit them to a neutral arbitrator. I asked him to whom. He said, 'Who is there in Philadelphia?' I spoke of Dr. Stengel as the head of medicine there, and he said, "All right, let's submit it to him.' So yesterday morning at breakfast we compared our respective statements."

Alfred Stengel, himself a heart specialist, accepted the referee assignment. He reviewed the opposing statements and briskly disposed of the matter in a letter to Gamble dated January 13, 1926. From Gamble's statement, the initiative was clear enough. He had suggested the vacuum tube possibility to Cabot and in 1920 had corresponded with the Western Electric Company, visited it twice in New York, and persuaded its engineers to take an interest in the development of an electrical stethoscope. He continued to make trips to New York for the next three years while the problems of amplification and filtering out extraneous noises were being worked out. Not until April 1924 were the first satisfactory phonograph records of heart murmurs produced, using patients that Gamble had obtained with the cooperation of another medical giant, Dr. Robert Loeb, from Columbia-Presbyterian Hospital in New York. It was Gamble who demonstrated the results at the A.M.A. meeting in 1924. It was he who worked closely with the engineers in the pursuit of a variety of mechanical details, including the need for greater volume. Gamble himself designed both the listening device applied to the patient's chest and the method by which the student could listen in by pressing the transmitting bell on his own stethoscope against a rubber washer in the face of the receiver outlet. It was Gamble who designed and installed the distributing wires for his first demonstration of the electrical stethoscope before Cabot's students in 1923.

Accepting the fundamental importance of his knowledge of heart sounds and their significance and of his role as teacher, Cabot's case for primary credit in the development of the electrical stethoscope was nonetheless weak. From 1919, his interest was prompted by Gamble. Stengel, in his letter to Gamble, pointed out that Cabot had been interested in the reproduction of heart sounds for teaching purposes for many years, but so had he, Stengel, and others.

"The later development of the method and the final recording of sounds upon wax plates have been largely due to the cooperation of the Western Electric Company and your own close attention to the details, and to some extent original contributions by you," Stengel wrote. "My conclusion would be that the fairest way all around to present this work would be to have it come out as by Gamble and Cabot."

Cabot acquiesced in this judgment and authorized the change when Gamble asked Columbia to name its heart murmur records "Gamble-Cabot." On January 13, after seeing Stengel's letter, Clarence wrote his mother: "I feel better. Of course, getting the records published is the important thing, but I do feel that Dr. Cabot has been sitting back and doing nothing and taking as much credit as possible." Not all junior investigators have fared as well, but it was clear now that Clarence Gamble was not a man who would back off from any position simply to avoid unpleasantness.

Paul Dudley White, the famous Harvard cardiologist, was at Massachusetts General Hospital at the time and was both a witness and a user in the development of the electrical stethoscope. In an interview in 1971, Dr. White said that the instrument is still "a very important" teaching aid in the demonstration of heart sounds in live patients, just as the act of listening to heart sounds is still important in the diagnosis of heart disease, despite the development of the electrocardiograph. Various modifications of the original Gamble-Cabot electrical stethoscope are used everywhere in the teaching of auscultation—the art of listening to body sounds in medical diagnosis. The seats in the Ether Dome amphitheater and one other classroom at M.G.H. are wired for the use of stethoscopes in cardiac grand rounds and the teaching of physical diagnosis.

Death of David Gamble

Returning east in the spring of 1923 and seeing his brothers and Cecil's children, the post-convalescent Clarence developed an urge to assemble the Gamble clan once more in their respective cottages on Little Traverse Bay for the summer. It did not seem that he had any premonition about this reunion but was nostalgic about the many good times he and the family had had together at Harbor Point. Cecil and Sidney, at any rate, were quite ready to go. Clarence wrote his mother and father in Pasadena. The whole family could be together. His father had had influenza and a cold on his last trip to Cincinnati that winter, and now was bothered with a recurrent kidney ailment. He did not feel well and did not want to travel.

True to his budding reputation as a man who would not take no for an answer, Clarence persisted in repeated letters and telegrams in trying to persuade his father to change his mind. For example, he wrote to Aunt Julia: "It's a shame Father doesn't feel that he can do it, for I'm sure there's no real physical reason."

Clarence had been at Harbor Point three weeks when the telegram came. Their mother now informed the brothers that David Gamble was about to undergo surgery. He had developed a jaundice without fever three weeks before and had an enlarged liver. This news caused Clarence to remark to a friend: "There are times when one would rather not know quite so much medicine. One was when I was in the hospital last summer, and another is now, for although I haven't heard all of the details, I can't be very optimistic over the ultimate outcome." He suspected his father might be suffering from a metastatic cancer of the liver, in which case there was no hope of recovery. This, in fact, proved to be the case.

Clarence and Sidney left immediately for Pasadena and were enroute there when their father died on July 15, 1923, two days after the operation. He was seventy-six years old.

Sarah Merry Bradley

Sarah Bradley was one of the first persons Clarence saw when he got back to Boston in the spring of 1923. He took her to a dance at the Harvard Club and subsequently to dinner on several occasions, and drove her to Brattleboro, Vermont, where her family had a summer home.

It was plain: The rich young doctor had overcome his previous disappointment in courtship and also his deep-seated suspicion that young ladies were interested in him for his money. He had fallen in love. For some three years the only members of the opposite sex who had interested him were nurses; a few at M.G.H. had become his close friends. There, however, he felt compelled to keep his guard high and his exit clear. It was well established that pretty young nurses were out to capture eligible young doctors, and his mother warned him against marrying one.

Indeed, Mary Gamble had laid down ten fairly exacting requirements for her youngest son's bride. In the first place, he had to feel that he could not live without her. She had to have *background*, and *not* be a nurse. She should be the only girl he'd want for the mother of his children. She should be interested in the same things as he was. She should, as he put it, have "much Pollyanna spirit." She should be the right age, a college graduate, have *ideals*, and a sense of social service.

Sarah Merry Bradley, then twenty-five, had a quiet beauty. One, in the idiom of that day and time, might have called her serene and also wholesome and decorous. She had an oval face and dimple on her chin; her nose was straight with an upturned tip;

her jaw had a firm set. Her widely spaced eyes were blue and her hair brown; at five feet five inches in height, she was two inches shorter than Clarence.

Sarah was born in Boston on March 9, 1898, the daughter of Richards Merry Bradley, a native of Vermont, a Harvard graduate, and a Boston realtor. The family—there were five sisters and one brother, but the latter died as a small child—lived on Beacon Street in Boston and summered at the Bradley Home Place in Brattleboro. Sarah was appropriately educated at Fiske and Winsor, and then "made the usual kind of debut in Boston," she said. Her mother, who was Amy Aldis, died of influenza in 1918. Her older sisters, Amy and Helen, did war work in France; so it fell to Sarah to keep house for her father and two younger sisters, Mary and Edith. She attended Radcliffe for two years, taking a particular interest in English and writing and playing on the College's field hockey and basketball teams. Meanwhile, with a friend, Grace Holbrook, and with the help of her father, she started and directed a summer camp in Brattleboro for culturally and socially deprived Vermont country girls, an activity she continued each July until her marriage. She still serves on the board of the camp, as did her sister Edith, until her death in 1974.

After the war, Sarah Bradley transferred from Radcliffe to the Simmons College School of Social Work, taking a two-year course, ending with a certificate in June 1924. As Clarence Gamble would tease his mother, Sarah failed in this one require ment—"she was not a college graduate, but had tried twice." ·

Gamble had met Sarah at Alice Forbes's coming-out party in 1918, but in later accounts he expressed no recollection of this casual meeting. He told his mother they met at a house party at the Forbes's summer home on Naushon Island, near Woods Hole, in the fall of 1921.

Sarah Bradley went horseback riding; the saddle girth broke and she was thrown; the horse came home and she eventually walked in, unhurt. Clarence said he was disappointed that he could not practice his medical skills on her. He did note that one of the pupils in her blue eyes was larger than the other. The next time they met, he found they were the same size, so he said that he would have to inspect them a third time. This was how romance began. They saw quite a little of each other during his final year of internship. The tragic accident with Zenos Miller in the summer of 1922 delayed the next meeting of Sarah and Clarence until the following spring, when Clarence was ready to pull his life together again. During 1923, he often came up from Philadelphia and saw her on weekends. He kept the latest of his Fords in Boston, but when he went to the Bradley house he parked it around the corner. He later told Sarah, "The reason he drove a disreputable-looking Ford was that he did not want anyone to marry him for his money."

Clarence's diary notes for March 1924 contained the following entry: "20th Thursday. Luncheon with Sarah downtown, then jogged out the Charles again to anchorage where the great news emerged most unexpectedly. Little memory of the rest of the day."

Clarence was sensitive to the stimulation of coffee, cocoa, or tobacco and therefore usually avoided them (for a time, in medical school, he smoked a pipe). Before making a speech, however, he sometimes smoked a cigarette or ate chocolate for the special stimulus of it. At lunch that day, before proposing, he drank two cups of cocoa. Sarah observed this and remarked about it. He turned red, doubly stimulated.

After returning to Philadelphia, he told his diary: "24th et seq. Spent most of week recovering from chocolate. 27th. Looked at solitaires. 28th. Examined design. 31st. Ordered ring. Ran out to Strafford to consult Ib on ways and means of proposing. Supper with them."

The explanation of this cryptic note lay in the fact that Clarence was not too giddy to play a practical joke. Sarah was coming down to Philadelphia on April 4 to receive the ring. Elizabeth ("Ib") Diament was a Quaker friend of Sarah's who had married and lived in Strafford, where Sarah would be staying. Clarence wrote his mother on April 1 about Mrs. Diament: "With Sarah's encouragement, I've had a heart-to-heart talk with her, telling her

The Gambles on their honeymoon,
California, 1924

how interested I've become in Sarah, and asking advice as to how and when to propose—as to whether to buy the ring first or not and other such foolish questions. She was so thrilled over the romance and so sympathetically helpful I couldn't get even a tinkle of a laugh from her—that will come though, when Sarah tells her that we've been engaged two weeks."

Clarence took Sarah off the overnight train from Boston and drove her to the Diaments. After dinner, the Diaments thoughtfully went out and returned late, leaving Clarence and Sarah alone and setting the scene so that he might find courage to pop the big question. The next morning Clarence came down to breakfast first. Ib Diament greeted him expectantly; Clarence looked depressed and then, with some skill, dramatized the part of the rejected but inarticulate suitor. Then Sarah came tripping down joyously, extending her ringed finger and exclaiming: "We are engaged!" The young Quaker wife looked at Gamble severely: "Clarence Gamble, *thee is a devil*." Sarah later would recall: "It is a phrase I have used frequently with him since."

Sarah Gamble remembers Mary Gamble as "a rather frightening person with very high principles." But Clarence, even closer to his mother after his father's death, was fully confiding.

He had wired his mother of the engagement and then, on March 24, wrote her a lengthy description of Sarah Bradley and her family, beginning:

Such a week! Full, wonderfully full of good times, and happiness that I hadn't dreamed of. In the days before and after she told me the all-important word we dug rather deeply into each other's make-up, and thoughts and desires, and all I found seemed pure gold. I thought I couldn't be happier than when she said yes—but the days since have made me much more so—made me love her tremendously more than I ever thought I could. She asked me if I thought I could stand 3650 breakfasts with her in the next ten years and I don't see how I can get along without them.

On March 28, his mother telegraphed a night letter:

Rejoice with you in your thrilling success have proved stethoscopes bring forth obscure murmurs and profound heartbeats research often leads into unexpected paths if you are happy there I am I have many questions not foolish hope my stated requisites are there. . . . Much love. . . . Mother

The next night, Clarence got down to a letter demonstrating that Sarah met the ten requisites, except that she was not a college graduate. Quite delicately, he refrained from pointing out that Mary Gamble was not a college graduate either.

In the month or two before the wedding, Clarence wrote his mother frequently and at length, reflecting a continuous state of overstimulation and hyperactivity. Not the conventional male animal, he became thoroughly involved in wedding preparations. Typing a letter to his mother, he babbled: "I'm so excited I can hardly tell the *a* key from the *z*." An accomplished correspondent, however, he wrote scores of letters to Pasadena, Cincinnati, Chicago, and Boston relatives and friends. It was as if the prospect of the impending plunge tightened, rather than loosened, his family ties. On May 26, he wrote his mother a long, sentimental letter in anticipation of her birthday, on June 1, which he signed, "Your baby, Clarence."

Clarence sent Sarah a list of 400 Gamble relatives and friends for wedding invitations. Mrs. Gamble came east for the event, and Cecil was best man. The wedding took place on June 21, 1924, at the St. Michael's Episcopal Church in Brattleboro with a reception at the Bradley Home Place.

The newlyweds honeymooned at the summer home of a friend near Mount Monadnock in New Hampshire. From there, on June 23, Clarence issued his first bulletin to his mother. "We're a bit sleepy after all we've had to do, but tremendously happy in spite of it." In another letter, on June 25, he conceded he still lacked enough energy to climb Monadnock. For the rest of the summer, they toured the country from coast to coast, introducing one another to their respective family networks. In mid-September they settled in a modest two-bedroom apartment in Philadelphia amid six barrels and fifteen packages of wedding presents but without beds at first—only mattresses.

Gamble was thirty and Sarah, twenty-six, when they married. Her entrance was one of three dramatic turning points in his life, over and beyond the crucial fact that he was born a Gamble. The first was when he decided to enter medicine and the third, yet to come, was when he committed himself to birth control. As his letters to his mother quite plainly showed, Sarah worked a great change in his life. As friends later recognized and remarked, Sarah was Clarence's balance wheel. "Sarah Gamble, beloved friend of so many, possesses a natural genius for human relations together with brains, intelligence, and creative imagination," Emily Mudd wrote many years later.

University of Pennsylvania

The next five years were as difficult for Clarence Gamble professionally as they were fulfilling in his romantic and family life. Training under Dr. Alfred Newton Richards (1876-1966), who was director of the department of pharmacology at the University of Pennsylvania from 1910 to 1946, was a singular privilege. But it could hardly have come at a worse time for Gamble, coinciding as it did with the long period of energy deficit that he experienced following his airplane accident and also with the period in which the "man's estate" settled on him by his father in 1915 multiplied many times.

Richards was one of the early twentieth-century heavyweights of American medical science. A biochemist by training, he focused his interest on physiological research in a setting of clinical pharmacology—the study of the action of drugs on the human organism. This interest dated from his work, as a member of the British Medical Research Committee in 1917 and 1918, with H. H. Dale on the role of histamine in shock, an original contribution that established Richard's reputation in cardiovascular research.

At the time of Gamble's coming to Philadelphia, Richards's attention was turning more and more to studies of heart function but he was still interested in the kidney, where his laboratory had made a breakthrough in basic knowledge.

Richards insisted that his major function was teaching, but he achieved the fame that attracted graduate students to him in experiments settling an old medical controversy: whether the kidney secreted urine—that is, manufactured it chemically—or simply acted as a mechanical filter in extracting waste products and fluids from the blood. He began his experiments in the fall of 1920, with the aid of a talented young associate, Dr. Carl F. Schmidt.

They chose the green leopard frog (*Rans pipiens*) as their subject, and performed an operation of consummate delicacy, using up many frogs to achieve a successful procedure. Schmidt anesthetized the frog, made an abdominal incision, tied off some blood vessels and cauterized others. He exposed the frog's kidney, an organ smaller than one's little fingernail. He then focused a microscope on the kidney, employing an arc lamp casting a beam one-fifth of an inch in diameter for illumination and passing the beam through a wall of cold water to keep the lamp's heat from stewing the kidney. All this done without mishap, one could see the organ at work.

Blood, pumped in through arteries from the heart, moved with "bewildering rapidity" through a maze of pathways. Richards and Schmidt spotted, just under the kidney surface, a cluster of blood vessels—the glomerulus—knotting up to form the entrance to one of the kidney's filter tubes and collecting chambers—the nephron. The filter tube emptied a thin, clear plasma into an even finer-gauged tube draining into the collecting chamber and then on to the urinary bladder, holding back thick blood that circulated into the filter tube and out through tiny veins that wound around the tube like a snake. There are thousands of these glomeruli in a kidney. The scientists observed that while some filters worked, others rested.

They had seen a kidney filter something, but *what?* Dr. Joseph Wearn, who had graduated from Harvard Medical School three years ahead of Gamble, now joined Richards in an even more exacting experiment. When Wearn came to work for Richards and inquired as to what he should do in the laboratory, Richards told him to sit there and look at the frog's glomerulus and think. What Wearn thought of was the microdissection needle invented by Dr. Robert Chambers of Cornell. Wearn wondered if he could sharpen this glass pipette so fine that, working under the microscope, he could puncture the nephron, draw off the fluid and determine what was in it through chemical analysis. This would be quite a feat, because the frog's nephron is less than a hair in width. Richards and Wearn had their first success in October 1921, using a capillary pipette of quartz 1/25th of an inch in diameter, drawn out to a point, sharpened, and held in a standard with a screw device permitting it to be moved 1/39,000,000 of an inch at a time. At the other end of the pipette was a suction device. A stream of air played across the kidney to dry off surface fluid. When the pipette finally hit the spot, the fluid drawn up was hardly enough to wet an eyelash.

Human application, by Dr. Homer Smith of New York University and others, of the basic information produced in the frog experiments revolutionized medical knowledge of kidney function.

It was a stimulating atmosphere for a young man who had set his sights on a research career. Following his arrival in Philadelphia in April 1923, Gamble had written his father: "Since the second-year medical work, I haven't had much contact with the 'pure science' basis of medicine, and I find that I can compete fairly well on the theoretical arguments with those in the departments who have been steadily immersed in it. I've always been so much interested in the 'how it works' side of the things I meet."

Following his marriage and honeymoon, Gamble returned to work in September 1924. He was on morning duty in the hospital and worked afternoons in the laboratory. On September 25, he wrote his mother: "I've been spending a good deal of time reading up what others have done to defenseless frogs and have wrecked a few myself. It is quite a delicate operation to get a glass tube into the fine arteries and veins, especially without losing any blood. If even a full drop of blood leaks out most of the vessels collapse, so there isn't any hope of getting into them."

The frog work continued for several months. "We ate frogs' legs quite often," Sarah Gamble remembered. She also remembered that their first year or so in Philadelphia was not easy for Clarence, because of his limited staying power and his efforts to conceal it. "I don't think we ever went out in the evening during the first two years." But he continued putting glass tubes in frog kidneys and in December wrote his mother: "To make a complete experiment I have to get six tubes in succession without a miss. Yesterday was the first time I've done this and I feel quite encouraged." He was now at a point where he could consider questions to be answered, and discussed with Richards the possibility of measuring function by circulating gases and fluids such as oxygen and saline solution through kidney. Richards suggested one method but "I was able to convince him that I had planned a better one—and by night I had fixed it up." Progress however was exasperatingly slow. On December 28, he reported: "Friday and Saturday I celebrated with my frogs. They behaved in true Christmas style. Yesterday, for instance, I succeeded for the first time in getting all six tubes into the beast without a miss and without letting him bleed to death. His kidney refused to produce anything to analyze, but perhaps that was because I was too slow with the work. Next time it will go more easily, I am sure."

In March, he went back on hospital duty. This brought his frog work to an end. Between fall and spring, he had two offers of assistant professorships elsewhere, at the University of Illinois and Dartmouth College at $2400 a year or thereabouts, but chose to stay on as an unpaid instructor with Richards. "I'm not ready for independent work yet," Clarence told his mother.

In May 1925, Richards set him to a new task. Richards turned to a subject that long had interested him: cardiac output. The problem was to find a practical method of measuring the volume of blood pumped by a patient's heart. A Yale group had devised a method of using ethyl iodide, breathed in and absorbed in blood passing through the lungs, as a marker that could be measured after passage through the heart by analyzing blood samples from the arteries. It was a question of confirming how accurate this method was, and also of competing in a new field.

Richards asked Gamble to work with Dr. Issac (Jack) Starr, Jr., who had been one step ahead of Gamble in clinical training at Harvard. They were to perform as a team, and did so for the next three years, producing three highly technical papers. They concluded that through a new, modified approach the ethyl iodide content of arterial blood in the dog and man could be correctly estimated from the content of this drug in a sample of alveolar air—that is, air taken from the air sacs in the lung where the blood-gas exchange takes place during respiration. Because they differed with the Yale group on how fast the body disposed of ethyl iodide circulating in arterial blood and, as they found, remaining in venous blood returning to the lungs and heart, the effect of these studies was to refute the Yale findings—a scientific blow roughly equivalent to a knockout in prize-fighting.

The authorship in all three Pennsylvania papers was "Issac Starr, Jr. and Clarence James Gamble." The order was not of Gamble's choosing and, indeed, reflected much friction between Starr and Gamble. Their personal feelings were spelled out in Gamble's letters to his mother.

The Starr-Gamble relationship, or "Jack" and "Jim" as they were known in the department of pharmacology, began amicably enough, but joint progress was slow and it was understandable that Starr associated the fact with Gamble's inconsistency as a worker and would resent that he, Starr, had to carry the burden of continuity. In an interview in 1970, Starr gave his estimate of Gamble in retrospect:

You want to know what I think of him? He had a very brilliant mind. He could do some things I couldn't think of doing, like mathematical calculations in his head. In that sort of thing he was extraordinarily competent, but he had little mental staying power. After hard mental work for a month or two, it sort of used him up, and he would have to go away or take life easy, and would be unable to do mental work for a period of time, sometimes months. . . . His health was irregular. That, of course, made it difficult both for him and for me. My guess is that the reason he got out of scientific work eventually was because of limitations of this kind. He would come back from a long vacation in fine shape, raring to go, and, as I say, mentally extremely brilliant and alert, and about Christmas time, he had a way of not arriving at the laboratory and I'd find he was having trouble sleeping . . . . There was no doubt he had a problem there. . . . I think there is some reason to believe that the tendency was there before the head injury. . . . He was an irregular worker.

. . . It was certainly much worse after the accident.

Despite Gamble's usual winter colds and lack of energy, Jack-and-Jim teamwork underwent a short-term revival while they combined efforts in January 1928 to bring a sheep's lung from the slaughter-house fast enough to keep the tissue alive by pumping blood through it. These efforts failed; "Jack is getting a bit discouraged." Jim saw a bright side: "The chief advantage . . . though, is that it will cut down the life of the partnership. I'll be glad when it's over."

By February the relationship rapidly deteriorated again. In March, Gamble talked with Richards about the need for a mathematical correction in their data that Starr would not agree to; it reflected on the quality of their measurements in a series of dog experiments. In the absence of any opportunity to refine these measurements, Richards agreed a correction factor was desirable.

Gamble asked Richards to tell him how he could avoid irritating Starr. "You don't know what the trouble is?" asked the professor. "No," said Gamble. Richards then explained that he had gathered that Starr felt Gamble's technical work wasn't quite as accurate and reliable as it might be; that there was some dissatisfaction over Gamble's going to Boston at Christmas-time without much warning, and that Starr "felt that research should proceed down just one track and the things I suggested from time to time were merely tangents leading nowhere." Richards said, "Now that he has come to writing up this work Jack rather feels that he has the weight of the world and of science on his shoulders, and he isn't apt to have much patience with outside suggestions."

Richards had another talk with Starr. Gamble observed that Starr's mental attitude changed for the better, though he doubted it would last. On April 27, Clarence wrote: "And we're gradually getting the final paper written. . . . I found a surprising thing . . . he really seemed to take my suggestions into account."

In May 1928, Richards had another talk with Gamble. He told him that he was being removed from hospital duty. "Their reason, I think, was quite a good one—'that I didn't have enough to contribute.' It has grown to be just too big a job for me." Richards asked Gamble if he had ever considered a job outside of Philadelphia—"I don't see how under the circumstances I'm bothering him enough to make him want to get rid of me, and yet it almost sounds so."

Then, for the first time, the subject of Gamble's wealth came up. Richards said, "He had heard it rumored that I could do whatever I wanted to even though it involved a good deal of expense such as building my own laboratory, and finally asked directly if that were true. I hardly knew what to answer to that. I hadn't then, and haven't yet, seen any place where the knowledge would affect his decision, so I answered, 'I've heard that question a number of times, suggested I suppose by Ivory Soap, and thus far I've found it better not to answer it in either way.' (Very likely that does answer it for him). And went on to say if he needed the information for some particular decision I could probably give it to him."

What Gamble really wanted to do, he told his mother, was to stay and work with Richards. "I still think I'm on the right track, money or no money, and besides what I can get here I want as much energy as possible before I jump to another job."

By June 1, Gamble at least had gotten his immediate future straightened out: "I've had another talk with Dr. Richards and have decided to stay for one more year. The thing that disappoints me the most is that after coming here for training by him in research—when I asked him how my work could be improved he answered that he didn't feel he knew enough about my work to answer. . . . Just as you do, I wonder what part the financial element plays in it all. Perhaps he thinks that I haven't spent any money in his department [and this] confirms a suspicion based on my lack of activity that I'm not intensely interested."

The point was less as described, almost surely, than that Richards was worried about the aftereffects of the plane accident. In fact, Richards recommended that Gamble go to a private mental hospital (the Austen Riggs Center) at Stockbridge, Massachusetts, for a psychiatric evaluation. Gamble agreed to do this, as soon as he and Starr had finished writing their report.

En route to Harbor Point, Gamble went to the Austen Riggs hospital in Stockbridge and told his mother of the visit in his letter of July 17. He had two sessions with Dr. Lawrence Lunt:

> I told him the tale of the accident and the progress since. He wrote down my biography at great length, asked all about my medical associates, how I got on with my wife, what I did with my vacations and a lot more. When he got through he said as far as he could see the main difficulty was the residue from the concussion, and that would continue to get better as time went on. On the whole, he said, he though I'd met the handicap well, but he felt that two or three weeks at Stockbridge in the fall might help me be more efficient with the energy I had available. To me it doesn't seem very necessary, but it might help satisfy Dr. Richards. All through the questions he [Lunt] seemed to be wondering whether I was magnifying my difficulties for some reason, or perpetuating them longer than they deserved. I told him I didn't think so, but naturally the patient's opinion isn't very conclusive on that. I asked him, as I have others, whether recovery from such injury would be more rapid with mental activity or mental rest, and like the rest he couldn't say—"A balance between the two" was what he suggested.

Gamble returned to Stockbridge for the first week of October and wrote his mother about it: "Well, here I am getting all cured."

A careful physical examination by a neurologist failed to reveal any nerve damage from the accident, at least any "accessible from the outside." The psychiatrist "spent quite a bit of time telling of the prejudice of everybody in general against the person who merely thinks himself sick, and who has nothing to show for it. I don't see that that applies much to me, though maybe Dr. Richards thinks I've merely gotten into the habit of being lazy. . . . Having run out of tennis partners, I tried golf today. . . . It's not nearly as good a game."

At the end of the week, he was discharged back to work. One of the Riggs's psychiatrists explained to Sarah Gamble, who was in Brattleboro, not far away, that Dr. Gamble had a compulsion towards perfectionism. At first puzzled, Sarah then exclaimed: "Oh, I know. When he is sailing and comes around a buoy, he has to miss it by a half inch rather than two feet."

Death of Mary Gamble

Gamble, his mother, and Aunt Julia had a little joke about the danger of "barnacling," or vegetating, from too sedentary a life. A Gamble was expected to keep on the move, even if one was over seventy-three. In October 1928, he wrote his mother from Stockbridge: "What's this about your not coming east? Of course you are. . . . You mustn't barnacle." Mary Gamble was persuaded. She made the familiar circuit to Chicago and Cincinnati and then came to Philadelphia for Christmas, rising above whatever feelings she had about the climate. Staying with Clarence and Sarah and their two small children in their home in Germantown, Mrs. Gamble was content to remain indoors most of the time. Christmas was on a Tuesday.

The following Monday, she awoke early with a chill. Clarence examined her; she had a temperature of 101.5 and severe pains in her leg muscles. Listening with his stethoscope, he detected a few rales at the base of her right lung but hoped that he was dealing with no more than a mild influenza. In those days neither sulfa drugs nor antibiotics had been discovered, and doctors were wary of pneumonia, still a leading killer with or without influenza.

Gamble called in Dr. Bradbury, head of the Pennsylvania Hospital out-patient department, and they took her to the hospital. Her white blood cell count was 28,000—not encouraging at that high level. By the end of the second day, they knew she had a blood infection, at first believed to be streptococcus but then pinned down as Type III pneumococcus, an especially dangerous one. Her white blood count dropped to 3,000—this first line of defense was being overpowered. A blood transfusion, a major undertaking at that time, restored the count to 25,000.

"When I got the news of the positive blood culture I telegraphed for Cecil to come on," Clarence later wrote to Dr. Lorena Breed, his mother's physician in Pasadena. "When he arrived the smile and the tone of 'Oh, Cecil' was worth a lot to hear. She had some difficulty with her tongue: 'They've given me so much dope I can't handle my tongue,' she said—it was lack of oxygen, not narcosis, that did it. . . . We did most of the talking."

Starting with those few small rattles, her lungs gradually filled during the week. "In the meantime," Gamble wrote, "I had ordered an oxygen tent, and as the lung space grew less and less we found this most comforting. There was no one in the hospital who knew how to run it. . . . I trained Sidney and Cecil in the analysis and adjustment, and we all agreed that it gave her at least 24 hours more than she would otherwise have had—and this might have meant the crisis (a sudden fall in temperature and the beginning of recovery). . . .

"Once, when we were putting her in the oxygen tent, she pointed to me and said, 'He's just experimenting with me—he always was an experimenter, you know.'"

In a way, this was true, because Dr. Baruch, the inventor of the oxygen tent, told Gamble that he had seen only one out of seventeen Type III pneumonia cases pull through.

Mary Gamble recognized the seriousness of her illness. She remembered that Sidney had had pneumonia and had been in an oxygen tent, and told him: "Well, I suppose one doesn't often get well from this trouble."

Twelve hours before her death on January 5, 1929, "Even though she was fighting for breath, she had Cecil get out the latest plans for the Y.M.C.A. building in Cincinnati." This was to be a combined Gamble family gift. She was unconscious at the last.

His mother's son, Gamble was still able to look on the bright side: "She had just had a good visit with all the children and grandchildren. . . . It all seemed such a well-rounded life and such an easy way to go—though of course that doesn't make the missing of her much easier," he wrote Dr. Breed.

part 2 birth controllers, U.S.A.

chapter 5 Sex and Society in the 1920s

In the 1920s contraception was not a subject that a young man readily could discuss with his mother. Clarence Gamble mentioned birth control only once in his correspondence with Mary Gamble; that was when he had lunch in 1925 with Dr. Robert Latou Dickinson, a prominent New York gynecologist and pioneer American sexologist. Thus, while Clarence was happily pursuing the Gamble tradition as a family man and meanwhile struggling to establish himself in medical research at the University of Pennsylvania, he was developing an interest that he did not mention to his mother. In 1926, he wrote her that he was interested in specializing in heart disease and in 1929 he told Dr. A. N. Richards that his primary interest was medical research. Following his mother's death, however, Gamble's unspoken interest became his life. Even then, he hesitated to mention the subject to his elders in academic medicine.

Birth control emerged only gradually as Gamble's *cause célèbre*, so gradually that his wife, Sarah, reflecting back on their eventual total involvement in the movement, said: "I can't think how it crept up on us."

Harvard Medical School provided no formal instruction in the anatomy and physiology of reproduction and methods of preventing conception—what, in general, we would now call sex education. Outside of what his own curiosity and initiative might provide in his exposure to genito-urological literature, obstetrical training, or personal adventure, the medical student in the 1920s was hardly in a position to become more sophisticated about the risk and prevention of pregnancy than any other intelligent, educated person. In fact, except in childbirth when even a Comstock might consider the woman momentarily safe from the adult male's presumed ever-present aggressive urges, the prudent general practitioner avoided any show of interest in the genitalia of his female patients.

The abysmal backwardness of the medical profession on the subject of sex in the early twentieth century must be fully appreciated to understand the heterodoxy and daring of physicians like Dickinson and Gamble, who expected, accepted, and experienced opposition as well as isolation and insult from the medical majority. Incredible now, the opposition was quite understandable then. For one thing, birth control began as a non-medical movement. The traditional physician is hypersensitive to any lay challenge to his authority in the diagnosis and treatment of human disease—in part because the average layman is ignorant about the structure and function of the human organism, in part because the quack, lay or medical, feeds and fattens himself on this ignorance, and in part because the limitations of the physician's knowledge and skills in changing the course of much disease make him habitually defensive in asserting his authority. At the same time, the fee-for-service practitioner must be responsive to public demand and prejudice if he wants a large following of patients. In religion, politics, law, economics, the community, and often also in what he does or does not do medically, his values must closely resemble, or at least must not openly offend, those of the prevailing social system. His professional survival depends on such conformity.

Thus, if Victorian morality and the laws shaped by this morality dictated that sexual intercourse was permissible only in marriage and then only if the purpose was reproduction, that the primary role of women was to marry and bear her children, that it was an unmarried girl's duty to preserve and defend her chastity, that it was a wife's duty to submit to her husband, and that any artificial interference with the conceptive outcome of intercourse was, as Pope Pius XI said in 1930, "a sin against nature," then inescapably the typical physician would comply. Perhaps it would not be so much through cowardice, as Margaret Sanger charged, but through common sense and the fact that he shared this system of belief wholehartedly or, if not sincerely, at least officially. Doctors themselves often repeated that consummate male conceit, that marriage, meaning regular sexual intercourse with a good man, plus having babies, would straighten out any young woman's nervous or other health problems. Such statements seldom referred, of course, to the maternal mortality rate.

The controversy over birth control, when Gamble came on the scene, was a stormy one, full of turbulence, downdrafts, crosscurrents, and cyclonic effects. Both proponents and opponents tended to be 100-percenters in the positions they took. As is characteristic of crusaders, Margaret Sanger habitually overstated her case. The birth controllers—including upper middle-class educated women, social workers, nurses, some sociologists and biological scientists, some clergymen, and a few physicians— liked to think that with the various methods of contraception at hand or others still to be discovered society could limit family size among the poor, improve maternal and child health, weed out the physically and mentally unfit, and control the size of selected populations. These were legitimate goals, but often were stated in terms of social revolution, including abolition of poverty and war, liberation of women, universal human happiness, improvement of the human race, and so on. For example, in 1918 Mrs. Sanger said, "All our problems are the result of overbreeding among the working class." The reformers' enthusiasm and hope

were part of their bias, but to practicing physicians, whose attendance on the sick gave them ample cause for realism and pes-
simism, a single solution for all problems was not credible, it
being difficult, often impossible, in medicine to find one solution
for one problem. Most doctors disliked Mrs. Sanger not only as an
interfering layman but also in the same way that they disliked
radicals, propagandists, sensationalists, and publicity-seekers of
any kind.

The medical profession's reasoning was not above reproach, to
be sure. When women asked their advice, doctors habitually told
them that they knew of no safe, reliable method of contraception
except complete abstinence from sexual intercourse—nothing
that was 100 percent. Dickinson himself said in 1924: "A guaranteed technique of contraception is not yet worked out." Few
doctors were interested in contraceptive research.

Margaret Sanger brought the Mensinga vaginal diaphragm to
the United States, and it remained the only contraceptive officially approved by national and international birth control organizations for many years to come. In England in 1915, evading
the efforts of Anthony Comstock to bring her to federal trial in
New York, Mrs. Sanger met the great patriarch of sex psychology,
Havelock Ellis, and he sent her to see Dr. Johannes Rutgers,
director of a birth control clinic in The Hague, Holland.

In Family Limitation, her federally banned pamphlet, she had
recommended the Mispah cervical cap pessary. Dr. Rutgers
showed her the superior Mensinga diaphragm, invented by a
German doctor a quarter-century before. The Mensinga diaphragm is a thin, circular cap of rubber two to four inches in
diameter loosely spread over a circular watch spring concealed in
its rims. The woman inserts this device, lubricated with spermicidal jelly, into her vagina so that it covers the cervical canal to the
uterus. The diaphragm can be put in place in the afternoon and
left until the next morning. Neither partner can detect its presence when the diaphragm is correctly positioned.

Rutgers said contraception was a medical problem, something
with which most American physicians in those days did not

agree. He convinced Mrs. Sanger that the Mensinga method was both safe and effective, but insisted that it should be preceded by a gynecological examination to rule out female organic conditions incompatible with conception and contraception, or even inter-course, as well as out of respect for the woman's general health. These conditions satisfied, the physician then could fit the pa-tient with a pessary of the proper size. Dr. Rutgers did not object to the fitting being carried out by non-medical personnel and in fact trained midwives in his clinic for this purpose. Because Mrs. Sanger was a nurse, he was willing to teach her, and finally allowed her to work with clinic patients on her own. Unfortu-nately, the Mensinga diaphragm could not legally be imported into the United States, and at that time no American company had seen fit to manufacture it. It was virtually unknown to American doctors.

Mrs. Sanger did not object to the ideal first step, a gynecological examination, but there was no Johannes Rutgers available in the United States. Thus, when she and her sister, also a nurse, started the first American birth control clinic in Brooklyn in 1916, they did the examination and fitting themselves, using diaphragms smuggled into the country. Following their arrest and trial, under a state "little Comstock" law, it became of strategic importance for her to seek American medical support of birth control.

In 1918, the New York Court of Appeals upheld the convic-tions, but broadened its interpretation of the state law which already permitted physicians to prescribe contraceptive devices for patients for the prevention or cure of disease. The Court's opinion interpreted *disease* to include any alteration in the state of the body or its organs causing or threatening to cause pain or sickness. In other words, the Court opened the way for physicians to operate a clinic offering birth control for anything they judged to be *medical* reasons.

Only a few physicians, such as Dickinson, greeted this relaxa-tion of the law with enthusiams. Organized medicine, medical specialty societies, and hospitals adopted a hands-off attitude, fearing that promotion of contraception would lead to female promiscuity, encourage immorality, and undermine the American home and the nation's strength.

Mrs. Sanger, following the founding of the American Birth Control League in 1923, opened a new clinic in association with the League. The medical profession objected, even though her stated plan was to make the clinic a center for medically supervised study of contraceptive techniques. In fact, she called it the New York Birth Control Clinical Research Bureau, later the Margaret Sanger Research Bureau, which continued in operation until the summer of 1973.

First headed by Dr. Dorothy Bocker and after 1925, by Dr. Hannah Stone, this was the first physician-directed birth control clinic in the United States. It adopted, as its most effective weapon, the Mensinga diaphragm combined with a spermicidal jelly also of German origin. The clinic's supply of diaphragms was first smuggled into the country with the help of Mrs. Sanger's second husband, J. Noah H. Slee, who arranged for them to be shipped from Holland to one of his factories in Canada and then brought into the United States. In 1925, Mrs. Sanger encouraged the Holland-Rantos Company to manufacture a pessary of the same type and quality in the United States. Manufacture was legal in contrast to advertising or distribution by mail. Restriction on mailing of contraceptives for medical use was relaxed by a federal court decision in 1930.

Dickinson's objectives were similar to those of Mrs. Sanger, but he was a physician and proposed to work within his profession and seek to persuade other doctors. It took from 1923 to 1937 for the medical profession to change its official mind.

In 1923, Dickinson formed the Committee on Maternal Health, made up of a few New York obstetricians and gynecologists. The Committee (after 1930, the National Committee on Maternal Health) wanted to do clinical research in contraception and publish results through medically approved channels. With rather lukewarm endorsement of obstetrical and gynecological societies, it opened an office "for reference and record." This office referred the women who sought advice to seven cooperating New York hospitals. The hospitals were supplied with case-history forms, condoms, and spermicidal jellies, but no cervical caps. Inquiries were few, the hospitals were indifferent, and most applicants wanted a special clinic, like Mrs. Sanger's.

Dickinson had sold his colleagues on the need for the Committee on Maternal Health with the argument that he wished to rescue contraceptive research from "some Sanger group." In 1924, however, he recognized that the Sanger clinic itself was the proper setting for this work. He visited the clinic, together with other Committee members; they were troubled because the Clinical Research Bureau had only one unknown doctor and were shocked to see propaganda posters on the wall and find that women who had no medical reason to practice contraception were receiving diaphragms. The Committee now undertook to establish a clinic of its own.

Margaret Sanger, recognizing that her clinic needed a good deal of improvement to achieve professional respectability, shrewdly proposed that the Committee simply take over the Clinical Research Bureau. Representatives of each group agreed to set up a new governing body for this purpose, the Maternity Research Council, to provide contraceptive advice to persons legally entitled to it and to undertake scientific investigations under the supervision of a medical board. Conservative doctors on the Dickinson committee stipulated that the new clinic should obtain a medical dispensary license from the State Board of Charities. "Moving," as David M. Kennedy said in his book about birth control,[1] "with the cautious agility of a nineteenth-century dip-

---

[1] David M. Kennedy's *Birth Control in America* (Yale University Press, 1970) contains a detailed review of the development of "Birth Control and American Medicine." The story centers on a complicated organizational courtship between Dr. Dickinson and Mrs. Sanger that, in seven years of flirtation and flight on her part and of diplomatic and gallant effort on his part, failed in consummation. A woman's intuition seemed to warn Mrs. Sanger against trusting the future of birth control to the medical profession, although she led, and eventually won, the fight to overthrow the Comstock law. This effort ended with the federal court ruling that gave physicians the unrestricted right to import, sell, and prescribe contraceptives for their patients (The United States vs. One Package of Japanese Pessaries, 1936).

lomat," Dickinson obtained American Medical Association and gynecological and obstetrical society moral support, plus $10,000 in Rockefeller money, and applied for the license.

Regrettably, the Board of Charities deferred to Roman Catholic Church opinion and in 1926 turned him down. One Board member pointed out that the only excuse for such an independent clinic was that the medical profession was unwilling to foster such clinics through hospitals and its own professional societies. In the following years, a series of efforts were made to bring together the Margaret Sanger Research Bureau and the Committee on Maternal Health or some successor of the Maternity Research Council. For various reasons, all efforts failed. Sanger and Dickinson respected one another, but like politicians, each had his own constituency to satisfy. Her constituency was, first, women volunteers in birth control and then, the social and biological scientists whom she put on her own board. His constituency was his gynecological colleagues and their medical societies—the doctors he was trying to involve in birth control. But it was the Catholics who blocked the dispensary license in the first place, and the Catholics who caused another police raid on the Sanger clinic in 1929. Ironically, they brought down the wrath of the Academy of Medicine because the police seized confidential medical records.

Mrs. Sanger longed for medical cooperation but felt that the risk of losing control over her clinic was too great. Paradoxically, it fell to her to frustrate Dr. Dickinson's earliest efforts to make contraceptive research acceptable to his profession, during a time when its officials were repeatedly rejecting proposals that the A.M.A. study birth control—"too controversial," they said.

Such was the character of the people and the times when Clarence Gamble went to see Dr. Dickinson in New York. Why he did so is a matter of conjecture. There appeared to be at least two reasons. One was a matter of personal interest. Gamble investigated the subject of conjugal relations, including family planning and contraception, pretty thoroughly in anticipation of his own marriage in 1924, as he told Sarah Gamble. He came across Dickinson's writings, among others. In 1924, Dickinson published in the *American Journal of Obstetrics and Gynecology* the first illustrated description of how to fit a diaphragm. He mailed out 3,000 copies of the article in defiance of the Comstock law.

Secondly, as Gamble later related to one of his fieldworkers, Edith Gates, the medical students coming into the Laboratory of Pharmacology at the University of Pennsylvania put him on the spot. One day a group of students was in his office; the subject of the cap diaphragm and its drawbacks came up. It did require a certain robustness of outlook and a dexterity in manipulating it into place not then considered to be wholly characteristic of the female, who also had to foresee its need and remember to remove and clean it afterwards. A valid objection was that use of a pessary required the privacy of a bathroom, a convenience not generally available to the poor or to outdoor lovers. There was many a slip-up of omission and commission.

The walls of the laboratory were lined with bottles containing hundreds of chemicals. A student turned to Dr. Gamble and said that there ought to be something on those shelves that would do the trick and not involve a messy and inconvenient mechanical device. There was raillery, and the comment that if he could not find anything there, pharmacology was not worth much. He did some library research on contraception and, although the literature was scanty, he dug up a few of the fascinating items that Norman E. Himes would eventually report.[2] Since the beginning of civilization, women with or without the encouragement of men have been plugging and dosing their vaginas with all manner of objects and potions in the hope of preventing pregnancy—pebbles, cotton-wool balls, sponges, half a lemon, honey, seed pods. The ancient Egyptians used crocodile dung and then shifted, for some reason, to elephant dung. The Greeks tried salt solutions and vinegar; these were found to be effective spermicides; a small sponge or cotton ball soaked in saltwater or vinegar made a

[2] *Medical History of Contraception* (Gamut Press, 1963; first edition published by the National Committee on Maternal Health, 1936).

simple, cheap contraceptive. Noting that Robert Dickinson recommended the cap diaphragm, Gamble wrote him for information and went on to ask what, if any, research had been done on
the simpler methods.

Their meeting took place, and we can safely assume it was a
memorable occasion. Dickinson was a surgeon, a graduate of and
former professor of obstetrics at the Long Island College Hospital.
He was an impressive gentleman with a Van Dyke beard and, as
one observer said, had a "controlled exuberance," with an active
intellectual curiosity and a fearless determination to understand
human sexuality in general and the female sex in particular.
"Glory to God" was his favorite remark when in high spirits, and
birth control was his favorite topic; he was compulsive about
bringing it into any conversation. As an early ally of the feminist
movement, he had other interests. He had investigated lady's
fashions and come out against the corset and the hour-glass figure
as inimical to normal breathing. He favored bicycle-riding for
ladies, something that had been viewed with dark suspicion as a
shameful opportunity for female masturbation. He was an authority on that subject.

Dickinson said that sex fears and maladjustments were the
leading cause of mental strain in married women, and physicians
were failing to meet the problem. There was need for sex counseling by physicians "clean of mind and happy in marriage. . . . What
I teach," he said, "is based, each clause of it, on the wreck of some
marriage or some mind." The crux of the problem was society's
mistaken notion that it was immoral for women to find pleasure
in sexual intercourse. On the contrary, he said the mutual satisfaction of man and woman was necessary. Sexual adjustment was
the key to happy marriage. Birth control made that adjustment
easier. His own wife had been free from child-bearing after three
pregnancies and their marriage was blissful. He advised that
physicians take the initiative and seek permission of the bride's
parents to give her basic instruction a day or two before her
wedding. Her fiancé could be advised separately.

Dickinson had succeeded in his plan to engage a fashionable clinical practice in order to amass sufficient capital to retire early and acquire the freedom to go into sex and contraceptive research. After developing an income of several thousand dollars a year he moved from his office-home in Brooklyn to a Manhattan efficiency apartment.

All we know specifically of Dickinson's meeting with Gamble was a letter that Clarence wrote to his mother on October 4, 1925.

I had lunch with Dr. Dickinson, father of Jean Dickinson [a Christian missionary] whom Sidney knew in China. He is extremely interested in the study of birth control. Thinks it is socially much needed, but the study of it is seriously interfered with by unnecessary laws. He says there is distressingly little scientific information (chiefly because of the laws) on the efficacy and desirability of the various methods, and he is trying to collect what he can. He says he has almost unlimited funds available from interested organizations, but that he can't get the scientific personnel that he wants. All the good young doctors that he would like to get are afraid of the effect of being connected with such an organization on their practice. He said, "I'm 64 and can't go on forever. My independence gives me a chance to do what I can, but young men like you, who are also independent, ought to take up the work. Don't you want to help me, and keep on with the work when I'm through?" He says that it is terrible that such a humanly important subject should be so covered with ignorance and mystery. A lot of colleagues will let him speak on the subject, but the college profs and doctors who ought to do it don't dare touch it for fear of losing their jobs.

Lovingly, Clarence

We have no record of Mrs. Gamble's reaction. Clarence made no statement of his own interest in birth control, but it is of some significance that he felt compelled to write his mother about meeting Dickinson. He could hardly escape an interest in pregnancy at the time because he was about to become a father.

On October 31, 1925, Sarah bore him a daughter, Sarah Louise, whom they called Sally.

Gamble gave his mother a full report of the event, remarking: "Such an exciting day! I wish you could see the latest Gamble.

Dick and Sally with Sarah B. Gamble

She's a pink baby, much whiter than the usual cranberry shade, but the redness is there—in her hair."

Neither Sarah nor Clarence had red hair or sandy, freckled complexions, but all five of their children did. It was a genetic mystery. In general, they resembled their father more than their mother, some observers thought; Elsie Wulkop, later a Gamble fieldworker and devoted friend of the family, imagined them all to be a throwback to some fierce Scottish chief. What was even more remarkable was that all of the Gamble children were planned.

Thus, the Gambles carried out the slogan of Mrs. Sanger: "Every child a wanted child" and the dictum of Dr. Dickinson that children should be well spaced, both for the sake of their health and their mother's. Dickinson advised that a bride should not seek to become pregnant until at least six months after marriage, and therefore should employ contraception during that

The Gambles with Sally and Dick

time because there was enough strain on the woman in adjusting to married life—homemaking, cooking, love-making—without superimposing pregnancy and its effects at the outset. He said that a mother should not have babies more frequently than every two years at the least.

Sarah and Clarence were exacting in heeding this advice. They agreed that they would have six children (her sixth pregnancy was a miscarriage).

Sally was born sixteen months after they were married.

Richard Bradley Gamble was born on April 9, 1928, about two and a half years later.

Walter James Gamble was born December 1, 1930, two years and nearly eight months after Richard.

Mary Julia (Judy) Gamble was born on May 14, 1934, three years and almost six months after Walter.

Robert David Gamble was born on March 9, 1937, two years and about ten months later.

The children, like their parents, lived up to the Gamble family crest, a stork carrying a stemmed rose in its beak. Sarah and Clarence have seventeen grandchildren, including one by adoption.

The influence of Dickinson on Gamble's interest in sexology may be judged from a series of undated letters Gamble wrote to the wife of a close friend who had asked him for advice, probably doing so because he was a physician and possibly because she had learned of his and Sarah's interest in family planning. Mrs. B., as we shall call her, first asked Clarence to recommend a book that would tell her what she wanted to know about sexual relations and contraception. He wrote her back in December (probably 1925) stating: "I haven't been able to find the kind of book that I should like to recommend to you. . . . So I think I shall be forced to write the textbook for you myself."

Gamble then went into some frank and detailed discussion of female and male sex anatomy and function, revealing his own attitudes as well as the state of the art in pre-Kinsey, pre-Masters and Johnson, pre-Sherfey times:

One thing of great importance to learn is that the feminine processes of sexual enjoyment are almost identical with the masculine, although much slower. . . . Rumor has it that the feminine mind appreciates a slower reciprocal motion in intercourse than occurs spontaneously with most men. . . . The orgasm of sexual climax in the female is quite similar to that in the male, and is a thing of which little is known by the average man. In mathematical terms it is the point where $dx = 0$, that is, the maximum of sexual experience. Like in the male, it is accompanied by a catch in the breath and often by muscular movements or twitchings, and as in the male, by the ejaculation of a small amount of fluid, whose function seems to be chiefly lubricant. . . . Care should . . . be taken that the male orgasm should not occur too early, for after this the female orgasm becomes impossible, while the reverse is not the case. Probably the greatest satisfaction comes when the two are simultaneous, and by care and mutual information this is said to be easily attainable. . . . The feminine orgasm is important for several reasons. Primarily for the physical enjoyment of it. Then it is usually followed promptly by refreshing sleep, but the sexual excitement gives nervousness and sleeplessness if it does not occur. and finally if the excitement occurs habitually without complete satisfaction it may give profound and long lasting nervous disturbances. . . . One other bit of advice—don't be in too much of a hurry. The caresses, the physical contact are probably worth more than the actual coitus. The very act itself may if desired last hours. One author says that if properly done it should last two hours. . . . As to frequency all medical authors are agreed that there is no set rule—that it varies greatly with different persons and different couples. A case is known where it occurred three times every night for seven years or more. Most seem to consider twice a week a fair average. . . . All emphasize that it should not be marked up on the calendar in advance like Wednesday and Saturday bath nights. . . . One man recommends that it occur after an hour or more of sleep when both will be well rested and in a position to enjoy it more. This sounds theoretically good, but practically a bit difficult. . . .

Don't forget that all of us ignorant males have a lot to learn in regard to the mental reactions and training of girls. Take, for instance, the simple matter of nakedness. We think nothing of it . . . and you'd think that might be the attitude of the other half, but not at all—they are shocked, tremendously so, or at least claim to be. How much more strange must it seem to them if it is bisexual. . . .

Finally I would urge that you both break over as much as possible the barriers erected around the things that are not to be spoken of, for unless you are both willing to there is absolutely no way in which you can interpret the proper application of the golden rule, and without that you will miss much that you might otherwise have had.

I'm sorry not to have sent this earlier, but spare moments for cerebral work are still limited. I hope you may find it useful, and that it may arrive in time to be useful from the beginning. If there is anything small or tremendous that you want to know, be sure to write. I'll try to tell you anything except how to control the sex of your children.

Gamble strongly recommended reading *Married Love: A New Contribution to the Solution of Sex Difficulties*, by Marie C. Stopes (London, 1918), although it was difficult to obtain in the United States. This book contained the bad news—for males— that a woman's response to sexual stimulus and receptivity varies greatly in the course of a month—"La donna e mobile." Ignorance of this fact or indifference to it makes for resentment and incompatibility as well as contributing to the Victorian female conclusion that men are beasts.

Gamble prepared a description of contraceptive methods, using Dickinson for the "best information." The methods included withdrawal before ejaculation, condom, douche—these three in those days were by far the most common—lactic acid jelly, and pessary. The Mensinga diaphragm was "the most satisfactory method in every way, but . . . not obtainable in this country."

Gamble felt compelled to write a sequel to the above letter. "Since it seems probable that the masterpiece I wrote in December may be used again, I enclose an appendix to form a new edition." The main purpose of his second letter appeared to be to drum up a subject for study:

Dr. Dickinson who has been much interested in the scientific and sociological aspect of the question has investigated the literature extensively and finds practically no authentic scientific information on the effectiveness of the methods suggested. He has started in a very careful way to acquire some. He feels that the lactic acid ointment preceding, with douche succeeding, has great possibilities. His only failure in preliminary work with it occurred because the patient thought it was for subsequent use. He is anxious to secure reliable data on it. Would you want to help? This would mean a record of the number of times used . . . in such a way that it could be connected with subsequently discovered conception, if any. . . . Dr. Dickinson and I would both appreciate the statistics, if you care to keep them.

But the lady didn't care to; she wanted no part of such an experiment.

There is no recorded moment when, or if, in response to Dickinson's quest for a doctor of medicine to assist and succeed him, Gamble ever said, "I'm your man." But their relationship steadily grew warmer, and it is evident that Clarence Gamble was the latter-day torchbearer of Dickinson's cause.

chapter 6   A Rebirth in Birth Control

The prevailing opinion as the United States entered the Great Depression of the 1930s was that a growing population was good for the country—for business, agriculture, politics, the church, national defense, and even for women's health. The long-time decline in the birth rate, especially manifest among Anglo-Saxons of the middle and upper classes, was viewed with some alarm. Hence, birth control, while increasingly popular among feminists and women professionals, was not commonly championed by men in high office. The rigors of the Depression, however, provided a countervailing argument for birth control. To the weight of ill health that long had fallen on the multiparous mother and the father's burden of many mouths to feed was now added the load on taxpayers as public relief rolls swelled. The birth rate for families receiving relief was more than fifty percent higher than for self-supporting families. It is easy to count relief cases and assign dollar costs to them. Typically, around half the persons on relief are children. It was self-evident that every additional baby in a relief family represented an additional public expense, and that sexual intercourse in the absence of conception control could be taken as an indicator of irresponsibility.

Gamble often argued that money spent on birth control clinics could be seen as an investment resulting in predictable savings to taxpayers. Speaking of the Michigan experience (see Chapter 7), he said: "Since many of the mothers to whom information has been furnished have used it for a period of more than one year, and since most of them belong to the dependent families, it seems allowable to estimate that the information given each mother is responsible for at least one less dependent child in the community." Putting the cost of the dependent child at "the extremely low figure" of fifty dollars a year, "the savings resulting from the 4,500 cases which have been given contraceptive information in the charitable clinics in Michigan would amount to nearly a quarter of a million dollars annually—an important item in these depressed days."

The Detroit Council of Social Agencies had figured that pre-natal, obstetrical, and nursing care for the mother of a dependent family cost the public eighty-nine dollars for each child born. "This might be taken as a justifiable basis for an estimate of a saving of $400,000 annually to the cities in which the clinics are now located," said Gamble. "In other studies, it has been estimated that the cost to society of raising and educating a child in a dependent family to the point of self-support is approximately $5,000. There are few investments which give the thousandfold yield which this immediately suggests." His calculation was based on a cost of five dollars or less per patient treated.

Gamble first became interested in birth control clinics in Philadelphia and Cincinnati. It was largely through his Princeton and Harvard classmate, Dr. Stuart Mudd and his wife that Gamble became involved in Philadelphia. Mudd, a microbiologist in the University of Pennsylvania School of Medicine, and Emily Mudd, a marriage counselor, had organized the Southeastern Pennsylvania Birth Control League, affiliated with the Pennsylvania Birth Control Federation and centered in Philadelphia.

Gynecologists and obstetricians on the faculty of six Pennsylvania medical schools formed a Committee for Maternal Health Betterment, with Dr. A. Lovett Dewees as chairman. This group started a Maternal Health Clinic at 69th and Market Streets early in 1929. A recognized gynecologist agreed to accept the legal risks, then thought to be considerable under the state's laws, and headed the clinic on a part-time salary.

A research problem drew Gamble into the program. His interest began, he later recalled, "when I was teaching at the University of Pennsylvania Medical School, with a request for advice from a birth control clinic which was being opened by charitably minded persons. They wanted to know which of the birth control jellies would be most effective. I found that the only criterion was the claims of the various manufacturers, and each of these claimed that his product was perfect and the only one that was perfect."

The 69th Street clinic revealed a strong demand, serving 500 patients in its second and 800 in its third year. In the next five years, eight other branch centers were opened throughout Philadelphia, including one in a settlement house, two in Young Women's Christian Association buildings, and two in black physicians' offices.

A five-year review, 1929–1933, reported 5,500 women served, stating: "Practically all of these women are of the underprivileged class. Although the function of the clinics is primarily philanthropic, some women come to use it because few private physicians are trained to give proper instruction. About two-thirds of the patients come referred by hospital and social agencies of all kinds. The remaining third come from private physicians, visiting nurses, labor unions, church organizations, and from grateful friends who have benefitted from our help."

Of the 2,280 treated in 1933, 44 percent were Protestant, 38 percent Catholic, and 18 percent Jewish; the racial division was 54 percent white and 44 percent black. Two-thirds of the husbands were unemployed. Eight of ten women had used some contraceptive before coming to the clinic, but found it unsatisfactory. Two out of ten had not known there was any way to control the size of their families. One out of ten admitted having abortions, mostly illegal. Many complained of marital maladjustment. By 1933, these were being referred to a psychiatrist; however, a dependable contraceptive was often a factor in stabilizing the family.

The fecundity of some of these women was startling. A woman, thirty-six years old, with an unemployed, tuberculous husband, was pregnant twelve times in seventeen years; seven children survived. A woman, thirty, had five living children and ten abortions by a midwife. A woman with a husband unemployed and on relief had been pregnant twenty-two times in twenty-one years. Fourteen of her children were living.

"It is obvious," said the report, "that with so many women coming to us through the welfare agencies the clinics cannot be self-supporting. It is, for this reason, all the more surprising to note that during the past year one half of the running expenses of the clinic was met by the patient's fees. Rigid economy has lowered the overhead expenses steadily in the last five years, so that the original cost of $10 per patient has now been reduced to $3.85."

In 1933, nine clinics were operated on a total budget of $10,832, with about $6,200 coming from contributions and $3,200 from patient fees, the remainder from miscellaneous sources. A small group of wealthy men and women, among them Clarence and Sarah Gamble, had pledged to meet the deficit for three years following their original gifts during the first two, experimental years.

In this experience, the Gambles came to the conclusion that it was more efficient to give money to birth control clinics to prevent the production of relief babies than to the Community Chest to care for them. At the same time, they found that those who choose to give to a specific cause can expect to be asked to keep on supporting that cause; in other words, those who start projects may have to keep them going. As he developed a philosophy of philanthropic pathfinding, Gamble came to recognize this as a cardinal difficulty—that is, making sure that his initial grants, or seed money, stimulated others to support the birth control clinics he got started and did not leave him with the task of planting the same crop in the same place year after year. This was particularly a problem in Cincinnati, a city long accustomed to the generosity of the Procters and Gambles, whose company, despite the stock market crash, continued to grow and show profits during the Depression years.

Following his mother's funeral in January 1929, Gamble had a talk with Mary Gamble's old gynecologist and friend of the family in Cincinnati, Dr. Elizabeth Campbell. They discussed birth control. Dr. Campbell wanted to get the doctors in the Cincinnati Academy of Medicine interested in starting a Maternal Health Clinic that would simultaneously provide contraceptive advice to the overly fertile and treat sterility in women unable to have a child. This was a strategy that Dr. Dickinson had adopted to take the wind out of opposition sails. Catholic doctors were happy to treat sterility. Dr. Campbell wanted to operate a clinic with the cooperation of the Department of Obstetrics and Gynecology of the University of Cincinnati College of Medicine, but keep it outside of the University so that doctors in the community would send patients to it and even come themselves for training without running into a town-and-gown conflict.

As a means of pulling a group together, Dr. Gamble suggested that Dr. Campbell invite Dr. Dickinson to Cincinnati to speak, and she did so in April 1929. Clarence's brother Cecil attended this Academy meeting. In a letter to Clarence, Dr. Campbell happily recounted Cecil's remarks about the well-attended meeting: "I remarked to him, 'Wasn't this perfectly fine; I am simply thrilled'. He yawned and said, 'You are a funny bunch. I do not see anything so thrilling; it looks to me like pure common sense.'"

Unquestionably, one of the most commonsensical aspects of what Clarence Gamble described as his "new adventure in Cincinnati" was his gift of $5,000, through the National Committee on Maternal Health, to meet the first year's expenses of the Maternal Health Clinic.

By and large, hospitals in those days were chary of operating birth control clinics as part of their out-patient departments or anywhere else within their walls. Dependent on Community

Fund aid for treating charity patients, they were ready targets for criticism by representatives of the Catholic agencies, as well as from their own like-minded trustees and medical staff members and local politicians interested in the Catholic vote. Robert Dickinson had experienced an indifferent reception from New York hospitals, and was persuaded that the Sanger model, a free-standing clinic, was the better course, although this approach had the drawback of placing the birth control effort outside of the normal institutional channels of medicine. Nevertheless, under the direction of Dr. William E. Brown, the first Cincinnati Maternal Health Clinic opened in the Cincinnati General Hospital, a city institution, in November 1929. The first patient, the clinic reported, was "a colored woman of 40—married at 15 and the mother of 11. She said she'd be honest, she'd tried everything she knew to get rid of the last baby—'cause she thought it was wrong to have more children than they could feed—and anyway her back ached so.'" The doctor fitted her with a Mensinga diaphragm.

On the whole, the Cincinnati clinic and its supporting community organization got off to a slow start. The opportunity to put the clinic in the City Hospital had been too appealing for Drs. Campbell and Brown to pass up, but Catholic politicians gave them cause for regret. Under vigorous attack at the end of 1931, the clinic was forced to move out of the City Hospital, but was fortunate in finding permanent quarters in the private Children's Hospital across the street. Subsequently, branches were opened in other parts of Cincinnati and the development of Gamble-stimulated clinics extended to Columbus, Springfield, Toledo, and other Ohio cities.

Gamble undertook the entire budget for the Cincinnati Maternal Health Clinic for the first year, but he offered only half that much, or $2,500, for the second year. He expected the people of Cincinnati to raise the remainder and thereafter provide the entire support. As he wrote Dr. Brown at the end of 1930, Gamble looked on the first year as a demonstration of "what the clinic could do and how the morals of the city might escape corruption in spite of it. This winter, I think, should be an advertising winter in which the actual number of patients treated is relatively unimportant." By advertising, Gamble meant any kind of published information or attention-getting devices for stirring public interest and thereby forming a basis for a fund-raising campaign. He got his faith in publicity from three sources: from P. & G., one of the earliest companies to engage in national advertising to sell its product, from Margaret Sanger, and from Dr. Dickinson. Mrs. Sanger could draw attention, crowds, and money wherever she went because she was the heroine who had so often gone to court and to jail for what she believed, and continued to make a good story by plain speaking and bold action. Dickinson, while himself quiet and dignified, conceded the value of being publicly attacked.

Dr. Brown, however, expressed serious doubts about an advertising campaign, arguing that it would arouse and focus opposition and be counter-productive. He, Dr. Campbell, and Dr. Boughton had a $9,000 budget in mind for the second year. He complained bitterly about their having to use their time for fund-raising, and wrote Gamble: "I do not think you can expect us to put our time in organizing the clinic, building up public interest, getting the proper agencies in line, getting the Academy support, and doing all the things necessary to enable us to function in a field where opposition is abundant, and then in addition to ask us to become 75 percent independent in the second year. It is asking too much."

Gamble did not mind "asking too much"; he knew what he wanted to see happen. Early in 1931, he wrote "Dear Bill" that, "Although the process of money-raising must seem a hard one, I feel that it is very essential for the success of the clinic."

All in all, the Depression was a propitious time for the promotion of birth control clinics. It was the time that Clarence Gamble chose to commit himself, his money, and innumerable future family dinner-table conversations to birth control and to his conviction that more is not necessarily better and may be worse. In the end, he and his family would establish a philanthropic foundation, the Pathfinder Fund; but until his death he resembled nothing so much as a one-man band.

From his home and office in Philadelphia until 1937, and after that from Milton, Massachusetts, and during vacation periods from the Gamble house in Pasadena or from Cottage 75 at Harbor Point, Michigan, he ran a nationwide program by mail with the help of one secretary plus a scattered assortment of women doctors, nurses, and others who served as clinic and community organizers in the field. Throughout this effort, continuing in the continental United States and Puerto Rico for the next twenty years, he indulged his daily urge to type or dictate long letters, his absorption with small details, and his inclination to manipulate people to do good, all by employing two or three and sometimes five or ten workers whom he might not see more than once or twice a year, as well as by corresponding with local birth controllers whom he did not meet at all.

Gamble, in later terse, somewhat cryptic, resumés of the genesis of the Pathfinder Fund, traced his interest in the birth control movement as follows: "Although the Pathfinder Fund was formed and incorporated in 1957, the work which it continues began in 1929. For the most part it was carried out under the National Committee on Maternal Health." The earliest work of this sort concerned "the organization of contraceptive services and associations to provide them." In other words, more people—both professional and lay—were responding to the trend by becoming interested in starting birth control clinics and voluntary community organizations to support them. Beginning with the first medically directed clinic in 1923—Margaret Sanger's Birth Control Clinic Research Bureau in New York—the number grew to between seventy-five and one hundred by 1930.

Gamble in the early years used three organizations as channels for transmission of many of his gifts. The National Committee on Maternal Health, of which he became a member in 1929, was the most satisfactory one, particularly after Gamble became its chairman of field service (1934) and then treasurer (1935). His brother, Sidney, succeeded him as treasurer in 1937.

Thanks to his friendship with Margaret Sanger, her Clinical Research Bureau provided him an excellent port of call for several years. In 1937, Mrs. Sanger designated him medical field director and encouraged him to give the Bureau money and direct its expenditures on fieldwork pretty much as he pleased.

Gamble was president of the Pennsylvania Birth Control Federation in 1934 and, as Pennsylvania delegate to the parent body, a vice-president and member of the board of the American Birth Control League. He became regional director of the South for the League at the time of its reorganization in 1939 as the Birth Control Federation of America. This volunteer relationship constituted an uneasy alliance, however, for Dr. Gamble insisted that his grants go to projects that he personally directed. Whereas Dr. Dickinson and Mrs. Sanger were prepared to accept and admire Dr. Gamble as a lone prospector and definitely treat him as a special case, he did not fit well in a large national organization's board-and-staff need for corporate control over program and participants and repeatedly found himself in conflict with the power structure of the establishment.

It makes some difference in what category a philanthropist gives, of course. When Gamble began, a gift to a birth control organization, so-called, was not deductible from taxable income, whereas one made to a nonprofit institution organized for a medical or health purpose was. Financially, it made good sense to fight for birth control in the name of maternal health and under medical direction; it also was sound political strategy since it is more difficult to be against the good health of mothers than against their practice of contraception.

Contraceptive Research

While having problems with his duodenal ulcer during this period and in 1934 undergoing a gall bladder operation, Gamble showed no lack of vitality or attention span in family planning work. His new interest exposed him to one further disappointment in the department of pharmacology at the University of Pennsylvania.

One problem that concerned Dickinson and Gamble was that there was no generally accepted method for determining the effectiveness of chemical contraceptives—mainly the spermicidal jellies. The Council on Pharmacy and Chemistry of the American

Medical Association performed an approval role for medicines as a whole, but the A.M.A. at that time did not approve of contraception as a respectable field of scientific and clinical interest. Doctors looked on the manufacture of contraceptives as something on the verge of quackery. In 1934, Gamble gave the National Committee on Maternal Health (NCMH) $5,000 "for the investigation of contraceptive materials and devices, and for the improvement of publicity in connection with them." This became the Standards Program, the tax-exempt vehicle for his increasing investments in laboratory and field testing of contraceptives. Stuart Mudd in due time used an A.M.A. change of policy accepting contraception as a medical problem (1937) as a leverage point in persuading the Council on Pharmacy and Chemistry to set up an Advisory Committee on Contraceptives and make Gamble chairman.

Meanwhile, Gamble needed a laboratory not unlike the one the A.M.A. had for drug investigation, but restricted to contraceptive testing. In 1935, he approached Richards by letter to see if the latter might be willing to furnish supervision, space, and perhaps personnel for such a laboratory under the general sponsorship of Dickinson and the NCMH. "I might help out in a limited way," said Gamble in a characteristically cautious attitude toward major-scale spending of his own money. He looked to foundations for more adequate financing. "There is, as yet, no secure future for any worker in the field, but the demand seems to be growing." Richards wrote Gamble a note: "I know so little about the whole birth control problem and the implications of such a program of research as you suggest that I prefer not to say anything at all until we can talk about it and get deeper into your thoughts." There ends the information. It is self-evident that Richards, or, if the proposal went higher, the dean, the faculty, or the president, turned Gamble down. It is doubtful that in those days any faculty, medical school, or university would have welcomed a designated contraceptive testing laboratory on campus.

Yet Dr. Royal L. Brown and the department of zoology did provide the laboratory facilities for the 1936–1938 collaboration in the development of the Brown-Gamble test for the spermicidal effectiveness of commercial contraceptives. In this procedure, ejaculates from youthful donors were mixed with the spermicide and measurements made of the time required for immobilization of the sperm. The test was widely used in the years of birth control when spermicidal jelly was for a time hoped to be the answer to the search for the "perfect" contraceptive. Gamble, through the NCMH, also financed and occasionally appeared as co-author in several small studies of contraceptive qualities made in other university laboratories, but it was not until 1952 that he acquired laboratory space of his own, in the department of anatomy at Harvard.

Gamble terminated his pharmacology career at the University of Pennsylvania in 1937 and moved his family to Boston, the hub of Catholic opposition to artificial contraceptives, where there was a state law prohibiting their sale. Gamble's explanation of the move was that he wanted to get away from Pennsylvania's tax on capital wealth, and Sarah's was that she wished to be near her family. Never discussed was his lack of a future and satisfying career at the University.

A year or so later, he bought an old, ten-bedroom, New England white clapboard house in Milton surrounded by several acres of rolling meadow, woods and swamp. It was large enough to contain their five children, at that time ranging from one to twelve years in age, plus overnight guests from family planning around the world, and the English children who soon came to live with them as war evacuees.

Milton, U.S.A., remained for the next twenty-seven years supreme headquarters in his expeditions into a world that was as generally indifferent to Gamble as it was to the health and welfare of mothers and children. What the neighbors thought about the Gambles and their activities is not known. It is a matter of record that Gamble did not care much about what anyone thought. What was important to him was what he thought.

A life-long problem in his human relationships was a difficulty in articulating what he thought. As his friend, Mudd, pointed out,

Gamble would come to and act on a conclusion without revealing the steps by which he reached it, and indeed was impatient with any need for explaning himself. By not exposing his thought processes to critical debate, of course, he simultaneously avoided the suggestions and judgment of his peers.

Although he and his father joked in their letters about the handicap of being rich, Clarence thought it would help in medical research. Perhaps his greatest disappointment in life was the realization that this was not to be. Albert Einstein described research as a form of play, but it is play governed by the most rigorous, onerous kinds of rules if the player wants the acceptance of his fellow scientific investigators, for he must willingly submit his contributions of knowledge to their criticism and confirmation or refutation. Such discipline is the only way science can protect itself from fallacy and error, of which there is much.

Sailing at Harbor Point, Michigan; CJG with Bob and Sally

A rich man can build his own laboratory and library, and go it alone; some have done so successfully, especially in the invention of machines, where the answer to the question "Does it run?" may be the ultimate test of success or failure. Universities provide the ideal milieu for research in the life sciences, where humanity needs an advocate for its own protection. Here, the faculty provides the essential society and forum of one's peers. As part of the academic system of professor-and-student relationships, one wins recognition of his competency by accepting the drudgery and routine of hard work, including brain work and scut work. Money is a necessity in support of the research, most of all for salaries, and so are ideas and talent, but also necessary is the disciplinary system for proving competence.

It was in meeting this last requirement that Gamble faltered. He was exceedingly fortunate in his initial appointment as assistant professor of pharmacology. Gamble wanted to be accepted on merit and to work alone, and Richards agreed. But it gradually became apparent that Gamble did not really care to remain in cardiovascular research. He was too impatient and too much of a loner to accept and work within the confines of any establishment, to accept departmental discipline and climb the ladder to academic success. Financial independence failed to make it possible for him, as he had hoped, to do more medical research than others; it did enable him to keep others from hemming him in.

chapter 7   Elsie Wulkop in Michigan

Clarence Gamble was prone to look back on his internship at Massachusetts General Hospital as the "most varied and fascinating years of my life. . . . Nowhere can one secure a more complete and interesting tour of human nature. . . . " There, he came to know and admire one of the world's outstanding collections of doctors, nurses, and social workers. Among them was a social worker, of German extraction, Elsie Wulkop. As an intern, he made various small, anonymous grants to aid Miss Wulkop's social service projects and later, after going to Pennsylvania, a larger grant for her to study and improve the M.G.H. system of social service case records, under the supervision of Richard Cabot, Chief of Social Service, and the first of the modern medical social workers, Ida M. Cannon. A person with a sense of humor as well as exquisite sensitivities, Miss Wulkop enjoyed the mystery about her benefactor, whom she led people to assume was some wealthy old gentleman who had taken a fancy to her instead of, in fact, a pup doctor in his twenties.

By 1930, Elsie Wulkop had become superintendent of the Children's Island Sanitarium at Marblehead, a summertime responsibility that left her free for other work during the winter. Gamble commended Miss Wulkop to Dr. Dickinson and the National Committee on Maternal Health for her "personality, energy, and reliability" and proposed that she be sent to Detroit to establish a birth control clinic at Harper Hospital. This fitted in with Dickinson's research interests, particularly his development of a massive data base through the coooperation of birth control clinics in various parts of the country, each being called on to furnish 1000 case records showing the outcome of contraceptive advice and practice.

Elsie Wulkop scored a notáble success, impressing Middle Westerners simultaneously with her eager love of humanity and capacity to get along with its divisions and subdivisions as well as, under Gamble's close guidance, her capacity to be fair but firm about the spending of a dollar.

She was paid $250 a month plus expenses to act as the agent of an anonymous donor to offer seed grants for the establishment of birth control clinics and promote maternal health leagues that would hopefully assume future fund-raising responsibilities.

A Lansing woman told Miss Wulkop that she reminded her of her aunts in New England, causing Elsie to lament to Clarence— after a twelve-year acquaintance they began to call each other by their first names—"Have I taken on the protective coloring of my environment and am now a typical maiden auntie of classic form?" On another occasion, a patient who had just poured out her woes to Miss Wulkop concluded: "You are a sort of universal mother whose serenity is comforting." There was no question that Miss Wulkop, who helped raise her sister's child, understood motherhood.

Between 1930 and 1935, Elsie Wulkop worked in Michigan, Indiana, Iowa, Nebraska, and Kansas, providing personal or financial stimulus or sometimes both, in the establishment of clinics in twenty-two cities of these five states, including fourteen in Michigan, where she also played a key role in the establishment of local Maternal Health Committees and Maternal Health Leagues. The momentum of these efforts was evident in the 1939 report of the Michigan Maternal Health League. It showed twenty-eight birth control committees and twenty-two clinics in operation in Michigan since the League's beginning in 1931. Some 15,000 patients, half of them on relief, had been served. These were married mothers with an average of three living children at the time they sought contraceptive help. In the Detroit experience, Gamble was amused to note that 40 percent were Catholic, a percentage not dissimilar from the Philadelphia experience.

Gamble became interested in Harper Hospital because of his acquaintanceship with three of the doctors there, including the other survivor of his 1922 airplane crash, Dr. Ralph Miller, whom he had aided in medical school and in getting established in practice as a specialist in diseases of the eye, ear, nose, and throat.

At the time Miss Wulkop arrived in Detroit, in November 1930, Detroit and Michigan had only one small birth control center, the Mother's Clinic, established in 1927 with the support of the Jewish Welfare Federation and others.

Establishing a birth control clinic in Harper Hospital was not an easy assignment, as the frequent and lengthy correspondence between Gamble and Miss Wulkop disclosed. He had instructed her to offer a year's support of a weekly clinic that two of the medical staff, Drs. George Kamperman and Harold Mack, were ready to undertake as soon as they had hospital approval and the money. The Hospital's director, Dr. Stewart Hamilton, opposed the plan. He said that he too frequently had been offered one-year support of various projects and then had been left with a failure on his hands when further support was not forthcoming. This was not his only objection. As Miss Wulkop wrote Gamble: "He struck his fist down and said, 'This matter is playing with fire. . . . It will get beyond control as Prohibition has and besides it is assuming to control human destinies.' "

But Kamperman and Mack wanted the clinic and Dr. Hamilton's attitude softened when Elsie Wulkop offered a two-year grant of $3,500. The trustees procrastinated for two months but the president, R. H. Webber, the head of one of Detroit's largest department stores, appreciated the desirability of birth control. The board acted to accept the offer of an "anonymous donor" to finance a Maternal Health Clinic to be operated under the supervision of the medical staff for two years "with the understanding that the Hospital may at any time discontinue the operation thereof and return to the donor the pro rata amount of the gift."

Miss Wulkop, who meanwhile had been courting the Woman's Hospital in Detroit with Gamble's encouragement, wanted to withdraw the Harper offer because of this restriction, but he dissuaded her: "It would not seem quite reasonable to allow an anonymous and unknown donor an opportunity to wreck the whole operation of the hospital merely for the contribution in question. I would expect that any clinic we start might be discontinued should the effect on the hospital donations or influx of patients prove markedly undesirable. . . . The only loss would be the one which you point out of having the birth control movement receive a black eye. I feel hopeful that you will be able to prevent this disaster."

The Harper Clinic, operating two hours a week at the outset, opened in January 1931, somewhat inauspiciously. It had three patients. The first was already pregnant, and the third, probably so. The second patient had such severe lacerations of the cervix, as well as possible inflammation of the oviducts, that she needed a hysterectomy.

Woman's Hospital was more enthusiastic in its plans for a birth control clinic, and shortly had one underway with a seed grant from Gamble of $900. These two hospital clinics survived and prospered, after shaky starts due to two needs: for patients (solved without much difficulty) and for money (a never-ending quest).

At the end of Harper's second year in birth control, in late 1932, Miss Wulkop and Dr. Hamilton began a subtle duel, the former backed by her unnamed "principals" and the latter, by his trustees. She wanted authorization from the Harper board to make a specific fund-raising appeal for the birth control clinic. Dr.

Hamilton figured that the donor would not let the clinic collapse, but would come through with third-year support. He did not know Clarence Gamble. In August, the Hospital informed Miss Wulkop it was closing the clinic. Though a cool hand, she showed some anxiety: "I feel that I have failed to organize this first of your clinics in Michigan," she wrote Gamble. But he stood firm. In the end, the trustees capitulated and approved of the special fund-raising appeal. The clinic continued in operation, and grew as a teaching clinic to become the largest and best-known in the state. It found local support, proving that Gamble was right.

Gamble urged Wulkop to push on to other cities as quickly as possible—to Grand Rapids, Jackson, and Pontiac as well as Toledo and Indianapolis. Some were ready for birth control, others not so ready. From Lansing she gave Gamble bad news in November 1931:

Lansing is in a bad situation as the only [general medical] clinic there has been closed for nearly three months as a result of the drive of private physicians against *any* free clinic, which they claim is militating against their earning a living. The city physician is incompetent and indifferent to public health so I hear, so the local social agencies are faced with a choice of paying for private office treatment for their clients or letting them go without care entirely. In spite of this demand on their meager funds for general medicinal use, they have already brought fifteen patients to our Harper clinic. . . . I hear one Lansing man asked $9 for giving contraceptive advice to a patient who was pretty near penniless and [he] expected the agency to pay this which of course was out of the question. . . . It seems to me that until the medical forces of Lansing settle this the entire question of clinics should be left severely alone. . . . To try to establish a contraceptive clinic in a city of nearly 90,000 inhabitants where no clinic for matters of life and death is permitted to function because of opposition of the medical profession is bad tactics.

Gamble agreed there was "no immediate need for action," but wanted to see a birth control league or relief organization do some group bargaining with the doctors, conceding that free clinics were out but offering to pay doctors. "It seems to me that with the present difficulty in securing practice a doctor could be found who would do the work for a dolwlar per case, plus the cost of supplies and, if necessary . . . of a nurse to . . . conserve his time."

Lansing provided a severe test of Gamble-Wulkop patience and perseverance. Originally, in 1931, they offered the Lansing Maternal Health Committee $400 against $200 in local money for the operation of a weekly clinic in Lansing for one year. This was comparatively generous, for he already had worked out a one-for-two formula elsewhere, offering from $300 to $500 against $600 to $1,000 of local money, always emphasizing that he was not trying to buy contraceptives for the people of Michigan but to educate them in the social results that could be obtained through this kind of investment.

But the vast majority of Lansing doctors were so opposed to a charity clinic that the Committee had to refuse the offer, and it was not until more than three years later, or the end of 1934, that Lansing got its first birth control clinic. Gamble's contribution then was $175 against $75 raised locally. Lansing social workers had been paying transportation expenses to send some indigent women to the new clinic in Grand Rapids for contraceptive advice, meanwhile paying local doctors a fee for such service to other poor mothers; inevitably, the private fee was from 50 to 100 percent higher than the clinic cost of $4 or less.

Gamble's correspondence with Elsie Wulkop exhibited many of the characteristics that became familiar to all of his fieldworkers as time went on. For one thing, while he often was both considerate and generous, he exhibited an insistent need to consider and have accounted for, not just dollars, but every penny. Contrasting his Detroit and Cincinnati experiences, he realized that he did not have to pay a community organizer a big salary or give a clinic a big budget to achieve maximum activity. In Cincinnati, he paid the community organizer $333 a month and granted the clinic $7,500 over two years whereas in Detroit, he got a more efficient job done for a field director's salary of $250 a month and a two-year clinic budget of $3500. As a matter of fact, Miss Wulkop was more highly paid than other fieldworkers to come; in the late 1930s, others received from $100 to $200 a month, plus travel and living expenses abroad.

Dr. Gamble was a bear on detail. In one letter in 1931, he rebuked Elsie Wulkop: "I am glad to get the answers to some of my questions but please look over my letters more thoroughly when you write. For example, you didn't tell me how many patients turned up at the clinics subsequent to the first." Later he wrote: "I suppose you think I spend most of my waking hours thinking of things for you to do. Perhaps this letter will confirm your suspicion."

One thing that bothered Miss Wulkop and was the subject of much comment in her letters was his insistence on remaining anonymous. It imposed a hardship on her. For the birth control fieldworker to approach a hospital or committee and offer money from a secret source created a mystery that begged an explanation; if one was not forthcoming, it would be manufactured. The most common rumor, encountered in Ohio as well as Michigan, was that Elsie Wulkop's silent partner was a manufacturer of contraceptives—of which a considerable number had sprung up in the past few years—and was using these clinics as a means of distributing his product. The fact that the allegation did not withstand scrutiny made no difference in the need to dispose of it. Trustees and administrators of reputable institutions, such as Harper, felt a responsibility to know where gifts were coming from.

Gamble did not agree:

> I think I would rather not use any identifying details by way of 'guaranty' accompanying my gift. During the time the gift is under discussion we are, of course, asking the hospital to devote the time necessary for its consideration with only your verbal assurance that the gift is available. After the gift, however, is definitely in their treasury, it seems to me that it should make no difference from what person or organization it comes.

Miss Wulkop told Gamble that she found it difficult to tell fibs in his behalf. That there would be any need to at Harper Hospital would seem to have been eliminated when, in September 1931, returning from Harbor Point to Philadelphia, Clarence and Sarah Gamble visited Harper Hospital and talked to Drs. Hamilton, Mack, and Kamperman. As Gamble wrote to Elsie Wulkop: "Each . . . expressed gratitude for what I was doing for the hospital and to each . . . I admitted nothing (unless by silence)."

That was not the end of it. At a meeting in Indianapolis, she met Dr. Brown, director of the Maternal Health Clinic in Cincinnati. Brown did not know her connection with Gamble, but frankly and cheerfully related that Dr. Clarence Gamble was financing his clinic in Cincinnati. This caused Gamble to reply to Miss Wulkop: "It annoys me a good deal that he published the fact that I am one of the Cincinnati angels."

One way or another, it is evident that Clarence Gamble's identity as a birth control angel became one of the worst-kept of secrets, by himself as well as by others. As time went on, he became more relaxed about public identification.

What is of more interest is why he felt this need for anonymity, and why one so insistent on accountability could fail to understand its need by others. Much of his modesty in giving he quite surely acquired from the example of his father, of whom the pastor of the Pasadena Presbyterian Church had said, "His left hand never guesses what his right hand is about." On the other hand, if one philanthropist wanted to educate others to give to the birth control movement, as Gamble said he did, and also believed in the power of advertising, as he said he did, why would he try—however ineffectively—to keep his giving secret?

Doubtless, Miss Wulkop identified one reason: he did not want more people hounding him for money. Possibly, too, he shared the realization of many men in the high income tax brackets—there is nothing to be gained by attracting attention to one's financial affairs. And possibly he felt the need to protect—through anonymity concerning how and where he spent his money—his research career while he was at the University of Pennsylvania. Also, what he was doing was an experiment; when one is unsure how one's efforts may turn out, one can do without kibitzers; if one is bent on satisfying one's curiosity, being a target of other people's curiosity does not help.

chapter 8   Lena Hillard's Kentucky Jelly

Program

It was ironic. The doctor and nurse Gamble most admired, Dickinson and Sanger, had worked for twenty years or more to persuade the medical profession that contraception was its legitimate concern. By mutual consent, they built the birth control movement around the doctor and the vaginal diaphragm. This campaign came to its climax in 1936, with the United States Circuit Court of Appeals decision approving the medical dissemination of contraceptive devices and information. This was followed in 1937 by the American Medical Association's approval of contraception as a subject for medical research, education, and practice, an action representing a complete turnabout from its official disapproval in 1936.

But now it was becoming perfectly clear that a birth control clinic headed by a doctor was more of a detour than a direct road to effective family limitation among the poor, of whom God

118

continued to make so many. The birth control clinics were valuable. The fact that there were far too few of them was being remedied, as fast as Gamble and birth controllers of like mind could work, but they were located in cities and the major portion of the population then lived in the country. Then, too, there were the problems of motivating disadvantaged mothers to go to the clinics and of solving transportation to and from the clinics. Dr. Gilbert W. Beebe, statistician and a Gamble-sponsored colleague in numerous scientific studies made by the National Committee on Maternal Health, touched on a sobering truth when in 1942 he reflected: "The epic decline in fertility which has been reshaping Western life has been accomplished almost entirely by the use of simple methods and without benefit of medical service." He referred to withdrawal, the condom, and illegal abortion.

Dickinson in 1941 wrote something that came close to an epitaph to the diaphragm as a mass source of birth control when he said: "Clinics everywhere thought they had a method so generally applicable that the extension of conception control required merely multiplication of centers. The diaphragm, correctly used, had a failure rate of only one per fifty couples per year, or two percent. Diaphragm and jelly looked effective enough to be exclusive. Follow-up study has given this comfortable belief a jolt. The *protection rate is high*, but the refusal-rate is disconcerting when, except for selected groups, a considerable proportion of those instructed decline to begin or continue with this method."

Dickinson summarized the real need when he said, "Contraceptives must be certain, simple, harmless, not unpleasant, cheap—easy to get, easy to keep, easy to use."

The diaphragm was best suited for use by the better-educated, self-sufficient, highly motivated, middle-class woman whom authorities were criticizing for having too few babies. Many women in the poverty group could be persuaded to try it—particularly after rapid child-bearing had made them desperate—but its good results depended on correct use, foresight, initiative, will power, manual dexterity, and the availability of a private bathroom. The device is not easily manipulated in a one-bedroom house or an outdoor privy. The poor woman's day was apt to consist of serial and multiple distractions from her main chance of preventing further pregnancy; the pursuit of a wearing, wearying life left her ready for bed but not ready, according to the classic old English expression, to have her good man "surprise" her. Already, Margaret Sanger, the true prophet, was talking about the need for "a pill" or better still, a vaccine.

Meanwhile Gamble fully appreciated Dickinson's remark that 4,000,000 American couples each night made the decision in coitus to procreate or not to procreate, an event more crucial for the urban and rural poor because they reached the decision to do so more often than middle or upper classes. NCMH studies showed that the average occurrence of sexual intercourse among economically depressed couples was twice a week, with an extreme range of once a month to once a night. Here—one had to face it—was a factory for poverty culture. Whatever the social and economic forces that denied these people the comfort, freedom, and dignity of self-sufficiency, they were highly efficient in the reproduction of their own kind—generation after generation born, raised, and dedicated to the perpetuation of squalor and misery.

The Kentucky mountain people were a dramatic example, and it was among them that Gamble decided to test alternative methods. He chose two alternative methods (condoms were impractical because of their cost). One was the use of a spermicidal jelly—the same lactic acid ointment used with the diaphragm—injected about a teaspoonful at a time into the vagina with an applicator immediately before intercourse. This method had received a small amount of testing encouraged by Gamble and Beebe among the patients of a birth control clinic at the Episcopal Hospital in Philadelphia in 1933. It had also been introduced in Logan County, West Virginia, in 1933 by a Gamble disciple from Maine, Doris Davidson, a public health nurse with the American Birth Control League, working in cooperation with the American Friends Service Committee. Conclusive scientific evaluation was lacking.

A second alternative was insertion in the vagina of a small sponge covered with a spermicidal powder that foamed when mixed with air and water. Dr. Lydia DeVilbiss had tried this method with patients of the Mothers' Health Clinic in Miami, Florida. It, too, required evaluation. Gamble did not regard either method as holding promise of complete effectiveness, but "If carefully used, children probably do not arrive oftener than once in twenty years," he estimated.

Gamble chose to organize a "jelly program."

He had heard about the human condition in the Appalachian mountains from Dr. William Hutchins, president of Berea College, Kentucky, a small college for Southern farm boys and girls who worked out part of their expenses under a program conducted by a "Dean of Labor." In 1927, Gamble, pursuing his early interest in aid to deserving students, gave Berea stock valued at $1,378.20 to establish a fund to make small, short-term loans (usually $1 to $15) for urgent, incidental needs, such as shoe repairs, textbooks, and railroad fare. He approved of the College's emphasis on teaching its students business methods and ethics, including paying interest for the use of money.

In 1936, Gamble found an opportunity to develop a new program in the surrounding counties—Madison, Jackson, and Rockcastle—with the stimulus of Phyllis Bache Page. Mrs. Page, then in her early thirties, was the attractive, articulate, Boston-bred, Smith College-trained wife of Richmond Page, librarian of the Pennsylvania School of Social Work. In later life a gifted teacher of problem children in the Winchester, Massachusetts, public schools, Mrs. Page's main interests until she met Gamble and kindred spirits in Philadelphia birth control circles had been arts and crafts and, by necessity, the frustrated ambition of her husband to be an author. Childless after several years of marriage, she was looking for a job. One of Margaret Sanger's attorneys described Mrs. Page as a "soft-eyed siren;" she had the kind of engaging personality and surplus of energy that Gamble wanted in his birth control workers. He offered her a job as his secretary of birth control "at $30 a week for not more than 44 weeks, 8 weeks vacation without salary," as he wrote in the job description he sent her.

Mrs. Page quickly demonstrated a *de rigeur* requirement in Gamble workers—a capacity to tolerate his close supervision and teasing ways with grace and good humor and, where necessary, to argue with him. She immediately became involved in his correspondence crusade, and also his style. From the Hotel Victoria in Nassau, Bahamas, he in March 1936 instructed his new secretary, back in Philadelphia, to write him airmail "at 10 cents a half ounce," to type double space on thin paper. A year later, when she wrote him on a Washington hotel letterhead, she reflected his training by automatically apologizing: "Have no thin paper tonight—please excuse extravagance."

At the outset, Gamble presented her with "Plans for Birth Control Activities, with Help of Mrs. Page." He wrote that the main objective was "to discover the most economical and effective way of making 'Every U.S. child a wanted child,'" a sizable assignment even for a Phi Beta Kappa scholar from Smith College. His list of things for Mrs. Page to do was sufficient to encompass the career of a Margaret Sanger, including the continuing task of stirring up interest in birth control among women's clubs and an immediate need to "look for new jelly centers."

Gamble sent Mrs. Page to the Conference of Southern Mountain Workers at Knoxville and then on to Berea. His instructions for both visits were explicit. She was to ask specified questions of conference delegates and "To answer questions asked by the delegates: Dr. Gamble, whom you represent, is interested in securing a clinical test of the efficacy of simple contraceptives." This was a departure from Gamble's earlier image as an anonymous instigator and initiator of public interest in birth control. From this point on it was apparent that—perhaps in part from Elsie Wulkop's complaints—he was resigned to the inevitable association of his name with his workers and his works.

Secondly, he wanted Mrs. Page to go to Berea and form a charitable organization that would supervise a public health nurse who would visit impoverished mountain women in their homes. "Call it something like 'Maternal Health League of Kentucky' or 'Mountain Nursing, Inc.' Make no promises but suggest salary and expenses, including automobile, for nurses would be available."

The leading women and a certain few doctors around Berea proved to be as well informed, interested, and progressive as those of Michigan or Ohio, although Berea, south of Lexington, was a town of only a few thousand population. They founded the Mountain Maternal Health League, and eventually affiliated it with the Kentucky Birth Control League and the American Birth Control League. The usual counterpart medical committee likewise was organized, headed by Dr. Helen Ruby Paine. A clinic was established in Union Church.

The local leaders agreed that Lena Gilliam (later Mrs. Ernest Hillard) would be an ideal choice for the visiting nurse. Then twenty-three and working in the Brooklyn Hospital in New York, Miss Gilliam had a commitment to mountain birth control. She told her story with Gamble's unacknowledged literary assistance in *The Survey* (September 1937);

Our family of nine, father, mother, and seven children, was living in a two-room log house on the Rockcastle River in Kentucky. I had just won a scholarship at Anneville Institute, but my mother could not let me go.

"There's another baby coming," she said. "My back aches all day long, and with all the cooking and washing and ironing and sewing I've just got to have your help."

"But why," I protested bitterly, "when it's already so hard to get food and clothes enough to go around do you go and have another baby? Don't you think we have a big enough family now?

I can still see the weary expression on my mother's face as she answered. "Yes, I've already had more than I wanted, though at first I was happy when they came. But what can I do—men being what they are? The doctor told me not to have any more, but he didn't say what I could do not to."

"I'll never get married," I told her, "or if I do, I'm surely going to find out how to keep babies from coming so fast."

During the day, while I was hoeing corn on the hillside, the thought of "babies and backaches" was continually on my mind. I resolved that same day, I'd find out what could be done.

Three years later my mother, who was only thirty-eight, though she looked years older, gave birth to her eleventh child—and died. When you find yourself at sixteen the foster mother of ten, the world seems nothing but trying to find food to fill all the children's stomachs and clothes to cover their bodies. . . .

Finally a friend made it possible for me to get to a New York Hospital for a nurse's training with an extra year on the obstetrical wards. I had planned to become a registered midwife and come back to the mountains. I learned in New York, though, that mothers really could be taught how to space their families. I knew that would help them more than all the care of the best midwives in the world.

Now Lena had her chance. Gamble offered her $125 a month, with employment not guaranteed beyond twelve months and she to pay her own living expenses. But she would have a car, and indeed could have one of Gamble's automobiles if she would come to Philadelphia and drive it out to Kentucky, and meanwhile register and operate it in her own name and assume all liability. Clarence mentioned Lena Gilliam in a letter to Aunt Julia in 1936: "I have just shot a birth control arrow to the mountains of Kentucky in the shape of an energetic girl. She had never driven an automobile before ten days ago, so to let her go off with our Chevrolet required a great deal of courage and a certain amount of practice."

Lena Gilliam made it to Berea and soon was seeking out mothers in the more inaccessible areas. It was uphill work and not only in a topographical sense. The hill people, in this section mainly farmers, in contrast to families living in coal mining camps elsewhere, depended more on creeks than roads as communicating links, inasmuch as the only land that would grow much of anything was in the creek bottoms. So people lived "up a branch" or in "the next holler." The visitor drove his automobile as far as he could and then proceeded, if he was that determined, on foot to his destination. The addresses of Miss Gilliam's patients were recorded in such terms as these: "A mile and a half beyond the letterbox Black Lick Road." "One mile up Jack Branch." "On side road one mile off from Bob Town." "One quarter of a mile in a log house above the school across the creek."

The drab women in the cabins seemed doomed to a perpetual state of pregnancy. The married ones ranged in age from sixteen to forty-eight and conceived on the average of once every twenty-eight months, those with less education having a higher rate than those with more. Some four out of ten admitted to having practiced contraception at some time before; usually the husband used a condom or withdrew before ejaculation, or the woman douched. If Miss Gilliam found the mother already pregnant, she put her down for a visit at some later time and moved on.

She was not an eager letter writer, like Gamble's other field workers; on a rare occasion when she wrote about her work, she said: "I spend my days in the mountain districts going from house to house. After discussing the children and the family health, I explain the purpose for which I have been employed and learn whether the mother is interested in contraceptive instruction. . . . As a rule, the mother is anxious to confide in someone and as a result I obtain the story of her desire not to spend her entire life in continuous pregnancies. I explain that I am working under the doctor's direction, and that the contraceptive is harmless and efficient as well as inexpensive.

". . . I find it usually takes nearly two hours in listening and explaining (chiefly listening) in order to give the information and establish the friendly contact with the mother which seems of great importance."

The public health nurse used an anatomical model of the vagina in teaching the mother how to apply the jelly. Each mother was asked to pay 10 cents for the applicator and 25 cents per tube for the jelly (Lactikol B) if she could; otherwise, she received it at Dr. Gamble's expense.

In the absence of the Catholic Church of the big cities, Miss Gilliam and other public health nurses and doctors promoting birth control in Kentucky, Tennessee, and West Virginia ran into little opposition to their work, other than passive resistance from the state health commissioner of Kentucky, who apparently took his lead from the conservative attitudes of the American Medical Association, the United States Public Health Service, and the

Children's Bureau. The celebrated Frontier Nursing Service of Kentucky—public health nurses on horseback—specialized in prenatal and newborn care of mother and child but shunned the contraceptive approach to maternal health. The mountain people were mainly Scotch-Irish and professed various Protestant revivalist faiths—Holiness, Church of God, Free-Will Baptist. Religious opposition was ineffective. One Kentucky mountain woman said: "The Holiness Church says it is a sin not to have children, but I don't think so."

The one force the women feared most was their husbands. A woman did what her man told her. Beyond those already pregnant, some women expressed an interest in using the jelly but did not follow through. Some were quite frank to say that they had to ask their husbands first. Typically, fathers were proud of fertility as an index to their virility—one man boasted about having twenty-six children. Some men forbid their wives to use the jelly. Occasionally, a man would apologize that other men would laugh at him if they knew his wife was using a contraceptive.

Miss Gilliam followed her patients eighteen months or more, seeing them on the average of about once every six months. Gilbert W. Beebe and Murray A. Geisler selected 400 of her cases for study under the auspices of the National Committee on Maternal Health.

Beebe and Geisler emphasized that the sample was biased from a scientific standpoint by the fact that the women studied were only those who volunteered—that is, were motivated to try contraceptives and had, in many instances, already used them. In other words, having more babies tends to stimulate interest in not having more babies.

Even so, of those women who accepted the jelly, about one in four never used or probably never used it. An estimated 40 percent were not using the method after one year, and 50 percent after two years. The reasons for non-use included lack of need, preference for other methods, lack of confidence in the contraceptive, undesired pregnancy, messiness, fear of injury, and a burning sensation from use.

But the pregnancy rate in the study group did decline, by more than half; and a continuation rate of 60 percent after one year and 50 percent after two years is not a bad record even today with superior methods. The hard facts of the kind Gamble liked to read, were as follows:

Before, the pregnancy rate of the study group was 66 pregnancies per 100 woman-years of exposure (to the risk of pregnancy), ranging from 78 in those making no effort toward contraception down to 27 among those using various methods—condom, withdrawal, douche.

After, the pregnancy rate was 26, the rate for those using jelly being 20 and for all other methods, 14, or an average of 17.

Overall, it was evident that the impact of contraception on the group was a 60 percent decline (from 66 to 26). It was also evident that the jelly method showed no superiority over other methods, leading the investigators to conclude:

"In general the interpretation placed upon the results is that a method was provided by which the patients secure a protection no higher than with methods of their own choosing, but that the service made a large contribution to the control of conception in encouraging the practice of contraception."

In more general experience, Gamble concluded that the jelly-only method was about 85 percent effective if faithfully used. He continued to support a jelly program for 700 women on the lists of the Mountain Maternal Health League until 1943. The League continued the work, establishing a clinic at Berea College Hospital in 1944, combining birth control with a broad program of maternal and child health and including both home and clinic visits.

Gamble was sufficiently excited about the work in Kentucky, as well as parallel activities in Tennessee and West Virginia, so that he visited the area several times, not hesitating, as it were, to show the Gamble flag. It was evident to him from this experience that the search for the *right* contraceptive for the masses must go on. The name of the game in birth control is perseverance. But from the start, he had another possibility to try. This was foam powder and sponge.

chapter 9 The North Carolina Story:

A Victory in Public Health

By 1937, Clarence Gamble had many irons in the fire. Lena Gilliam was spreading the word on lactic acid jelly in Kentucky, but in another year would marry and move to North Carolina, leaving her sister, Sylvia, also a nurse, to carry on birth control in Berea. Edna McKinnon, an attorney who had lobbied birth control bills for Margaret Sanger in Washington, went first to Montana and then Tennessee, where she aroused leading citizens and physicians in Nashville and elsewhere to start hospital birth control clinics. Phyllis Page, the artist and now Gamble's private secretary, and then Gamble himself went to Puerto Rico, in his first venture outside the continental United States (see Chapter 11). Hazel Moore, a Sanger veteran in stimulating group organization, was in Virginia badgering cautious public health doctors to swallow their fears of the Catholic Church and allow local health departments to offer birth control services. Doris Davidson, the nurse whom Gamble discovered in Maine, was in Raleigh, North

Carolina, in a roving assignment centered on community organization and contraceptive jelly experiments. Elsie Wulkop, the
Boston social worker and first of Gamble's fieldworkers, was
down in Tampa getting Joyce Ely, a public health nurse, started
on a small foam-powder-and-sponge study among employees of
the Dupont estate on Boca Grande Island. Frances Roberta Pratt, a
public health nurse from North Carolina, was also there, helping
out. Under one organization or another—the National Committee on Maternal Health, the Birth Control Clinical Research
Bureau, or the American Birth Control League—all eight of these
women fieldworkers were wholly or partly salaried or took all or
some of their direction from Clarence Gamble.

The Boca Grande project was completed some months before
expiration of the period for which Miss Pratt had been hired. Elsie
Wulkop, on her way north in February, thought it an opportune
time to talk to Dr. George M. Cooper, assistant director of the
North Carolina State Board of Health, who was in charge of the
state's maternal and child health program. Miss Pratt had been
born and raised in Raleigh; perhaps Cooper would give her a job
developing a sponge-and-foam-powder program.

In the foam-powder-and-sponge technique, the foam provides
the spermicidal action and the small sponge, either natural or
made of rubber, provides the receptacle for the powder. The user
is instructed that, not more than a half hour before intercourse,
she dip the sponge in water, squeeze it out, then sprinkle both
sides with the powder. She must gently knead the powdered
sponge to start the production of foam and then insert it as far
into the vagina as her finger can reach. Each thrust of the penis
squeezes foam out of the sponge. Spermatazoa are killed by the
foam; the sponge is left in place until morning and then pulled
out by an attached thread. In case of further intercourse during
the night, Robert Dickinson advised use of a second sponge inserted over the first.

Dr. Gamble was eager to get started a large, well-designed field
test of this method, one that would provide a scientific comparison of foam powder with jelly alone and jelly combined with the
diaphragm. More broadly, he nurtured the idea of integrating

birth control and public health in a program aimed at poor people. This was one reason for Miss Davidson being in Raleigh; she had found Dr. Cooper "a perfect lamb from the beginning," and, as she saw it, friendly toward the organization of an ABCL program in North Carolina.

Miss Wulkop, in a single conversation with Cooper, found a new opportunity for Gamble to demonstrate the virtue of striking while the iron was hot, always at the risk of miscellaneous burns, of course. The outcome was undoubtedly Gamble's most valuable birth control promotion in the United States.

North Carolina was historically an ideal place for the first merger of the birth control with the public health movement under state health department direction. Under the leadership of Dr. Watson S. Rankin, the state's first full-time state health officer (1909), the North Carolina State Board of Health was the first in the United States to develop a system of county health departments headed by full-time health officers. Their mission was to improve rural health.

The first county health officers themselves were merely practicing physicians paid small sums by the Board of County Commissioners to look after sanitation and the sick poor part time. Some became outstanding, but often it was the least competent physician in the county who got the public health job. By the 1930s, many of the more able took special training at schools of public health; their teachers, with rare exceptions, however, did not consider contraception a part of preventive medicine.

The circumstances under which the medical profession accepted local health officers in their communities were crucial in public health progress, and influenced the thinking in birth control of Cooper and his chief, Dr. Carl V. Reynolds, the state health officer. County medical societies went along with these health doctors on the government payroll on condition that they stay out of clinical medicine—"curative medicine" it was called then. The private physician's domain was fee-for-service care of the sick; there were institutionalized exceptions, such as the aged, tuberculous, insane, or others too poor to pay for their care. When the question of birth control arose, the same pattern prevailed. If the woman could pay, she was considered a private case. By and large, the private practitioners of North Carolina were friendly toward the state health department; it was important to do nothing that would offend them.

A correlative factor was the history of local autonomy among the country health departments themselves. The original county health units had no connection with the state health department, and resisted the direction and guidance of this "outside agency" as long as possible. County health officers had a deep-seated, residual fear of publicity; in the early years Dr. Rankin had criticized the quality of their work and threatened to develop a point system for evaluating their activities that could be used in publicizing the many defects in local programs. What gradually overcame their opposition to Raleigh "domination" was the offer of free state services, called "optional units" and including dental examinations for school children, immunizations against smallpox, diphtheria, and typhoid, free laboratory tests for infectious diseases such as syphilis and hookworm, and Adenoid and Tonsil Clubs (mobile surgical teams) offered in the name of public charity to the indigent.

Rankin and his successors recognized out-of-state aid as a key factor in gaining control over county health departments. The State Board of Health was able to augment state services to the counties in part through state tax appropriations and in part through grants from the Rockefeller Foundation and the United States Public Health Service. North Carolina in the twenty-five years prior to 1937 had become accustomed to accepting outside money from New York and Washington while loyal Dixiecrats in other sections of the South were still cussing the "damnyankees." It was practical to take advantage of this outside aid only if it could be done quietly so as to avoid stirring up any local political reaction.

By 1936, North Carolina had health departments in fifty of its 100 counties and the future looked good, thanks to a new federal aid. Under the Social Security Act of 1935, the Public Health

Service and the Children's Bureau had acquired funds to aid state and local health departments. This was the beginning of regular federal aid of this sort, but birth control was not on the list of categorical interests that could be supported by the so-called "formula grants." Cooper was quite sure, and told Gamble, that this exclusion was due to Catholic political influences in the Roosevelt Administration.

Birth control, nonetheless, was a matter of increasing concern in North Carolina. The state had shown great public health progress in some sectors. In 1920, for example, its death rate for dysentery was four times higher, but by 1940 it was somewhat less, than the United States average. But its infant and maternal mortality rates were higher than all but four or five other states; induced abortion and infanticide contributed heavily. As they acknowledged, Reynolds and Cooper received several hundred letters a year from "underprivileged, multiparous or organically diseased wives" asking if there wasn't some way they could be relieved from further childbirth. One woman had heart trouble and nine pregnancies in eleven years. A twenty-six-year-old mother, bedridden with kidney disease, was in her tenth pregnancy.

North Carolina, with a population of three and a half million, one million Negro, one out of five on the dole and more living in poverty, was ready for birth control. Ready or not, Gamble saw the possibility of action there as early as 1934, when his attention was drawn to the problems of unemployment and hunger in North Carolina in a fund-raising letter he received from the Church Emergency Relief Committee. He did not make a contribution, but offered to pay a portion of salary and expenses if the Committee's fieldworker in North Carolina would be willing to offer contraceptives to the poor. She did not accept his offer.

Liberal-minded people, such as social workers in the state and county welfare departments and sociologists at the University of North Carolina, favored birth control. The North Carolina Conference for Social Service endorsed public health contraceptive services in 1932, and was supported in this resolution by the State

Board of Charities and Public Welfare. Nominally sponsored by well-known physicians and leading citizens, the North Carolina Maternal Health League was organized in 1935. Its most active element, however, was social workers, led by Mrs. W.B. Waddill and George H. Lawrence, who had been a county welfare director and became a sociology professor at the University of North Carolina. Lawrence was also a member of the State Board of Health.

The seed for action had been planted some years before with the establishment of birth control clinics in Asheville and Fayetteville. These two had been privately organized but by 1937 were under county health department supervision. Reynolds and Cooper wanted to extend these efforts elsewhere. In discussions, they insisted that any public health birth control program should not only be sponsored but guided and directed by practicing physicians in cooperation with local health officers; the Maternal League readily agreed.

The only trouble was that neither the State Board of Health nor the Maternal Health League had any money for this purpose. Federal aid was not available, and Reynolds refused to take a budget request with a birth control item in it to the state legislature. The League was not organized for voluntary fund-raising.

Such was the situation when Elsie Wulkop walked into Dr. Cooper's office in Raleigh at 10 a.m. on February 17, 1937. She told him something about her work in birth control for Dr. Gamble. He told her something of the difficulties of fighting the runaway procreation problem among backward people in his state. They found they had a common dislike—the American Birth Control League. The doctors of North Carolina did not like it; nor did they care for Mrs. Sanger. She was too noisy and pushy. The doctors didn't like all this lay propaganda or, for that matter, any publicity they did not control. It became evident to Miss Wulkop that Miss Davidson, with whom she had breakfast that morning, had mistaken a friendly manner on Dr. Cooper's part for a willingness to ally the state health department with the Birth Control League. Indeed, Cooper was emphatic: it was Dr.

Reynolds's policy to accept financial aid from no one unless he had complete independence in spending it.

Miss Wulkop told him that Roberta Pratt, a public health nurse now trained in birth control, wanted to work for him. Why didn't Cooper hire Miss Pratt as his field representative in organizing contraceptive services as part of the prenatal and postnatal clinics in county health departments? Only complete lack of funds kept him from jumping at the chance, he said. What if Dr. Gamble put up the money for salary, travel expenses, and supplies? In that case, Cooper said, he was ready to move if he could demonstrate to Reynolds and the Board that certain conditions would be met.

These conditions were that there be enough support for one year and no pressure to continue beyond expiration of the grant. The state health department could use the money as it saw fit. There would be no publicity about the program and no alliance with a national organization.

As Gamble later told the League: "Miss Wulkop told me of this by telephone, and as I felt it to be a valuable opportunity, I agreed to furnish the necessary contribution."

At dinner that night, Miss Wulkop informed Miss Davidson of the eventful day. The next morning, Miss Davidson got off a telegram to Gamble:

MISS WULKOP YESTERDAY . . . ARRANGED WITH DR. COOPER . . . THAT YOU WILL PLACE PRATT THEIR DISPOSAL . . . WITHOUT MY KNOWING ABOUT IT DO NOT BLAME WULKOP GRABBING OPPORTUNITY AND WOULD PERSONALLY LOVE WORK WITH PRATT BUT AM SERIOUSLY DISTURBED HOW LEAGUE WILL REACT PROBABLY BADLY AS IT IS TAKING WORK I HAVE LABORED OVER TWO MONTHS . . . RIGHT OUT OF MY HANDS . . . HAVE NOT REPORTED SITUATION LEAGUE YET PLEASE ADVISE.

Gamble tried to restore Miss Davidson's wounded pride as best he could. He phoned her the evening of February 19, and in a letter the next day advised her to call him collect if she wished, but please do it at night. His letter explained:

"I . . . want to do everything I can to make things as smooth as possible for you. . . . I don't see how your suggestion of making the contribution through the League could be made acceptable to the State Board of Health since they want to avoid publicity and entanglement with propagandist organizations. It is possible, of course, that the outcome may displease the League since anything that has been connected with me seems to do this. I feel, however, that your part in it is above criticism."

She replied, "May I say that I find myself in a peculiar position. . . . I need not repeat that I think that what you are planning to do for North Carolina is simply magnificent and I am all for it. It will be a great thing for the state and for the countless poor women who are in desperate need of exactly this service. On the other hand, I do feel that the League had a right to be informed of such a plan before it was consummated, and consequently I must say that I cannot altogether blame them if they become indignant."

She said that she appreciated the way he sought to emphasize the good in a situation while disregarding other factors, and also his adherence to the old truth, "A soft answer turneth away wrath." Now, however, she would like to quit the League, where he had placed her, and work for him. Gamble reached new diplomatic heights in talking her out of this idea; he assured her that, whatever the hardship, her talents were of maximum value in trying to improve the League and therefore the sacrifice was worth it. As for her role in the new picture, he would like to see her doing public education and raising birth control funds in North Carolina. Gamble had had to give away two favorite aces, publicity and fund-raising, in dealing with Cooper but he hoped to find duplicates up his sleeve.

Meanwhile, financial and other details were worked out. Gamble agreed to give the State Board of Health, $4,500. For Clarence Gamble to put up that much without any word about matching funds bordered—for him—on fiscal recklessness.

Miss Pratt started work on March 15 at $150 a month. It was agreed that the program would target on indigent mothers and be carried out through a visiting nurse from the county health departments going into their homes, as well as by physicians and nurses seeing patients in the health department clinics. Cooper asked that Lawrence of the North Carolina Maternal Health League be drawn into the arrangements. This suited Gamble, in view of his own notions about future community organization and fund-raising, and he asked that his gift should appear in State Board of Health bookkeeping as "Maternal Health League Fund.

Gamble and Cooper were silky smooth with one another. "I would appreciate it if the knowledge of my financial connection with this work could be limited to as small a group as possible," Gamble wrote Cooper. The latter was pleased: "I am glad that you do not want too much said about this enterprise right in the start. It is our purpose to work very quietly through the State League for Maternal Health and . . . strictly through the organized health departments where there is one or more available physicians who are interested and competent to become responsible for the technical work."

The North Carolina birth control program began without a word of publicity. As a matter of fact, Cooper did not send out an information letter to county health officers until November, eight months later. Meanwhile Miss Pratt got services underway in six counties starting in Chapel Hill, where Lawrence lived.

Cooper said he would make monthly reports of progress to Gamble. What Cooper did not say, but Gamble learned indirectly, was that Cooper came close to being shot down, so to speak, when he brought the plan before the State Board of Health for approval. One board member strongly objected to acceptance of this outside aid. As Gamble informed the American Birth Control League, "Dr. Cooper said that his ability to tell the Board that the check for the contribution had been received that morning and that he had never yet returned a contribution turned objection into approval."

Thus began in North Carolina a milestone in the American birth control movement, the provision of contraceptive services by departments of public health—an unusual undertaking that could not get off the ground until a private citizen, not even a resident of the state, put money in the state treasury. It was Clarence Gamble's first experiece in working with government, and from it he learned a great deal about the advantages and disadvantages thereof. One thing he had to accept was the need for patience and perseverance, for, as one public health official said, "There has been no hurry."

As a state employee, Miss Pratt was in a different position than his other fieldworkers, except that, like the others, she had to face the reality of economic insecurity. She corresponded with Gamble, in a brief, formal manner; her narrative reports sounded pedestrian. She had some of the same problems as the others, such as a sense of being manipulated like a chessman in some master game plan, but she lacked the capacity of a Wulkop or Page to dramatize a situation; she tended to talk about places, rather than people. Most important, she accepted the bureaucratic working philosophy of a Cooper as opposed to the adventurous risk-taking of Gamble.

Cooper made the $4,500 last for eighteen months. During this period Miss Pratt traveled among the county health departments explaining the plan for contraception centers—or "prevenception centers," as she preferred to call them. She talked to the county health officer, special field nurse, supervising nurse, local physicians, and welfare workers, planning with them services adapted to local conditions. In all cases, the county health officer technically had to ask the state for her consultation and then obtain local medical society approval. Patients could be handled in a variety of ways, through home visits by public health nurses, by private physicians in health department clinics or hospital clinics, by family physicians, or by public health or welfare referrals to private physicians. Patients given contraceptive advice were not limited to those having medical reasons; they also were accepted if they believed they already had enough children, if they wished to space their children, or for mental health reasons. Foam powder and sponge was the method most often chosen, but the health officers and local physicians were free to recommend any method they wished.

In the beginning, March 1937, there were two diaphragm clinics with eighty-four patients. By October 1938, there were fifty-six contraception centers in fifty of North Carolina's one hundred counties. They had served 1,141 patients, according to the reports sent in. Five of the centers were using diaphragm and jelly and fifty-one, foam powder and sponge. Among these 1,141 patients, failure of method was reported for only six, three of these alleged to be due to low intelligence. Only twelve were reported to have personal objections to foam powder and sponge, due to unpleasantness, discomfort, irritation, burning, or pain.

Cooper had said he wanted no publicity and Gamble had agreed. Yet, thanks to stimulation by Gamble, no birth control program had drawn more attention since the days Irish Catholic policemen periodically hauled Margaret Sanger off to jail or to court.

To begin with, Gamble wrote and signed and Cooper approved an editorial about North Carolina's pioneers in birth control published in the January 1938 issue of the *Journal of Contraception.* Mrs. Sanger's Clinical Research Bureau straightway reprinted the piece and got out a press release. An Associated Press reporter brought the release to Cooper the morning after the doctor had addressed the Tri-County Medical Society in Raleigh about the program and Reynolds, his chief, had made the concluding remark: "Dr. Cooper has endeavored to carry this program on as a purely medical question, dealing only with doctors, and it is not a Margaret Sanger enterprise. If it were, we would have nothing whatever to do with it." Cooper protested the press release. Mrs. Cecil A. Damon, executive secretary of the Birth Control Clinical Research Bureau and a longtime close associate of Gamble, expressed her distress that anything might have happened to "gum up the works."

In May, Gamble spoke on "Contraception as a Public Health Measure" before the North Carolina Medical Society at Pinehurst. He gave Children's Bureau figures showing that infant mortality among brothers and sisters born a year or less apart was 147 per 1,000 live births but dropped to less than 100 with a two-year spacing and still further when there were three to four years between births. He spoke at one point of "the disease of unwanted children," but pleaded: "Don't go home and quote me now as saying that children are to follow syphilis as the next great plague to go. I don't put them in that class."

Gamble asked Cooper if he would deliver a paper before the annual meeting of the American Public Health Association so that public health doctors everywhere could hear what North Carolina was doing. Cooper assigned the task to Dr. Roy Norton, an assistant director and newly appointed professor of public health administration at the University of North Carolina. Norton spoke at Kansas City in October on "A Health Department Birth Control Program." Among other things, he said that careful records were being kept so that the effectiveness of foam powder could be evaluated; that birth control is an essential part of the maternity and infant program in a public health department and should lower morbidity and mortality rates, and that "there has been no fanfare, ballyhoo, or overaggressiveness" in the North Carolina program.

Cooper caught a little flak on this one. Norton's report made headlines in the Asheville *Citizen*, among other newspapers, and the secretary of the Catholic Study Club in Asheville wrote the president of the State Board of Health for "clarification." She wanted to know if the General Assembly had appropriated money for the support of the fifty-six birth control centers, "Or does this support come from the . . . fund . . . for the so-called maternity and infant 'health' program?" This so nettled Cooper that he wrote her a two-and-a-half page letter. "Not one penny" of government money had been used for birth control; support had come from a member of the University of Pennsylvania medical faculty, Cooper said.

The Asheville lady also wanted to know, since Norton said there had been no public objection to the operation of the Clinics, whether the public had been informed in the beginning. Cooper was vulnerable on this point, but owned up to the no-publicity policy, and admitted that he had not even sent a circular letter to the local health officers until "some of the health officers found out about the service from neighboring health officers and complained about the discrimination."

In regard to the complaint—the only letter of protest the program received—Cooper wrote Gamble: "The only thing we have to fear is too much publicity. Even now that would be extremely fatal to our enterprise for the simple reason that every reputable physician in the State would withdraw his aid at once.

Gamble was not alarmed. In early 1939, he succeeded in interesting the *Reader's Digest* in the North Carolina program. The magazine sent a writer, Don Wharton, down to do an article. Cooper cooperated reluctantly, with a mild protest to Gamble, and finally consented to publication of Wharton's article, "Birth Control: The Case for the State," with some changes. The *Digest* planted the article in *The Atlantic Monthly*, where it appeared in October 1939, followed by a *Reader's Digest* "condensation" in November. In this article, Gamble was identified as "Dr. Clarence J. Gamble, philanthropic heir to a soap fortune," and as the source of North Carolina birth control funds.

Cooper, too, seemed to warm under the spotlight, provided the light was medically tinted. He made his first report on "Birth Control in the North Carolina Public Health Program" in May 1940 at the annual meeting of the North Carolina Medical Society at Pinehurst. Emphasizing the spacing of children as an important part of preventive medicine and the desirability of having family planning "controlled by the medical profession instead of the laity," he confessed to utter amazement "that simple honesty and open-handedness in dealing with a vital medical and public health problem should stir up interest all over the world as being something unusual." As the result of the *Atlantic* and *Reader's Digest* articles, he said, "letters still come to the State Board of Health from many other states and a number of foreign countries, especially South America" asking for more information about the birth control program. He was surprised, too, at an unexpected show of interest on the part of Tarheel physicians and their reports of large numbers of patients coming to them privately for contraceptive advice. Cooper's three-year report led, in the next month, to a story in the Charlotte *News and Observer* headlined, STATE TAKES LEAD IN BIRTH CONTROL CLINICS OF SOUTH. The following year, Cooper in collaboration with Miss Pratt and Dr. Margaret G. Hagood of the Institute for Research in Social Science, University of North Carolina, did a more definitive report for the American Public Health Association, "Four Years of Contraception as a Public Health Service in North Carolina."

It was interesting: Both Cooper and Gamble could claim credit for their public relations policies, the former for "working quietly with the medical profession" and the latter for capitalizing on every chance, medical or lay, to spread the news.

The same might be said on the matter of financing, where they also locked horns. The program was barely more than a year old when Gamble pressed Cooper to raise money for half of Miss Pratt's salary and change her assignment to public education, including the organization of community groups and fundraising. This proposal found Cooper in a huffy mood.

Gamble closed a letter in July 1938 with one of his usual cheery notes: "How are you celebrating the summer? We are having a delightful time on the edge of Lake Michigan. Boating and swimming and tennis keep the children busy, and a porch overlooking the Lake makes typewriting endurable in spite of the distractions."

Cooper replied promptly: "I do not believe I have ever had a more strenuous summer and one with greater anxiety than I am having this summer. About two months ago, Mrs. Cooper was stricken with pyelitis and a number of complicating conditions. We took her to a hospital and she is only now beginning to gain a little strength. . . . I have had additional work of various kinds. In the middle of it all Dr. Reynolds has been in a 'war' with certain elements in the profession here over his syphilis program. A good many unpleasant things have happened. . . . Vacation even for one day has been out of the question just as it was all of last year and the year before. . . . You will understand from the above that I can

The Gamble home in Milton

appreciate what it means for a man to have his family in such a place as you describe.... For me that would be heaven right now."

Cooper conceded that Lawrence and the North Carolina Maternal Health League could probably raise half the money needed, but said he simply did not have the time to negotiate the matter. In October, when the first $4,500 was gone, Miss Pratt faced a payless payday while Cooper and Gamble sweated one another out. Cooper didn't want to give the program up; neither did Gamble. He did offer to tide it over with $200, for the sake of Miss Pratt, but repeated his demand for matching funds. In December, Lawrence sent out an appeal to a considerable number of persons in the state. The return was small; Gamble relented and continued his support on a month-to-month basis.

A different kind of financial crisis occured in 1939, associated with the reorganization of the American Birth Control League as the Birth Control Federation of America. The board of directors, of which Gamble was one, now imposed the regulation that a member had to make his contributions for birth control through the organization. Gamble went along with this. When in February 1939 the Birth Control Federation sent Cooper a check for continuing support, Cooper referred the matter to Reynolds. This was too much. Reynolds said to return the check. Cooper did so. As they had said before, the State Board of Health would not take money from a national propaganda organization. Cooper wrote Gamble: "We began this work with a direct understanding with you as an individual physician. . . . If we could continue on a while longer with you as an individual, we should be grateful." Gamble discussed the dilemma with the new officers of the Federation, and obtained their special dispensation in this instance to give directly. In March, he sent Cooper a check for $1,000 and agreed to cover Miss Pratt until January 1, 1940. At one point, unable to stand the uncertainty, Miss Pratt resigned, but Gamble talked her into staying through 1939. As 1940 began, the crisis recurred. Gamble said he would support her until the end of March. In April, she was out of a job, and left the birth control field.

One hard fact of grantsmanship is that cool courage is not enough. There comes a time when the supported must recognize that the supporter feels used up. This was it.

Primarily, Gamble's decision to terminate his North Carolina support sprang from his philanthropic philosophy of the stimulating grant—a small seed once planted and cultivated is supposed to grow and stand without propping up. To some extent, however, his decision may have been conditioned by certain kinds of disappointment. The failure of the program to become self-supporting was one; other disappointments fell under the headings of market penetration (population covered), scientific experimentation, and evaluation of results. Gamble did not talk of disappointment or failure, but the facts were plain enough.

Writing to Cooper in August 1940 about the need to give every mother in North Carolina the contraceptive information she ought to have, Gamble said: "Perhaps if I say I'd like to see further progress in this regard, you'll think my appetite insatiatable." He was then pushing for both an appropriation by the legislature and for voluntary fund-raising. In reply, Cooper said he and Reynolds opposed both courses. The state government was hard up, and they feared that public fund-raising would stir up bitter opposition.

Gamble, proverbially mild in his insistence, now remarked on the possibility that there was more interest in vaccination against smallpox—a rare disease—than in preventing unwanted pregnancies. He pointed out that despite North Carolina's (by then) sixty-one contraception centers, the state had instructed fewer mothers in contraception in 1939 than had Texas (where the state health department was notoriously weak).

Cooper took the rebuff civilly, although defensively. He replied that his reports did not reflect everything done because he preferred understatement to exaggeration. What he wanted for the future was the continued support of a public health nurse as a coordinator, funds for contraceptive supplies, and, as new additions, a traveling physician to consult with local doctors and health officers and money to hire more nurses for the county health departments.

They were still debating the future in October. Gamble, persevering, offered to send in Mrs. Edna McKinnon for community organization and fund-raising work. She had been quite successful in Maine, another poor state. Cooper was stubborn; he liked it the way things were: "Dr. Reynolds . . . still feels, as I confess that I do, that the finest approach is just as we went at it before on an independent basis with you putting up the funds. . . ." That was the end of it.

Happily, the contraception centers did not die. Some county health departments scratched around for money in various places to continue birth control services with existing personnel, as before. One county used federal aid from a Farm Security Admin-istration homestead project for this purpose. Some secured con-traceptive appropriations from their county commissioners. Other obtained donations from local individuals and organiza-tions such as women's clubs. Some simply took money for supplies from their regular health department contingency funds. A few counties asked patients to pay anything they could.

The North Carolina Maternal Health League attempted to raise money but it was, as Gamble suspected, more or less a captive of the State Board of Health and lacked roots in independently or-ganized community birth control groups; there was also the in-herent difficulty of interesting any private group in supporting a public agency.

By 1942, birth control found its way into the regular health department budget system, in keeping with Cooper quietness. The State Board of Health permitted county health officers to include contraceptive items in their projected budgets and acted on these requests according to its own good judgment.

Thus it became possible with the passage of time for Roy Norton to report in 1959 on "Twenty-One Years' Experience with a Public Health Contraceptive Service." This review confirmed one source of Gamble disappointment—the failure of the program to achieve coverage of the population of indigent mothers at risk. They rose from 236 patients in 1937 to 3,000 or so in 1940, sagged between 1,800 and 2,800 during the 1940s, climbed into the 4,000's in the early 1950s and then dropped under 3,000 in 1957.

In his four-year report in 1941, Cooper had said "70 percent of the underprivileged mothers of the state may now receive in-struction and supplies," but this was a deceptive statement and merely said that sixty-one contraception centers were to be found in eighty-one counties containing 70 percent of the population. In 1940, only "about one married woman of child-bearing age out of 100 in the areas covered was receiving contraceptive services through these public health centers," he acknowledged. However, since only about one out of four were financially eligible for free care, it appeared that about 4 percent of the needy group were served. There was a sharp fall-off between pregnant women who came to the prenatal clinic and those who came back after childbirth for "prevenception."

The contraceptive service averaged two visits per patient in 1940, either at home or in the clinic. Nurses were responsible for 67 percent, private physicians for 15 percent, and social workers for 12 percent of the referrals. The choice of methods was foam powder, 72 percent; diaphragm and jelly, 27, and condom, 0.5. Fifty-seven percent of the mothers were instructed in health department clinics, 35 percent in home visits by nurses, 3 percent by private physicians, and 1.6 percent in hospital clinics.

In early 1940, Gamble and Donald Klaiss from the Institute for Research in Social Science at Chapel Hill went over some of the clinic records and were displeased with what they found. One reason was that the clinic and visiting nurses, handling birth control as part of their maternal and child health duties, were not making an intensive effort to instruct mothers in the need, value, and proper use of contraceptives.

Because of his devotion to research, Gamble's biggest regret about the North Carolina program probably was its failure to measure the effectiveness of foam-powder-and-sponge method on a mass basis. Gamble at the outset emphasized to Miss Pratt the importance of keeping careful records. When Gamble and Klaiss looked into the clinic records in 1940 they found them incomplete. Miss Pratt said she had tried to persuade local health officers and nurses to be more painstaking but had been told that birth control records must conform to all other records kept by public health nurses. Gamble in his gentle way took Cooper to task for what, in other circumstances, might have been simply denounced as sloppy work. Cooper protested that his "chief interest is still on the scientific end," and he hoped they would be able to develop fully controlled methods of data collection. It was pretty late in the game, however, to be talking about research methodology.

As a superficial example of the difficulty, early in the course of the program Cooper had decided that numbers of contraceptive patients should be included in the maternal health section of the standard reporting form for county health units. Eventually he found—and also found he had to defend himself on this score—that the numbers of patients served probably were underreported. But a separate record form was not provided until December 1940. This particularly illustrated the fact that birth control fell into the category of an extra duty rather than a special task.

Whatever the case, the research dimension of the program was not safeguarded—a triumph of bureaucracy over science. When Cooper made his three-year report to the Medical Society in 1940 it contained many generalities and few particulars. He lacked a data base on which he could build the story of foam powder's effectiveness or lack of it.

In a preliminary analysis of individual records at two selected centers the previous year, William P. Richardson and Donald Klaiss claimed "satisfactory results from the foam powder and sponge technic." In 1959, however, Norton reported: "Most of the clinics now use either the jelly alone or with a diaphragm." While test-by-test effectiveness was not determined conclusively, it appeared that in the long run foam powder and sponge fell by the wayside on acceptability.

From reports he received, Dickinson placed the effectiveness between 80 and 90 percent. Nurses said the method had a high acceptance rate among interested farm women who lacked the advantages of privacy and plumbing. On the other hand, some regarded it as troublesome and messy. Its great advantage, like jelly alone, was that it eliminated the need for a prior examination by a physician.

As Gamble told North Carolina doctors in 1938, the methods available are "not perfect, any of them." In retrospect, Norton passed judgment: "No attempt has been made toward exact determination of clinical effectiveness of the various methods." For Gamble, this made poor reading.

One great good to emerge from the North Carolina program was acceleration of public health interest in birth control in other states. In due course, health departments offered contraceptive services in South Carolina, Alabama, Texas, Virginia, and Florida, as well as Puerto Rico.

Whatever the outcome, Clarence Gamble never accepted defeat. He just moved on to something else. He still had a condom project in North Carolina up his sleeve.

chapter 10   A Confidence in Condoms

A dedicated birth control worker who becomes pregnant unaware might evoke some analogy to a safety expert overtaken by an accident. While it is true that Clarence Gamble steadfastly favored the concept of every child a wanted child, the fact remains that he lost two of his best birth controllers to motherhood.

The first was Phyllis Page, who, after several barren years of marriage, bore children in 1938 and 1940 and departed from the field of conception control.

The second was Lena Gilliam Hillard, who became pregnant but miscarried in 1940 and then in 1942 bore the first of three children, in the midst of a scientific study in which it was her mission to convice the farm women of Watauga County, North Carolina, to try condoms or foam powder. Momentarily, the scientifically impeccable Dr. Gilbert Beebe of the National Committee on Maternal Health wondered if the employment of a pregnant fieldworker might bias the study in some way. Almost certainly it did not, but by the time Mrs. Hillard had her second baby she was feeling depressed. "It's time to tell you the big news," she wrote Gamble in 1944. "Lactikol B failed and I'm the victim." In her third confession, in 1945, she wrote: "Yes, and once again you will say, 'I'm disappointed.' So am I. The truth is I'm pregnant—Imagine three babies and support by the nurse who's teaching child-spacing. I never heard of such a case history in *all my life.* Sorry I've again messed up our project. . . . Please try to forgive me." Gamble, always cheerful and not unappreciative of a good practical joke, forgave her, and, being in a giving mood, soon took a financial plunge in the Hillard's turkey farm, an unsuccessful enterprise that eventually strained their friendship.

Before these mixed blessings befell her, Mrs. Hillard delivered the desired data on 658 couples for one of Gamble's high-priority ambitions, the first good field study of condoms.

Gamble was aware that, during a period when he and others had been trying to persuade underprivileged mothers to come into a clinic and have a physician fit them with a diaphragm, the condom with no professional or public encouragement had become the most popular American device for contraception, even though birth control clinicians disdained it. In 1936, Norman E. Himes reported United States sales of condoms to be almost 317 million. The first vulcanization of rubber in the 1840s had made such a rubber sheath for the penis practical but of limited appeal. With the use of liquid latex and manufacture by machine in the early 1930s the device became less expensive and more popular. In this new form, it was thin enough to transmit sensation and yet strong enough not to puncture or tear. It also was less subject than the old crepe rubber condom to aging. The remaining problem was one of quality control, to eliminate the risk of failure due to built-in defects in the rubber. Most condom companies were interested in high production and low cost and sold an inferior product, but a few took product testing seriously.

The condom of good quality offered distinct advantages. It was available as a "whisper item" at any drug store, to the unmarried as well as married. Drug stores were not the main outlet; the bulk of condoms was sold in gasoline stations, cigar stores, or pool halls, often through vending machnes. A packet of three, rolled, could be carried in one's watch pocket. The sheath could be quickly slipped on, and required less preparation than other contraceptives. The condom also had the advantage of offering protection against veneral disease.

It had some disadvantages, in addition to its general disreputability as an agent of carnal sin. It placed prevention of conception in the hands of the man, who cared less about the consequence of intercourse than the woman and who also often complained about the rubber's reduction of pleasure. Males, doubtless millions of times, repeated the question: "Who wants to take a bath in a raincoat?" But female insistence constrained many men to provide this protection.

From the standpoint of the poor, the retail price was not right. Condoms could be manufactured for a fraction of a cent per unit. This provided an enormous profit margin on an item selling under highly competitive conditions for 8⅓ to 33⅓ cents per sheath. Actually, by elimination of the middleman, the item could be sold at a profit for four or five cents each.

For the previous two or three years, Gamble had been in touch with officials of the Youngs Rubber Company, New York manufacturers of the Trojan brand, one of the higher grade and more popular condoms. Youngs officials assured him they would supply condoms free in gross lots for a mass field test carried on under scientific auspices.

When Lena Gilliam married Ernest Hillard, a high school agriculture teacher, and moved to Sugar Grove in Watauga County after having done the preliminary work in the Berea, Kentucky, study she provided precisely the opportunity Gamble was looking for.

Watauga County, in the heart of the Southern Appalachian Mountains, lies in northwestern North Carolina, on the Tennessee line. In 1939, the county had a population of 15,000, nearly all white and mostly farmers. Boone, the county seat, had only 1,800 residents and the next largest community, Blowing Rock, a summer resort, only a few hundred.

While the Allegheny-Ashe-Watauga three-county district had a health officer, Dr. Robert R. King of Boone, it had no birth control program. This, as Gamble saw it, made an ideal situation for an experiment with different methods. He discussed the proposal with his collaborator in the state program, Dr. George M. Cooper, who said the State Board of Health would have no part of it. Cooper was still haunted by the specter, later proven unwarranted, of unfavorable publicity provoking some Jehovah-like wrath in the medical profession. Nor was King, the local man, friendly to the project. Gamble wrote him in the spring of 1939 and told him about the availability of an "interested and energetic trained nurse" capable of carrying out medical recommendations. King was not interested in providing local supervision of such a study.

But Lena Hillard was resourceful. She made friends with Dr. John B. Hagaman of Boone, who with his wife, Lynn, delivered 200 babies a year, about half the county's total. "I will be glad to assist Mrs. Ernest Hillard," Hagaman wrote Gamble in July. "I do not have much time for anything except my practice, but will back her up in the work, and help supervise."

Organizational sponsorship was also nominal, under the National Committee on Maternal Health. Actually, Gamble financed the study and Beebe designed it (the latter, working on his West Virginia study, soon joined the staff of the Milbank Memorial Fund). In the end, Gamble was left with the chore of finding a biostatistician to tabulate and analyze the data. He went to the Johns Hopkins University School of Public Health and Hygiene and found Dr. Christopher Tietze, who later joined the staff of the National Committee on Maternal Health (NCMH) with headquarters at the New York Academy of Medicine. Beebe planned the study well. Both he and Gamble made periodic visits to Watauga County during the condom portion of the study, September 1939 to October 1941.

The condom is a male contraceptive but, because a public health nurse was their only communicating link, Gamble and Beebe decided to attempt to reach the men through their wives.

Mrs. Hillard offered instructions to the wives and a dozen condoms to start for all willing to use the service. A representative sample was obtained by dividing the county into twenty-six sections with approximately equal numbers of families; thirteen sections were chosen at random and in these the nurse visited every home. The original plan was to conduct a foam-powder-and-sponge experiment in the remaining sections simultaneously, but the latter task proved too big for Mrs. Hillard.

On the first visit, Mrs. Hillard explained the need for birth control and the use of condoms but often found the farm wives explaining *to her* why they needed contraception. She was even more surprised that among those who had used a contraceptive the condom was the most popular, being preferred by two-thirds.

The Tietze analysis showed that, among the 658 couples in the survey, 409, or 61 percent, did not practice contraception at the time of the initial interview. Of the 249, or 39 percent, who did, 163 used condoms compared with 43 who withdrew before ejaculation and 13 who used a jelly. The diaphragm attracted only four users. Evidently, the condom was better suited to a rural environment.

Mrs. Hillard was most explicit in her instructions:

READ THESE INSTRUCTIONS CAREFULLY
TO AVOID FAILURE

1. These condoms are the finest obtainable, but the protection they will give depends on you and your husband. They must be used *every* time you have intercourse.
2. The condom is put on the erect penis (male organ) just before intercourse begins. If put on later, only just before ejaculation, it may already be too late.
3. If entry occurs again after ejaculation, another condom should be worn to keep any remaining sperm (male germs) from entering the vagina.
4. Many persons do not realize that extra lubrication may be needed to avoid discomfort on entry, and that ordinary saliva (spittle) is useful for this. Greasy things like vaseline should *not* be used because they might harm the rubber, perhaps causing it to leak or break.

5. Some men complain that the condom slips off when they withdraw after ejaculation. Of course the longer one waits to withdraw after ejaculation, the easier it is for the condom to slip off and spill, but this will not happen if the condom is held to the base of the penis (near the body) by the hand at the time of withdrawal.

6. Give the method a fair trial at least, and if you have any trouble ask your nurse to help you. Don't let your supply run out without getting more from her.

Mrs. Ernest Hillard, R.N.
Sugar Grove
North Carolina

Proceeding on this basis, the nurse was able to persuade 387, or 59 percent, of the couples to give condoms a trial. For 163, of course, acceptance simply meant continuing to use condoms, now free of cost. Some 253 women refused to accept condoms in the first interview, and 18 accepted them but did not use them. The main reasons for rejection were religious or moral objections, known or assumed inability to conceive, preference for another method or source of supplies, and desire for a baby.

During the study period and for some time after, Mrs. Hillard corresponded regularly with Gamble and Beebe, sending them weekly reports and transmitting anecdotes as well as data and requests for more supplies. "I have one patient who has a queer husband. He has refused to touch her since the baby came four years ago." He was "afraid she will die if she gets pregnant." The woman reported success when she explained to him that they could depend on birth control, but she insisted on using two methods.

Mrs. Hillard had another mother who had received a false report that the nurse had stopped doing birth control work. "She said she told her husband that she would simply catch up a hen and take it to the store and sell it in order to get money to buy some Trojans." They sold in the Boone druge store at three for fifty cents; Mrs. Hillard estimated that her condom families used an average of three a week.

One husband, after the nurse visited his wife, got up in church and testified: "The devil has been to my house and tempted me in my weakest spot." Nonetheless, he kept on using condoms; his wife was in poor health, physically and mentally.

Making her rounds on first and follow-up visits and delivering condoms as called for, pushing her Ford over icy, snow-covered roads in the winter and through mud and around washed-out bridges in the summer, Mrs. Hillard, then in her late twenties, sometimes felt like complaining to the world, even when not pregnant and vomiting. She appreciated it when Beebe suggested that she cut down from full to half time, and see about bringing her sister, Mrs. Sylvia Gilliam Payne, over from Kentucky to help.

But she did get results previously not expected of the condom. As noted, six out of ten couples accepted the method (387). Of these, 69, or 27 percent, stopped using it, despite a continuing risk of pregnancy. Interference with coital sensation and religious objections were the leading reasons. Only five stopped use because of pregnancy—that is, failure of the method. There were an assortment of other reasons: Too much bother, no confidence, neighbors' criticism or gossip, "mother-in-law objects," "no place to hide condoms." After three years, 73 percent of the original acceptors continued to use the condom.

The study's purpose was "to secure an estimate of the acceptabiliity and effectiveness of condoms under conditions resembling those of a public health program." After determining acceptability of the method, the study looked at how long the method remained in use, or its continued acceptability. Calculating expected against actual pregnancies, Tietze and Gamble found condoms reduced pregnancies 81 percent. Limited to second and subsequent pregnancies and using the appropriate pre-interview rates during noncontraceptive exposure as a basis for comparison, all but 68 of 367 expected pregnancies were prevented. However, those who used this method both before and during the study demonstrated that experience was a good teacher: their effectiveness rate was 92 percent. These figures, of course, referred to effectiveness in actual practice and not to physiologic reliability under ideal conditions. Couples admitted irregular use in almost three-quarters of the 72 unplanned pregnancies.

"The high degree of confidence the condom enjoyed among users in Watauga County appears fully justified," the investigators reported.

Among those who accepted condoms, the pregnancy rate had been 65 per 100 years of exposure before the study in women with no experience in the use of contraception and 13 in women with preclinic contraceptive experience. The pregnancy rate for all users during the three-year study was 11 per 100 years of exposure, being only 6 for those with contraceptive experience beforehand and 16 for those without.

The conclusion that here was a good a method for preventing unwanted pregnancies and one requiring little of a physician's time touched on the one instance of criticism encountered during the course of the condom study.

Dr. Cooper told Dr. King, the health officer in Boone, that a preliminary statement by Gamble on "A Clinical Trial of the Condom" had to be approved by him before publication. King wrote Gamble: "I did not feel that it had any real value statistically or otherwise." He said that he did not approve of the Watauga County Study, nor did local doctors: "I have talked with three of the . . . leading physicians in the county, and none of them are in favor of the program as it is conducted. . . . The feeling . . . is that any program of contraceptives should not be carried on through nurses except under the direct supervision of physicians; also, that this work would best be carried on through physicians themselves in their offices, and not through what is practically a house-to-house canvass."

Gamble and Beebe were at this time, in June 1941, preparing to start the foam-powder study in the other half of the county. Gamble wrote Dr. Hagaman about King's criticism, and drew this reply: "I would advise that you go on . . . as planned, and say very little to Dr. King . . . as I don't think he will be able to influence the public, the medical profession, or the State Board of Health in the future. Dr. King has been acting on the advice of one man in the town, who he thinks has political power, but he is badly mistaken. Mrs. Hillard has handled the work very efficiently and gained the confidence and respect of the public in a way that has made Dr. King very jealous, and he would like now to take the work over and kick her out, which would then mean failure. His contention that the work affects the income of the physicians is unfounded."

In October, Gamble visited Boone and Mrs. Hillard took him to see every doctor in the county. "Each said that his practice was not interfered with by the contraceptive program," Gamble noted. Nevertheless, when informed that the Watauga County study was ready for publication, Cooper remained on the same track. He wrote Gamble in 1944: "You will recall that I did not approve this project and I would like you to know that there has been quite a lot of criticism from the medical and nursing profession in Watauga County." He did concede that these were oral reports from his field representatives and he had nothing in writing. Cooper said he did not want the study published. The decision, however, was not his to make.

The foam-powder-and-sponge study had quite a different outcome. As before, it was doomed to failure as a scientific experiment. Mrs. Hillard (and Mrs. Payne for a time) offered this method in the thirteen untapped sections of Watauga County. They met with many rejections and, among those who used it, some failures. The popularity of the condom in the studied sections, it appeared, had influenced attitudes in the unstudied; it seemed possible that Mrs. Hillard herself may have biased the reception of foam powder, by reflecting her patients' lack of confidence in the method.

In mid-1942, Mrs. Hillard complained bitterly about foam powder in her letters to Gamble. Four of her patients had become pregnant while using the powder, she said; as for others, "I am sick of attempting to persuade them to use foam powder." In July, she threatened to quit her birth control job; another patient on foam powder was pregnant. Mrs. Hillard asked Gamble to let her drop the method: "If you don't, I may quit and raise babies and rabbits." In August, she demanded: "Why haven't you answered my letter? Even though you are on vacation you should have

responded when a friend is in trouble." Gamble apologized: he
had been out to California to see Aunt Julia, who had had a stroke
and on the way back he stopped in Oklahoma to look at his oil
wells; they were "producing gas delightfully." At the moment,
Mrs. Hillard was more interested in keeping her breakfast down;
she was pregnant again.

Underlying Mrs. Hillard's problem was a conflict of interests
that spread her energies too thin, as indicated in her letter in
January 1942: "I guess I am selfish for I want the following: 1.
Ernest's exemption from military training. 2. A baby. 3. To continue doing birth control work. 4. To be a Red Cross nurse. 5. To
get out of debt. Some of these conflict, as you can see. I did get the
two sets of tires and tubes and chains."

This was not all. During the war, the Hillards became preoccupied, in addition to their regular jobs, with buying a farm,
raising chickens, and canning fruit and vegetables, as well as
finishing their house and raising a family. The condom study,
having been completed, and the foam-powder study having dwin-
dled away, Mrs. Hillard reduced her Gamble-supported birth control work to one day a week; she operated a Saturday clinic in
Boone for her loyal following of condom-minded mothers.

chapter 11 Catching the Boat for Puerto Rico

Puerto Rico was a special case. As the Depression in the United States receded, the Biblical virtues of populating the earth repossessed the official American mind. It was true, relief families were reproducing themselves in large numbers at the taxpayers' expense, but the declining birth rate among the "right people" could be viewed as a greater cause for alarm in an economy based on growth of the Gross National Product; the right kind of people educated themselves, found work, earned, consumed, invested, and turned a profit. They also voted, a trait of some importance to New Dealers up for reelection in 1936.

Yet it was clear to those who had social, economic, and demographic eyes to see that this small, hilly, tropical island on the Atlantic edge of the Caribbean Sea, east of Cuba and Haiti, was suffering from overpopulation. It was elementary arithmetic. Puerto Rico has an area of 3,400 square miles, less than half the

With Antonio Roig, Puerto Rican benefactor

size of New Jersey. Its Spanish-speaking, predominantly Roman
Catholic people were packed in, at about 500 persons per square
mile. The population increased from about one million in 1900 to
two million in 1940. Puerto Rico in the mid-1930s had an annual
death rate of around 20 per 1,000 population, about twice that of
the United States; but it also had a birth rate of around 40, more
than twice that of the mainland. Later, Christopher Tietze estimated the island's rate of natural increase (the difference between

the birth rate and the death rate) for the 1900–1940 period as 2.5 percent per year, a large increase when it is considered that the gain accumulates in the manner of compound interest. Actually, the average Puerto Rican woman's reproductivity declined about 25 percent in this period, but was balanced by an increase of married women in the child-bearing ages. The net population increase was mainly due to a declining death rate. The size of the population would have been far greater but for the fact that Puerto Ricans, having been recognized as American citizens since World War I, were free to emigrate to the United States. Many did.

For some years, there had been concern about the poor health of Puerto Ricans, particularly on the part of the Rockefeller Foundation and the Public Health Service. The peasants, whose main occupation, when employed, was cutting sugar cane, had one of the highest tuberculosis death rates in the world, five times as high as the United States. Malaria and hookworm infestation, both a common source of anemia, reduced the capacity of the people to work. The incidence of syphilis, a tragic crippler of mother and child, was three times as high as in the United States.

But neither Rockefeller nor Puerto Rican public health doctors were interested in birth control, either from the standpoint of maternal health or economic rehabilitation. When the subject arose, they tended to be either indifferent or opposed. The prevention of unwanted children was not a part of their training in preventive medicine, and politically they took their cue from the ruling class. In Puerto Rico, the government was strongly influenced by the Catholic hierarchy in the Church, politics, and business. One of the peculiarities of Puerto Rico or, for that matter, any underdeveloped country with a low per capita income is that there were relatively few taxpayers; those who paid taxes were well-to-do and usually conservative in their beliefs. Unquestionably, it was the Catholic bishops who imposed and reinforced the morality of unlimited multiplication and, as an eventual consequence, unlimited unemployment, hunger, ill health, and emigration. Today in New York City live Puerto Rican emigrants almost equal to the entire population of the Island in 1900.

Puerto Rico had been since 1899 a territorial possession of the United States. For the first fifteen years of American occupation, the commercial relationship with the United States blossomed, and there was much optimism about the arrival of the Industrial Revolution and dawn of a new era. There was no attempt to balance population growth and means of support, however, and the hope for a prosperous economy wilted. It became a commonplace to say that Puerto Rico had a scarcity of all natural resources except climate and people.

Not all Puerto Ricans were overpowered by the authority of the Church. Though Catholic, many were religious only in a formal sense and were tolerant and all-embracing in the universal, humanistic sense. They were actually divided on the subject of birth control, many educated laymen and physicians being in favor of contraceptive practice and willing to see it extended to the peasant families, apathetic from the grinding poverty of their lives. The first attempts to organize family planning leagues in 1925 and again in 1932 failed. Of these early efforts, Celestina Zalduondo, Puerto Rican family planning leader in more recent times, remarked: "The pressure of the Church and apathy of the people put a quick ending to the efforts of the League."

During its first term, the Roosevelt Administration committed itself to the spending of federal funds for relief, favoring work relief but embracing any kind, direct or indirect, to help needy people. One of the agencies created was the Puerto Rico Emergency Relief Administration (PRERA). In 1935, Gladys Gaylord, executive secretary of the Cleveland Maternal Health Association, visited Puerto Rico and persuaded the PRERA administrator and his wife, Mr. and Mrs. James R. Bourne, of the desirability of establishing a chain of maternal health clinics offering contraceptive advice without charge. The program began in May 1935 with the opening of a pilot clinic in San Juan at the School of Tropical Medicine. This clinic was placed under the direction of Dr. Jose Belaval.

Belaval was no ordinary physician; he could be called the Robert Dickinson of Puerto Rico. The leading obstetrician in San

Juan, not a Catholic but in good social standing, then in his late fifties, he devoted to birth control all the time and energy he could spare from his practice, spurred on by the many poor women who crowded his office for help.

The demand was brisk in the San Juan clinic, and by December the PRERA boldly launched an island-wide program, the plan being to expand as rapidly as possible into the seventy *municipios*, or municipalities, making up the island, with maternal health clinics serving as delivery points for contraceptive advice and supplies. In this ambitious effort, two competent and energetic Catholic social workers, Candida Campos de Cordova and Carmen Rivera de Alvardo, served as leaders with Belaval as medical director.

At the outset the diaphragm was considered to be the preferred method, because, as Miss Gaylord wrote Gamble: "The percentage of success of the diaphragm method in Puerto Rico would probably be higher than in the United States, due to the lithe figures of the women, their long fingers, lack of inhibitions in regard to sex, and their teachability."

The acceleration of the program was phenomenal—indeed much more impressive than the State Health Department program in North Carolina. On the other hand, it was subject to a forbidding array of political and bureaucratic impediments jeopardizing its future. Belaval summarized the period from December 1935 to June 1936 as follows: "Instruction was given to twenty-four doctors, fifty nurses, and seventy social aides. Within six months we put in operation forty-five clinics in different municipalities, where 3,404 patients received birth control advice."

In view of the upturn in American economy, the United States government meanwhile decided to terminate the PRERA. Recognizing the continued depression in Puerto Rico, however, the Department of Interior established a new agency, the Puerto Rico Reconstruction Administration (PRRA).

"The idea," Belaval continued, "was to open one clinic for each town, so as to extend the work through the whole Island, but on

June 15th, 1936, when we were most enthusiastic with the work being done, an order for liquidation . . . came from Washington. The whole program of birth control came to a standstill; the personnel had to be discharged, and the clinics closed."

Dr. Ernest Gruening, PRRA administrator in the Department of Interior and later senator from Alaska, was interested in the birth control program but too busy with agency reorganization to do anything about it until the end of July.[1] Then, said Belaval, "I was ordered to reorganize the project with a budget of $250,000 for the first year. Again we began . . . now on a larger scale. Just when we were beginning to open clinics on the Island, on September 15th, 1936, the order came to stop work again—this time on account of legal technicalities, or at least that was the reason given us."

Belaval, among his other attributes, had the spirit of a scientific investigator. From those first 3,000 cases, thanks to good data collection, he learned something about the characteristics and behavior of the average Puerto Rican woman. The woman coming to the free clinics was twenty-seven years old, had been married nine years, and had five living children.

"There is the lay idea that the frequency of coitus among the lower classes is very remarkable," remarked Belaval, "but our statistics . . . show differently, the average being twice a week." No appreciable difference in sexual activity could be correlated to race. As regards their reactions to coitus, 72 percent of these women said they derived pleasure, 27.5 percent reported they felt "absolute indifference," and about one-half of one percent stated they had "painful or disagreeable sensations." These reactions, it was found, were not influenced by the use of contraceptives: half of those who got pleasure used contraceptives of some sort, whereas none of those with painful sensations tried to protect against pregnancy. Two-thirds of San Juan women used contraceptives compared to about one in four in the small towns. The most frequent forms of contraception were withdrawal, condoms, douches, and suppositories in that order. Counting stillbirths, spontaneous abortions, induced abortions, and deaths in infancy,

[1] Dr. Gruening was a prime mover in one of the first bills passed by Congress for domestic birth control.

Belaval found a total loss, or fetal wastage, of one out of every three pregnancies.

The majority of Puerto Ricans were on federal relief. Now, with no birth control aid, they were in effect required to remain on relief and multiply. The "legal technicalities" mentioned as the reason for the government's closing of the birth control program proved to be mainly political. Mrs. Alvardo, in a historical sketch, said this: "A fatal blow was struck in Washington. The opposition, although ineffective in Puerto Rico, made itself felt on the mainland in this year of a presidential election, and in October 1936, the maternal health program of the PRRA was suddenly terminated. This event marked the end of the federal government's efforts to help control the birth rate of Puerto Rico and to counteract the dangerous population increase it had originally helped to release by its successful attack on mortality."

Phyllis Page, investigating the situation on behalf of Clarence Gamble, talked to Dr. Gruening in Washington and learned that two Catholic bishops had brought pressure to block the birth control appropriation, quite in disregard of the welfare and wishes of Puerto Rican women. Political candidates are proverbially sensitive to the emergence of touchy issues before election time; thus the Democratic Administration, fearing Catholic Democrats, found cause to back out of this first federally sponsored birth control program.[2] Mrs. Page asked how Catholic opposition in Puerto Rico best could be met, and Gruening replied: "By going in as soon as possible and starting work—a boat leaves every Thursday and arrives Monday."

Gamble had received news of the collapse of the Belaval program from Dr. Eric Matsner, medical director of the American Birth Control League, who recently had been in San Juan helping restart the demonstration clinic there. Gamble now took action in a manner that almost invariably offended the top officers of the League, with whom he sat as a Board member. He told a meeting

---

[2] The U.S. Circuit Court of Appeals decision pulling the anticontraceptive teeth of the Comstock Law was not handed down until November 30, 1936, three weeks after Roosevelt was reelected and far too late for any possible stiffening of liberal Democratic spines.

of the League's Executive Committee that it was expedient to send a representative to Puerto Rico to see whether the clinic program could be saved. He asked if the League would like to share with him in support of such a mission. Some Committee members thought the League might provide aid from its Clinic Fund. No action was taken, however. On the same day, Gamble wrote Belaval offering to pay half the cost of one demonstration clinic if a committee of leading citizens was organized to operate it. Mrs. Marguerite Benson, executive director of the American Birth Control League, wrote Gamble the next day: "We are eager that the good work done by Dr. Matsner should not be lost. . . . Fortunately you are able to handle the peculiar circumstances in a way that nobody else connected with the League can do."

Belaval promptly replied that a demonstration clinic could be reestablished at the Presbyterian Hospital in San Juan at the cost of $200 a month. He also said he would like to form a local chapter of ABCL.

At a meeting of the ABCL Board in November, Gamble announced that he was putting Mrs. Phyllis Page on the boat to Puerto Rico, and again asked what share of the action the League would like. The Board appointed Matsner and Gamble as a special committee to handle the League's communications with Puerto Rico and deferred action pending further correspondence with Belaval. Gamble wrote Belaval, telling the obstetrician of his interest in rural tests of foam powder and sponge with careful recording for research purposes, but not excluding help with the city clinic, and offering to send Mrs. Page down as his personal representative as well as expert in community organization.

Receiving a carbon copy of the above letter, Matsner now made his position unmistakable: "In my opinion it would be a great tactical error for anyone from the States to go to Puerto Rico unless it was at the specific request of Dr. Belaval. . . . In view of Dr. Belaval's . . . specific request for affiliation with the American Birth Control League . . . should he request a worker from the States that person would have to represent the American Birth Control League." Matsner therefore recommended to the Executive Committee that the ABCL either "withdraw completely from any participation . . . and . . . communicate this fact to Dr. Belaval (or) if the ABCL should sponsor the establishment of a Puerto Rican maternal health association, that any and all activities of direction, policy, activities of fieldworkers, etc., be handled directly through the office of the medical director of the League."

"I am sure," Matsner wrote Gamble, "that you will realize that I am motivated . . . entirely by my desire to see that the maternal health program of Puerto Rico be established on a firm basis which will continue constructively and not meet the same tragic fate of the two previous programs. May I again reiterate my definite conviction based on the knowledge of local conditions that no worker be sent from the States to Puerto Rico at this time."

Gamble wasted no time analyzing Matsner's motives. The next boat was leaving on November 12. Gamble asked for and obtained a conference in New York attended by ABCL top officers and himself plus Mrs. Page and Mrs. Bourne, the wife of the former PRERA administrator. Mrs. Bourne took sharp issue with Dr. Matsner; she urged that an American community organizer be sent for the reason that she doubted the Puerto Ricans could develop a sound voluntary maternal health association themselves. The ABCL executive committee met the next day and refused to give its blessing to Gamble or to his attractive, young birth control secretary.

Mrs. Page caught the boat and the League missed it. She was on her way but had not arrived in San Juan when Belaval wrote Gamble: "I will be very glad to have Mrs. Page come here and study our peculiar situation . . . and see for herself if it would be convenient for you to back our plans. . . . We are in need of simpler contraceptive methods for our poor ignorant classes and will be glad to give them a trial."

Phyllis Page spoke Spanish as well as Boston English. A week after she arrived, she had a new birth control organization in San Juan underway. Along with others, Mr. and Mrs. Carlos V. Torres, a well-known attorney and his wife who had been among the founders of the short-lived Birth Control League of Puerto Rico

(1932), backed the new effort, Mrs. Torres becoming its president. Mrs. Alvardo was executive secretary and Dr. Belaval, medical director, of the new organization—the *Association Pro Salud Maternal e Infantile*, or Maternal and Child Health Association. Mrs. Page brought with her a copy of the constitution of the birth control organization she had helped organize in Berea, Kentucky; the Puerto Ricans adopted it, so the Association was a replica of the Mountain Maternal Health League.

In a blithe mood, Gamble replied to Mrs. Page's letter reporting the good news and teased her about her typing accuracy: "I'm glad to see evidence in the pied line that you are really using the Touch System. It sounds as though you hadn't absorbed any of the Mañana Method. Don't increase the Puerto Rico death rate by overwork."

Gamble offered $200 and a shipment of diaphragms so that the San Juan clinic could get underway immediately. In December, he wrote Mrs. Page: "Your progress sounds splendid, and the idea of having Dr. Belaval's writing Dr. Matsner a paean of thanks for your coming is the greatest triumph of all. It seems almost unbelievable! Do you suppose the League will ever learn?"

Gamble began with support of $100 a month for a social worker, Rosa A. Gonzales, at the Association clinic in Lares, a rural district. He likewise underwrote the $150-a-month salary of Mrs. Alvardo. Once more emphasizing the public educational value of fund-raising, he insisted that the Maternal and Child Health Association ought to raise some money, particularly for the operation of the city clinic in San Juan. There was no public campaign, but Antonio Roig and a few other wealthy Puerto Ricans made contributions. Meanwhile the Puerto Rico Reconstruction Administration found post-election courage and undertook to supply contraceptives and personnel for birth control services in three of its rural medical centers. Gamble went to the Rockefeller Foundation and proposed it spend $100,000 a year to provide 100,000 Puerto Rican women with contraception at the cost of one dollar per woman, but the Foundation declined this unusual opportunity.

In the next year, there were seventeen birth control clinics in operation. The Association sponsored three of these. The San Juan clinic emphasized diaphragms, but the one in Humacao offered foam powder and sponge exclusively for its rural clientele, and the clinic in Lares tried spermicidal jelly. The PRRA, or federal government, operated nine clinics in rural districts. The sugar planters sponsored three programs for their workers, and planned more.

Meanwhile Mrs. Page returned to Philadelphia and had a baby. Miss Gonzalez wrote her congratulations: "I can already see what a wonderful, sweet, little mother you will make. . . . I thank God for the privilege of having met you and corresponded with you for a year and I shall certainly miss you more than words can tell."

So often frustrated in putting across the message that only population control could assure Puerto Rico a prosperous future, the Belaval-Torres group in early 1937 took their case to the Insular Legislature. The Chamber of Delegates and the Scientific Committee of the Puerto Rico Medical Association was on record as favoring legalized birth control and a public health department contraception program for the poor. The Legislature got the message this time and passed the Maternal and Child Health Association's bill eliminating penalties for giving contraceptive advice from the territory's obscenity law, authorizing the Commissioner of Health to establish maternal health services in public health units, licensing doctors and nurses working under their supervision to provide such services, and legalizing sterilization. Actually, the main thrust of the act was to create an Insular Board of Eugenics that would authorize sterilizations on a voluntary basis. However, contraceptive instruction of persons requesting and needing it was permitted. In addition to various medical reasons for birth control, the law recognized "economic poverty and social conditions." The Acting Governor, Rafael Menendez Ramos, signed the bill into law on May 1, 1937.

The Catholic opposition did not accept this defeat without one last counterattack. Not long after Dr. and Mrs. Gamble visited Puerto Rico and saw how well their timely aid had borne fruit,

Mrs. Torres wrote them that Catholic opponents had found a new way to cause trouble. As a result, the Insular Health Department was not going ahead with the program. The critics argued that the new law violated a federal obscenity law prohibiting the use of contraceptives in any United States territory. The federal law supervened, they held, inasmuch as the Puerto Rican Charter granted the Insular Legislature the right to pass only those laws not contrary to the acts of Congress.

The United States Attorney in San Juan, Cecil Snyder, told Mrs. Torres that he was receiving daily demands stimulated by the Church that he do something to stop the birth control movement. He acknowledged that the 1937 Puerto Rican law in his opinion was null and void, but said he was stalling because it was also his opinion that contraception was necessary.

The Maternal and Child Health Association asked for a test case. In December 1938, a grand jury found no grounds to indict Mrs. Torres and a physician and nurse for operating a birth control clinic, but Mrs. Torres insisted on being tried. She summarized the situation in a letter to Gamble:

> The PRRA cannot continue giving us their aid if we are to be involved in a court case which would necessitate their being mentioned. . . . We went to see Mr. Snyder and he . . . is very friendly to our cause, though of course this has to be kept secret. . . . He will prosecute us on a stipulation of facts, and subpoena us for several test cases instead of making a raid. . . . We shall limit our defense to the medical aspects of these cases, and shall not mention population or economic questions at all.

Gamble sent Mrs. Torres "Best wishes for the trial," adding, "I hope I shall not have to visit you in jail." She collected four heartbreaking cases of mothers whose lives were jeopardized by pregnancy and made them a part of a brief presented before Judge Robert A. Cooper of Federal District Court in a ten-minute hearing. In January 1939, Judge Cooper upheld the Puerto Rican law in so far as contraception was undertaken under a doctor's supervision for the protection of the patient's health, but ruled out contraception for social or economic reasons. Since the interpretation of medical reasons were left to the doctor, it was a major victory.

The Health Commissioner, Dr. Eduardo Garrido Morales, now found courage to implement the 1937 law and establish a public health system of free maternal health clinics offering contraceptive advice throughout the Island. Dr. Belaval became the medical director, and Mrs. Alvardo and some of her specially trained nurses were transferred from the Maternal and Child Health Association to the Health Department to supervise the work.

This development provided a fitting climax to Dr. Gamble's start-up support. By the end of 1938 he was writing typical "the-time-has-come" letters to Mrs. Torres about the need to make the Association program self-sufficient. Mrs. Alvardo, whose contract was about to expire, wrote him of her concern about the future: "I think that your participation has been wonderful to the development of the work. Sorry to say I doubt very much that any Puerto Rican would have done the same. But, I am sure you understand that in case you can't go on helping, I must look for some other job." Gamble paid part of Mrs. Alvardo's and all of Miss Gonzalez's salary through 1939. The Health Department program then accomplished his aim of self-sufficiency.

Clinical testing

Meanwhile Gamble had found in Puerto Rico what he lacked in North Carolina, an ideal environment for the painstaking conduct of field studies, thanks to the scientific and robustly cooperative spirit of both Belaval and the team of the social workers and nurses who collected the data. As a result, Gamble financed a wide variety of clinical trials of contraceptives in Puerto Rico for the next quarter-century.

Gamble was particularly pleased to find a young Mexico-born, United States physician, Dr. Charis Gould, at Ryder Memorial Hospital in Humacao, and after visiting him wrote congratulating Gould on the "delightful way you please and persuade the patients." Gould was co-author of the first published paper covering experience in 1937. Three methods were tested—diaphragm and jelly, jelly and syringe, and foam powder and sponge—at San Juan, Lares, and Humacao in a total of 360 cases. The pregnancy rate for all the women dropped from 104 per 100 years of exposure to 40. The differences in the effectiveness of the three methods were insignificant.

In 1939 Gamble asked Dr. Gilbert W. Beebe of the National Committee of Maternal Health for his estimate of the clinical effectiveness of foam powder and sponge in comparison with other methods. Beebe replied that there had been "no definitive experiment" that could be accepted with confidence. He recommended that it was highly desirable to design and conduct studies that would provide evidence that foam powder and sponge or jelly alone was or was not as effective as other methods.

Gamble in response launched Beebe in collaboration with Belaval on a two-year study of 1,962 couples in four urban and nine rural districts of Puerto Rico. The three methods were again tested and together reduced the rate of *embarazos* among *mujeres* (pregnancies among women) from 70 to 39 per 100 years of exposure, or 44 percent. The rate for diaphragm users was 29; for foam powder, 33; and for jelly alone, 40. Obviously, there was not a great deal of difference in actual use among these groups in the effectiveness of the diaphragm versus foam powder, and their acceptability did not differ greatly. The dropouts, or rate of rejection with the passage of time, amounted to 48 percent overall.

Beebe and Belaval concluded that it was possible to get approximately a 50 percent reduction of births with these methods if their use was maintained. But with a dropout rate of nearly 50 percent, this meant a net reduction of only 25 percent, so it was apparent that these methods did not offer an effective means of controlling population. Beebe and Belaval recommended that not one but a combination of methods be used in the birth control program.

Gamble was not altogether satisfied with this study. He was inclined to make a stronger case for foam powder, concluding that "the powder clearly merits inclusion in the armamentarium needed by the physician seeking to protect underprivileged patients against the chance of conception." But he still faced the obstacle of obtaining more general acceptance of foam powder.

Unfortunately, there was a slackening of effort in the Puerto Rican birth control program during World War II. After the war, Gamble became interested in evaluating the impact of the birth control program on a selected population, and sent Christopher Tietze to Puerto Rico in 1946 to explore the possibility.

Tietze noted that almost 50,000 women had passed through the Puerto Rican Health Department contraceptive clinics since their inauguration in 1939, or about one in ten of the adult female population. Paradoxically, during this period condoms had become the most popular method of contraception, even as in the hills of North Carolina, followed by a spermicidal jelly called Cooper Creme, diaphragms, and foam powder in that order. He also noted that tubal ligation, the female operation producing sterilization, was more widely known among Puerto Ricans than the common methods of contraception. But the number of operations done amounted to only several hundred per year. Few men were interested in the much simpler male sterilization operation, vasectomy, due to the widespread but, of course, unfounded fear that it would impair their capacity for sexual intercourse. At this point, the birth rate in Puerto Rico had remained practically unchanged for forty-five years.

In a joint report, Mrs. Alvardo and Tietze observed that "critics have felt that birth control has failed in Puerto Rico and that it will not be possible—under present social and economic conditions—to reduce the birth rate to a point where further population growth is prevented." They pointed out, however, that there never had been an intensive public educational campaign to supplement the clinics—"Such a campaign would have to include home visits by competent nurses or social workers to all families believed to be in need of pregnancy control and careful follow-up work with those who had received advice at the clinic."

Further studies supported by Gamble served mainly to confirm the validity of the above observations and reinforce the fact that, prior to the advent of oral contraceptives and intrauterine devices, the condom was the most acceptable and generally the most effective contraceptive among the poor.

chapter 12   Back to Harvard

In 1942 the Harvard Medical School offered Dr. Gamble a temporary appointment. While tenured professors were in military service, Gamble became an instructor in physical diagnosis, at Boston City Hospital, continuing until 1945. Students, now professors, remember him as an excellent teacher.

Gamble found a sympathetic ear in Dr. George B. Wislocki, professor of comparative anatomy, who informally invited him into his departmental laboratory at the Medical School for two or three years, and then provided him laboratory space and a non-salaried appointment as research associate in anatomy from 1952 to 1958. During this exciting period, Gamble became involved in a dispute arising from his concern for the future of American intelligence, and in two other controversies involving his laboratory work.

College Graduate Study

The nearest Clarence Gamble ever came to alarmist behavior was in his anxiety that Harvard and other college graduates were not reproducing themselves. In 1946, he wrote an editorial, "Harvard—a Dying Race," for the *Harvard Medical Alumni Bulletin.* He spoke of the "threatened extinction" of American colleges and "the impending damage to the nation" on the threshold of a period of unprecedented expansion in college enrollment.

The following year, he spoke to the University's president, James Bryant Conant, about the genetic tragedy of declining American intelligence. Conant did not take him seriously. This did not deter Gamble, who for the next decade was college project director of—and, as such, something of a problem to—the Population Reference Bureau, a voluntary information agency in Washington, D.C. In this capacity, he staged an information campaign among the nation's colleges to increase the fertility rate of their alumni, not neglecting his own alma mater, Princeton. In 1946, in an article in the *Princeton Alumni Weekly,* he cried, "Attention, Sons of Nassau!" and called on them to help save the future of Americans by more frequent reproduction of intelligent children who would go on to assume positions of national leadership. College graduates, he said, were falling short of the 2.1 children they needed to replace themselves. At one point in the contest, the Boston *Globe* published an editorial captioned, "Yale 2.03, Harvard 1.7."

Thanks to nature and pure circumstance, Gamble's campaign met with success. War-weary veterans of the Armed Forces returned and took advantage of the G.I. Bill of Rights to go to college; within a few years, married students with children substantially contributed to the housing problem on every campus. By the time they graduated, the birth rate was pushing onward and upward, and some of the nation's intellectual leaders were up in arms about the population explosion.

This was pure Gamble: rarely, if ever, did he encounter an interesting problem and not assume he could do something about it. From an intellectual standpoint, he encountered the Perils of Pauline in the college project. Staid members of the American Eugenics Society were startled at his audacity. Robert C. Cook, editor of the *Journal of Heredity,* who became director of the Population Reference Bureau in 1951, challenged the validity of his assumptions. In 1956, the PRB board of directors dropped Gamble from his seat among them for violation of its rule that no officer could write or speak in the name of the Bureau without clearance of his material. The rule had been adopted in the hope of controlling the press releases issuing from Milton.

No scholar or scientist questioned the human race's need for higher intelligence and higher education. In fact, the general attitude of American eugenicists was that low fertility among college graduates was a calamity. Larger families for bachelors of arts and sciences could be a step in the right direction. Gamble, however, came to the conclusion that graduation from college was an adequate criterion for the selection of parents who would reproduce more intelligent offspring. Curiously enough, he became convinced of this despite the fact that neither his father nor his mother, nor Sarah, his wife, was a college graduate.

Gamble set forth his rationale in two articles, both stressing the need for more intelligent and more highly trained specialists in an increasingly scientific and technological society. The first, "The Deficit in the Birthrate of College Graduates" (*Human Fertility*, June 1946) stated:

> If a wholly accurate test of intelligence, uninfluenced by environment were available and could be applied to the entire population, it would be logical to look for the heredity required for future intelligent leaders among the children of those who had passed such a test with a high score. In the absence of such a test a partial substitute may be assumed to lie in the ability to graduate from college, indicating as it does a mentality above the average of the population. Needless to say, such a grouping is incomplete in that for economic reasons it has not been applied to many who could have passed it. It must be remembered, too, that because of hereditary variations the intelligence of one generation may be either above or below that of the parents. Even though we must recognize that there will be frequent exceptions, it seems probable that in a statistical sense the heredity of children of college graduates will make them of greater average value than others to the population as a whole.

In a second article, "The College Birthrate" (*Journal of Heredity*, December 1947) he consolidated his position:

The greatest single reservoir of those possessing the requisite abilities to plan, to guide, to execute with intelligence, is the group of college-trained citizens. The higher intelligence is not the magical effect of the sixteen years of education which leads to a college degree. It is that sixteen years of progressively more advanced learning constitutes a more or less rigorous selective process, and those who vault the final hurdle to achieve a diploma tend to be the cream of the crop that started the race back in kindergarten. This was confirmed by the results of the 10,000,000 intelligence tests given the selectees by the army. In these tests, the college graduates had an average record better than 94 percent of all men examined.

Obviously this does not mean that all the intelligent citizens of the United States have attended college. As a matter of fact, of the highest six percent in the army tests, only a quarter had college diplomas. The remainder, distributed throughout the entire population, are of equal eugenical interest but data on them are harder to obtain. College graduation is a criterion that is readily applied in selecting those of high intelligence. It is a convenient sampling-technique—and one widely used—which serves perfectly the ends of this paper.

By reasons of these considerations, the fecundity of this group is a matter of great significance. Since children tend to inherit the intellectual capacity of their parents, the average of the children of graduates will be above that of the national as a whole.

Gamble originally learned his genetics and eugenics under the distinguished Princeton biologist, Edwin Grant Conklin, who regarded men's college and women's college graduates as particularly remiss in their responsibility to perpetuate themselves. Even in the nineteenth century, Harvard graduates averaged only three-quarters of a son and Vassar graduates, but one-half of a daughter, he pointed out.

Conklin derived his outlook from Francis Galton, the younger cousin of Charles Darwin, who originated the theory of evolution by natural selection, popularized as "survival of the fittest." Galton introduced the word *eugenics* ("well born") and, from his studies of British aristocracy, embraced the concepts of "stock" and "breeding" as the sources of superior human strains, which he hoped would supplant the inferior. He did not consider environmental stimulus and such contributory influences as wealth and family connections. Naturally, his bias in favor of the well-born was not well received in the revolutionary societies espousing egalitarianism—whether democratic, socialistic, or communistic. The United States, for example, cherished the doctrine of equal opportunity and success through individual merit, offering every barefoot boy the hope of rising from log cabin to White House, or from mechanic to head of the Ford Motor Company.

So it was that Gamble, in choosing the college graduate as his intelligence reproduction model, succeeded in linking one unpopular cause with another—intellectual elitism and family planning.

He was interested in the management of reproduction at both ends of the survival-of-the-fittest ladder, in those with "inferior genes"—dysgenic—and "superior genes"—eugenic. For some years, he had sought to suppress the hereditary forms of mental retardation and mental illness by publicizing state laws providing for the sterilization of these classes of institutionalized patients. He frequently wrote and talked on sterilization, and became one of the earliest exponents of vasectomy, in those days directing it at the male deemed unfit to become a father.

At the eugenic end of the spectrum, it had become well established that intelligence, as measured by the Intelligence Quotient (IQ), was largely inherited. Eventually, psychologists were able to say that intelligence was about 80 percent inherited and 20 percent the product of environment. A basic drawback of the IQ, however, is that it does not define intelligence; its test scores simply evaluate individuals as members of the test group, taking the median score of 100 as normal and measuring how much the individual falls below or stands above "normal" in comparison with others. The IQ says nothing about the various identifiable components, or qualities, of intelligence, or the obvious fact that some people are bright about numbers and stupid about words, and so on.

The IQ test has been called psychology's greatest scientific contribution, but many who speak for it as experts become extremely tentative when asked to apply it to such thorny questions as what social group is more intelligent than another, or which individuals should have babies. It is infinitely easier to prove in the study of large population groups that intelligence "runs in families" than to reduce this truth to operational terms and breed individuals for intelligence. As indicated, one unanswered question is "Intelligence for what?" Another is, "How do you select and mate the breeders of intelligence?" Also, "What do you do with those who do not breed true—inevitable in any kind of cross-breeding?"

A final question is more subtle and more formidable in a democratic society. How do you get around the experience that the average differences in hereditary capacities between any of the conventional social, economic, or ethnic groups is less than the actual differences in hereditary capacities for individuals within any of these groups? Discrimination against the individual would be built into any system of selection based on group experience. Gamble recognized that he was speaking in the statistical sense about averages and not ranges, but did not perceive this as an objection.

The American Eugenics Society had long talked about the need to establish a eugenics policy in the United States, but on the basis of geneticists' understanding of the limitations of their knowledge, as well as of public opinion, stopped short of recommendations, much less planning any course of action. Reading AES literature, prepared under the auspices of Frederick Osborn, Chauncey Belknap, Henry R. Fairchild, Frank Lorimer, Clarence Cook Little, and other impeccable academics, we can imagine Gamble, the disciple of trial and error, growing increasingly impatient with all this indecision. He could not tolerate inaction.

In 1945 he won the approval of Guy Irving Burch, president of the Population Reference Bureau, for a project that Gamble would finance—a study, college by college, of how they were doing in what he happily called "the stork derby." On the face of it, his proposal was modest: "Fundamental objective: To initiate discussion of differential birth rates. Possible secondary result: Slight increase in birthrate of college graduates."

The major tool of this project—essentially one of public education—was different kinds of awards and honors to those alumni, viewed as classes, who had the best fertility records. As a matter of fact, he asked the Planned Parenthood Federation of America to give an annual award. The PPFA turned him down.

The Gamble Papers in the Countway Library show that he first decided to do something about reversing white Anglo-Saxon Protestant "race suicide" twelve years earlier, in 1934, when he was president of the Pennsylvania Birth Control Federation. In his opinion, one unfortunate outcome of the fusion of intelligence, woman's emancipation, and birth control was that graduates of women's colleges were the least fertile; some, more interested in professional careers, were not getting married at all. Gamble arranged with the president of the American Association of University Women so that his Pennsylvania Federation could give a reward to the Bryn Mawr College class having the highest birth rate in the first ten years after graduation. The Class of 1914 scored the highest—1.22 children per graduate. He gave $25. Gamble at that time offered to turn over the award program to the American Birth Control League, which rejected it.

It was his idea to raise the award to $50 and repeat the competition in all women's colleges, but interest dwindled. It was particularly difficult, he said, to get responses to the survey questionnaire from "recalcitrant virgins and newlyweds." He became occupied with other irons in the fire.

One of Gamble's traits was that he would never totally abandon an idea, good or bad, but would return to it again in different forms, times, or places. Under the auspices of the Population Reference Bureau and with the assistance of Mrs. Betty U. Kibbee (McNeely) in his Milton office, he focused on Harvard, Princeton, and Yale as a pilot project and, when the statistics on their alumni's natal sins of omission were in hand, sent out the news to alumni magazines, the Associated Press, and others, framing the project as a new form of inter-collegiate competition. His main intent was to honor the class of an American college with the highest number of children per graduate. The Gamble-Kibbee team generated a tremendous volume of information, but there is no indication that this particular award was ever made. As it turned out, Brigham Young University in Utah was to fertility what Notre Dame was to football—a perennial champion. Closely following the Mormon institution were Catholic and rural sectarian colleges, with the Ivy League trailing.

As far as the record shows, only the College of the Pacific adopted a related proposal for the university to congratulate its alumni on each newborn contribution to American intelligence. There was much correspondence about whether to give them a silver or gold spoon, the cheaper silver winning out. Gamble considered the minutest detail in his college project, including printing on both sides of the pages, envelope-forming sheets, and gummed versus non-gummed envelopes.

It was a different idea, however, that brought Gamble to see Harvard President Conant. Gamble first talked it over with George Wislocki, chairman of the Department of Anatomy, and Dr. C. Sidney Burwell, dean of the Medical School. This was to establish a Eugenics Fund to be used to encourage professors to engage in tax-exempt conception, so to speak. Gamble described it to a friend thus:

> Professor John Smith with a salary of $3600 is to be raised to $4000. . . . This would increase his income tax by approximately $80. Instead of this the president of the college suggests to a committee in charge of the Eugenics Fund that $200 be appropriated for each of John Smith's two children. There is in consequence no increase in income taxes and the Smith family income is increased by Eugenics Fund procedure to the extent of $80.

Baby bonuses were not a new thing. Various governments of Europe worried about low national birth rates and had provided such benefits, but not on the basis of intellectual or other merit.

Gamble offered $750 to start a Eugenics Fund, but the treasurer of the Harvard Corporation refused to approve of such a salary arrangement. Gamble decided to go over the treasurer's head and one day found himself in Cambridge explaining this proposal and also his college project to Conant, who was a physical chemist:

"When I presented the plan," Gamble wrote, "he laughed at me and said he thought there had never been a demonstration that the children of college graduates were more intelligent than the others. I am planning to see the presidents of Princeton and Oberlin before long." Gamble encountered "irritation instead of cooperation at Princeton," and no taker anywhere.

While no one challenged Gamble's grand assumption that intelligence and education, as well as stupidity and ignorance, have reciprocal relationships, it should be noted to be critically precise that he did qualify his proposition, "it seems probable . . . in a statistical sense," yet he adduced no statistical evidence to prove his proposition. But he had fun.

Diffusion Test

Gamble became dissatisfied with the Brown-Gamble test for the spermicidal potency of chemical contraceptives. Technical detail is not appropriate to this account; in the main, his objection was that the test depended on mixing sperm and spermicide—"a stirring not present in the vagina" following coitus, he said. Another objection was that the mixture had to be diluted to prevent the sperm being killed too quickly to measure a time interval.

He consequently developed a diffusion test avoiding both stirring and dilution, whereby tiny amounts of semen, obtained from medical students, were brought into contact with a spermicidal jelly in a capillary tube; the time it took for the sperm to lose their motility was measured. Because the new test, published in the *Journal of the American Medical Association*, was slower and the results were difficult to replicate, some British and American users of the test expressed dissatisfaction with it, saying that they preferred the older mixing test.

The controversy, however, rose from the question of how the millions of sperm ejaculated into the vagina made their way into the uterus. Gamble did not explore the question in his report, but appeared to hold with the assumption that the microscopic sperms slowly migrate from the vagina to the fallopian tubes in the manner of salmon swimming upstream on their way to spawn. His son Richard remembers in one group discussion his father saying: "Think of yourselves, gentlemen. How much stirring is there after ejaculation?" He ignored a certain amount of evidence supporting the competing "insuck theory," holding that muscular contractions of the uterus, acting as a pump, drawing sperm—and presumably the spermicide—quickly and en masse into the uterus. Such a possibility might account for the unreliability of the old-fashioned douche following intercourse.

Dr. Carl G. Hartman of the Ortho Research Foundation attacked the Gamble view caustically in 1957:

> This pioneer worker in the contraception field (coinventor of the excellent Brown-Gamble test) . . . now argues that no test is valid that depends on mixing of semen with the contraceptive. . . . In Gamble's aboutface, he naively and deliberately ignores the fact that semen and the contraceptive do mix during ejaculation and pelvic thrust. He also remains indifferent to the essential anatomy and physiology of the lower segment of the human genital tract.

The evidence for the insuck theory was clear in some animals, but suppositional in humans at the time; later, the theory had greater acceptance but is now passing out of favor except in some women's liberation circles concerned with the politics of sex. It is, of course, less romantic and appealing to males than the vision of a multitude of sperm seeking to overcome tremendous obstacles in a race that only one can win. In spite of man- and womankind's endless fascination with the theories and metaphors of procreation, spermicidal testing became of less value with the advent of the pill and the IUD and a diminishing interest in the diaphragm and jelly.

Gamble gave up his work in spermicidal testing. His son Richard remembers the day he came home and announced that he had thrown away his lab equipment. It was, Richard said, a poignant moment, which told him a great deal about the satisfactions his father gained in life, as well as his seldom-shared inner struggles concerning his work and the life-choices surrounding it.

"What he was experiencing was the end of his career as an experimental scientist. Despite all the work he had done with people in the field, starting family planning associations and the rest, there was in him I feel the dream of the satisfaction of being a laboratory scientist where precise measurements could be made, things could be tested and proved, a world of hard facts and concreteness, and the excitement of working on the frontiers. His decision to throw away his laboratory equipment meant he never again would be doing that."

Salt as a Spermicide

The fact that common table salt (sodium chloride) dissolved in water kills sperm long had been known. Until Gamble, no one did anything much with this information. Dickinson accepted it, but did not address himself specifically to the question of whether a 10 percent solution of sodium chloride in water would be injurious to the vaginal mucosa; he implied that it might produce irritation. Gamble, however, was eager to find a cheap, simple contraceptive that could be used vaginally by farm women unable to afford the one-cent cost of a contraceptive foam tablet, and that would be available in any household, however, poor. What he wanted was a homemade spermicidal jelly. He tried rice jelly. Every home has salt and, in the rice-growing areas of Asia, should have rice. He cooked up salt and rice flour in a double boiler and tried it in the laboratory in the course of testing sixty-eight commercial contraceptive preparations with his diffusion test.

Gamble was delighted to find the rice jelly containing a 30-percent salt solution in water had a faster immobilization time (twenty-seven minutes) than any of the commercial jellies. Rice jelly with a 20 percent salt solution ranked fourth and, with 10 percent, ninth. He duly reported these facts in 1953, and also that the 10 and 20 percent salt-and-rice jellies had been tested on three women at the Margaret Sanger Research Bureau in New York for subjective discomfort and physical evidence of irritation. Despite daily vaginal doses of 5 cc. each for twenty-one days, no discomfort or irritation was observed. He also recommended, as an alternative, the use of a small vaginal sponge or pad of cloth dipped in a salt solution of 10 percent or stronger.

Gamble meanwhile began to preach the use of this salt-and-sponge method in the Far East. Margaret Roots, his fieldworker, recommended the method and persuaded many to try it. George and Barbara Cadbury, representatives of the International Planned Parenthood Federation, also were moving about the Far East and, wherever they went, opposed the use of salt. The situation degenerated into a bitter conflict, echoes of which still can be heard after twenty years.

Dr. Helena Wright, London gynecologist and a leading feminist, then chairman of the IPPF medical advisory committee, a devotee of the traditionally approved vaginal diaphragm and jelly, was the first to challenge Gamble. She told him, in 1952, that his salt solutions were hypertonic and therefore osmotic pressure would draw an excessive secretion of fluids from the vaginal membranes, causing discomfort and irritation.

Insofar as the record shows, except for the small empirical test at the Margaret Sanger Research Bureau, neither Gamble nor any recognized laboratory investigator addressed himself to the logic of her criticism, derived from the ancient knowledge that salt or brine preserves meat, due to leeching and drying effects, not to mention the common urge to take a shower after swimming in the ocean. The facts are simple enough. A physiological, or isotonic, saline solution contains 0.9 percent salt. Roughly speaking, for it varies, seawater has been calculated to contain about 2.6 percent salt, three times as much as blood serum. Gamble variously suggested 10 to 30 percent solutions of salt in water as a spermicide, but seemed to prefer 20 percent—that is, more than twenty times as much salt as found in body fluids, or eight times as much as in average seawater.

Gamble in the late 1950s developed a salt-and-sponge, or salt-and-pad, following in scattered parts of the world. He dropped the rice jelly method; because the tropics generally lack refrigeration, the jelly soured and became unusable in two or three days. But he gladly supplied sponges, natural or plastic rubber, and offered instructions on the use of salt.

He and Mrs. Roots in their correspondence developed a remarkable lore concerning the technique. He raised such questions as whether the peasant women should keep a dish with salt water and a sponge in it beside her sleeping pad, or a bottle containing salt solution with the sponge handy, and how big the bottle should be so the sponge could be dipped into it and gently squeezed before insertion.

A few missionary doctors in India swore by the salt method, one writing that he considered it his "standard contraceptive" when his women patients asked for advice. These doctors and others to whom Mrs. Roots talked said that they heard no complaints from their patients. There were reports of enthusiastic use among small groups of women in Taiwan, Lebanon, and Chile. In contrast, salt received a poor reception among the Japanese and Koreans, and encountered a similar low acceptability among the Punjabis in the India-Harvard-Ludhiana study. Consumer objections tended in the direction of "messy" or "too much trouble." The obstetrics and gynecology department at Yonsei University in Korea tried salt and sponge on women patients without much success. Dr. Kang Joon Sang, a Korean field director and Pathfinder Fund grantee, said that the women complained that the salt solution felt hot. Doctors found some tissue erosion. Husbands complained that the salt irritated the penis.

In scientific research, the burden of proof falls on the claimant and any claim is open to challenge until confirmed. The trouble was that no investigator had taken the salt method seriously enough to make a systematic and comprehensive study of its safety, effectiveness, and acceptability. The chemical contraceptive testing standards that Gamble helped devise for the A.M.A. Council on Pharmacy and Chemistry required, as evidence that a preparation was without irritation or injury, daily vaginal application in twelve or more women for twenty-one successive days, as observed from the subjective viewpoint of the women and the medical specialist's objective examination with a speculum. Gamble had reported only three such cases. A British physician, P. Eckstein, tested a 20 percent salt jelly in the vaginas of three monkeys for a six-month period. Two showed no reaction, and the third, a slight irritation.

Eckstein in 1959 suggested that Gamble might want to finance further tests, at an estimated cost of $750. "I told him," Gamble later wrote, "that I was fully satisfied with the non-injuriousness of 20 percent sodium chloride and that if further investment was made it should be the International Planned Parenthood Federation's investment. Unfortunately . . . I have been given no connection with the IPPF."

Gamble authored one cooperative study among Indian and Pakistani women (1955). While he did not regard it as conclusive because of the limited number of cases and possibly other defects, it contained a surprise. It showed that vaginal foam tablets inserted immediately before intercourse produced a pregnancy, or failure, rate of 9 per 100 women per year—only a third as high as the salt and the diaphragm methods, which were about equal. (The diaphragm failure rate of 27 per 100 women per year could be attributed to failure to use the method.) Gamble responded by distributing hundreds of thousands of free foam tablets as the preferred method. He agreed that salt was "perhaps less pleasant" and "not apparently as acceptable," as he admitted in one letter in 1956.

At the same time, he refused to back off from salt as a highly effective alternative method "when used." The issue was never resolved in the scientific literature of contraception. Salt was strictly a home remedy, requiring no physician and no prescription, and therefore beyond clinical and pharmaceutical as well as research interest.

School of Public Health

When one mentions the name of Gamble around the Harvard medical campus, the hearer, if an older physician, is quite apt to say, yes, he knew Dr. James L. Gamble and admired him very much. James Gamble, Clarence's cousin, was professor of pediatrics at the Children's Hospital. He did lifesaving research work in the correction of fluid balance in children with diarrhea. As Clarence would explain, "Cousin Jim is the dehydration Gamble. I am the contraceptive Gamble."

When Dr. John E. Gordon, professor of preventive medicine and epidemiology at the Harvard School of Public Health, became interested in population problems following World War II, a friend suggested that he talk to Gamble. The meeting led to the seven-year demographic study in the Punjab State known as the India-Harvard-Ludhiana or Khana study, and to the entry of the School of Public Health into the population field. Gamble financed Gordon's initial survey, an additional $5,000 for one year's training at the School of Public Health for Dr. John Wyon, a young British missionary doctor who spoke Hindi and had been working in rural India, and another $10,000 to send Wyon back to India and see the study through its first year of 1953–1954. Gamble's pump-priming was sufficiently successful that support for the study eventually included the Rockefeller Foundation, the government of India, Indian Council on Medical Research, Population Council (New York), Higgins Fund of Harvard University, National Science Foundation, Ford Foundation, and pharmaceutical companies which furnished the contraceptives. Planned by Gordon and Wyon, the study lasted seven years, was staffed by 47 persons, involved 12,000 Punjabi villagers, and produced some three dozen articles and a book over the next seventeen years. The total, long-term impact of the study from the standpoint of health education as well as contraceptive effectiveness appeared negligible. Its most significant conclusion, and one that provided a guideline for much sociological research to come, was that "Motivation appears to outweigh method in importance." It ultimately proved Gandhi right in one underlying aspect: birth control is a matter of choice—of the will power to do or not to do something.

In 1958, Clarence Gamble transferred from the department of anatomy to the Harvard School of Public Health, a close ally of the Medical School. He became research associate in population studies, keeping his same rank and continuing the same self-supporting arrangement, making grants for his laboratory staff and equipment through Harvard.

So it was that he found and rented his own space for a laboratory on the second floor of Sparr's Drug Store, at Hungtington and Longwood Avenues, next to the old Huntington Building, then mainly occupied by the department of epidemiology. Gamble continued his contraceptive research, as already described, in his new location and, beginning in 1962, made it the base for his IUD evaluation and distribution program.

Hardly anyone knew what went on over Sparr's Drug Store. There was an in-group joke that Gamble's contraceptive advice might not be too good, because all his lab technicians and secretaries—there were not more than two or three at any time—got pregnant. The observation was not wholly accurate. His daughter Judy worked in the laboratory for several months after her marriage, while her husband, Stanley Kahrl, was studying at Harvard. She already was pregnant when she started work. Some staff did become pregnant after accepting employment, but this related, more significantly, to the fact that they were the wives of medical students or young faculty members and at the summit of the child-bearing years.

Retirement from the faculty overtook Gamble in 1962, but he continued to maintain his laboratory at the corner of the Harvard medical campus until 1965, when the Pathfinder Fund moved into larger quarters on nearby Tremont Street.

Meanwhile Gamble saw a long-time dream of making family planning a center of attention in medical education and public health education come true. He encouraged Dr. John C. Snyder, dean of the School of Public Health, to establish a department of demography and human ecology in 1962. This was made possible by a large contribution from some of the Gamble family—not from Gamble. From this beginning, in what is now called the population sciences department, Harvard moved on to the establishment of a university-wide center for population studies in

Cambridge. All candidates for the Master of Public Health degree at Harvard now take the course on population growth and fertility control.

Always the loner, something of an outsider, and considered an eccentric, Gamble regarded his acceptance by the Establishment and the emergence of conventional organization features in his own Pathfinder Fund with some sadness and, at best, mixed feelings. His job, as he remarked toward the last, was unfinished; meantime, it appeared, the fun was going out of it. He was in serious danger of becoming respectable and only escaped this fate by a narrow margin.

Experiment in International Living, Austria, 1947

Gambles—An Experiment in Living

The Gamble family compensated Clarence for whatever recognition he lacked from the rest of the world. The Gambles, including
an extended family of parents, brothers, their wives and children,
aunts, uncles, cousins, and friends were a family—one of a van-
ishing race—of long letter writers.

Everywhere he went, by automobile, train, boat, or airplane,
whether on business or vacation, Gamble carried a portable
typewriter. As soon as he settled in his seat—preferably with a
view of a harbor, mountain, lake, or whatever was there—he
opened his typewriter and pounded out long letters to be mailed
at the first opportunity. As a matter of fact, voluminous corre-
·spondence became the backbone of communication in programs
in family planning development and contraceptive trials that he
conducted through fieldworkers, friends, and missionary doctors
first in the United States and later many foreign countries, beginning in the Far East and subsequently in Africa and Latin
America.

Once, on the way from home in Milton, Massachusetts, for a
summer in Harbor Point, Michigan, Gamble got into his pajamas
and knocked off a letter in his roomette in a night train standing
in the station in Detroit. He pulled on his trousers and shoes and
got off to mail the letter. The train rolled out, taking Sarah and
their cook with it but leaving Clarence behind. Fortunately, he
had his wallet, so he could pay for a hotel room and the trip to
Traverse Bay by bus the next day; the hotel demanded payment in
advance since he had no baggage.

Gamble was a dependable source of instruction and amusement
to his five children, who never ceased to wonder, "What will
Daddy do next?" It might be anything—investing in a North
Carolina turkey farm, helping the boys install an electric-shock
machine in the sofa to surprise unsuspecting guests, rigging a rope
tow on the hill behind the house, buying a motorcycle to save on
gasoline during wartime rationing, planting a wartime Victory
garden, raising baby chickens, ice-skating on the flooded tennis

court, racing pigeons, wiring the dove coat so that every time a racing pigeon arrived at dawn a bell sounded in his bedroom, or requiring the children to drive him to some destination and find their own way.

His redheaded children, the products of family planning, were raised on its terminology so thought nothing of it. As a physician, Gamble had a precise, proper way of discussing the structure and function of the reproductive system, and it never occurred to them that there was anything obscene about sex. It was simply what Daddy and sometimes Mummy, too, talked about with other grown-ups who came to dinner and stayed to discuss birth control. According to one medical acquaintance, "Dr. Gamble either talked about birth control or remained silent." But this was not true as his five children saw him.

Five children, in an era when the American family commonly had three, was the cause of raised eyebrows among fellow birth controllers. Emily Mudd, herself a marriage counselor, and mother of four in the course of paying a tribute to Sarah Gamble in 1965, pointed out that the birth rate in the Gamble family, including children and grandchildren, was twice that for the nation. Gamble was not disturbed by questions about practicing what he preached. In his view, he did practice what he preached, as all of his children were planned and wanted. People of good stock should have more children. It was not wholly clear to all whether his was a scientific, ethnic, or social class judgment. There was not the slightest doubt, however, that Gamble considered himself and his wife to be the right people to become parents, and happily, as it turned out, this proved to be the case. As friends said, the Gambles were "a real family."

One projection of the Gambles' sense of family was their interest in the Experiment in International Living, a program initiated by Donald Watt of Putney, Vermont, in the 1930s. Its purpose is to send groups of youths each summer to live as members of various families in selected foreign communities. All five Gamble children took part. Sally and Dick went to Austria, Walter to Germany, Judy to France, and Bob to Holland and as a leader to

Poland; Sally and her husband later led a group to Holland; Dick was a leader in Norway and Finland and with his wife led the pioneer group to Nigeria; Walter led a group to Germany. Dr. and Mrs. Gamble became board members of the Experiment in International Living and she succeeded Watt as chairman of the board in the 1960s.

While all the Gamble children respected their father and, like their mother, defended him against his critics, they developed individual views of him, depending in part on what point in his career they arrived and how much time he could spend with them. As a father, he enjoyed guiding, instructing them, and playing with them. Recreationally, this was mostly to the good, for he himself was eager for sailing, canoeing, tennis, horseback riding, swimming, skiing, mountain hiking, in fact anything that took him outdoors and into the sun.

In the judgment of Sally, the eldest, he overdid it. "It was not comfortable growing up with him," she said. "He drove me to be independent before I was ready for it." As a little girl would, she liked pretty, feminine things, but he ridiculed them and tried to make a tomboy out of her, she said. He wanted her to become a physician, but she resisted and, as she grew up, became more rebellious toward his efforts to manage her interests (in the end, she became a wife, mother, and not only a contributor to family planning in the District of Columbia, but a very active voluntary leader and worker).

The Gamble children speak of "Gamble silence." By this they mean that, although their father could be infuriating in his unrelenting efforts to persuade others, if someone just as stubbornly held to an opposite position, he would fall silent, and his adversary might understand this silence as consent. But it wasn't. At some later time, Gamble would return to the subject, restating his proposal as if it was a fresh idea. This was a burden to Sally, who admitted that she may have inherited her father's obstinancy.

She remembers with discomfort Sunday afternoons at their home in Milton. Gamble would invite a select group of Harvard

medical students to dinner, "I hated being paraded as date material," she said. Sally, in retrospect, realized it was partly an act of
defiance as well as good judgment when she fell in love with a
young Jewish Harvard law student, Lionel Epstein. Her father and
her husband became good friends, and soon Gamble was writing
his son-in-law letters beginning "Dear Li" and signed "Daddy."
Birth control friends of Gamble said that he always asked for
advice but never took it. This was not so in his relationship with
Epstein. Gamble believed in keeping his financial affairs to
himself—he did his own income tax returns and those for all his
children and his grandchildren for many years with the help of
only one secretary. But Epstein specialized in tax law, and Gamble did take his advice. It was his son-in-law who suggested in
1957 that the Gamble family form a foundation. Epstein's father
was a New York garment trader. When Gamble found himself in
the City one rainy day he rushed down to the Epstein warehouse
and bought a raincoat off the rack. Proving that family ties were
for him stronger than prejudice, Gamble made a point of visiting
his son-in-law's family whenever he was in New York.

The other children lacked Sally's first-child outlook. Robert,
the fifth, while confessing that he hardly got to know his father,
observed that "Each of the Gamble children was encouraged to
pursue his own line of interest." It is conceivable that Gamble
may have learned with Sally the mistake of trying to run one's
children's lives. Whatever the case, Richard and Walter, the second and third, had a much easier relationship with their father
and, indeed, were permitted to go their own way. Both followed in
their father's steps to Princeton. Richard studied international
relations and then went to Columbia and the University of
California in Berkeley where he earned a Master's degree in social
science. He made a commitment to family planning when he
made two Far East trips with his father and studied sociology and
demography in graduate school. He then became interested in the
development of small industries in Nigeria, where he lived and
worked for nine years. Four years after his father's death, he

became executive director of the Pathfinder Fund, of which he is now president. Walter went on to the University of Pennsylvania and became a physician. He then, as his father once had, turned to cardiovascular research, a career that he pursues as assistant professor of pediatrics at Harvard and the Children's Hospital in Boston. When Walter showed his father his first paycheck, the latter said, "That is more money than I ever earned in my whole life."

Richard's and Walter's recollections fairly well square with those of Judy, the fourth child. Judy was fond of her father and remembers him as a patient teacher. "He read aloud to us a great deal—I can still hear him," she said. A mathematical wizard, who could do calculus in his head, he helped the children with their homework, encouraging them and directing their attention to what they had overlooked with a "Yes, but," providing them the opportunity of telling each other, "Daddy has just yes-butted me." At dinner, he might discuss an article he had read in the *Reader's Digest*, *National Geographic*, or *Things of Science*.

He tried to stimulate the children to figure out problems for themselves. He taught Judy to fix the electric pump, first showing her how to take it apart. He then sat down and watched her try to put it back together. When she said, "Come on, Daddy, help me," he said, "If you figure it out for yourself and later forget, you will be able to do it again." This method did not work well with Robert, who said: "Daddy was big on having you figure out something yourself. I would ask how something works, and he would say, 'Well, you tell me.' He wanted you to fool around until you learned how to handle it. It worked perfectly well for Walter and Judy, but not for me. This is not the best way for me to learn. To some extent, I would be scared of a piece of equipment."

As his father had with him, Gamble drilled his children in keeping account of their money. For example, when Judy was seven, he allowed her twenty-five cents a week plus ten cents for charity. When she was eight, he doubled her allowance. But she received it only on condition that she kept track of how she spent it. "I got two cents a week for bookkeeping. I showed him my books every two weeks. If I . . . waited three weeks, I forfeited the last two cents."

As for wealth, "I had no idea of what was awaiting me until I was married. . . . I never felt any career pressure. There was a family standard that whatever you do should contribute something to the community. It was different from other families. We did not have to think of a career in terms of the money we could make. . . . He felt that conspicuous consumption was a very bad thing. At Harbor Point, we were the 'crazy Gambles.' We only had a sailing canoe rather than a yacht."

"The question was not whether he could afford it, but whether we could afford it spiritually—what it would do to us. He couldn't see why the boys should have a car of their own, but when they insisted and made it clear that it would make them more independent, he said, 'Fine.'"

Judy's husband is an English professor who teaches at Ohio State University in Columbus. Robert upheld the strong Protestant tradition of the Gamble family in becoming an Episcopal minister; he now has a church in Grinnell, Iowa. In 1974, he married Antonina Spisak of Krakow, whom he had met when leading an Experiment group to Poland.

Clarence's grandfather, James, sired ten children; his father, David, four (one of whom died in childhood). His brother Cecil had six and his brother Sidney, four, and Clarence, of course, had five. Among his children, Sally has five (one adopted); Richard, four; Walter, three; Judy, four; and Robert, one.

Sarah, who herself was one of five children, complained during her child-bearing days that every time she became pregnant she felt like an elephant. Consequently, on each wedding anniversary, Clarence gave her a miniature elephant.

No one took Gamble for a natural genius in human relations. He struck some as totally lacking in empathy or rapport. Mentioning that everyone in birth control seemed to have a collection of little stories about Clarence Gamble, mainly dealing with his capacity for giving offense, Robert C. Cook, onetime president and director of the Population Reference Bureau, said: "Mrs. Gamble seemed to be a nice, sensitive person, and I couldn't help but feel that she was being dragged through one after another of these crashing outrages." When accused of being indifferent to others' feelings, Gamble would protest that he had the best of intentions, and this was true. He was never able to appreciate that others had needs, motivations, and goals of their own which might conflict with whatever he wanted done at the time.

Yet Gamble, as a family man, was sentimental and loyal, and in his never-take-no-for-an answer way, attentive and loving.

part 3 pathfinder overseas

chapter 13 Dr. Koya vs. Japanese Abortions

Clarence Gamble began his major overseas adventures as a front-running birth controller in the smallest possible way. In 1950 he tossed a $700 chip on a gaming table where the future health and happiness of more than a billion persons, or half the human race, was the ultimate stake. This was then the population of Asia. With an annual growth rate of more than 2 percent, this population would almost double in the next twenty years. Gamble became identified with early family planning organizations and field studies of contraception in Korea, Taiwan, India, Pakistan, Ceylon, Japan, Indonesia, the Philippines, Thailand, and elsewhere.

The first of these was the so-called three-village study in Japan, a classic in the literature of contraceptive field work carried out under Japan's foremost public health leader in family planning, Dr. Yoshio Koya. This collaboration of money and ideas, continuing through the 1950s, took place against the backdrop of a relatively small nation that had committed itself to population growth and territorial expansion but had seen its dream of a Pacific empire and *Lebensraum* incinerated in the radioactive ashes of Hiroshima and Nagasaki.

In the humiliation of American G.I. occupation and the chaos of unemployment and hunger, the Japanese government was ill-prepared for a population explosion or the determination of its people to avoid reproducing the children they could no longer support. Yet by the 1960s the world acclaimed Japan as one of the first countries to embrace birth control as a government policy, and the first Asian nation to get its birth rate under control. No one, paradoxically, was more surprised by this success than Japanese politicians themselves. Just as in the United States and elsewhere in the world, the notion of family or population limitation was still repugnant to many of these leaders long after the people whom they presumed to represent were practicing effective birth control.

Japan had provided a clear-cut example of how population pressures act, if not as a direct cause of war, as a force that moves a people to accept war as an instrument of their destiny. Conversely, Japan exemplified how the aggressive military mind of any nation, with all its purblind limitations in social problem solution (do or die), uses the manpower demands of war and territorial expansion as justification for population growth. This was not always the case, despite a warlike tradition dating from the early shoguns, who were local military dictators. A census of the Japanese islands in 1726, during the era of the Tokugawa shogunates, showed a population of about 26 million; in 1846, 120 years later, the population was still 26 million. According to Dr. Fumiko Y. Amano, "Each family usually raised two offspring. The rest were sold or became victims of infanticide and abandonment. Even euthanasia was a common practice." The equation of a closed population was as simple then as it is now: where deaths equal births, or births minus deaths equal zero, there is a zero growth rate.

By the early 1920s, when the Japanese birth rate reached an alltime high of 36 per 1,000 population per year, the population had doubled: 56 million. In total area, the four Japanese islands approximate two states of Missouri. Soon, this dense, insular population—characterized by an energy for work unsurpassed anywhere, a fierce need for personal achievement, a love of nature and artistic and technical excellence and beauty, a singular homogeneity in race and culture, and strong cultural traditions of male superiority and female inferiority—became the impetus for Nippon's twentieth-century ambition to build an overseas empire, quite in the same manner that Western powers had done. During the 1930s and until the climax of World War II, it appeared that Japan might have its Pacific empire, including Manchukuo, Korea, North China, Okinawa, Formosa, and various bites of Southeast Asia.

To rule all this, the Emperor and his generals believed they needed many, many Japanese as well as ships, bombs, machine guns, and cartridge belts. Hence, the militarists emphasized what Japanese rice farmers long had believed, the Kodakara concept, meaning "Children are the greatest wealth of family as well as country." The Japanese law of primogeniture fitted well with the policy of world conquest; all members of the family must honor and obey their father, but only the eldest son could inherit his property. Younger sons were obliged to work for their eldest brother, hire out to a neighbor, or migrate. Many went to the cities and worked in factories, but many also became colonists in conquered territories.

Before World War II, Japan prohibited contraception and abortion. Public discussions of birth control were banned. In 1936, police closed the Tokyo birth control clinic operated by a follower of Margaret Sanger, Baroness Ishimoto (Mrs. Shidzue Kato), arresting her in a round-up of 300 persons accused of "dangerous thoughts." It was not a matter of morals. Buddhism and Shintoism, the predominant religions of Japan, unlike Catholicism, do not concern themselves with sexual "sins against nature." Political and economic considerations, combined with the sexual drive, determined the country's capacity to produce babies. Four years after Pearl Harbor, the Rising Sun could shine overseas only on distant graves of the war dead—more than a million products of Kodakara.

War is a costly and therefore undesirable means of population control, however effective it has been in certain nations and in certain historical times. The loss of many hundreds of thousands of men in combat was the price of the vastly reduced population in Russia following World War II, as in other countries in the postwar period, particularly France, which failed to achieve expected population growth. In some countries such as the United States, furthermore, the phenomenon of the war baby boom ultimately produces a population increase. The men come home and the women are glad to see them. The reunion produces a sharp increase in marriages and births and the children create a bulge in the age distribution of population that may manifest itself in a second wave of babies coming some twenty to twenty-five years later.

Some six million Japanese—soldiers and settlers—returned from overseas in the three years following the surrender in 1945. The women at home were tired, hungry, and undernourished; often homeless as the result of bombing raids, they were no less responsive to their men, if the statistics are any index. The birth rate, 25 per 1,000 population in 1946, rose to 34 in 1947, the highest in twenty-five years. The population of Japan increased from an estimated 72.4 million in 1945 to 82.6 in 1949, a gain of more than ten million in four years. The growth rate reached 3 percent, and continued to rise at a more gradual rate in the next twenty years until it passed 100 million and provided Japan with more than 700 persons per square mile, one of the highest densities in the world. Crowding became a way of life.

The Japanese people, rich as well as poor, paid for the madness of their militarists. The wealthy lost property and money as the Supreme Command for the Allied Powers (SCAP) at first seized industrial machinery as war reparations and broke up feudal land rights. Prime Minister Tojo and other convicted war criminals were hanged or imprisoned; many public officials were ousted from office.

The new democratic constitution in 1947, written by the United States government and imposed on Japan, terminated the

sole right of the eldest son to inherit his parents' property, requiring equal distribution among all children; this often produced
shares of farms too small to work, and so, as some saw it, accelerated rather than slowed the trend from rural to urban life. Unemployment and underemployment in the cities were high; in
bombed areas housing was scarce or totally lacking. Some re-
turnees found their houses taken over by people who had lost theirs,
and so were obliged to leave home again.

Fraternization of Japanese women with American G.I.'s produced ostracism plus babies, and also stimulated racial prejudice
against the half-caste progeny. Added to this was the plight of
young girls sent back from the China mainland settlements who
were pregnant as the result of mass rapings. Suicides of unmarried, pregnant women became daily news. Infanticide, usually
through abandonment of newborn infants, was commonplace.
Despite the prewar Japanese law making interruption of pregnancy a crime unless it was to save the mother's life, a black
market in induced abortions spread throughout the islands. An
illegal abortion by midwife or doctor could be had for 2,000 to
3,000 yen, or about three to five dollars. The leading Japanese
newspapers, *Mainichi* and *Asahi*, appealed to mothers not to
bring any more babies into such a hard world. Hundreds of
women wrote in from the farming and mining areas asking how
they could avoid babies. Over and over, Japanese repeated to one
another the sentiment: "Life is more tragic than death."

Contraception was much in some people's minds, although
only opportunistic manufacturers of condoms, jellies, and pow-
ders were prepared to meet the demand. Relatively few husbands
and wives practiced contraception, an estimated 5 to 15 percent
in the farmlands and 20 to 25 percent in the cities. Birth control
was a matter of crisis intervention, approached after the fact of
pregnancy rather than before, and mainly through the method of
"take-out babies," as the Nipponese termed aborted fetuses.

Many good people, including birth controllers, regarded the
abortion phenomenon with horror. A number of pregnant women
die from abortions. In clean, well-trained hands, the possibility is

rare, but the Japan Academy of Obstetrics and Gynecology would find that, even when treated by doctors designated and supposedly qualified to do abortions, women died at the rate of 2 per 1,000 induced abortions, while an additional 3 per 1,000 had ill effects. Some doctors had records ten or twenty times as bad. Women who had abortions kept on getting pregnant, and therefore faced the need for repeated operations—these were commonplace. Beyond all this, the thought of destroying an unborn human being is not a pleasant one—for some, it is emotionally traumatic. This approach often led to wrathful, punitive social judgment of the mother as a fallen woman, even though in reality she was usually married and had numerous children, and even though, under the environmental circumstances awaiting it, the fetal human had little prospect of health or happiness—in fact, might itself become a casualty after birth.

It became apparent to the authorities that abortions should be legalized, so they could be brought under the control of the government and the medical profession. No less than thirty Japanese birth control organizations came into being in 1947 and the five years following, but they were almost as much in conflict with one another as they were with the bitter tea of Occupation.

Dr. Fumiko Amano and her husband, Kageyasu, both American-trained physicians, and Dr. Kan Majima, another ardent birth controller, went to see the SCAP chief medical officer, General Crawford Sams, who told them: "Only an effort to raise the standard of living and culture through intensive industrialism will help the Japanese with their over-population problem." "How about birth control?" the Japanese asked Sams. "That is for the Japanese to decide," he replied. In short, SCAP was ducking the issue.

The Japanese Diet, urged on by its doctor members, faced the issue. In May 1948, the Diet enacted the Eugenic Protection Law, stating its object to be: "To prevent the increase of inferior descendents from the standpoint of eugenic protection and to protect the life and health of the mother as well." The felicitous phrasing did not disguise the fact that the "eugenic operations" authorized by the law were induced abortion and sterilization. An indigent woman could have such an operation at government expense for any of several reasons; these were at first genetic or medical, but later the law was amended to include economic or social reasons. The operation could be performed by physicians designated by local branches of the Japanese Medical Association at their own discretion in some circumstances or with the authorization of a District Eugenic Protection Council in others.

During the first month the law was in force, 6,400 legal abortions were recorded and the number climbed steadily each month thereafter. It was estimated that there were nearly 100,000 legal abortions in the last seven months of 1948. Meanwhile, illegal abortions did not disappear. The Japanese government now faced a new crisis. The Japanese people's growing dependence on abortion as birth control could be likened to a kind of social iatrogenic disease which can—and does—occur when planners do not foresee all the consequences of their good intentions toward the very people their policies are intended to help.

Dr. Gamble, the faithful Princetonian, learned about the Japanese situation in 1949 at his thirty-fifth class reunion. He went to see Dr. Frank W. Notestein, director of the Princeton University Office of Population Research, later president of the Population Council founded by John D. Rockefeller III. Notestein in late 1948 had headed a Rockefeller Foundation survey team sent to the Far East to investigate population problems. He reported that "The Far East is rich only in people . . . whom pain hurts and death robs, however inured they may be to their lot."

Notestein told Gamble that Japan had no birth control program, but was ripe for one. The demographer would recommend that the Rockefeller Foundation accept population control as a major field of interest and mount a program of research and aid throughout the Far East. Rockefeller himself favored the proposal, but other Foundation trustees and officers were not of like mind and decision was postponed. This led Rockefeller to establish a new and independent Population Council in New York in 1952; the old Foundation did not declare population to be of major program interest until 1963.

General Douglas MacArthur, Supreme Commander for the Allied Powers, likewise dragged his feet. His policy, as carried out by General Sams, was "hands off." They wanted no outside interference on birth control in Japan. The New York *Times* in 1950 commented that Occupation authorities were "sometimes under pressure by Catholic agencies." The New York *Herald Tribune* had reported on charges from the Vatican in Rome that American experts were trying to turn Japan into a scientific laboratory for contraception. The Vatican newspaper, *L'Osservatore Romano*, agreed that Japan had population and food problems, and suggested the way to solve them was for underpopulated countries such as the United States to reduce race prejudice, change their immigration laws, and admit Asiatics. The Japanese, more realistic, saw little hope in that direction. Catholic defenders of the faith for Buddhists and Shintoists made the charge that there was "a well-organized plot" to give the false impression that the Japanese people wanted birth control. In fact, the practice of abortion proved their desire for birth control.

One American expert on the spot was Dr. Warren S. Thompson, a leading demographer at the Scrips Foundation for Research in Population Problems at Miami University, Oxford, Ohio, who had recently been a consultant on MacArthur's staff. Thompson contradicted SCAP. He stated that birth control offered the only hope of solving the Japanese population crisis, but agreed that the Occupation could not force such a program on the Japanese.

Notestein told Gamble that a Japanese program, whether of public education or of research, would require some American initiative to get it started. Gamble immediately wrote Thompson, in June 1949, and asked for suggestions of how he might give a Japanese birth control program a push with "A few hundred dollars, a thousand or less." Thompson sent Gamble the names of two Japanese birth controllers, Professor Jitsui Kitaoka and Mrs. Kato, and told him how he could communicate with them both for a nickel (then the cost of a domestic air mail stamp). He should write these people letters and enclose them in an envelope to a certain doctor in the National Resources Section, GHQ, SCAP, who could be reached through APO 500, San Francisco, California, whence mail would go by military air transport. Regular air mail to Japan took a month or six weeks and at that time cost 30 cents an ounce.

Beginning in 1949, Gamble made a number of small gifts, usually from $200 to $400, to three or four Japanese birth control organizations, mainly to finance the printing and mailing of their publications. Mrs. Kato cooled Gamble off somewhat. She proposed that he help her start a traveling birth control clinic that would cost $500 a month. This was, said Gamble, "beyond my financial capacity." She had explained to him that the government, under the Ministry of Health and Welfare, operated some 700 health centers, but only twenty had birth control clinics. She quoted Dr. Koya as reporting that these clinics served an average of only four women each. This led Gamble to suggest that Mrs. Kato publicize the government clinics and see if she could not devise a program to increase the patient load of one such clinic, as a demonstration.

Meanwhile, by mail Gamble met his Japanese equivalent, one of the most astute family planners in the world. This was Dr. Yoshio Koya, then going on sixty years old and director of the National Institute of Public Health, a training and research bureau under the Ministry of Health and Welfare.

Koya, who died in the spring of 1974, was a short, owlish-looking gentleman in dark-rimmed glasses, prideful but friendly, a man who despite his dignity could see the humorous side and who laughed easily.

Koya had been in the government a long time, pre- and postwar, but was no ordinary bureaucrat. He was born in 1890 in rural Japan, the eldest of a local medical doctor's nine children. As a youth, he supposed he would become a physician but he was lazy and inclined to spend his time reading German novels. Koya managed to graduate from Tokyo University in 1916. If he was to become a doctor, he decided that it would be in public health because there "I would not have to see blood."

As a matter of fact, Koya's main interests were art and literature; he lived in an intellectual colony, *Nakai, Shinjuku-ku,* Tokyo, and was one of a circle of Japanese authors and painters who achieved national and international distinction. While still in college, he wrote a first novel, *One Who Inherits the Earth*. It went through twenty printings and brought him a good deal of money, enough so that he could marry and buy the home in which he, his wife, and two children—a son, Tomohiko Koya, is a doctor—were to live for more than a half century. The novel was never translated into English. When interviewed as an elder statesman in 1969, Koya refused to mention its subject, implying that it was something risqué, if not pornographic. After college, he decided to become a writer, and studied for two years in France, Germany, and Italy. He read Tolstoy's *War and Peace* with deep regret, realizing that he did not have that kind of talent.

Returning to Tokyo, he took up painting; he recalled one early effort called "Onion and Lamp." He showed it to an art critic who said, "It looks like an onion on a lamp." True to Japanese appreciation of life's esthetic dimensions in art and nature, Koya continued to paint in later life as an accomplished amateur, but meanwhile was appointed professor of microbiology in Tokyo Medical College. He now decided to study public health intensively and became particularly interested in biostatistics. He wrote a manual, *Methodology of Vital Statistics*, that sold well.

In 1932, when he was forty-two years old, he received his M.D. degree and became professor of public health at Kanazawa University. For several years, he studied and wrote on the epidemiology of tuberculosis, Japan's leading killer before the war. In 1939, he was appointed chief health officer of the Ministry of Health and Welfare of the imperial government. The next year, the Ministry ordered Koya to draft a National Eugenics Law bidding Japanese mothers to be fertile for the good of the empire. This law made abortion a crime. Following the war, Koya escaped the purge of public officials considered to be resistant to democratic reforms.[1] As he recalled, "My attitude about birth control changed 180 degrees. Having more babies was a Fascist idea."

As the public health and welfare arm of SCAP, General Sams in 1946 selected Koya as director of the National Institute of Public Health. In early 1950, MacArthur sent Koya with other Japanese doctors to the United States to study modern public health methods. Koya was particularly advised to visit state and local health departments in the American South, on the supposition that the backward rural conditions there were comparable to those in Japan. On the other hand, the Japanese have no race problem. Koya was particularly interested in the North Carolina public health program in contraception, and it was Dr. George N. Cooper who "set up my mind about family planning." Koya also visited the well-established birth control clinic in Cincinnati. He was not aware until interviewed in 1969 that the North Carolina and Ohio projects were among the first financed by Gamble.

Koya credited Dr. Oliver H. McCoy with bringing him and Gamble together. McCoy was the Rockefeller Foundation representative in the Far East and acted as liaison between SCAP and the Japanese Ministry of Health and Welfare. Gamble wrote McCoy, offering him $200 or $300 to translate American birth control pamphlets into Japanese. McCoy assured Gamble that, while Koya was already training doctors in birth control, a public education program in family planning was much needed. He said it was highly unlikely, however, that the Japanese government would undertake it. Apparently, Koya heard about Gamble from McCoy, but the latter in 1972 had no recollection of introducing the two.

Gamble-Koya correspondence for 1950 is missing from the Countway collection, but it was in the late summer or early fall that Koya wrote Gamble for financial aid in the village study of

---

[1] Hearing that SCAP was reading what Japanese authors had published prior to Japan's defeat and, if it disapproved, blacklisting them, Koya made a vigorous effort to round up all copies of his many published works, mostly in public health, and indeed bought all those he could find on the shelves of Tokyo bookstores. Later, when he visited Washington, D.C., he found all he had published were on the shelves of the Library of Congress!

Sarah with Judy and Bob in Japan

birth control that he wished to undertake. Gamble would have
preferred to go to Japan and explore the situation, taking his son,
Richard, who was about to graduate from Princeton and was eager
to go abroad. SCAP however, in June refused the Gambles permission to visit Japan, as it had Margaret Sanger several months
earlier. MacArthur was interested in planning Japan's industrial
and economic development—but he did not care about the size of
its families. He rationalized that if SCAP admitted birth control
propagandists it would be under pressure to accept their Catholic
opponents, too. In any event, without outside help the Japanese
were already further advanced in birth control legislation than
most countries, he said. It was a clever argument and effectively
postponed the arrival of Mrs. Sanger as well as Gamble and other
American birth controllers until 1952, when the new peace treaty

CJG with Japanese children

was in force and the Japanese assumed responsibility for foreign visitors.

Meanwhile two trends, one gratifying and one alarming, were already in evidence. In the first place, Japan's birth rate dropped from the high of 34 per 1,000 population in 1947 to 28 in 1950 (it continued down, reaching 20 in 1954). The reduction of population growth was offset to a considerable extent by a parallel downward trend in the death rate, from 14.6 per 1,000 population to 10.9 (and on down to 8.2 in 1954). The fall in the general death rate appeared mainly attributable to improved nutrition and the control of tuberculosis and other infectious diseases.

The "take-out baby" explosion surprised Japanese and foreign observers alike. There were 246,000 legal abortions in 1949, the first year after the Eugenic Protection Law took effect. The total by 1954 stood at about 1.2 million. In fact, by 1955, induced abortions equaled live births—that is, approximately one of every two pregnancies ended in abortion. The popular belief was that young, unmarried women were having all these abortions, but Koya showed that the majority of induced abortions occurred among married women, aged 30 to 40, who had two or more living children.

The high abortion rate supplied a powerful argument for contraception, and Dr. Koya made the most of it in his discussions with Ryugo Hashimoto, Minister of Health and Welfare. In 1949, Hashimoto persuaded the Cabinet to form the Population Problem Council, of which Koya became a member. The Council had a short life. It recommended that the government carry on a contraceptive program for married couples through the Eugenic Protection Consultation Offices of government health centers, and promote both professional training and public education in contraceptive techniques and the provision of advice and supplies to parents free of charge. Diet members from rural areas did not believe their constituents would accept contraception, however; Koya himself was not certain. The Council's recommendations were rejected, and it was dissolved less than a year after it began.

What Koya needed, he now saw, was a field study to test the acceptability of contraception among rural Japanese. That was a key question; one way or another, the answer could be used to determine government policy. Secondly, if contraception was acceptable, he wanted to know what methods would be most appropriate. Lastly, what kind of results could be expected if a representative group of people did accept guidance and supplies?

There was only one problem. While he had physicians in the Institute who were trained in public health research, and it would be possible to hire nurses and midwives from the local health centers to do the fieldwork, Koya had no money in his budget for research. Nor was there the slightest hope of obtaining any from the government. In 1950, Japanese philanthropists interested in birth control were impossible to find, and American foundations had not yet surfaced in the international field of family planning and population control.

But Clarence Gamble had a long experience in financing and supervising birth control field studies. Koya wrote Gamble. Gamble was immediately interested but, as always, cautious. In the past, he had some bad luck in paying doctors $250 or so for small field tests of contraceptives—studies that were never finished or published—and was inclined to offer to pay expenses only on completion and delivery of the published report.

There was an exchange of views by letter during 1950, but even by airmail it took weeks to get a reply, so the opportunity for a full understanding at a distance of 9,000 miles was not good. Koya in 1969 recalled that Gamble contributed good ideas to the design of the three-village study. In his earlier studies, Gamble had insisted on field testing one contraceptive at a time. Koya wanted to offer his subjects a free choice of methods, to avoid criticism that he forced the use of any method. Gamble was satisfied with this approach; at the time he was interested in moving on from studies of contraceptive method in essentially self-selected samples to determining the effects of contraception on the population of an entire community.

At some point, perhaps September 1950, Gamble advanced Koya $700, as Koya recalled it; there might well have been another out-of-pocket donation during the first year; if so, it was small. Koya, in 1969 at the age of seventy-nine, was emphatic in his recollection that the money was not enough, and at times he had to dig into his own modest salary to meet expenses.

It is probable that Gamble promised more support if Koya and his associates showed good results in the first year. He placed the project under the sponsorship of the National Committee on Maternal Health in New York in November 1951, the same month Koya published his first report. Gamble then sent along a bank draft for $1,300.25. From 1951 through 1962, Gamble gave the Koya group more than $37,000, at the rate of $3,000 to $4,000 a year. After 1958, the grants came from the Pathfinder Fund.

Meanwhile, the new Population Council in New York, funded by the Ford Foundation, the Rockefeller Foundation, and the Rockefeller Brothers Fund, adopted this rising Nipponese public health star, and Dr. Koya presumably had no further complaints about "not enough."

Koya repeatedly expressed his gratitude to Gamble, as for example in a collection of fourteen papers on family planning programs and research conducted in Japan, published in English: "Dr. Clarence J. Gamble was the person who guided us in many ways in the early period soon after the war, when it was most difficult to carry out studies of this type. His assistance in our experiments in three villages and on the contraceptive foam tablets made our achievements possible."

Koya published his first report, "The New Population Phenomenon and Its Counter-Measures. A Study of Three Rural Villages," in 1951. Gamble asked that he not be identified with the study, not only to avoid any negative reaction about American interference in Japanese affairs, but also, as Koya later marveled, because he felt no special need for credit. Koya meticulously gave Gamble acknowledgment for financial assistance in a footnote, however.

Three villages in the Kanto District were selected for study:

Minamoto-mura, a mountain-side hamlet engaged in raising wheat, barley, potatoes, sweet potatoes, and other food crops. These, during the war, had replaced the previous mulberry tree and silk-worm culture. The people were poor but fairly well informed. Minamoto had been a model village in a voluntary maternal and child health program.

Kamifunaka-mura, a typical, lowland, rice-growing community on a railroad, meaning that one of five was otherwise employed, mainly on the railroad. One in three husbands had finished middle school (equivalent to junior high school) compared to only 13 percent in Minamoto.

Fukuura-mura, a fishing village on the sea, essentially a crowded cluster of small houses on the cliffs and point of land on each side of an inlet into Sagami Bay. Only 12.5 percent of the men had completed middle school. Deep-sea fishing was their main occupation, most of it by hand-lines and far offshore. The topography of the village prevented the addition of so much as one more house.

The three villages together, had a population of 6,978. The average length of marriage was sixteen years and the average number of children, four per family. One fact struck the demographers early in the study: some kind of fertility control was already in operation. The villages' annual population growth rate had dropped from 1.88 percent in 1948 to 1.35 in 1950.

Fieldwork began in November 1950 with one public health nurse in each village making home visits to talk about the various methods of contraception and continuing these visits about once a month. Koya's instruction to the nurses was "motivation first, methods later." Three methods of guidance were employed: general education, individual instruction, and delivery of contraceptive supplies. General education consisted of group lectures, the showing of lantern slides and a movie donated by Margaret Sanger, and distribution of a pamphlet written by Koya.

In May 1951, physicians from the Institute of Public Health visited 1,069 families, gathering base-line data, including what Koya called "the speed of childbearing." They again described the contraceptive methods available. These were five: condom, diaphragm, jelly, foam-powder-and-sponge, and safe period. Contraceptive supplies had been made available free of charge by the visiting nurses from the outset. The consumers were allowed to make a free choice of methods and to change methods if desired. Koya was insistent about this.

The researchers were disappointed to find that after six months' information and discussion only 507, or about 47 percent of the couples expressed a desire to practice contraception. They then decided to analyze the 562 families, or 53 percent, who were not interested. Nearly half of the women in this group, they found, were past the menopause and needed no contraception. Also, there were quite a number of widows and widowers, plus some husbands and wives not living together, a few single women, and four who had been sterilized. Excluding these and women with one or two children—three was then the customary rural Japanese goal—92 percent of the remainder—the number at risk of conception—wanted contraception.

Not all of the 92 percent were actually practicing contraception even after ten months of guidance, for various reasons including not menstruating since last delivery, already pregnant, or desire for another child (especially a boy). However, 266 families, or more than half of those who wanted to, were actually using contraceptives.

Koya found all this "rather amazing," and he made the most of it politically. He now had data showing a high degree of acceptability and substantial use of contraceptives among rural villagers. He took this information to Minister of Welfare Hashimoto in October 1951. Hashimoto took it to the Cabinet. The Cabinet accepted his recommendation: "Abortion has undesirable effects on maternal health. It is therefore necessary to disseminate contraception to decrease these undesirable effects." Encountering no repercussion to this position statement, the Ministry of Health and Welfare sent a specific plan for contraceptive promotion to the governors of the forty-six prefectures in June 1952, and then obtained Cabinet and Diet approval for an annual national budget of 22,400,000 yen—about $60,000. The joint federal-state plan called for two-for-one matching by the prefectures, so the potential maximum was around $180,000. The money mainly went for the operation of free birth control clinics in the government health centers. "From that time on," wrote Koya in his second report, "everything went smoothly and rapidly."

Koya felt it wise to explain why the Japanese chose "protection of mothers' health" rather than "limitation of size of population" as a national policy. "The limitation of size of population can never be said to be an eternal truth which contributes to the betterment of a nation. In order words, today's Japan might be in a position that requires the limitation of size of population, but she would be able to have a national policy of increasing population again in the future if her economic rehabilitation could be accomplished satisfactorily." Thus, he recognized that for some the dream of empire was at that time still not dead. In any event, he was happy to supply this rationalization for any who still believed in more babies, such as the mother-in-law or the father-in-law who scolded their son's wife about interfering with nature's way.

This was one aspect of resistance to those methods requiring the woman to make some preparation immediately preceding sexual intercourse. As Koya pointed out in his first report: "The greatest reason is, we presume, that the structure of Japanese houses is a powerful obstacle to the use of such a method since it cannot be used without others noticing it . . . Sleeping rooms in a farmer's house cannot be locked or lighted when needed. Incidentally, 80 percent of the married couples in our villages use the same sleeping room with their parents or children."

These, briefly, were the steps by which the Japanese government embraced family planning—not population control! It was clear, too, that a man from Milton, Massachusetts, provided the initiative, the encouragement, as well as the financial spark— several hundred dollars followed by some thousands more, as the need demanded.

As 1952 began, Koya started the Association of Population Health, a voluntary group supporting the Institute of Public Health. Gamble, through the NCMH, sent it $1000 in February and $2800 in December. This gift, more eloquent than words, expressed how pleased he was with Koya, whom he met for the first time in October 1952. Gamble returned to Japan in 1953, 1954, and 1955. The Japanese birth controllers honored Gamble as the first American, or indeed only foreigner, to offer them help when they most needed it. The inscription on the trophy-cup read, "Dr. Clarence J. Gamble, the Benefactor of the Family Planning Movement in Japan." One Japanese newspaper exuberantly called him "soap king of America."

They were likewise impressed with Mrs. Gamble, as Johns Hopkins-trained Dr. Minoru Miramatsu, who acted as interpreter for Koya and Gamble, remembered. Koya took the Gambles to visit the three villages. At one health center, in Odawara, Gamble made a speech to thirty or forty Japanese housewives. "All during Gamble's speech, Sarah Gamble was knitting some small thing," said Miramatsu. "That was very impressive. A few Japanese women remarked about it to me after the meeting. It was a little strange to them to see an American woman knitting while listening to her husband's talk. The comment was, 'She must be a very good housewife.'"

Miramatsu was amused that Gamble often began his birth control speeches at luncheon or dinner by quoting Mark Twain to the effect that everyone talks about the weather but nobody does anything about it. He then added that the same had been true about population. This first led the Japanese, he said, to believe that Gamble was more interested in the weather. They quickly learned better.

What impressed Koya was Gamble's single-minded dedication to family planning—not to controlling world population but to helping mothers, he said. When Koya showed Gamble a magnificent view of Fuji—there was not so much smog then—Gamble talked about family planning. When Koya pointed out the flower gardens, Gamble changed the subject to contraception.

Although the plan was to give the women of Minamoto, Kamifunaka, and Fukuura a completely free choice of methods, Gamble persisted in his eagerness to test simple, cheap contraceptives that villagers might make from materials at hand. In 1952, Gamble urged Koya to try salt-and-sponge. Three months later, he proposed the use of the salt-and-rice jelly. Koya was open to the suggestions and cooked up some jellies himself, trying both a salty seaweed food called *nori* and rice flour. He preferred rice flour, he said. The salt-and-rice jelly was squirted into the vagina with a syringe. Gamble recommended development of a bamboo applicator. thinking again of something the Japanese could make for themselves. He also suggested a glass tube containing the jelly that could be opened at both ends. The woman, he said, could insert a finger into the tube as a plunger. But this, for some, may have evoked the vision of a woman at the height of sexual foreplay with her finger stuck in the tube.

Gamble and Koya resembled two master chefs exchanging recipes. Koya, getting into the swing of things, noted some interest
among primitive farmers in the withdrawal method. Preferring
wherever possible to help people do it their own way, he came up
with another suggestion. This was a stiff rubber cap made to fit
over the head of the penis: "It is placed at the end of the penis
immediately before ejaculation and is left inside the vagina with
its shape unchanged, thus the ejaculate is retained in the cap." He
hoped Gamble would let him use some of the money for a trial of
this method. The advantage was not apparent. Gamble declined.

Reading the *Japan Planned Parenthood Quarterly*, published
by the two Doctors Amano with his aid, Gamble was curious
about one of several advertisements for contraceptives, the Sampoon foam tablet. The tablet mainly consists of potassium bitar-
trate, sodium bicarbonate, and satarch, plus 0.2 percent of the
chemical spermicide, phenylmercuric acetate. The women inserts the tablet in her vagina just before intercourse. The tablet
produces carbon dioxide when moistened by semen or vaginal
fluid.

Attracted by the great simplicity of this technique and always
persevering in single-method testing, Gamble persuaded Koya to
make a field study of the Sampoon tablet in Kajiya-mura, a
seacoast village south of Tokyo. The tests involved 82 women
over a four-year period, 1955–1958, and produced a remarkable
result. In the five years before the study, these women had 128
pregnancies at a rate of 53 per 100 years of exposure; during the
four study years, they had 19 pregnancies, or a rate of only 11.9,
somewhat lower than for the condom in Koya's other studies
(13.1). As a result, Koya recommended the foam tablet for general
use.

Koya warned Gamble that what people liked or disliked in
contraceptives was quite beyond reasoning or theory. At the end
of the first year of the three-village study, 128 out of 266 were
using the sponge with foam powder or jelly, followed by condom,
87, and safe period, 34. At the end of the second year, the condom
(125) had moved to the fore, with safe period (46) second and
sponge (44) third. Whereas foam powder or a chemical jelly had

been recommended for use with the sponge in the first year, a 10 percent salt solution was recommended in the second.

After seven years, the quickly applied condom clearly established its superior utility. In 1957 it was preferred by 38 percent, or by 50 percent counting those who used it in combination with the safe period. Among eight methods, the sponge-and-salt method dropped from 22 to 1 percent and the jelly-and-syringe from 20 to 1 percent. Diaphragm and jelly rose from 4 to 13, sterilization of the woman from 0 to 13 percent. The safe period began at 12 and ended at 10 percent. Withdrawal increased from 1 to 8 percent. Foam tablets increased from 0 to 4 percent. In toto, this was the most comprehensive study of people's habits and preferences in contraception up to that time.

Koya explained the predominant preference for the condom to Gamble thus: "It is due to that more men are cooperative when the education gets into the people." To what extent male bias crept into his observation is difficult to judge, but there can be no doubt that in the condom's use the Japanese breadwinner demonstrated an active desire to limit the number of children he had to support.

The rice jelly method, alone or with sponge, did not work out, because the cooked rice flour had poor keeping qualities. Simply soaking the sponge in brine became the recommended approach. But acceptability again was low. "One reason," wrote Koya, "appears to be that few couples have a separate bedroom, and treatment with salt solution in the night without its being known to others is difficult. Furthermore, the sponge may be seen by others when it is being dried."

The grand objective of the study was to replace induced abortion with contraception as a birth control method. Consequently, an increase of abortion among village women in the first two years gave Koya much concern. Induced abortions rose from 1.9 per 1,000 population before the study began to 4.8 in the second year. After that, however, the village rate regularly fell until it reached 1.2 in the seventh year. The induced abortion rate for Japan consistently climbed during this period, from 6 to 13.

Koya investigated the 31 abortions occurring in the three villages in 1951–1952 and found that 28 were among women who had used contraceptives but became pregnant. These failures appeared to be mainly due to faulty technique or irregular use. As the subjects became increasingly motivated and proficient, the demand for abortions to back-stop contraception lessened—in fact, the village abortions were only one-eleventh as high as for Japan as a whole.

At the end of the seventh year, 75 percent of the village families exposed to the risk of pregnancy used contraceptives. Most of the remaining 25 percent wanted more babies. It was found, not unexpectedly, that the proportion of contraceptors rose in direct ratio to the number of children, reaching 97 percent among families with five or more children.

The villages' crude birth rate of 26.7 per 1,000 population in the year before the study began fell to 15.4 and 14.6 in the second and third and 13.6 in the seventh year. Most of the impetus from guidance by the nurses and doctors occurred in the first two years. Experimental increase or decrease in the intensity of home visits beyond that point, it was found, made little difference as long as contraceptive supplies were available in the villages.

The 50 percent drop in the three-village birth rate was substantially paralleled but not equaled throughout the nation, where the decrease was from 33 to 18.4 during the same seven years. As indicated, however, in the villages the reduction was largely due to contraception, whereas for Japan as a whole legal abortions were the main instrument.

Acceptance of sterilizing operations showed a parallel trend in the villages and the nation, beginning with relatively few and steadily increasing. By 1957, more than 250,000 Japanese women had been sterilized. Men, on the other hand, showed little desire to take this exit from fertility.

The three-village study demonstrated that a well-motivated people could control their population by free choice and regular use of contraceptives, in the absence of an "ideal method," and irrespective of the comparative effectiveness of the methods available. The villages' population growth rate fell from 1.51 percent the year before the study to 0.81 percent in the seventh year. Had a national application of Koya's guidance program been possible and had the same results been obtained—he did recommend that it be attempted—Japan would have been spared the massive problems resulting from the birth of approximately 3,700,000 unplanned babies during this period.

Koya had the opportunity to prove that the three-village study was no fluke through further studies, supported by the Population Council, among coal miners and city relief clients. In 1956, five years after the Japanese government adopted family planning as a national policy, Koya, then, sixty-six, retired from the Institute of Public Health. He retired, in a manner of speaking, as an undefeated champion of action research in birth control. He became professor of public health at Nippon Medical College and president of the Family Planning Federation of Japan. For some time to come, he remained the only Asiatic birth controller with the capacity to stage a contraceptive program that could make a dent in a community's birth rate.

Koya conscientiously avoided taking credit for the general decline of the birth rate in Japan, the only Far Eastern country to succeed in cutting its rate of population growth in the 1950s. He sought to correct the general misunderstanding that "the dramatic decline in the birth rate in Japan after World War II was due to the measures taken by the Japanese government on a basis of population policy. So far as the initiation of family planning in Japan is concerned," he said, "it is essential to comment that the people started first and the government followed them." Koya did not mean to deny that the government encouraged birth control, first by making abortions legal and then by adopting an affirmative policy on contraception. But it was not true, he said, that these measures were aimed at population control. Government action was the result of the rapid increase in abortions. The stated objective of the Japanese government in 1951 was to protect mothers' health by substituting contraception for induced abortion; the purpose of the three-village study was to determine whether this was feasible.

The approach, as it turned out, was feasible. In the early years of the national program, abortions continued at a high level, but after 1962 the numbers receded. In 1970 Dr. Minoru Tachi reported that the annual total of legal induced abortions had dropped to about 750,000, a reduction of some 450,000 from the high point in 1955. Tachi estimated that, whereas in 1955 fertility limitation was 70 percent due to induced abortion and 30 percent contraception, in 1965 the situation had reversed—70 percent due to contraception and 30 percent to abortion. This was what Koya had hoped for.

For some years now, the annual birth rate in Japan has varied between 16 and 18 per 1,000 population, a rate comparable to many of the Western nations.' Japan's estimated growth rate in recent years has been in the vicnity of 1.1 percent. At this rate, its population would double in sixty-three years, as compared to 2 percent (thirty-five years) and 3 percent (twenty-four years).

Although the population by 1972 approached 105 million and crowding increased commensurately, the country's enormous economic growth and relative prosperity somewhat relaxed the determination of some Japanese families to limit their offspring to two; there was more talk of the desirability of three. Indeed, Prime Minister Eisaku Sato in 1969, reflecting the demand by some business interests for an increased supply of young, limited-skill, low-paid workers, called for a higher birth rate. Sato drew on a report by the Population Problems Inquiry Council showing that Japanese women of child-bearing age were not reproducing themselves and that this, in a long-term view, meant the population would decline rather than become stationary. This information received an alarmist press reception that shed more heat than light. If the proportion of females of child-bearing age rises, then the birth rate may rise; if the proportion declines, then the birth rate may drop.

The concept of a controlled population still troubles Japan, whose people's determination to limit family size has been exceeded only by small nations of Europe with growth rates of 0.5 percent or less. It is likely that in the future, as in the past, the people will decide for themselves.

How they have carried out their decision is also a matter of some fascination in the age of the pill (oral contraceptives) and IUD (intrauterine devices). Surveys by the Population Problems Research Council conducted by the *Mainichi* newspapers have shown that more than 50 percent of Japanese married couples practice contraception and 70 percent have used contraceptives at some time. As a rule, there contraceptors use more than one method. The condom is king (used by 65 percent). The safe period, or rhythm method, is second (37 percent). From 5 to 7 percent each use withdrawal, jelly, foam tablets, diaphragm, or intrauterine ring, and only 0.4 the sponge method.

The pill and IUDs, the widely publicized contraceptive advances of modern times, have not played a significant role in Japanese birth control. The Ministry of Health and Welfare prohibited their use in the government's more than 1,300 health clinics and maternal and child health centers, on the basis of insufficient experience and the possibility of harmful side-effects. Also, with abortion readily available there is a tendency for couples to use less-effective methods and to risk omitting contraception occasionally. A private physician, however, may prescribe either an oral contraceptive or an IUD upon the patient's request, and they are readily available in drug stores.

In 1970, on the basis of a birth rate of 18 and a death rate of 7 per 1,000 per year, the United Nations estimated that Japan's population would be 121 million in 1985. There is no reason to expect any sudden reversal of the low fertility rate. Since World War II, the Japanese system of stem, or extended, families has shifted toward the formation of small, nuclear families not interested in producing children to maintain the family line. There is less interest in the inheritance of family property and in looking to children for support in old age. With higher incomes, and more social security, parents have tended to choose durable consumer goods in preference to expenditures for the upbringing of large numbers of children. The expense of educating children presses on the household budget; in fact, "better education for children" is offered as a leading reason for keeping family size small.

chapter 14   India and the IPPF

In April 1940, Margaret Sanger wrote Clarence Gamble:
"India, in my estimation, is a bottomless sink as there is no limit to the amount of money that you can put in there. They need birth control on a large scale. . . . If I am not too old when this war is over, I should like to make my next epoch's work China and India. Don't you want to come along? It is a wonderful place to bring up those five children."

In November 1952, Dr. and Mrs. Gamble joined Mrs. Sanger in Bombay, India, where they met their daughter, Sally, and son-in-law, Lionel Epstein, and attended an international conference (Richard met his father later in New Delhi). At this meeting, the International Committee on Planned Parenthood, founded in 1948, reconstituted itself as the International Planned Parenthood Federation (IPPF). Mrs. Sanger was installed as honorary president; Lady Dhanvanthi Rama Rau of India became chairman; Dr. C. P. Blacker of Great Britain, vice-chairman; Mrs. Vera Houghton of Great Britain, executive secretary, and Dr. Helena

Wright, chairman of the IPPF medical advisory committee. Gamble's inclinations and idiosyncrasies were, of course, well known to Mrs. Sanger, but these others had not met the man. For them, in the next few years, he served by turns as gadfly, hair shirt, elephant prod, and *bête noir*.

Gamble had no official role in the IPPF, either then or later, but he was as busy as a fox in a chicken coop recruiting Christian missionary doctors who would carry out field trials of his simple vaginal contraceptives—salt rice jelly, salt and sponge, and foaming tablets—with the peasant woman who came into their mission hospitals and health centers and who had no alternative contraceptive methods available. As a matter of fact, he soon lined up a dozen cooperating physicians in such exotic places as Lahore, Madras, Ajmer, Bangalore, Kasganj, Mainpuri, Bareilly, Sholapur, Marehra, and Bombay.

In this pursuit, Gamble within the next year or two found himself in conflict with Lady Rama Rau and the London headquarters of the IPPF.

In 1952 and 1953, when he took the first of his five trips to India, Gamble could not precisely be described as a newcomer to the promotion of birth control in that area of Middle South Asia, about one-third the size of the United States but with two and a half times its population. Gamble inherited from his parents a charitable interest in the Christian missionaries of the Far East, and by 1933 narrowed this attention to the supply of birth control information and contraceptives—mainly diaphragms and jelly—to the medical missionaries whom he wrote about this offer. He had several takers, and by 1936 was corresponding with Dr. Carol E. Jameson of the Missionary Medical College for Women in Vellore. "I would like to finance some project for testing in India methods of contraception adaptable to the local situation, and was hoping you could tell me how this could best be done," Gamble wrote. He was, he said, a disciple of Dr. Robert Dickinson in his search for inexpensive contraception. Dr. Jameson told Gamble that the national hero of passive resistance against British authority, Mahatma Gandhi, when asked to endow a Gandhi bed in the Vellore Hospital, replied that if he had the money, he would rather endow a spinning wheel or a cow—"Hospitals are the invention of the Devil." In contrast to his distinction as a spiritual leader for freedom, the Hindu lawyer was a substantial drag on the birth control movement. In an interview with Mrs. Sanger in 1936, Gandhi agreed that the women of India should be free to control their fecundity but disagreed that they should practice any method of contraception other than total sexual abstinence—"If they will only learn to say 'no' to their husbands. . . . The real problem is that they do not want to resist them." Thus Gandhi extended the philosophy that made him famous— civil disobedience. Neither the Hindu nor the Moslem religions, on the other hand, actually forbids man's burning the bridge between sex as recreation and sex as procreation if he so desires. India was the first country in the world whose government recognized that it was overpopulated and in need of birth control.

In 1938, Gamble began sending $450 a year to Dr. Victor Rambo, who operated a hospital and dispensary for the Disciples of Christ at Mungel, in Bilaspur. "I am primarily interested in knowing how the foam powder works in India," wrote Gamble, "and this can only be learned from an accurately kept case history of all cases." This was not an easy assignment. Much later (1954) Dr. Gladys Rutherford wrote that it was almost impossible to obtain menstruation dates from Indian women: "The usual history is that menses cease as soon after marriage as they go to live with their husband, and after a baby is born scarcely return before the next pregnancy. It may be considered a denial of woman's chief function in life to admit menstruation." One already pregnant woman in Uttar Pradesh produced a momentary stampede away from foam tablets, telling others: "The tablets are no good. I swallowed ten of them, and nothing happened. The next night I swallowed ten more, and again NOTHING HAPPENED." Misunderstanding their purpose as well as the correct orifice of application, she thought the tablets were supposed to induce abortion.

In 1949, Rambo wrote Gamble's secretary, Sue Search: "We are not good reporters for we are overworking, all of us. . . . P.S. Why do you not come out and help us?" Rambo did find time to instruct Gamble on Indian folklore and tradition, and Gamble

learned something about local habits from this doctor who, for a
good part of every year, was taking care of a daily load of eighty
sick patients with only forty hospital beds. Rambo wrote, "A
woman came to me in the hospital just day before yesterday four
months pregnant nursing a ten-months-old infant," by way of
illustrating two points: (1) illiterate peasant women believed they
could not get pregnant as long as they were nursing a baby, a rule
that contained some truth but some exceptions as the period of
nursing was prolonged; (2) to keep on nursing the baby was
lifesaving for it, because the people were too poor to buy milk; yet
this practice was nutritionally disastrous for the nursing woman
and the oncoming baby in utero. Chronic pregnancy was only one
of the many problems to be treated, however; these ranged from
leprosy to opium addiction in infants. Skin infections and related
eye infections were most common, as typical in any unsanitary,
insect-ridden, tropical environment. The causes of seventy-five
percent of all deaths were simply lumped together as "fevers."

Ghandi was right, of course, in suggesting a lack of motivation
on the part of the uneducated Indian woman. When writing Gamble for more foam tablets, Dr. Marian B. Hall of Ajmer said:
"Some women use them, some are irregular users, some throw
them away, and some swallow them!" From Kasganj, Dr. Mildred
B. Ogden wrote: "We find they simply tire of using any method."
Whereas endemic malaria frequently acts as a biological destroyer
of fertility, Dr. Ogden found that the rise of malaria during the
monsoon season interfered with the women's contraceptive practice: "They did not feel well enough to bother."

The intolerable heat as well as dampness likewise undermined
the best of contraceptive intentions. Jellies formed molds or fer-
mented, chemicals deteriorated, and plastic spoons dried out and
curled up in a few months. In addition, the one-room peasant hut
was not an ideal site for contraceptive preparations. There was no
privacy, no plumbing, and no place to store contraceptive supplies
out of reach of the curious hands of small children or roving
monkeys.

In any event, the house was not necessarily the scene for sexual intercourse. The Indian farmers frequently lived huddled together in walled villages, not only as a traditional feature of feudal agriculture but as a means of protection—in the mortality lists "killed by wild beast" was a not infrequent cause of death in tiger country. The farmers owned or leased small landholds outside of the village and left for the fields early in the morning. They frequently had sexual intercourse in a rice paddy or pea patch when the women brought them lunch. The provident woman might carry foam tablets tied in a corner of her sari, but such preparedness would be unusual. Many a medical missionary threw up his hands in despair when a woman, having used up her free contraceptive supply, simply failed to come back to the dispensary for more, and got pregnant again.

In contrast, the high-caste, English-educated Indian woman knew about family planning and practiced it. Such cities as Madras and Bombay had municipal maternal and child welfare centers offering instruction on contraception. Their standard method was the "Dutch cap," as the English called the vaginal diaphragm.

The political as well as medical attitudes toward birth control among most educated Indians were different from those in the United States, where the medical profession had dragged its heels until late in the 1930s and the federal government did not adopt a nonobstructive public health approach to family planning until the 1940s. Indian leaders, other than Gandhi, exhibited no inhibitions about contraception; they frankly discussed the combined health and economic problems of over-population. The upper-class knew what it meant when public health doctors said the infant mortality rate in India was about 125 per 1,000 live births and, in some sections, ran as high as 200 to 400, as compared to a reasonably good rate in Western countries of 25. Or that, in the long run, a birth rate of 40 to 50 per 1,000 population per year represented a social and biological effort of poor people to balance these infant losses with surviving children. They knew, too, that it was a vicious circle. The total annual death rate of around 20 per 1,000 population, including mothers and fathers, was about twice that of Western countries. Adult life expectancy was short; characteristically, even an enlightened Indian woman may speak of herself as old in her forties. Likewise, the rigors of life are such that the Indian laborer after he reaches the ripe old age of forty-five, is inclined to sit back, and if possible live with his children and merely contemplate life.

Lady Rama Rau, a Brahman and professionally trained social worker, was founder and president of the first national voluntary birth control organization in the Far East, the Family Planning Association of India, started in 1949. She was the wife of Sir Benegal Rama Rau, born in 1889, son of a physician, and likewise of the highest Hindu caste. Sir Benegal went to King's College in Cambridge, joined the Indian Civil Service in 1913, and was knighted in 1939. He rose in the Indian government, holding various high commissions in its financial affairs, becoming governor of the Reserve Bank of India in 1949 and at times serving as Indian ambassador to the United States and Japan. Lady Rama Rau, who was born Dhanvanthi Handoo and wed in 1919, bore two daughters. Her own mother, married at eight, had twelve children.

Lady Rama Rau exerted some influence in the decision of the National Planning Commission to make a countrywide family planning service a part of India's First Five Year Plan. Thus, in 1951, several months ahead of Japan, India under Prime Minister Nehru became the first government to adopt birth control as a national policy; the restrictions on methods, however, probably set back many years the implementation of an effective program.

Lady Rama Rau likewise was a central figure in structuring the International Planned Parenthood Federation. The IPPF news letter described her at the Bombay conference as "one of the world's most remarkable women . . . Lady Rama Rau possesses the ability to command with all the charm so necessary for success in a woman. Tall, noble in appearance, always exquisitely dressed, she has a warm deep voice. . . . No comment was more generally heard than this: 'How can Lady Rama Rau do all she does and remain so serene and poised?'"

To anyone who knew Clarence Gamble's desire to take the shortest paths in spite of organization regulations, and to persuade others to do what seemed to him best, it would seem inevitable that he would come into conflict with an organization set up with rigid divisions headed by a strong, authoritative, if charming, personality. The regional system of jurisdiction developed by the IPPF also became a critical factor in the operation of his contraceptive enterprises. At the IPPF top was the governing body, made up of the officers and a council. This group of nearly fifty persons represented four parts of the globe: Europe, Near East, and Africa (office: London): Indian Ocean area (Bombay); Far East and Australia (Singapore), and Western Hemisphere (New York). These regions in turn were made up, at the outset, of seventeen national planned parenthood associations and these, of a larger number of local family planning associations. The organization resembled the Planned Parenthood Federation of America, a national alliance of state and local chapters, except for the IPPF's interposition of regional offices. These were considered to have jurisdiction over voluntary birth control organizations of countries within the region.

Considering that the world family of nations numbers roughly 150 and that the distances were great, that IPPF members were few, and that their dollars, crowns, yen, rupees, guineas, and lire were meager, the IPPF was an exceedingly ambitious undertaking. It was impractical for its governing body to meet more than once or twice a year; going to meetings meant the channeling of large chunks of every budget into travel expenses, in effect giving travel a higher priority than contraceptives. It was necessary in the meantime to depend on correspondence for communication, a laborious and time-consuming process that as easily leads to misunderstanding as to agreement and action. Often, the problems that were being raised at the beginning of the year were still being considered at the end of the year, and into the following year.

Such an organization requires dependability of its officers, a steadiness in its course, and administrative willingness to refer and defer, often euphemisms for much red tape and little progress.

Altogether, to make such an organization operate smoothly the emphasis has to be more on form than on substance. As an ectoplasmic extension of international travel, the social and cultural seemed to be the more important, or at least more conspicuous, aspects of each international conference, as if the high-born and well-met got together to taste the roast beef and wine and discuss the plight of the low-born, ill-born, or not born. Some participants, of course, were objective about it. Mrs. Dorothy Brush, rich but sensible and plainspoken, pointed out that the era of Lady Bountiful was fast coming to a close; in her travels, she found poor and less-favored races bitten by the bug of nationalism and independence, hypersensitive about white condescension and belligerently demanding a part of the action.

India, Pakistan, Ceylon, and Burma comprised Lady Rama Rau's IPPF domain. It was this area, more or less by virtue of the squatters' rights common to all evangelical Christians, that Gamble chose for the next extension of his own ideas about birth control. These were mainly two: wherever he could find them, to bring interested citizens of the community together in family planning associations that would support public education, clinics, and services to women in their homes, and to continue his search, through laboratory and field tests, for a cheap, simple, safe, effective contraceptive that would help poor parents regulate the size of their families. While population control might be a desirable and inevitable result, and he personally regarded genetic improvement of human stock as a desirable goal, he put his emphasis on the health of mother and family, aware that racial and national groups did not like to be told that it would be a better world if *they* cut down on *their* kind. When Mrs. Brush, editor of the IPPF news letter, *Around the World News of Population and Birth Control*, seemed to put too much emphasis on population reduction, he told her so. And when asked by nationals of another country, "Are we overpopulated?", his answer was, "That's for *you* to decide."

On the other hand, Gamble—always the doer, never the diplomat—could hardly have picked a less propitious moment in

India to spread the news of the Great Cause. Typically, he did not seem to realize, or at any rate, admit that he was "batting on a sticky wicket." He almost invariably reported his activities as "hopeful," "promising," or "progressing"—this in a twenty-year period in which India's population grew from an estimated 350 million to 550 million, an increase equal to the population of the United States.

Gamble worked mainly with white medical missionaries, sometimes themselves the objects of suspicion or resentment in the eyes of Hindus and Muslims. As he came on the scene with his salts, sponges, and jellies, the Indians and the Pakistanis had, in 1947, just won independence from the British Empire. For all students of India, insiders and outsiders, Harvard public health doctors, Rockefeller Foundation experts, or others, there was the "bottomless sink" riddle—the problem that India could not solve its difficulties because they were too big to solve.

At this juncture, Clarence Gamble chose to see what he could do about freeing the poor women of India from the grind of overreproduction. At first, he got on well with Lady Rama Rau. In November 1950, he had a cable from his brother, Sidney, who was in Bombay and said she was in desperate need for a gross of diaphragms and jelly tubes. He quickly obliged her, and also sent his recipe for a homemade contraceptive, salt rice jelly. She appeared quite open to his proposal for experimentation, and wrote him that she had a village in mind—"We have the confidence of the women in this area and could instruct them to use this homemade jelly. . . . I shall look forward to getting the details from you." In 1951, he wrote her: "Have you thought further about the possibility of trying an experiment? . . . I believe that I can find the funds to hire an Indian woman to visit families and give them birth control instruction and supplies." A month later, she wrote him that plans for an "experimental center" near Bombay were well advanced and she hoped to start a study of various inexpensive contraceptives as soon as the monsoon rains stopped, in October: "We are trying to keep to the lines you suggested." Manpower was available, and she did not need financial aid at the outset—"We hope to take you up on your offer of financial help for a second experiment in another rural area. . . . I shall let you know as soon as I get news." Months later, Gamble wrote asking for news. She replied inviting him to the international conference on planned parenthood in 1952, but not mentioning the proposed experimental center. Dr. Abraham Stone from the Margaret Sanger Research Bureau, she said, was in Bombay as a birth control consultant to the goverment, and helping Dr. C. P. Blacker plan a pilot study using the rhythm system. "I myself have little faith in it, and rather deplore the time and money that the authorities are prepared to waste on these experiments," she said. Gamble replied: "Like you, I have little faith in the rhythm method, especially for use in India. . . . What is the news of the village experiment for which you said you had funds?" The correspondence petered out at this point and nothing came of their proposed project.

The Procter & Gamble heir soon became a source of irritation to the Brahman lady. Anticipating the upcoming conference in Bombay, Gamble in 1952 wrote William Vogt, national director of the Planned Parenthood Federation of America in New York: "The Family Planning Association of India on which much of the responsibility for the November meeting will fall seems to be a rather weak organization. Dr. Hannah Peters, 'writing for Lady Rama Rau,' said they did not have funds enough for a survey of contraceptive services in India." Gamble proposed to make a grant to the FPA of India, both for research and to help with conference expenses, and did give $1,000. He sent copies of his letter to Mrs. Ellen Watumull, president of the Watumull Foundation of Hawaii, who gave $5,000 for the conference, and also to Mrs. Vera Houghton in London. It is not improbable one also fell into Lady Rama Rau's hands. If so, she could hardly have found Gamble's estimate heartwarming.

A few days later, he wrote Lady Rama Rau a fairly sharp note: "Mrs. Sanger tells me that you have been discussing a birth control clinic in Bombay under the Family Planning Association where various birth control methods can be tested and compared.

I . . . think that funds for testing of birth control methods can be much more effectively expended through other clinics. I have been told that Indians will hesitate to come to a clinic which is exclusively for birth control instruction. . . . More serious than this is my discovery in this country [United States] that if one method is advocated in any group it is almost impossible to persuade other members of that group to use a different method." This comment bore on the fact that Bombay had diaphragm-and-jelly clinics only.

Lady Rama Rau, it became apparent, was not going Gamble's way. The precise nature of his discontent was not articulated in the record—she was, unlike him, not eager for argument. The logical deduction is that not only did he irritate her but that they represented opposites in approach, methodology, and rationale in the delivery of contraceptive services. She meanwhile listened to Dr. Helena Wright.

Dr. Wright, a practicing gynecologist in London and an outspoken leader in the emancipation of woman, was convinced that indoctrination of a woman in pregnancy control should begin with a medical examination by a specialist in gynecology—not just any physician—and then proceed with the fitting of the contraceptive implement of choice, the diaphragm, and should involve appropriate instruction in its use. Any alternative approach simply did not show proper respect for the woman as an individual. In the absence of a gynecologist, it was better to do nothing at all.

In India, this was tantamount to doing nothing at all. Dr. Wright's preference for the diaphragm-and-jelly method and insistence on a gynecological examination persisted, even when it became widely recognized that such an approach was impractical in any country with vast numbers of indigent women in need of services, and with few trained physicians—much less gynecologists—to provide such services.

Dr. Wright, surely as outspoken and strongminded in her beliefs as Gamble was in his, had a way of contemplating the American doctor as if she had just caught him walking down

Harley Street flagrante delicto. In an interview in 1970, Dr. Wright was still steadfast in her view that contraceptive practice should be undertaken only under direct supervision of a practicing doctor and that this effectively eliminated Dr. Gamble and his "simpleminded methods" from serious consideration. "The first point and one to which no one has given proper attention . . . is that Dr. Gamble was not a real doctor," she said.

Such a statement might surprise anyone who knew that Gamble graduated second in his class at Harvard Medical School and trained in internal medicine in Massachusetts General Hospital, but it was not inconsistent with the common viewpoint of practicing physicians that a doctor is not a doctor unless he sees patients. "As far as I know, he never treated a single patient for contraception," Dr. Wright went on. "This is basic. . . . In a way, it is the proper explanation of what happened. My first clash [with him], and this was a clinical clash, was in Bombay in 1952."

Dr. Wright was there for the conference and to teach Indian doctors the diaphragm method. She said that Dr. Gamble sought her out, questioned IPPF contraceptive policy, and quickly came to the subject of salt as a spermicide. All one had to do was increase the concentration of salt in the vaginal fluids and the sperm would be killed "as if almost physiologically," she quoted him as saying. "Surely you realize," she said to him, "that if you put a hypertonic solution in the vagina you will produce such an excess of the vaginal secretions that it will be intolerable to the patient."

Whatever the irritability of salt in the vagina, it was plain that Dr. Gamble irritated Dr. Wright. Gamble, she said, would not listen to her. So they disagreed from their first encounter. "There was no way of stopping him," she said. "But there is a curious thing about that man. We disagreed, not exactly in a friendly way, but in a quite different way that had no enmity in it. He could not move me in what I thought was right. I couldn't move him because I didn't think he knew what he was talking about." In retrospect, "You have no idea how glad we were when that man was gone—all the harm he did. I'm a living fossil though, and when I meet him again we'll have some wonderful conversations."

Gamble and Lady Rama Rau had no opportunity for a meeting of the minds at the seven-day Bombay conference. She was occupied as chairman and hostess and he, among other things, was busy lining up missionary doctors for field tests. He paid the expenses of several of them to come to the conference, and daily invited them to lunch. This gave Sarah Gamble and Sally Epstein enjoyable opportunities to predict how soon after they sat down at the table the topic of conversation would turn to contraception, and to see what would emerge from Gamble's coat pockets; he habitually stuffed them with whatever he wanted at hand. In due time, he was bound to bring out a sponge, jelly tube, plastic syringe, or a letter.

Lady Rama Rau—not a doctor, of course—did seem to demonstrate an appreciation of Gamble's broader outlook in her review of family planning in India at the IPPF conference in Stockholm in 1953:

> We are today only tackling the cities. . . . We cannot at the present moment reach out into the villages. The villages have no communication. It takes a very strong person, and people perhaps much younger than myself, who could be able to tramp for miles or go by bus or by bullock cart into the villages to reach the people there. Conditions in the villages are very different also. There is no privacy; there are no lavatories; they use the fields. You cannot use contraceptives . . . that today are in use and which we are recommending in our clinics.
>
> . . . I would like those of you who are research workers, who are experts . . . to devote a little more time, a little more energy, to the search that we are clamouring for to make contraceptives easier, so that we might be able to spread them with less trouble than we can possibly do at the present . . . so those who have neither doctors nor nurses, nor hospitals to go to, might still be able to use some sort of contraceptive method that would not require the aid of doctors and nurses. If it is necessary to have doctors and nurses it will be a long time before these people can be served, for doctors and nurses do not grow on trees; they have to be created.

This, surprisingly, was far more a Clarence Gamble than a Helena Wright message. The first and second annual reports of the IPPF, 1953 and 1954, likewise showed a friendly attitude toward Gamble. In the 1953 report, under "Field Work," was the following excerpt:

Following the Bombay Conference, Dr. Clarence J. Gamble (U.S.A.), and his son Mr. Richard Gamble, a graduate of Princeton University and a candidate for a Ph.D. in sociology at Columbia University, toured extensively in India and Pakistan, and visited also Ceylon, Hong Kong, Japan, Singapore, and Thailand. In India, a number of experimental studies were instituted into simpler methods of contraception. The formation of family planning associations was assisted in Ceylon and Pakistan and other financial aid was contributed by Dr. Gamble and his son for setting up of clinics. In Bangkok (Thailand), where the first family planning clinic had already been started . . . application has been made to the Government for a charter for an association. In Japan, representatives of various organizations were brought together to discuss a national federation. The Singapore Family Planning Association was enabled by Dr. Gamble to send its Vice-Chairman, Mrs. M. K. Butcher, to Kuala Lumpur (Malaya) to help form the Family Planning Association of Selangor.

In the same spirit of approbation, the IPPF annual report for 1954 made a longer statement on Gamble's work under "Field Activities":

Dr. Clarence Gamble and his son, Mr. Richard Gamble, in a four-month's trip around the world from January to May 1954, visited 13 countries, representing the International Federation in the following seven: Ceylon, Hong Kong, India, Japan, Malaya, Pakistan and Singapore. Exploratory visits were made to the remaining six countries of Burma, Egypt, Formosa, Indonesia, Lebanon and Thailand.

Dr. Gamble and his son found everywhere many people interested in birth control and of the opinion that contraceptive advice should be made available for health and economic reasons. . . .

In Pakistan, Dr. Gamble and his son were able to review the progress made by the Family Planning Association which had been formed in Lahore during their previous visit in 1953. A new association was moreover formed in Karachi. . . .

In Ceylon, Dr. Gamble arranged through the New York Committee on Maternal Health for the Family Planning Association there to have the assistance of Mrs. Margaret F. Roots. . . .

In Burma, family planning was found to be a new idea and, as in Thailand, there was the feeling that the country could support a larger population. For families with more children than they can afford to support, it is hoped that guidance on family planning can be made available through existing health centers.

Dr. Gamble reported that many leading citizens in Indonesia favour a family planning programme. Although some islands, like Sumatra, have room for more people, there is little hope of being able to transfer families from the more densely populated islands, such as Java.

Dr. Gamble, in his report, warmly commended the work being done both in Singapore by the Family Planning Association, then operating nine clinics, and in Hong Kong where the Kowloon clinic of the Family Planning Association had the biggest number of attendances ever previously encountered at a single clinic session.

Kuala Lumpur, the capital of Malaya, was also visited where the Family Planning association of Selangor had been formed the previous year and two clinics are now active.

While Dr. Gamble was in Formosa a petition of the Government by 34 people for the registration of a family planning association was granted.

"Much valuable information was collected," the report concluded, "and new names added to the mailing lists as a result of this four-month's trip. . . . To Dr. Gamble and his son the International Federation is indebted."

From the standpoint of promotion and organization, Gamble and son had done a rather remarkable piece of work in their two trips. At the same time, the IPPF carefully disclaimed any connection with fieldwork done by private individuals who did not have the full authorization and sponsorship of the national or regional organizations in the areas concerned.

Throughout 1953, Gamble looked for a way to integrate his fieldwork with the IPPF. The organization struck him as being in a "nebulous state." As an opener, he suggested to Mrs. Sanger that "Dick and I might be field workers for the . . . Federation." Mrs. Sanger replied that she would be glad to appoint the Gambles as field representatives but didn't think it a good idea. She offered two reasons. The first was that the Planned Parenthood Federation of America, although an IPPF member, did not relish competition from the IPPF for American contributions. Secondly, said Mrs. Sanger, "I hope you are not getting yourself involved in red tape . . . I am willing to sign this agreement for you and your son

Dick, but I tell you, frankly, I do not like it. I would like you to be a field organizer definitely for the International Federation, with no strings tied either financially or otherwise with any local group."

As the IPPF's 1953 conference in Stockholm approached, "It was in my mind," wrote Mrs. Sanger, "to propose . . . that you take my place as President . . . There is no one I would like to see or who could do this job better than you. I do not want to see the International controlled by any national organization, either of the FPA of London or the PPF of New York . . . The International must be over all and if it is properly organized we could even have contributions to this organization exempt from taxation and financially independent of any local group." (Mrs. Sanger was persuaded to stay on, despite recurrent ill health, until Mrs. Elsie Ottensen-Jensen of Sweden succeeded her as president in 1959).

Gamble did not take Mrs. Sanger's advice. In September, he wrote the IPPF Executive Committee proposing that he and Richard represent the organization on visits in 1954 to India, Pakistan, Ceylon, Burma, Thailand, Singapore, Indonesia, Hong Kong, Taiwan, and Japan. He also planned to go to Egypt and Lebanon, where there were no FPAs. In December, he wrote again that they were leaving for Cairo on January 16, 1954: "Are we to represent the Federation?" The London office was now sufficiently moved to ask its executive committee for a mail vote. The consensus was favorable, with the usual conditions—that the Gambles obtain regional and national clearances of their birth control activities in countries where there were FPAs and, in countries where there were no FPAs, that they act wholly in a private capacity.

Meanwhile, Dr. Gamble had given Lady Rama Rau further offense. At some point, probably in Stockholm, he had mentioned that he could not test the salt-and-sponge method on American women because they would not accept it. Gamble wrote Mrs. Sanger in 1953: "I heard that Lady Rama Rau felt that I was using Indians as guinea pigs with a birth control method that had not been tested either for safety or effectiveness. She may not have heard of the test by the Margaret Sanger Research Bureau and I hope the enclosed letter will reassure her." Gamble wrote Mrs. Rama Rau a fairly exhaustive letter; the following paragraph was most pertinent:

> To test a new and untried method in the United States is at present almost impossible. The knowledge of birth control is so widespread that most people know of the condom and the diaphragm techniques and are not ready to accept anything else. . . . Even if the salt method could be tried in this country it would not give information as to whether it was acceptable and effective under Japanese or Indian conditions.

Only the uninformed could accuse Clarence Gamble of class discrimination in his choice of guinea pigs. From time to time, he attempted to test various aspects of contraceptive application on his wife, the wives of friends, his fieldworkers, and his secretaries. He was not uniformly successful in obtaining their cooperation, to be sure.

Also at Stockholm, he encountered some resistance to his conviction that the best way to promote birth control of any kind was to send out fieldworkers to find the interested people, lay and medical, and bring them together in community organizations and clinics. If there was anything that he had learned in his long American experience, this was it. Opposition or ignorance tended to isolate and neutralize local interest; it took an outsider, someone interested in the Great Cause but detached from local conflicts and jealousies, to furnish the spark and initiate action, often with the help of a little outside money to stimulate local giving. It wasn't important that this particular person be (or not be) a doctor, nurse, or social worker. More important was that the person, usually a woman, should be enthusiastic and energetic and have an agreeable personality. The combination of qualities desired were those of a missionary and salesman. One might add, it would help if she loved to travel and loved to talk.

The value of such an outsider—not to come in and arrogantly take over, but to act as a catalyst, bringing in the latest information from other parts of the world and seeking to identify local counterpart persons and stimulate community support for

The Bangkok meeting, 1963

Christopher Tietze

Margaret Sanger's last trip to Hong Kong, 1963

Yoshio Koya, 1950

them—had been established by large private philanthropists for a half century. By design, the outsider displaces the power and the glory from himself to local leaders and their communities. This approach had worked well over the years for the Rockefeller Foundation in its international health program. Modesty was an essential. Credit-grabbing for the outside sponsor spelled failure.

In any case the point for Gamble was that mankind needed family planning everywhere but was not practicing it in most places; the thing to do was go look for opportunities and to get something started wherever and whenever possible.

If Gamble had been highly verbal, if he had forensic talent and interpersonal skills matching the energy and enthusiasm that burned within, he might have captured the IPPF. But he was not, he had not, and he did not. When he found IPPF leaders resistant to his precepts, he conceived it to be his duty to teach them the value of fieldworkers by example. Unfortunately, the questions of outside intervention and high professionalism, plus related issues, became awkward and indigestible bones of contention between the individual—Gamble—and the organization—the IPPF.

Some of the IPPF leaders—they included distinguished and accomplished persons and, of course, as honorary president, Margaret Sanger—saw their goals and objectives from a different viewpoint. This was mainly that of international relations and the diplomatic, perhaps more precisely, the bureaucratic, process. The British, who tended to dominate, were painfully conscious that they were no longer welcome in some of the most romantic places on earth, and that indigenous people of the underdeveloped countries were becoming actively resentful of exploitation or intervention by foreigners. No matter what their intentions, do-gooders from outside could easily be construed as mainly doing good for themselves *en passant*, if not actually assisting their own governments in the fight against communism. Increasingly, tropical countries with predominantly black or brown races were rebelling against their white rulers and their power groups competed for control. Nationalists took pride in their independence, but lacked economic resources. The necessity of having to accept foreign aid, much of it from the United States, denied their self-sufficiency and mocked their dignity.

The International Planned Parenthood Federation, a rudimentary replica of the World Health Organization of the United Nations, tailored its regional organization accordingly. The central organization did not initiate plans and actions to be carried out by the organizations of the member nations but rather looked to them, acting singly or as members of a region, to decide what they wanted to do. The IPPF functioned more as an agency of review, standardization, and certification, while offering what modest financial aid it could in projects that had been thoroughly debated and approved at national, regional, and international levels.[1] One difficulty of such a highly structured system was that it lacked the dynamics to move promptly. Another was that the members of an artificially structured region did not have common interests, capabilities, or rapport. Who would believe that Lady Rama Rau's region—India, Pakistan, Ceylon, and Burma—could work together. Mrs. Sanger wrote Gamble in 1955: "As I look back upon the rules and regulations and dividing up the world as we did . . . it seems to me rather a weakness to have the large areas in the hands of one or two individuals to decide what should be done and who should do it."

In brief, the IPPF told Gamble that it (a) had no objection to fieldworkers but (b) their use was entirely up to the national and local family planning associations, and (c) the International Federation would not interfere with self-determination.

In the spring of 1954, Gamble typed letters to Mrs. Sanger from various parts of the world, expressing his disappointment that there was no fieldworker in the new IPPF budget and hoping that "International may start a fieldworker soon."

Had Clarence Gamble been a bugler in the cavalry, he never would have learned "retreat." He now, in rapid succession, hired three fieldworkers of his own, Margaret Roots, Edith Gates, and Parry Jones. (Edna McKinnon did not rejoin him until 1960.) He

---

[1] With the availability of more funds, the IPPF changed its operating procedures substantially in the 1960s.

was determined to demonstrate to the IPPF what fieldworkers could do. In the trouble that ensued, IPPF leaders demonstrated, in the face of such *faits accomplis*, that they did not believe this chap would ever learn cricket.

chapter 15 Margaret Roots in Ceylon

Gamble liked to say that he met Margaret Roots on a tiger hunt and Edith Gates steaming down the Volga.

Clarence and Richard Gamble took two weeks from birth controlling for a tiger hunt in February 1954 in the South Khotir Block of the Indian jungle. They did not see a tiger, but they did bag Mrs. Roots, a Canadian widow of fifty-eight years who, with a woman friend, joined the hunting party of medical missionary friends. Mrs. Roots, mother of three grown children, left the table with her friend the first time Gamble lectured on contraception, with Dick bringing in a vaginal diaphragm to be passed around for the guests, all doctors, to inspect.

Gamble, as we have seen, had his own ideas about the qualifications of a good fieldworker in birth control. Following the hunt, Clarence planned to fly to Colombo to follow up on the Family Planning Association of Ceylon, whose members had received his support and encouragement the year before. By the time the party emerged in New Delhi, Gamble was convinced Mrs. Roots was a fieldworker at heart and invited her to come along to Ceylon, on a tryout. There was no time to coordinate with the IPPF in London or negotiate an invitation from the FPA in Colombo. Margaret Roots needed to make a decision about her future right then, so he helped her make it. He recruited her into the Great Cause, where, first with the National Committee on Maternal Health and then the Pathfinder Fund, she worked for him for the next twelve years.

Gamble did take Mrs. Roots to Bombay and introduce her to Lady Rama Rau. Not unaware of the latter's preference for professionals of her own nationality, Gamble provided Lady Rama Rau a sort of trade-off, although he did not specify it as such. He had discovered a Dr. Devi Krishna Rao, a well-trained Indian health officer in Bangalore. She had reached the compulsory retirement age for women—fifty-five. Gamble recommended Dr. Rao to Lady Rama Rau, and the latter soon hired her as medical director of the Indian Ocean Region.

Lady Rama Rau was not, in contrast, taken with Mrs. Roots. She was, as always, polite, but pointed out that Margaret Roots was not qualified to work in India—she was not trained in birth control and did not even have a college degree. If Ceylon wanted her, that was its affair. She reinforced her position on Mrs. Roots in a letter to Gamble in Singapore in April 1954: "Our work lies with doctors—and no doctor will cooperate with an untrained worker." In a letter home, Gamble happily noted that he, a doctor, had married a Simmons graduate in social work. "Two blasts have come from Lady Rama Rau," he wrote, "so I'm thoroughly in disgrace." The second was her reaction to Gamble's letter to Vera Houghton in London saying he would have Mrs. Roots keep the IPPF informed of her activities, but neglecting to mention the FPA of India.

What attracted Gamble to this gray-haired, blue-eyed grandmother was, as he wrote Mrs. Sanger, "her personality, energy, and interest." What must have immediately appealed to him was that she was a sort of walking *National Geographic Magazine*, or rather a motorized one. She and two New Zealand women had spent five and a half months motoring through sixteen countries from London to New Delhi. They had tented and cooked their meals all the way, routing their odyssey to see the work of the Save-the-Children Fund and the United Nations Children's Fund (UNICEF), which had provided her letters of introduction.

Margaret F. Roots (1895-1971) was one of those rare, blithe, but canny spirits who learn to overcome difficulties by refusing to get into a flap or accept defeat. She was born in Toronto, Canada. Ill health forced her father to move his family to Banff, Alberta, where she dropped out of college to help support the family. She married in 1918 and by 1929 was a widow with three small children. Mrs. Roots supported her two sons and a daughter through any work that gave her some freedom to be with her children. Her sons became distinguished in geology and geography and one took part in an Antarctic expedition, 1949-1952. During this period, following her daughter's marriage in Vancouver, British Columbia, Mrs. Roots served on the staff of the Royal Geographic Society in London, where the urge to travel overcame her.

Mrs. Roots traveled with the Gambles for two months, first visiting some of his Indian missionary doctors in the villages and then the FPA in Bombay. She began work in Ceylon in March 1954 and stayed until August. Uninvited the first time, she returned by invitation of the FPA of Ceylon the second time, in December 1955, and stayed a year.

In Colombo, she was staggered at the statistic that the average Ceylon village woman had eight to ten pregnancies by the age of thirty. Ceylon, now the Republic of Sri Lanka, is small in size but rich in sapphires and rubies, rubber, tea, elephants, Buddha idols, and people. Its population had grown to ten million people in large part due to the use of DDT in control of malaria. As a result of DDT spraying against mosquitoes, the death rate was cut 40 percent in one year, from 1946 to 1947. It continued to drop to a modern world level while the high ancient birth rate persisted and brought Ceylon population dynamics to the point where births were out-numbering deaths three, and eventually four, to one.

The FPA, stimulated by the Gambles, had established a birth control clinic in the lying-in hospital in Colombo. Mrs. Roots's first major assignment was to organize the Family Planning Association of Jaffna, Ceylon's second largest city. While letters began to fly around the world about this unqualified American woman's invasion of the island without advance clearance by the Ceylon FPA or coordination with the Indian Ocean Region and the IPPF in London, Mrs. Roots was enjoying the sponsorship of the Rotary Club of Jaffna. Her identification with an all-male group raised some eyebrows, because many Tamil women were still in purdah, veiled and screened from public gaze. But Mrs. Roots followed Tamil custom and asked another woman to accompany her when she met Dr. Gunarathnam Cooke, chairman of the Rotary Club's social advancement committee. As would become customary in her community organization work, she met through him a great succession of physicians and health officers, government officials, business men, school principals, and leaders of social and church groups. She was called on to give her first talk on family planning at a Rotary Club dinner in May 1954. The members outdid themselves with a record of 78 percent attendance, plus ten Rotary-Anns as guests. It was not often that these women had an opportunity to meet with men to hear a woman speaker, nor was it any too frequent that Mrs. Roots had an opportunity to carry her message to a male audience. Both Westerners and Ceylonese had told her she would not be able to reach the men at all, yet she did so on this first occasion and the result was the formation of the Family Planning Association of the Jaffna Peninsula.

She soon encountered a familiar Indian refrain in Ceylon: "The West should only give Ceylon their BEST." This put her at a disadvantage in promoting Gamble's salt-and-sponge method—"or if you don't have a sponge, a homemade pad of old sari cloth will do," she would tell the village women. The fact that this method cost nothing worked against it.

From Singapore, Gamble advised Mrs. Roots:

Now I have another job for you. I've tested the laboratory aspect of salt, but I haven't worked on the acceptability. Please use your head extensively on how to make it easy for the natives to use it. How much should they squeeze out to keep from dripping on their bodies? Should they keep a coconut shell at their bedside with salt solution in it? Should the sponge be sunk in it ready for instant use? Would a wide-mouth bottle be better? Perhaps you can try some personal experimentation—you're one sex closer to the users than I am. A report from India says that one tester found 30% salt jelly uncomfortable. Have you tried saturated salt solution and sponge? Did your system protest? Perhaps you can learn something by talking to those who are distributing sponge-and-salt if any have started. This is an important job which I can't do. I hope you can."

There were other ways to take salt, as Gamble pointed out in noting that Mrs. Roots complained about the heat: "I think you should take at least a week in the hill country. . . . You speak of nausea. This is sometimes connected with the loss of salt which occurs from continued perspiration. I suggest that you try putting large quantities of salt on your food. Also, see if at the drug store they have coated salt pills. Try swallowing some of these to see if they make you feel better."

As so often happens to white persons in the tropics, Mrs. Roots suffered from more than one complaint during the punishing summer heat. She developed a skin cancer on her nose. A doctor advised her to go to London for radium treatment, and she did so. Altogether, her tryout was a success. Dr. Gunarathnam Cooke told her, "It was your quiet and open way of speaking that broke down all barriers." Also one Tamil physician told another: "Mrs. Roots is remarkable. We don't think of her as a foreigner."

But a letter from Mrs. Sylvia Fernando, head of the FPA Ceylon, to Gamble in August 1954 was the best testimonial both to Mrs. Roots and to Gamble in his policy which kept him a long jump ahead of the IPPF. In it, Mrs. Fernando divulged that one source of Ceylonese concern about unsolicited American aid was the hope of Ceylon's becoming a part of a Swedish adopt-a-country plan; under it, the Swedish government was trying out a different approach to foreign aid, under which it would become the sponsor of small, developing countries and, through their governments,

provide continuing financial and technical aid in health and welfare. Mrs. Fernando wrote:

> I do hope Mrs. Roots will be able to take up her work with us again in a
> few months. . . . When you first brought Mrs. Roots here I was against it
> as I felt that the money so spent would act prejudicially to any chance we
> had of being adopted by Sweden. I have set my heart on this because what
> we need is trained personnel for a period and money. The "felt" need is
> not there but easy to arouse and Mrs. Roots is the ideal person for this.
> She is not trained and my original feeling was that if you wanted to spend
> money we could have at least two trained people for less than the money
> you would spend on a western women [Mrs. Roots received $6,000 a year
> in salary]. This still remains true but it is no argument I now know—we
> want someone like Mrs. Roots to go into the highways and byways and
> tactfully put the idea across. Then it is that the trained personnel come
> in and these we have not got and that is why I am still hoping for Sweden.
> In the East just now there is a violent dislike of "white" people telling us
> about a "better way." . . . Of "whites" the most disdained are the Ameri-
> cans. There is the feeling that Americans more than any other will
> suggest things that are good for the world but not for the individual
> "black." That is why we wanted real tangible data about the salt and
> sponge. We did not want the idea to get about that we did not mind if the
> vaginas of poor women were irritated because they were inured to hard-
> ship. . . . Mrs. Roots, however, is a Canadian, she is grey haired and
> inspires confidence. We could not replace her with a Ceylonese because
> we could not find one who would be so efficient and ready to travel. . . .
> As an outsider, she would not suffer any inhibitions in approaching
> people with different religion or nationality or social status.

Talking to people in Ceylon was a matter, as a minimum, of
knowing Tamil and Singhalese as well as English. When Mrs.
Roots returned after her cancer cure, she got down to the business
of learning enough language to get by and of studying Ceylonese
customs. Later she recalled: "As in all countries, I learn at least
three words at once—a greeting with appropriate gesture; "thank
you, that is very good;" and "where is the p.o.? At the post office,
there is always a person speaking English."

Lady Rama Rau had said at Stockholm that it would take a
strong person, someone perhaps much younger than herself, to
take to the road and go back into the villages. Mrs. Roots did it at

the age of sixty. Of course, she had the good sense to organize herself for this undertaking, in which she was technically under the supervision of the Ceylon FPA on loan from the National Committee on Maternal Health. She chose as her requisite woman traveling companion and national counterpart Mrs. Devi Pathmanathum, a Tamil Hindu from the FPA in Colombo. She rented an automobile and hired as a combined driver, assistant, and interpreter a man named Samarasinghe, who was Singhalese and Buddhist. With them, she traveled the back roads of Ceylon.

Mrs. Roots visited the rubber and banana plantations and the tea estates. She talked to the managers, overseers, workers, and the Commissioner of Labor. She talked to paddy field workers, gem diggers, fishermen, physicians, health officers, mayors. In one summer month in 1956, she talked to more than 1,000 of such people. She made a point of talking to religious leaders. She talked to Muslims, Hindus, Sikhs, Buddhists, Taoists. At the cost of some study, she found in each relevant religion the exact working of their own texts bearing on marriage responsibilities and contraception. Often the local priest's knowledge was based on hearsay, or garbled tradition. When Mrs. Roots quoted the Koran to Muslims, she felt a bit like the Devil quoting Scripture, she said.

In talking to people, she tried to do so in their level of experience. "What is your most vaulable crop?" she would ask rice workers, and they would answer, surprised at her ignorance; "Can't you see? Rice, of course?" "No, no" she would say, "it is not rice," and then in response to their puzzlement, "Is not your most valuable crop your children?" They would laugh and agree. She continued: "Do you plant your rice close together?" The villagers would explain how rice should be planted and grown—with adequate spacing between rows. Finally she would come to the point: "And should there not also be spacing for your most valuable crop, your children?"

Mrs. Roots used the special techniques in getting along with doctors that had originated with Elsie Wulkop and been passed on by Gamble. The problem was to avoid having the physician look down on her as an uninformed layman posing as an outside authority on birth control. One way was to say that she was there, wherever she was, not to teach but to learn from the professionals. In fact, of course, she did wish to teach. Another way was to hand them reprints of some relevant information written by physicians.

Politically, Mrs. Roots found cooperation from the start. The Ceylon government neither openly opposed nor espoused family planning. Like good American politicians, Ceylonese officials waited to see what the people wanted before committing themselves. When she sensed one was resistive, Mrs. Roots would maneuver her argument to prevent him from saying, "No." Her best argument was an economic one; the more children, the more schools would be required; the more schools, the higher the taxes. If she encountered a Minister of Finance who looked on mothers as the source of much-needed soldiers for defense of the country's borders, she would point out that a baby now was not of much use to the army until fifteen or eighteen years after he was born; and meanwhile the advancing technology of warfare required smaller numbers of highly educated men to operate its tools of destruction. The more schools a country had to build, the less money it would have for defense now.

From the standpoint of folklore and custom, Mrs. Roots felt that she never could learn enough. She was careful not to walk into a room ahead of the man; in Ceylon, the women were followers. On one field trip, she was accompanied by a pretty, dark-haired American girl, Mimi Coletti. They stopped at a temple to see one of the enormous statues of Buddha. A monk, brown-skinned, wrapped in an orange robe, with one shoulder bare, wanted to show them some relics. They waited for him on the verandah of his house and Mimi, seeing a cot, sat down. "Mimi, don't sit there," exclaimed Mrs. Roots. But it was too late. The monk saw her as he came back. He subsequently followed her around, wrote her letters, and offered to give up the cloth to marry her. Mimi had given him the sign that she was willing to share his bed.

Mrs. Roots's enthusiasm for travel adventures was so infectious that the IPPF could not resist news letter publication of excerpts from one of her reports (October 1965):

A day in the field with her Ceylonese colleague, Mrs. Devi Pathmanathum, is described by Mrs. Margaret Roots who was lent to the Family Planning Association of Ceylon by the National Committee on Maternal Health (New York).

Many mothers in our area have 5 to 10 children, a very low salary and poor health. Can you please send someone to talk to us? Such calls come daily now. This was from a public health inspector at Apanayaka, about 68 miles from Colombo. We arrived at his office, but chickens, a dog and a child who 'didn't know' were the sole occupants! Kindly villagers thought another office was 5 miles further on 'just past the bridge.' We came to four bridges! Finally we found his sign—on a coconut palm behind bamboo, pepper vines, orchids and cannas. D.P. knocked and shortly the PHI appeared—young, goodlooking, sleepy but pleasant. Although he had forgotten the meeting, 'Oh yes, it is all arranged.' 'How many mid-wives are there?' 'Oh, one lives vnear here—shall we get her?' Roused from her siesta, in a very becoming blue-bordered white sari she silently joined us.

Before long, the car stopped. 'We must walk about a mile, I hope you do not mind.' D.P., fighting a cold, cowered but assented. Soon a 20-foot flight of iron steps faced us and on top—a long swaying suspension bridge. We rubbed our eyes! Fifty feet below, the Maha Oya foamed over rocks where villagers beat their endless wash and bathe their persons.

Along a single-file, jungle footpath, our perehera (procession) trailed—we four and our driver-assistant with the supply bag. We crossed over paddy fields, through groves of golden coconuts like footballs (no, none dropped on us), among rubber trees and between lovely scented frangipani. Polished by many bare feet, the hard-packed path was treacherously slippery. Then a river! Off with sandals or shoes, up with saris, skirts, or trousers and we waded through it knee-deep. 'What? No end to this mile?' 'If I had said nearly two miles you probably wouldn't have come!' Although poor D.P.'s throbbing headache got steadily worse under the blazing sun, she only remarked, 'Even the climb up Mt. Everest DID end sometime.' And so did our family planning trail—at an open-sided mudwalled school. A very small boy with a very large knife, chopped open cocnuts for us—a welcome pick-up.

This 40 by 60 foot schoolroom daily holds 350 children with the overflow on woven mats in the clean-swept yard. Today it was filled with parents and tiny tots—most mothers with one at the breast (literally), fathers with one on the knee and older children outside the school fence. We rested briefly on the school benches, chatting with the district Headman and very intelligent village selectmen. The talk in Singhalese aroused keen interest and many questions. The procuring of supplies, etc. was arranged. Then we left among smiling, cheery calls of "Ayubo-van" (may you live long), said with joined palms raised.

We were tired! The river wade was refreshing and most of the way back we carried our shoes in our hands. The PHI gave us tea at his bungalow—that PHI whose caring for his people meant new freedom and independence for them. Then came the long drive to Colombo in the sparkling tropical night while D. P. nursed her aching head and I removed a huge, full leech from my foot! It all added up to a day in a fieldworker's job in Ceylon.

Mrs. Roots made friends wherever she went, and, as she moved from country to country, acquired a large extended family of "adopted children" who wrote her as mother, sister, western grandmother, aunt, or simply "dear friend." Even elephants remembered her, according to one anecdote that she loved to tell. In Kandy, a city in the mountainous interior of Ceylon, where she talked, among others, to 450 policemen about family planning, an Anglican minister named the Reverend Ratnarajah invited her out to watch an elephant clear a wooded hillside for a new boys' school. The elephant, with an almost naked black mahout sitting on its head, knocked over trees and after they had been trimmed into logs carefully balanced and lifted the logs onto a truck. The elephant's name was Majah and the mahout's Mohammad Ali. Majah took a mid-morning break when she grew tired and Mrs. Roots made her acquaintance while the great beast was drinking water and eating bananas. "Her beady eyes looked steadily into mine as I talked to her," said Mrs. Roots. Some months later, as Mrs. Roots was driving through Kandy, the car stopped for a red light. Sitting in the back seat and talking to Mrs. Pathmanathum, she suddenly felt a gentle tug at her hand lying in her lap and looked around to see an elephant's trunk curling through the open window, over her shoulder, and nudging her hand. The light turned green and there was much honking at the elephant and car blocking the way. Mrs. Roots had Samarasinghe pull over and stop. They went back and discovered the elephant was Majah taking a break—Mohammed was nearby. He said Majah had never done anything like that before. Presumably she recognized Mrs. Roots by smell, laugh, or voice, they decided. Mrs. Roots rewarded Majah with a hand of fourteen bananas, which made one large mouthful for the friendly elephant.

In terms of birth control, it was hard, slow work, but here and there Mrs. Roots was able to point with pride. When she returned to Ceylon at the end of 1955, a Colombo City Mission worker paid by Gamble had 500 women on either salt-and-sponge or foam tablets. The Mission, at Mrs. Roots' suggestion, gave a Christmas Party in honor of all contraceptors who had not conceived during the previous twelvemonth. The Gambles—Clarence, Sarah, Judy, and her friend Mimi Coletti, and Robert—attended the party. Mrs. Gamble and Mrs. Roots gave out the prizes—material for a blouse—to those who had experienced the "new freedom."

Later, Gamble published a study of 694 foam-tablet users, showing a drop in their pregnancy rate from 96 to 17 per 100 couples per year.

Mrs. Fernando had invited Mrs. Roots back for perhaps two or three years, but concluded that the more Gamble shipped in simple contraceptives and the more Mrs. Roots persuaded Ceylonese to use them, the less chance there was for Ceylon to negotiate Swedish aid. At the end, the FPA board wrote Mrs. Roots a letter requesting her to leave, and she moved on to Thailand, Taiwan, Singapore, and Hong Kong. The Swedish government installed a resident representative but he left in three months, his furniture still unpacked, when the Ceylonese insisted that family planning be done their way, with "no strings attached." Ultimately, the difficulties were resolved and government-to-government assistance was established. This outcome was surely no discredit to Mrs. Roots. Often, when she finished talking to a group of women who never had discussed birth control even with each other before, they would crowd around her car, smile shyly, and push one woman forward to speak for them which the driver would interpret. One such farewell she recorded in her diary: "This woman has been chosen to go get tablets and condoms each month. Give in our names, and we will use all the sponges and salt you gave us. Because we will not have extra babies, we promise we will build a school. And we will use latrines in our village. Thank you."

chapter 16   Edith Gates in Africa

If Margaret Roots might be described as a mother-earth archetype, then Edith M. Gates might be thought of as a kind of high priestess who surveyed and managed that earth. Her profession was service to women; if credentials other than a medical degree and specialization in gynecology counted, she had them. Miss Gates was a health educator and administrator whom Clarence and Sarah Gamble first met in 1926 while traveling in Russia as members of a Y.M.C.A. sponsored study tour. Sherwood Eddy, an old friend of the Gambles, had invited Clarence to go along as the group's doctor.

A single woman who hesitated to put her birth date in *Who's Who of American Women*, Edith Gates was born in Scranton, Pennsylvania. Her mother was a pioneer in the Young Women's Christian Association and women's missionary work; her father, a physician and active church leader. She received her B.A. degree in physical education at Oberlin College in 1917, and her M.A. in adult education and health education from New York University in 1942.

Her first job was as a local YWCA health educator. She was a high school physical education teacher when she decided to enter foreign service with the National Board, YWCA, in program development and leadership training in Poland and Belgium (1921–1923) and in Russia, Estonia, Latvia, Belgium, Palestine, Syria, Egypt, and Turkey (1926–1928). She then became national director of health education for the YWCA in the United States and continued in this position until 1944. For the next three years, she worked with the American Christian Committee for Refugees in Cyprus, Switzerland, and Germany, concerning herself with the repatriation, vocational rehabilitation, and immigration of displaced persons.

She was executive director of the Volunteer Placement Bureau in Honolulu, Hawaii, when Dr. Gamble came across her again in May 1954, on his way back from the Far East. It is easy to imagine that the word "fieldworker" flashed through the Gamble mind when he sat down to talk to Edith Gates. True, she had no experience in birth control—the YWCA was then notably shy about this sort of thing—but Miss Gates did have the college degrees that Lady Rama Rau missed in Margaret Roots and, what was pleasing to him, she had a long experience as a health educator, administrator, and program organizer. And she was about the right age, the late fifties, to have an itch for world travel.

Gamble talked Miss Gates into making a trip through the Far East, "exploratory" for her but "follow-up" for him. He wanted her to take a look at activities he and Richard had stimulated six to eight months before. Lady Rama Rau was not encouraging, but, despite this, he wanted Miss Gates to see what more might be done in India. From September through December 1954, Edith Gates, informally attached to the National Committee on Maternal Health, toured Japan, Taiwan, Hong Kong, Thailand, Burma, East Pakistan, India, and West Pakistan and then jumped to countries more familiar to her—Lebanon, Cyprus, and Greece—ending in Switzerland.

Gamble's first impulse was to send Miss Gates back to India, but Margaret Sanger objected: "It is going to be another turmoil." In her talks with Lady Rama Rau it was her understanding "that while they need money . . . they would almost rather do without the money for field work if it has to be done by foreigners, and especially by Westerners. Perhaps I am more plain-spoken than Lady Rama Rau."

Miss Gates leaned toward the Middle East and Africa, and Gamble now thought to see if the IPPF would like her to become its field representative there. At that time, these areas were a vast birth control wasteland. The IPPF had a member organization in the Union of South Africa, but between there and Egypt was nothing. Egypt—the United Arab Republic—had no family planning association, but the government had become interested in the population problem and, following the visit of the Gambles, in late 1953 established a Joint Planning Committee to Study Population. Subsequently, it opened twelve government-financed family planning centers.

By offering Edith Gates to the IPPF, Gamble extended and amplified his whole argument with the IPPF about fieldworkers. Gamble, disinclined to wait on the IPPF, offered her a fulltime job as field representative of the National Committee on Maternal Health. He spelled out what he wanted her to do in a letter as 1954 ended:

The chief objective might be termed a group of active, intelligent community leaders, ready to join together into an organization to make birth control available to the citizens . . . Bisexual committees have been found effective . . . but these . . . may not be possible in the Near East. . . .

To provide the initial expenses and supplies needed by a new birth control committee is a very valuable investment. . . . Before you offer more than $300 in any one place, let's talk it over by letter.

Initial services should, I think, be centered around the diaphragm-and-jelly method. This is now the most widely known and is considered by physicians to be the most successful when used. . . . It also has the advantage of making the local doctors feel that they will be included in the new program. . . . The less expensive methods of foam tablets or salt can be discussed as a possible future project, if and when the local doctors approve. Supplies of these can be offered free for testing. . . .

For education of the physicians we are ready to send copies of Dickinson's *Techniques of Conception Control.* . . .

The length of time you will want to stay in any city will depend on local circumstances. . . . For a guess, I would say that if you meet a hopeful group . . . it may take a month . . . to help them write a constitution and make plans. . . . A subsequent return visit may be very advisable. Times in which it is necessary to await further developments can be spent in visiting other nearby countries. . . .

It will be helpful if you can give us an idea of the local public opinion by a brief survey of several or all of the various countries. . . .

Don't hesitate to give me your suggestions regarding this program and to improve it as your experience and local indications indicate.

Gamble sent copies of these marching orders to Mrs. Houghton, IPPF executive secretary, and Mrs. Nancy Raphael, European, Near East, and Africa regional director of the IPPF, as well as to Mrs. Sanger.

Edith Gates's first fulltime, six-months' exploratory tour, beginning in January 1955, took her from Switzerland to Greece, Egypt, Jordan, Lebanon, Syria, Iraq, Turkey, Cyprus, and Israel. Her second, seven-months' tour, from July 1955 on, took her to Egypt, Sudan, Ethiopia, Kenya, Uganda, Zanzibar, Tanganyika, Southern Rhodesia, and briefly, South Africa. Subsequently, she did the West Coast of Africa, and eventually returned to East Africa, and still later moved on to South America.

Many of the people in these parts of the world had not heard of family planning or birth control. Miss Gates amended the Gamble plan. Through lectures, conferences, and literature, she would introduce the subject in a short visit the first time around, then return for a second short visit to stimulate further interest, and come back a third time to organize a family planning association and stay longer. The concept of a voluntary organization was new to these cultures. Either the government carried on an activity or it wasn't done. It might not be done anyway; a tropical African "nation" in many instances was one large city surrounded by wilderness—civilization stopped at the city limits and so did the

usual modern resources and services. But a voluntary organization could stir up community and government interest in the
city.

The Gamble philosophy, of course, was quite the opposite of
the IPPF's, which was to wait for either the national family
planning association or the government to invite it in. Thus, in
the absence of an FPA and in the presence of an indifferent
government, there was no way in. If one was not overpowered by
the stereotype dislike for the white foreigner or by fear of giving
offense, however, a person—a Gamble type—could come in and
look up the few people who were interested in health and welfare
and try to get something started. If you were rebuffed—if people
believed the communist allegation of a white man's conspiracy to
commit genocide against blacks—you went somewhere else
where you were welcome. It was exploratory anyway. Whatever
done was "an experiment."

It was not all smooth sailing for Edith Gates. In 1955, Gamble
wrote Dr. Hanna Rizk of the Social Research Center at the
American University in Cairo, who was prominent in birth control, for an appraisal of Miss Gates and her work in helping to
establish the Family Planning Association of Egypt. Dr. Rizk
attempted an "objective opinion":

Everyone of those who got acquainted with Miss Gates admits that she
had a very pleasant personality and that she has been liked by all of those
whom she contacted. She did very well in arousing interest during this
preliminary stage. However, it is the general feeling that the actual
establishing of the Family Planning Association should be supervised
and carried through by the Egyptians. The reason for this is that the
opponents of the idea of family planning are numerous, and they would
attack the Association on the ground that it serves the purpose of Western countries. They even go to the extent of saying that the Western
countries are interested in weakening the Arab countries and that family
planning is one of the methods that achieve that end. Needless to say
that this is absolutely false . . . accusation . . . If the atmosphere were
different, I could not see a person who is more well-fitted for family
planning than Miss Gates.

Elsewhere, she received a more enthusiastic welcome. As she later wrote of her work in Kenya:

In Mombasa, it was the Aga Khan Moslem women that asked me to speak to them one Friday evening after their usual evening service. It was nine o'clock . . . the mothers had taken their children home from the service and put them to bed. As the young doctor drove me into town, I saw we were approaching the big central mosque. As the chairman of the group greeted me, I said in surprise: "Is the meeting in the mosque?" thinking this would not be allowed for a Christian. "Oh yes," she said, "I hope you don't mind, for you will have to take your shoes off." This I had done often in just visiting mosques, but never had I had the privilege of delivering an address at the same pulpit as the Moslem Immam had used just two hours before. It was a beautiful sight to stand up there facing some 250 women in their colorful saris or soft summer frocks, for we had the older Moslem women who kept their scarves over the tops of their heads, the next generation that only draped the scarves over their shoulders, and the modern Aga Khan ladies who wore European dress.

The notion of Edith Gates as a high priestess of birth control is not so farfetched. In Nigeria, she spoke in an Anglican church, on the invitation of the Bishop of Ibadan, before a large group of men and women.

As I drove up with my escort, I was surprised to find the dean of the cathedral awaiting my arrival at the steps of the church. Noting my surprise, he said, "I hope you don't mind but we realized the crowd would be too large, so are holding the meeting in the nave of the cathedral." . . . Though I did not accept the invitation to talk from the pulpit, I did feel the significance of the meeting where . . . such a delicate health problem could be discussed in the nave.

"As the result of these five years of work and travel," Miss Gates wrote in 1961, "there are now twelve voluntary Family Planning Associations in ten countries of tropical Africa—one in four West African states (Sierra Leone, Liberia, Ghana, and Nigeria); two in the Rhodesias (North and South), and six in four countries of East Africa (Kenya, Uganda, Zanzibar, and Tanganyika). And they all are serving the various racial groups in their countries, through their multiracial associations."

At the end of this Odyssey, Miss Gates in 1960 took over the far-ranging correspondence and educational activities of the Pathfinder Fund, in Milton, Massachusetts; she remained in this position until she retired in 1966.

When Edith Gates went into a new country, she said, the first thing she would attempt to find out was what the people *cared* about. To take one example, the Arabs were impassioned patriots. Egypt, another rebel from British colonialism, was in political crisis. King Farouk was overthrown in 1952, and Egypt in 1953 became a republic—later the United Arab Republic—with Nasser, the military rebel leader, coming into power in 1954. But the Arabs also cared a great deal about their religion and their virility, and indeed often claimed that contraception was against the teachings of Mohammed. The fact that this was *not* so gave Miss Gates a point of entry that she exploited to the fullest. One project in which Gamble involved her was the printing and distribution of a *fatwa*. A *fatwa* is a judgment made by the Grand Mufti, who is in the final authority on Moslem Law. Any Muslim who has a question about his religion may submit it to the Mufti and get an official interpretation, somewhat like a papal encyclical for Catholics.

Such a question had been asked in 1937 on birth control:

A married man has a child. He fears if he gets many children that he may be embarassed by becoming unable to bring them up and take care of them; or that he may suffer ill-health and a nervous breakdown from the inability to fulfill his duties and responsibilities toward them; or that his wife's health may be affected from repeated pregnancies and deliveries without having intervals for her to rest and regain her strength and compensate for what her body lost during pregnancy.

Does he or his wife have the right to take some scientific measures according to a doctor's advice which lengthens the intervals between pregnancies, so that the mother can have rest and regain her health, and the father would not be under health, economic or social stress?

Answer

It is allowed to take some measures to prevent pregnancy under the circumstances cited in the question, either by ejaculating outside the vagina, or by the woman inserting something to shut off the opening of the uterus to prevent entrance of the seminal fluid.

The principle is: that it is not the right of the man to ejaculate outside the vagina except with the permission of his wife and that it is not the right of the woman to shut off the opening of her uterus except with the permission of the husband.

But it may be allowed for the man to ejaculate outside the vagina without permission of the wife if he is afraid of having aberrant offspring, e.g., due to bad living environment; or due to the man being in far travels and being afraid about the child.

By analogy, it may be allowed for the woman to shut off the opening of her uterus without permission of husband if she has reasons for that.

To sum up: either husband or wife, with the permission of the partner, is allowed to take measures to prevent entrance of the seminal fluid into the uterus as a method of birth control; and either of them may take such measures without permission of the partner if there are reasons such as cited or similar ones.

Is it permissible to do a therapeutic abortion? According to the great authorities in Islam, it is permissible for a pregnant woman to terminate pregnancy in the early months before fetal movements occur, if the health of the mother is endangered.

The above *fatwa* was signed on 25 January 1937 at Dar el Efta by the Mufti of Egypt, Sheik Abdul-Majid Salim.

At the time he was in Egypt in early 1953, Gamble met Dr. Mohammed Kamel Abdul Razzak, Director of Health Education, Ministry of Public Health, who agreed to resubmit the question to the Fatwa Committee of Al Azhar University. The following additional judgment, signed by Mohd. Abdul Fattah el Enami, Chairman, was received on 10 March 1953:

The use of medicine to prevent pregnancy temporarily is not forbidden by religion, especially, if repeated pregnancies weaken the woman due to insufficient intervals for her to rest and regain her health. The Koran says: "... Allah desireth for your ease; He desireth not hardship for you. ... And hath not laid upon you in religion any hardship." ... But the use of medicine to prevent pregnancy absolutely and permanently is forbidden by religion.

Wherever she went in Muslim countries, Edith Gates carried copies of this statement, printed on a single sheet in Arabic on one side and English on the other. When she ran into opposition, she passed around the *fatwa*.

Edith Gates encountered another problem. Even the upstage IPPFers criticized her for not being married. Introduced as a birth control expert in one country, she was asked: "Did you say *Miss* Gates?" In reply, she carefully explained that following World War II she had done health education assignments for the American Cancer Society without having cancer, and likewise for the National Tuberculosis Association without having tuberculosis, and she certainly hoped that ministers had not committed all the sins they talked about.

chapter 17   No Organization Man

It is doubtful if any other American health movement has had a more turbulent course than that of birth control. The period of the embattled crusade was pretty much over and dignified management and peace-making efforts had superseded flagrant civil disobedience and confrontation by the time Clarence Gamble came on the scene. Nonetheless, as he established himself as a quick-acting strategist in getting fieldwork started, Gamble found himself in conflict with leaders of the American Birth Control League (forerunner of Planned Parenthood-World Population, Inc.), then seeking to establish its national supremacy as a federation of state and local chapters. It was a curious conflict inasmuch as Gamble and the League professed much the same family planning objectives. In a long series of incidents, alternately ludicrous and distressing, the Executive Committee of the League's Board of Directors by 1937 found it necessary to discipline him as a member of that Board. Since this involved telling a multimillionaire how he should spend his money, folly was exceeded by futility in the attempts to bring Gamble into line.

One source of these efforts was Mrs. Marguerite Benson, the League's executive director, who warned against "sacrificing the organization to the cause." To Gamble, however, the work of the cause was more important than any single organization, and not being dependent on organizations, he had little patience or understanding of their needs, realities, or viewpoints. The conflict had a rather complicated background. This was in some part related to Gamble's strong identification with Margaret Sanger and her Birth Control Clinical Research Bureau, a competing organization. The League's severest critic, Mrs. Sanger, was dividing her time between New York City, travel abroad, and her home at Willow Lake, Fishkill, New York. She was somewhat in the position of Napoleon at Elba, a general awaiting for his army to hand him back his horse and his sword.

Mrs. Sanger in 1915 had formed the Birth Control League of America, a small New York group with socialist, feminist, and labor roots. Later the same year, a more "reputable" and affluent group of New York women liberals formed the National Birth Control League. Both organizations existed more in wish than reality, and both faded from sight during World War I. In 1921, Mrs. Sanger staged a successful national conference and formed the American Birth Control League (ABCL), with herself as president. Two years later, she opened the closely affiliated Birth Control Clinical Research Bureau (BCCRB), a contraceptive clinic under medical direction and with an interest in research.

The League and Bureau operated from the same address in New York until 1928 when she returned from an eighteen-month absence in Europe and found herself in nonnegotiable conflict with a now well-established conservative board of directors. She resigned first as president and then as a board member from the League. Mrs. Sanger retained control of the Bureau, which had the financial support of her second husband, James Noah Henry Slee; meanwhile, an attempt to unite the Clinical Research Bureau with the National Committee on Maternal Health (NCMH) failed. The two principals, Mrs. Sanger and Dr. Robert Dickinson, remained both fearless and friendly toward one another. Regrettably, the same could not be said for Mrs. Sanger and certain socially prominent League ladies and professionally ambitious staff workers. On the one hand was the individual, the charismatic leader with a talented and loyal personal following and a worldwide reputation as a champion of mothers, and on the other a corporate organization with largely unknown leaders working together to structure and stabilize the birth control movement, but with no persuasive fund-raising appeal and little to offer to the many small maternal health associations operating local birth control clinics.

This is an all-too-familiar plight among national voluntary health organizations: the desire to lead interested people in one strong, unified effort; the need for a widespread constituency and the money and staff to attract it; the wish to render a service and meanwhile to impose standards and control; the problem of overcoming the opposition of older, successful, isolated local groups to superimposition of a national headquarters upon their own pioneering leadership, especially if the national headquarters is located in New York City and headed by prominent Easterners.

One problem of a national program is to get a local group interested in broader purposes than simply running its own show. Another problem is the continuous need for operating funds—for general contributions that can be used anywhere in the annual budget that the administrator and the board see fit. In fact, the most appealing kind of gift from the standpoint of the giver, the restricted or special-purpose gift, is the least attractive to executives assuming responsibility for overcoming deficits in the total operation, including the provision of regular supporting services for new and exciting programs.

All this is said here because, insofar as the record shows, Mrs. Benson never explained the position she was defending and Dr. Gamble at the same time indicated no awareness of her side of the picture. The fact was that he in a financial sense, just as Mrs. Sanger in a spiritual sense, posed a critical threat to Mrs. Benson, who had the misfortune to head a weak organization with a program usually discussed in terms of unattained goals.

Gamble first rose to prominence in organized birth control as chairman of the board of the Philadelphia Maternal Health Centers and then, in 1933, when he was not yet forty, as president of the Pennsylvania Birth Control Federation, a position from which he resigned in 1936 for the expressed purpose of admitting new blood and avoiding self-perpetuation at the top. As a matter of fact, this was one of his recommendations to the ABCL board in New York—that it limit all officers to two-year terms with the exception of treasurer. It is probable that advice of this sort did not make him popular with Allison Pierce Moore (Mrs. Louis deB. Moore), longtime chairman of the ABCL board.

Gamble first took his place on the large national board as a state delegate also in 1933, becoming one of five vice-presidents. He continued on as a delegate at large until 1946. He became a member of the Executive Committee in 1939, continuing in this position for three years. His position as ABCL board member and (after 1937) as medical field director of the BCCRB constituted a conflict of interest in the eyes of anti-Sangerites. His earlier identification with the National Committee on Maternal Health, as a member from 1929 on and as its treasurer from 1935 to 1937, posed less of a problem, since the ABCL recognized the National Committee's primacy in birth control research. The BCCRB in contrast actively dabbled in everything, including the development of clinics, community organization, and public education—whereas the ABCL quite emphatically claimed these activities to be in its jurisdiction.

It is impossible to state precisely when Mrs. Benson and Dr. Gamble first found themselves at odds. Gamble entertained his Aunt Julia with long, chatty letters on the subject. A letter in 1934, after he started attending ABCL board meetings, said that the League "is adopting a few of my suggestions." One was to hire Doris Davidson as field secretary and another was, he said, to get her out of the New York office and into the field. Miss Davidson organized a West Virginia League as a chapter of the national organization. This was something of a prize, for fewer than half of the forty-eight states had chapters at that time. Gamble himself, through Elsie Wulkop, deserved credit for three—Indiana, Iowa, and Nebraska.

Gamble pelted Mrs. Benson with questions, ideas, suggestions, and offers, during this period. For him, letter-writing was a way of life. For Mrs. Benson, however, answering his letters was a distraction that could easily have become a fulltime job. The League national headquarters in those years had only a tiny staff and an annual budget of around $100,000. In any event, keeping the Executive Committee happy had a higher priority in the executive director's list of important things to do. She often referred his letters to Dr. Eric M. Matsner, the medical director. This seemed to be a constructive course, inasmuch as Gamble and Matsner were both on the ABCL's medical advisory group, the National Medical Council on Birth Control, and could talk as one physician to another. But it was Gamble's purpose to stimulate Mrs. Benson and she could not escape his non-medical proposals. In sum, Mrs. Benson informed Dr. Gamble that he should mind his own business, and his reaction may be gathered from a letter he wrote to Aunt Julia: "The executive secretary of the American Birth Control League is proving more and more annoying. In February she sent me a letter rejecting with great superiority two personal contributions which I had offered her for special purposes. Apparently she thought me specifying the purpose meant she wasn't doing her work adequately so she went on with all the items she could think of in which the Pennsylvania Birth Control Federation wasn't as successful as it might be. I think you can see why I specify exactly what the contributions are to be used for."

Any opportunity for a Gamble-Benson friendship was rapidly receding, in sharp contrast to the cordial reception that he enjoyed at the Clinical Research Bureau from Mrs. Cecil Damon (Stenson), Margaret Sanger's executive secretary, and from Mrs. Florence Rose, her personal secretary. Mrs. Damon encouraged Gamble to pursue any project that showed promise of helping mothers. She did not hesitate to tell him when she thought he was being willful or was on the wrong track but nonetheless preserved a relationship of mutual hope that good would result.

Gamble now began to hit Mrs. Benson and the ABCL Executive Committee with some big projects—she did not put a gold star on his report card for such efforts. Instead, she and Mrs. Moore discussed his challenge to the authority of the officers, and brought a resolution before the Board of Directors on May 14, 1936:

> Resolved, that it is injurious to the progress of the birth control movement and to the American Birth Control League, and contrary to the League's policy, for an individual director to undertake, initiate or supervise any projects in relation to birth control unless authorized by the Board of Directors.

Aimed at Gamble, the resolution presented no problem to the rest of the fifty Board members; those present (Gamble was not) passed the resolution. It seemed logical that no one of them would do anything in birth control without the approval of the governing body of which they were a part. Gamble, on the other hand, was the only one with the money, time, and field staff to operate a program of his own.

Gamble enjoyed the esteem of various members of the Board, and it did not appear that Mrs. Benson had the muscle to enforce her May 14 injunction. He did however, keep her informed of what he was doing and offered the League opportunities to share in his activities wherever possible. A skeptical person might have wondered if there were not an impish defiance in the way he sometimes did it. Gamble confided to friends that he was trying to educate Mrs. Benson. Since she was trying to educate *him*, it was something of a stand-off. He did demonstrate that by taking the initiative and acting quickly Gamble and his fieldworkers were the real leaders in the field.

The fact should not have been lost on Mrs. Benson. During summer vacation in 1936, Gamble found an opportunity to talk to some ladies in Brattleboro, Vermont, Sarah Gamble's girlhood summer home, and in Harbor Springs and Petoskey, near the Gamble's summer cottage at Harbor Point, Michigan. The ladies became enthusiastic and wanted to know how to start birth control clinics in their towns. He wrote Mrs. Benson about it in September: "Since this is a project in relation to birth control as defined by the Resolution of the Board ... at their meeting last May, will you please ask them for authorization to answer these inquiries?" Mrs. Benson was not enthusiastic:

> Since you are able to travel and constantly make new friends for birth control, would you not be willing to do just that, and to leave it to the League to develop these contacts into group activity? ...
> Naturally, you were able fully to describe what was being accomplished in Philadelphia—*but* were you also in a position to acquaint the Harbor Springs group with their own state organization? ... Do you know what recent activities of Michigan are outstanding?
> ... Again I can only ask you to accept the virtually unanimous opinion of those most concerned that any procedure contrary to this code rebounds to the discredit of the movement and of the individual who fails to see its importance. Unfortunately, I am not in a position to reveal to you all the evidence which I might in support of this statement.
> There can be only two paths: one, wholehearted cooperation in the group effort. The alternative: a complete severing of all ties and becoming frankly a free lance. As you may well know, so difficult a subject as birth control hardly lends itself to successful free lance activity.
> ... I should dislike very much to bring this matter again before the Board.

Gamble replied, mildly, that he *had* put the Michigan and Vermont ladies in touch with their state leaders and they already were moving ahead with plans. He was not entirely ignorant of what was going on in Michigan: "I (CJG) have followed with interest the process whereby the seven or eight clinics organized by Miss Wulkop in Michigan have multiplied themselves to the present twenty-five. I showed the Petoskey and Harbor Springs group a map of the State with the locations of these activities." As a free lance, he had not done too badly.

At its annual meeting in January 1937, the Board reelected him as a delegate at large. To the Olympian observer it all might seem like much ado about little that could not be handled by open-handedness and mutual trust. But voluntary leaders and their professional staffs do, as a genre, tend to include people who develop what has been called "inner circle mentality," seemingly coveting and hoarding power rather than generating and transmitting it by encouraging others.

Mrs. Moore and Mrs. Benson now agreed that it was time Dr. Gamble was spanked. At a Board meeting on March 4, 1937— Gamble did not attend—they endeavored to sharpen the resolution of May 1936 condemning members who involved themselves in birth control projects not authorized by the Board. The Board, however, contented itself with an amendment: "Resolved, that nothing in this resolution applies to the regular activities of state league representatives in their own states." The Board also hedged on the question of discipline. It simply voted that if an infringement occurred, the Executive Committee would examine the facts and recommend action to the Board. It likewise was agreed that Gamble should have the opportunity to defend himself before action was taken. Thus armed, Mrs. Moore wrote him as follows:

> Certain activities financed by you in Kentucky, Florida, Puerto Rico, and North Carolina have not been cleared with the Board of Directors of the American Birth Control League. If knowledge has come to us of such projects it has been after they were initiated rather than before . . . This has embarrassed the Board and has caused in some instances considerable financial wastage in the field, time-consuming meetings and unnecessarily voluminous correspondence which could easily have been avoided had clarification of your projects been made at the proper time.
>
> The principle involved is not one of the relative merits of individual projects nor of the objectives sought. The principles with which we are concerned is that the sanction of the League is implicit in the activities of its individual directors in the field of birth control.
>
> Will you please let us have a written statement of explanation to present to the Board on April 8?

Gamble typed a precise, nine-page, single-spaced statement reviewing his activities and summarizing pertinent correspondence with ABCL officers. These, to our Olympian observer, might suggest that the League did not appreciate what an invaluable asset it had in Dr. Clarence Gamble. He was virtually a one-man birth control movement. And he did move. In his covering letter of April 5, 1937, he was a model of civility:

> By reference to this summary you will see that I reported each activity to some member of the Board, or to our Executive Secretary for transmission to the Board, before the work began.
>
> But discussion of meticulous points of chronological sequences is relatively unimportant. What is of great importance is the way in which the American Birth Control League can function most efficiently. It seems to me that we can reach the maximum of accomplishment only if every person interested in the cause of Birth Control does his part *whenever* opportunity offers. Not only does such individual activity give greater manpower for accomplishing the purposes of the League, but it also often enables individuals to open doors which are shut to "propaganda" organizations. Often, too, in situations requiring immediate action, individuals may move swiftly toward success, while a large organization, hampered by its necessarily ponderous progress, would fail.
>
> The best route, therefore, toward our goal of "every United States Child a Wanted Child," lies through a democratic state with active cooperation of all members, not through a totalitarian state in which individual initiative is rigidly controlled. . . .
>
> Our office system and procedures should contribute to, not dominate, the purpose of the League. With an ignorant, irresponsible Board of Directors, rigid control of projects might be required in order to ensure high professional standards in our clinics, but with a Board of the present caliber that is unnecessary.
>
> If we continued to restrict our activities to only those projects initiated by and in our Central Office, the net result will be a complete loss of many units of progress, and extreme retardation of others.

Gamble mailed his statement only three days before the Board meeting on April 8. It was Mrs. Moore's intention that he submit his statement to her and that it would first be referred to the Executive Committee. He made a neat end-run; he sent copies of her letter to him and his reply to every member of the Board. The Board meeting—he was there—"was to me rather amusing," he wrote in a confidential memorandum to his fieldworkers. On the agenda was "Dr. Gamble's communication to ths Members of the Board." Mrs. Moore explained, "in an irritated voice," that the Executive Committee had not had a chance to consider his statement and therefore had no report to make at that time.

Gamble's memorandum to his fieldworkers continued:

There followed a prolonged discussion of whether a member of the Board could start birth control activities or contribute to outside birth control organizations as an individual. It seemed generally concluded that he could. . . .

It was eventually decided that the motion quoted in Mrs. Moore's letter of March 10th was too drastic and it was entirely obliterated. . . .

Behind the whole discussion is the thought that I am cheering for methods which tend to remove birth control from the hands and budget of the physicians and the fear that my activities may furnish a precedent whereby persons or organizations other than the League may be allowed to organize clinics. Possibly it is more fundamentally anti-Sanger than anti-Gamble.

All in all, Gamble could count April 8 as a good day. Mrs. Sanger wrote him: "I understand that you came out a victor at the Board of Directors meeting of the ABCL. Congratulations. I trust that you will continue to press forward on getting out of that organization those who are not equipped with vision or selflessness sufficient to make the League anything more than a 'pink tea social centre' for pleasant conversation or gossip."

On April 21, however, Mrs. Sanger chided Gamble: "It discourages me to find that you still are inclined toward the policy of 'smoothing' the eternally ruffled feathers of Mrs. Benson. Frankly, Doctor Gamble, I am at a loss to understand why so much consideration must be given at all times to Mrs. Benson's wishes. She is, after all, but a paid employee recently come into the movement for the sole purpose of obtaining a good position."

In this letter, she also touched on what was soon to become the first order of business in American birth control organization—the merger of the ABCL and the BCCRB. This was a matter that had been under discussion for some time by certain members of both organizations who formed a committee of coordination to that end.

Both Mrs. Sanger and Gamble were on the coordinating committee as BCCRB representatives. Later she wrote him: "I want you to know that we all have such confidence in your judgment and ability regarding this work that you should not hesitate to make any proposals in my absence." In view of the fact that Dr. Gamble was the most active person in fieldwork in either the BCCRB or the ABCL in these years, Mrs. Damon followed up on her chief's endorsement by making him BCCRB medical field director.

Gamble was a key figure in softening Mrs. Sanger's mood to a point where merger became possible.

The merger process accelerated in the fall of 1938. Mrs. Sanger came along, protesting to Gamble: "I am the rebellious one against Boards and Committees, yet I know you have long wanted to have our own clinical work under group management [rather] than individual direction. I know the value of this but by temperament I am too impatient of its value."

The merger was consummated in January 1939 with the formation of a new Executive Committee. Kenneth Rose, who came from the professional fund-raising counseling agency of John Price Jones, was acting managing director of the Birth Control Federation of American (BCFA), combining the ABCL and the BCCRB. Mrs. Edna McKinnon wrote Gamble that Mrs. Damon saw him as a rising star: "Mrs. Benson is in the dog house with her group. . . . She is really leaning on you for support. . . . She will do anything you say for she feels that it is the only way to save her skin. My hope is that you will definitely stick to the things OKed by the board . . . and not try ANYTHING on the side for a year. . . . You will have the whole crowd eating out of your hand. (Please, that is not Dale!) "She referred to Dale Carnegie; it was a little joke they often made when they praised one another, in reference to How to Win Friends and Influence People.

Gamble wrote Mrs. Sanger: "A day in New York this last week makes me feel better about the impending merger. The Executive Committee, as Mrs. Damon tells me the names, sounds intelligent and reasonably neutral. It seems that you, with Mrs. Damon acting as proxy, are to be given a voice on a number of committees. . . . Mrs. Damon handles people well. She chaperoned and protected me in an interview with Mrs. Benson, at which the latter proposed 'burying the hatchet' and 'forgetting the past.' "

The reorganization, carried out under the strong hand of Rose, was far less an incident than a process. It continued throughout 1939 and 1940.

Mrs. Sanger became honorary chairman, bringing her name to the top of the BCFA letterhead. She surrendered all activities of the Bureau except the clinic; this, at Gamble's suggestion, became the Margaret Sanger Research Bureau and continued to serve its thousands of woman patients.

Dr. Richard N. Pierson, whom Gamble liked, became fulltime president at the outset. Mrs. Louis De B. Moore, replaced by Dr. Pierson as presiding officer on the Board, resigned from the Executive Committee and later from the Board. Dr. Robert L. Dickinson became a vice-president, along with four others. Mrs. Benson dropped down to the position of director of the Regional Organization Department. Mrs. Cecil Damon, acting for Mrs. Sanger, became a member of the Executive Committee and served temporarily as director of information. From the BCCRB, Mrs. Florence Rose was given a senior secretarial position and Mrs. Hazel Moore and Mrs. Edna McKinnon were made BCFA fieldworkers.

Dr. Gamble became a member at large of the BCFA board and a member of the Executive Committee, a position of unaccustomed power for him, and also a member of the Regional Organization Committee. He also was made regional director for the South, causing him to exclaim to Phyllis Page: "Have I told you that I am now working under our friend, Mrs. Benson? It's a fact! . . . And they tell me if I want to stay on the Board I must be a good boy and spend money for birth control only through their treasury."

Dr. Woodbridge E. Morris, who had been director of maternal and child health in the state of Delaware, became general director of the BCFA. Gamble was pleased with this appointment. Dr. Eric Matsner soon resigned as medical director.

There had been, as part of the merger plan, a call for coolheadedness. But subsequent to the first get-together of Gamble and Rose in the latter's office in early March, each wrote the other a letter on March 6, 1939, which made it clear that they had not quite got together.

Rose thanked Gamble for "your willingness to adjust your thinking . . . to the needs and requirements of the Federation," and then came to the crux of the matter:

> Let me endeavor to establish the principle . . . which I gathered . . . was acceptable to you. . . . May I add that I have checked this principle with a number of heads of comparable organizations and regular business organizations, and it conforms with the same policy under which they function.
>
> "Any individual who is actively identified with the establishment of policies or the carrying out of those policies on behalf of an organization, whether that individual be a paid or volunteer member of the organization, must necessarily represent in the public mind the organization he or she represents."

Rose went on to say that all financial or other assistance given by the above individual in the organization's field of interest requires the expressed approval of that organization's officers. Such financial assistance as approved by the organization should be provided through the organization itself and not through the individual, except under extraordinary circumstances where a committee in charge approves. "This would apply not only to you but to all other board . . . and staff members."

Gamble took a "states'-rights" position:

> You suggested that in the future I should refrain from making contributions for birth control to birth control organizations unless special consent were secured from the Federation. . . .
>
> Because I am intensely interested in making contraceptive information widely available, and because the Federation can be an extremely effective instrumentality in this process, the suggestion worries me a good deal. It indicates a tendency to centralization and regimentation which I fear may decrease the Federation's accomplishments. . . . Generally applied, such a restriction would limit much local interest. . . .
>
> Take, for example, the case of a person who might consider contributing the salary of a social worker to a birth control clinic. He or she would probably be much less interested in making an arrangement with a distant national organization. . . .
>
> There is also the fear that birth control groups of the plains and the cotton fields, and even those nearer headquarters, will resent the suggestion that censorship of their contributions by a national organization is necessary to make the country safe for contraception. . . .

Past history often furnishes a good guide to future action. Had the policy you suggest been followed in the past it would have made impossible many accomplishments which you and I now value. . . .
To me there appear to be a few advantages of the suggested plan to offset these obvious disadvantages. You were more optimistic in the matter, however, and pointed out that some of the disadvantaged of the past might not be met with in the future because [of] reorganization. . . .
In the hope that this may be true, and because my research training has led me readily to risk experiment, I told you I was willing to try the effect of carrying out your suggestion.

From this point on, Gamble asked the BCFA for a whole series of permissions to continue supporting his ongoing projects. In each case the Executive Committee gave prompt approval. During 1939, he made gifts to the BCFA totalling $4,390.53, all designated for expenditure by the Regional Organization Department. He continued to support birth control research through the National Committee on Maternal Health.

Not always informed of what was going on and, even when informed not at all reassured, the Gamble fieldworkers were nervous and jumpy. Mrs. McKinnon's basic personality traits were exuberance and self-confidence, although at times she might be depressed, outraged, cynical, humorous, or impertixnent. In from the field and fighting a lingering influenza, she exhibited the unexpected reaction of dark suspicion in a letter to Gamble in Pasadena:

I am certain that my confusion and failure to snap back, as it were, is largely due to the psychological tension that is bottled up in me over the work. I can't help feeling that you are secretly determined to make it appear that the merger just won't work. That you want to continue your private projects unmolested and that you are going to do it no matter what sacrifice you demand of others. And I'm about reaching the end of my resistance. You are making such an effort to show up Benson that you are making people, *your friends, believe* the stories she has told of your being a troublemaker. Won't you for all our sakes drop your trying to do things on the side . . . and try to play ball JUST FOR ONE YEAR! . . . You need the Federation and it needs you!

At this point, Gamble was preoccupied about the health of his family. In the preceding three months, two of Sarah's sisters had died of streptococcal throat infections and the daughter of one was ill with pneumonia. The antibiotic cure for such diseases was still to come. Gamble reassured Mrs. McKinnon: "You don't need to worry so much over me. . . . I'm not thinking that the merger is all wrong. It's only the one element in which my nose is being rubbed so constantly. As for private projects . . . I haven't spent a private nickel since the merger. . . . The thing that irritates me the most is that there is so little evidence of interest in results for the mothers. . . . The canyons of New York seem to obscure the rural needs."

Terminating his service as acting managing director, Kenneth Rose in May 1939 recommended to the Executive Committee that Dr. Gamble be dropped as regional director of the South and also as a member of the Regional Organization Committee. The Committee so acted. The reasons given were that he lived in the North, and the need was for a fulltime director working in the South. Gamble, who was not present at this meeting, was unprepared for this turn. While he continued on the Executive Committee, he was displeased. Receiving the news at the Oglethorpe Hotel in Brunswick, Georgia, Mrs. McKinnon, back on the job, gave way to "a flood of uncontrollable tears." She wired Gamble that she was ready to resign, but he wired back to hold on.

Mrs. Benson, director of regional organization, herself protested to Mrs. Henry J. Mali, chairman of the regional committee:

Being ignorant of the discussion which preceded this decision by the Executive Committee, I am inquiring, perhaps naively, why this step was indicated and whether you think the Executive Committee might reconsider the matter. Is it inconsistent with the present plans to retain Dr. Gamble as a member of the Regional Organization Committee, providing he is willing? . . . The loss of Dr. Gamble's influence as a Committee member is, I think, regrettable. His "drive" and ideas contribute a quality of freshness to our group thinking which I sincerely regret losing. I feel certain that Dr. Gamble himself would be the first to grant the right of the Committee to disagree sometimes with him on method in field work. Moreover, I know that he has made a great effort since the merger to adapt himself to organizational rather than individualistic patterns.

There is no indication in the Gamble papers that he ever commented on Mrs. Benson's belated defense of him. It appeared to be a case of love at last sight. Whatever its significance, Mrs. Benson now could count herself as well out of it—no one had asked her advice—and indeed she did count herself out. In July, she resigned from the BCFA, leaving the battlefield to any who survived. At this point, it was not at all clear who would survive.

Gamble had high hopes for Dr. Morris as the executive chief of BCFA. From the outset Morris treated Gamble as important, as did Cecil Damon. As with Mrs. Benson and Rose, Gamble bombarded Morris with letters, going into an incredible amount of detail about small matters that an administrative chief properly might be spared.

Morris reciprocated with more demands on Gamble's time than *he* could meet, an interesting switch from the era when all Mrs. Benson asked was that Dr. Gamble leave her alone. Morris did not thrive on administrative turbulence, however. Since the position of medical director was open and working with physicians was more to his liking, he opted for a more sedate level of activity when Kenneth Rose, who had been acting as fund-raising counsel, returned in April 1940 as executive vice-president of BCFA (later national director). Morris changed from "general director" to "general medical director."

The conflict between Gamble, the individualist, and Rose, the organization man, now resumed, and their relationship progressively deteriorated in 1941 and 1942. "I am much annoyed at the completeness with which I am being amputated from the field work," Gamble commented. Friction became evident in a circular letter from Rose to his staff restricting relationships between the staff and board members. When Gamble came to New York and had lunch with staff members they humorously discussed "the question whether, since the action of their taking luncheon with me had been suggested to staff members by a board member, the matter shouldn't be more properly handled by their requesting me first to take up the matter, preferably in conversation, with you," Gamble wrote Rose.

In no mood for joking, Rose sought the advice of Dickinson on what to do about Gamble, Dickinson wrote as follows in 1941:

Dear Mr. Rose:

You ask me about Dr. Gamble.

One who has given nearly twenty years to full time free service to medical marriage problems, including birth control, evaluates Clarence Gamble as follows:

No other physician has given years of exclusive service to the cause of birth control as has Dr. Gamble, except Hannah Stone, and she had not his university teaching standing. His wealth permitted him to start a lot of practical attacks on live problems of ours, either in rural work, or in laboratory research.

As examples, we owe to him the idea and the funds for studies of standards for our devices and chemicals . . . for inventing and financing a lot of rural projects;* for inspection trips, as to Puerto Rico and elsewhere, and articles in the medical press.

In the introduction to my book, *Control of Conception*, I place him, as initiator, next to Mrs. Sanger.

I agree with you that Gamble is a bother to Boards and to Committees. Anyone is a nuisance who insists on first things first; on simple solutions; on the poor as having first claim; and on most results for least money. He was too practical and economical for the Executive Committee of the National Committee of Maternal Health, and for the Federation he doubtless brings up troublesome ideas and decisions. But few know our field as he does. . . .

Gamble and I—one hopes—will some day be accredited with some nuisance value. Because of our loyalty to the cause, we carry on.

Yours, grateful for your energy and results,

      Robert Latou Dickinson

* Eg., beginning of work in North Carolina and in Alabama of which the Federation boasts now.

Dickinson sent Gamble a copy of the above letter and wrote him as follows:

Dear Clarence:

That clearance between us was worth while. Please never call me "doctor" again. "Robert" or "R. L." after an evening when we got near together.

You and I have had a long struggle to advance certain ideas. We have held to what we thought the line of progress so persistently—we call it patiently—that we have been pretty often persona non grata. So, rather often, we have had to go our own ways. Sometimes solitary ways. Governing boards have just tolerated us or not wanted us. They thought they could ignore us. To be asked to face facts, to do first things first, is not popular. We bide our time. If we happen to be right, the ideas will win out.

Please read over again my favorite poem—the one with the shortest title—Kipling's "If" . . . .

A year later, Rose persuaded the Executive Committee to pass a resolution preventing board members from discussing a possible financial contribution with a state League until the gift had been approved by the national director. Rose's view was that if a board member indicated readiness to contribute, as Gamble customarily did, it would make the Federation appear obstructive if it then disapproved. Gamble's view was that it was impossible to work out the potentialities of any possible opportunity in a state without discussing the possibility of a contribution to support it.

Gamble in 1942 wrote Mrs. Sanger: "I don't know whether it is worth our trying to educate the PPFA or not." (Backing away from a term Mrs. Sanger had introduced many years before, the Birth Control Federation of America in 1941 had renamed itself the Planned Parenthood Federation of America—PPFA). Mrs. Sanger replied: "Dear C. J. I'm just as discouraged and discussted [sic] as you are—not only about the limitation placed on persons like yourself but the limitations of the calibre of those in charge—to whom you must bow the head and bend the knee. . . . It begins to look as if some of us should have greater liberty to do good birth control work if we were *not* a part of the Federation."

The problems of the birth controllers in living together, or merely of tolerating one another, had come full circle in six years. But something new had been added—Mrs. Sanger had dropped the "Doctor" and now called Gamble "C. J." By 1949, he was addressing her as "Dear Margaret." So by then, after fifteen to twenty years of friendship, the three most creative leaders of American birth control—Sanger, Dickinson, and Gamble—were calling one another by their first names! They could, in a way, thank the

ABCL-BCFA-PPFA for stimulating this demonstration of mutual affection for one another.

Gamble wrote Margaret Sanger in 1942: "I have wanted many times this fall to . . . visit with you [about] the progress of the Great Cause. My duodenal ulcer hasn't let me be so active as I should like to be and, partly as a result of that, there have been no trips to New York. Then, too, I have started teaching some of the physical diagnosis at Harvard, which keeps me busy on Tuesdays and Thursdays, which seem to be the popular days for the New York meetings. The discussion over the dictatorship [at PPFA] continues, though I have tried to let it interfere as little as possible. . . . The thing that worries me most about it is that the spirit behind it . . . that wisdom is located only in New York and that all powers and decisions must be centered there—will annoy the local groups who should be encouraged to try their own wings and feel that they are important cogs in the local and national machinery."

Gamble Versus the IPPF

After World War II, when Gamble began to intensify his efforts overseas, he had similar problems with birth controllers in the international organizations. The point is impossible to prove but it seems certain that there were many occasions during the 1950s that officers of the International Planned Parenthood Federation spent more time discussing how to control Clarence Gamble than they did on how to prevent unwanted pregnancies. Mrs. Vera Houghton, IPPF executive secretary in London, wrote Margaret Sanger a confidential letter in early 1955: "The opposition which Dr. Gamble is building up against himself is reaching terrifying proportions. People just cannot stand this weight of correspondence and I'm afraid the result will be that his letters will remain unanswered. He is everywhere, into everything. In fact, he is trying to run the IPPF through any channel he can. He doesn't always stop to think whether what he is doing is wise. . . . I honestly believe that Dr. Gamble is moved by a generous and active spirit but there is another side to the accounts and I'm afraid the bad is balancing out the good. . . . There has to be an end to this correspondence and I promise you that this is the last letter you will get from me on it."

Lady Rama Rau wrote from India. "Dr. G in his great zeal goes ahead and although we appreciate his enthusiasm, we have to see that we do not tread on the toes of sensitive nationals." Mrs. Sanger replied: "I keep warning him that he must not step on people's toes with his enthusiasm." Mrs. Ellen Watumull, in a letter to Mrs. Sanger, quoted Margaret Roots as acknowledging that Gamble would accomplish more in India and some other Asiatic countries if he would be less aggressive and could persuade the people there to take the initiative. By getting so many missionaries to engage in the research projects. Mrs. Watumull wrote, he tended to separate himself somewhat from the important people in government. This, in early 1955, was the latest bone of contention.

Gamble wanted a good field study of the salt-and-sponge, salt rice jelly, and foam tablet methods of simple contraception. The salt methods had encountered low acceptability in Japan. In the three years following the Bombay conference of 1952, he and his collaborating missionary doctors in India and Pakistan were able to collect data on fourteen groups of women receiving contraceptive instruction in ten health centers, most of them rural in character.

Lady Rama Rau, as IPPF regional director as well as international chairman, regarded the trend in events with increasing indignation. First it was Margaret Roots. Then it was Edith Gates. Next it was J. Parry Jones, a Philadelphia Quaker who had been distributing surplus dried milk in a famine area near Amdras. As a new Gamble recruit in late 1954, Jones first was assigned to pull the field study material together. Gamble blandly asked Lady Rama Rau to show Jones her model teaching clinic in Bombay and to introduce him to various Indian birth control workers, in a routine request ignoring the fact that non-medical foreign field workers were a sore point with her, especially as in the case of

Mrs. Roots, where they had no professional background in birth control.

Lady Rama Rau complained to Mrs. Houghton and sent Gamble a copy of the letter. The burden of this letter was that Gamble and certain missionary doctors were doing contraceptive field tests without her consent. In reply, Gamble explained that the study was underway before he had formed any relationship with the IPPF—in fact, IPPF rules about working through regional and national representatives had evolved while the study was in progress. He sent her a draft copy of his study, published in Calcutta in June 1955.

The average age of the 876 women studied was 29: average length of marriage, 13 years. They had averaged 5.4 pregnancies, 5 babies being born alive and one of five dying in infancy or early childhood, leaving an average of 4 living children per family.

The pregnancy rate of these women had been 65 per 100 couples per year prior to the use of contraception and dropped after instruction to an average of 19 for all methods, meaning that the interval between pregnancies was increased from an average 18 to 63 months.

Four kinds of salt methods and two kinds of foam tablet were used. These were compared with the diaphragm and jelly method. The salt methods included pad and 10 percent salt, rubber sponge and 10 percent salt, cloth wad and salt, and salt rice jelly. There was considerable variation in results for any given method from place to place, apparently reflecting regularity and efficiency of use.

But the results were a surprise. Tabulation of the pregnancy rates during the use of contraception showed all foam tablets yielded the lowest pregnancy rate (9) whereas all salt methods (24) and diaphragm-jelly (22) offered little choice between them. However, Gamble cautioned that the number of patients and months of study were too few to conclude that any method was superior to another. What the study did show, as had the Japanese studies, was that any method of contraception *used* was far superior to none in reducing the pregnancy rate. Neither regularity of use nor acceptability was analyzed.

There is no indication that Lady Rama Rau ever commented to Gamble on his study. He did manage to corner her at a conference in Puerto Rico in May 1955, as he reported to Mrs. Sanger: "I'm afraid I failed to uncover much that she may have buried beneath politeness." She restated her objections to Mrs. Roots and Mr. Jones and her insistence that any IPPF representative in the Indian Ocean Region be a doctor of medicine. She felt that an individual from one of the countries in the region might succeed better. She would like to have earlier information from Gamble's Christian physicians in India. "To my mind, perhaps unduly Occidental, these don't add up to the irritation that I've sensed," Gamble wrote. "What have I missed?"

He could be exasperating. The issue had been stated and re-stated. What he had missed was that Lady Rama Rau did not want his help—American help—on his terms. Margaret Sanger had told him this. Parry Jones had reported this. Lady Rama Rau had shown him how she felt. Whether Gamble understood this problem in cross-cultural understanding—it seems doubtful that he did—was beside the point. He didn't want to get out of India.

One person who understood Gamble and said so was Mrs. Margery K. Butcher of Singapore, regional representative of the Far East and Australasian region of the IPPF, including Japan. She was well aware that he had helped finance FPAs in Solangor and Johore, Malaya; Taipei, Taiwan, and Bangkok, Thailand, as well as Japan. She said that Gamble and his money were welcome in her region, as was Mrs. Roots. Mrs. Butcher wrote a confidential appraisal of the IPPF program and its conflicts in which she made the following two observations:

In India's position it must be extremely difficult to isolate national from regional, and regional from international, especially as Lady Rama Rau is chairman of the IPPF, and also seems to be the link between the FPA of India and the Indian government.

I have re-read very carefully the report of the Program Sub-Committee at Stockholm. Dr. Gamble has really tried to adhere to what was suggested there, but the IPPF machinery was not really sufficiently advanced to cope with his ideas and suggestions, and as a result both he and IPPF are likely to be frustrated.

Meanwhile, as another case in point, a battle was in progress on
the Anglo-American front, centered on Edith Gates and the IPPF's
ambiguous attitudes about countries where it had no Lady Rama
Raus. There was no disputing that Gamble, in his desire to move
and make progress, presented the IPPF in London with two accomplished facts, Mrs. Roots and Miss Gates. Although he at first
had said that their appointments as NCMH field representatives
were independent actions and created no responsibilities for the
IPPF, he soon turned around and asked how their work might best
be integrated with that of the IPPF and, indeed, would not the
IPPF wish to appoint them as *its* representatives?

Mrs. Houghton parried the thrust. Her first point was well
settled: The IPPF insisted on prior consent from the region to
send in a field representative. The second issue was arising for the
first time—sending in a field representative where there was no
IPPF member organization. In the Middle East, "since the IPPF
knows far less than you do about conditions there, we do not
really think it possible for us to allow Miss Gates to represent the
regional organization. If you care to send Miss Gates as a representative of the National Committee on Maternal Health, we can
have no objection, though obviously Dr. Hanna Rizk should be
consulted before any work is done in Egypt." (Dr. Rizk was a
co-opted member of the IPPF Governing Body). Not a man who
could take "no" for an answer, Gamble came right back with a
request that the IPPF prepare a calling card listing Mrs. Roots as a
field representative or some equivalent term.

Gamble again wrote Mrs. Houghton in December 1954:

I must tell you about a dream. It is one built on the dreams of Mrs.
Sanger and many others, and shows the happy day when birth control
will be available to all families throughout the world.

As I have worked toward the dream over the years, it has seemed to me
an extremely important road to reach it is one built on the establishment
of birth control services. . . . To learn how best to establish such centers,
I have experimented in this country, doing some of the work personally
and some through social workers. Beginning with a clinic in Cincinnati
in 1929, I've helped to establish more than 40 pioneer clinics in 8
states. . . . With Richard's help, I have learned something of the procedures needed in other countries. For world-wide progress, this experience

has led me to believe that great effectiveness can be attained by the IPPF by enlisting, sending out, guiding, and encouraging field workers, especially in the countries where birth control services are not now available. . . . Is there any interest in the Federation's organization in attempting such a plan? Your last letter seems mostly built around the words, "no objection." It is possible that these are terms of approval in the British language, but they are not so recognized in the American language.

Mrs. Houghton replied:

I think we all share your dream otherwise surely we would not work so hard for the movement, and there can be no two opinions about the importance to the countries which are not yet organized for family planning of properly qualified field workers. Any difference of opinion can only lie in the method of appointment. . . .

You are in the very fortunate position of being able to get things done and I admire all the more your unfailing patience with us. We are not unimaginative, but in anything that we do we have to take into consideration the viewpoints of several nationalities and try to speak as one.

Also, Mrs. Houghton noted that the IPPF was an organization of "slender means." In fact, Dr. Gamble embarrassed the IPPF by showing how weak it really was. His strategy appeared deliberately provocative: he took action and then offered the IPPF the chance to share in it, and meanwhile asked the IPPF for suggestions of what to do next.

Gamble made a concession: "I agree . . . that a field worker should work only in territories where she is wanted by a local organization," but "new local groups, because of their inexperience, have no conception of what a field worker can accomplish." The "only way to ask them if they wanted the help she could give was to have her give a demonstration of her abilities."

Mrs. Houghton wrote Gamble that the British Committee, a sort of *ad hoc* overseer of the IPPF, discussed the employment of Mrs. Roots and Miss Gates. "The Committee considers that there are certain cardinal principles that must not be overlooked in the desire to advance the cause quickly in areas so urgently important. . . . The British Committee considers that the only acceptable course is for any interested individual to give money to the IPPF for work in any given area and for the IPPF then to ask the region concerned to administer the funds in any way it considers best."

There was one fresh note here. It was the first time that the IPPF in London said, in a flat, official way, what had previously often been suggested. In effect: "Give us your money and we'll decide how to spend it."

At this critical juncture, Dr. C. P. Blacker, vice-president of the IPPF, chose to enter the conflict. Gamble found in this fellow physician a sparring partner equal to the argument, as evident in the fact that they continued to agonize over one point for three years. Blacker was a London psychiatrist and secretary of the Eugenics Society, who had been interested in family planning and eugenics for thirty years. Margaret Sanger respected his objectivity, judgment, and diplomacy. Blacker, who robustly addressed himself to "Dear Gamble" wrote in February 1955:

> Like every other member of the Governing Body of the IPPF, I very much appreciate your efforts to spread and reinforce the family planning movement in the countries you have visited. Also deeply appreciated is your generosity in making grants and donations to encourage this work. . . . I am writing to you frankly and in what I know you will realize is a friendly spirit. . . .
>
> I think that you are following a mistaken policy, and one which imposes grave difficulties for the IPPF's Executive Committee, when you give assignments (and afterwards ask the Executive Committee to authorise such assignments) to persons such as Mrs. Roots and Miss Gates. . . .
>
> It is impossible for Mrs. Houghton, or myself, or, indeed, for the Executive Committee of the IPPF, to give recognition and status within the IPPF to these ladies—in short to accredit them—without seeming to override the susceptibilities of the responsible people in the National and Regional organizations concerned. . . .
>
> If you wish to spend money in encouraging family planning movements in Asian countries (but do not want to turn the money over the IPPF for use by the region in any way it considers best), why not consult first within the national and regional organisations? . . . Ask them to draw up and submit to you, for your approval, a proposition or programme, or perhaps more than one, which could serve the purpose you have in mind. The selection of the personnel to be employed in each project should be made *by them and not by you*. . . . If you had in mind

some person whom you thought competent to undertake a particular piece of work, I suggest that it would be best to ask the local people to arrange to interview that person without prior commitment on either side. . . . If either side had misgivings or reservations, that would be the end of the matter. What annoys Lady Rama Rau and raises insuperable difficulties for us is the procedure according to which you first select your candidates, then offer a grant conditional upon that person being employed in some Asian country, and finally request Mrs. Houghton to secure the authorisation of the IPPF for that person to act as its representative. . . .

But I well see that things would not be so simple in a country in which there existed no national or other relevant organisation. I have in mind the Near East. . . . All I can then suggest is that you consult the Regional Office and such responsible individuals or organisations with which you yourself might have made contact, and in whose judgment and sense you have confidence.

Please forgive my writing you in this outspoken and seemingly critical manner. I do so because, with Margaret Sanger, I realize how uniquely helpful you are able to be to the family planning movement in the world and how wonderfully generous you have in the past been. But I also know there has been some rather bitter criticism of your methods. . . . I seriously fear that if a clear understanding . . . is not soon reached there may be a serious rupture, as a result of which we would all be losers.

Quite unusual for him, Gamble only briefly acknowledged Blacker's letter and said he appreciated the spirit in which it was written. Margaret Sanger offered him moral support, saying it had been her experience, too, that as organizations expanded, they always made pioneer work more difficult, and in fact administrative types "always resent the pioneer spirit." Later she chided him: "I think there is one thing, Clarence, that I would like to say in all frankness. . . . Vera Houghton is practically alone in the headquarters in London. . . . The poor child is overwhelmed with correspondence, and I think your questions, that you put to her with tremendous pressure and persuasive power . . . upset her considerably. . . . She has not authority on her own to make any decisions."

Eventually, Gamble addressed himself to the heart of the matter in Blacker's letter of February 11, telling the latter in May 1955 of his aims and purposes:

One of my chief interests for the past 25 years has been the developing of a new birth control program. . . . I have felt that I have been in a unique position to do so. Charitable organizations and medical services . . . already in operation can raise funds by pointing to past accomplishments. It is harder to get contributions for new programs which have no record of achievement and cannot guarantee success even though the probability of accomplishment of the new is greater than that of the old. . . . Perhaps one could say that I have accomplished more by contributing "risk capital" and have left to others donations to "going concerns."

. . . Experience in this country had indicated that the best way, perhaps the only way, to get a program started is to put a field worker on the spot to get things organized and operating. When I began, a field worker was a "new program," which has since been followed by the Planned Parenthood organizations. . . .

My interests in Asia are roughly similar. . . . My limited experience in Asia indicates that there, also, the most effective ways to get clinical birth control service started is to send a field worker to the spot and contribute the needed initial expenses.

I feel that the IPPF can increase its effectiveness if it can provide a field worker who can be sent to various parts of the world where as yet no programs are in operation. . . . During our travels my son and I came across two people who were available and . . . well suited . . . Mrs. Roots and Miss Gates. In both instances an immediate decision had to be made. Because time was short and because they had as yet no demonstrated proficiency. . . . I did not ask the IPPF to accept them as field representatives. . . . I feel I should point out that when I suggested that the Federation might engage them for future work I did not ask it to take responsibility for their past activities. . . .

. . . I feel there are definite advantages to their being the Federation's representatives. The Federation will, I believe, find the experience of a field worker valuable in expanding its work. Perhaps it will [help] raise more money for more such workers. Secondly, I think it will be advantageous to the IPPF to have our contributions channeled through its Treasury. Both the larger budget and the record of direct accomplishment will help in fund raising. Foundations may hesitate to give a sum which would be a substantial portion of the budget and they usually prefer helping where success has been demonstrated. They would, I believe, rather contribute to a second field worker than for the first one . . . .

The English Committee made comment . . . suggesting that, if I would like to help, I should give unrestricted funds to the regional organizations in which I was interested. You will understand that, because of my belief in the greater value of new projects . . . this suggestion might involve a loss of effectiveness. New programs even though effective will seldom be envisaged by existing organizations.

Blacker replied to Gamble in July 1955 with an offer of a *modus vivendi* pending arrival, so to speak, at a formal peace treaty:

Your letter and my talk with Lady Rama Rau have led me to the conclusion that, in the interests of spreading knowledge of planned parenthood all over the world and in those of harmony between yourself and the IPPF, the best plan would be for us to work independently of each other, except as set out at the end of this letter, but with the closest possible cooperation between us.

. . . We all very greatly appreciate the energy and money which you have put in. . . . But serious difficulties have arisen over the method of selection of personnel and in the choice of their assignments. The Governing Body strongly supports Lady Rama Rau in thinking that the best way to find the right personnel is to assign the initiative to the national and regional organisations concerned. . . .

The Indians are moreover *exceedingly sensitive* to the way Europeans and Americans treat them. They bitterly resent the imputation that they cannot themselves find the personnel best qualified to solve their own national problems. . . .

. . . If I understand your position aright . . . you and your son will continue to make surveys of different parts of the world in the course of which you are likely to meet other people who . . . you may think well qualified to do work in the international field; and there may well be personal and other reasons which make a decision as to their future an urgent matter so that there may not be time or opportunity to consult the national or regional organisations in the manner I have suggested.

If I am correct in these assumptions, I have three proposals to make. . . :

1. If, on your own initiative, you make further appointments . . . I suggest that you make them under the auspices of the Committee on Maternal Health and that the IPPF should not be concerned. . . . But the closest consultation should be encouraged between the person you appoint and the national and regional organisations concerned. . . . I feel sure of the good will of our side in London. . . . Everything is to be gained by cooperation; everything is to be lost by friction and disputes. But the IPPF should have no responsibility for the person . . . who should not announce that he represents the IPPF. . . . The IPPF would have no power to control or veto. . . .

2. If, after appropriate consultations, you find yourself able to approve and subsidize a project or an individual recommended to you by a national or regional organisation of the IPPF . . . then the work could be made the responsibility of the . . . organisation and . . . the financial transaction could then be channelled through the IPPF.

3. As regard experiments on contraceptive methods or in other fields, as long as they are conducted under the auspices and control of the national and regional organisations of the IPPF, I see nothing but advantage in channelling the money through the IPPF.

. . . The proposals contained in this letter are my own. . . . Would they, do you think provide a basis for agreement and for future policy when your work comes up before the Governing Body in Tokyo?

Blacker's letter appeared to be a sensible statement. Technically, however, it left room for misunderstanding. The major premise stated at the outset was that "the best plan would be for us to work independently of each other." This was called a "conclusion," but the letter offered "exceptions" to the major premise and the real conclusion was that they should work independently under certain circumstances and collaboratively under others—a compromise solution. In his reply, Gamble accepted the major premise that they work independently because that most clearly described their past relationship, but he did not give up hope of bringing the IPPF to his way of thinking and doing. "Implicit in your suggestion is that of my freedom to correspond directly and to enter into financial relations with interested persons or groups," Gamble wrote in part, "and this will cut down the number of letters which I will need to ask you and the Federation staff to read. . . . In conclusion, let me say that I accept your recommendation . . . that the IPPF and we "work independently of each other. Let us do so, of course, with the fullest and most friendly cooperation."

Margaret Sanger, reading these letters, was as usual supportive: "This whole bickering attitude on the part of *someone* makes me sad and discouraged. Dr. Blacker wants to help in keeping the IPPF from discord within its ranks. . . . I personally do not like the present attitude of 'dog in the manger.' You have been too modest. Only a few of us in the movement knew that you were financing and guiding projects while credit for results seemed to be given others not so modest." Gamble appreciated her understanding and agreed, "Perhaps if I had used more publicity it would now be easier to persuade the people in the organization of the value of what I've learned over the years."

The Tokyo Decision

The Fifth International Planned Parenthood Conference in Tokyo, in October 1955, was an occasion for welcoming the new Planned Parenthood Federation of Japan into the IPPF fold. It also might well have been an occasion for celebrating the good works of Dr. Gamble. Indeed, some of the Japanese birth controllers regarded it as such. Dr. Kageyasu Amano, for one, gave Gamble the major credit for bringing the miscellany of conflicting Japanese birth control organizations together into one Federation, planned and then founded when Clarence and Richard Gamble were there in 1953 and 1954. As a matter of fact, Dr. Amano said as much on the last day of the Conference, the closing banquet attended by the entire conference including Mrs. Sanger and Lady Rama Rau, as well as Sarah and Clarence Gamble and two of their children, Judy and Bob. Mrs. Gamble that night wrote a letter to the "Dear Red Heads" at home describing Amano's presentation: "Some company here in Japan presented the Japanese Federation with an enormous silver cup, the Margaret Sanger trophy, to be presented to some doctor who has rendered outstanding service to Japan. So they presented it to Daddy at the dinner tonight, much to his surprise and mine. Daddy made an excellent little speech telling what had been accomplished by the Japanese doctors and that the trophy really should go to all of them."

It was about the only time all week that IPPFers gave Gamble any favorable attention, although he was permitted to present his report on the results of simple contraceptive testing in India and Pakistan, and the IPPF was well aware that he footed the bill for the conference to the extent of $3,000. On the other hand, his request that the 1,000-word reports of his three fieldworkers be published in the proceedings was rejected on the ground that they were, as Lady Rama Rau said, mere travelogues or of no scientific significance.

The Governing Body of the IPPF as a whole felt no desire to honor Clarence Gamble for his fieldwork, and, indeed at its closed meetings and in the hall of the Imperial Hotel, Gamble and his fieldworkers were a target of criticism. He was left to find out what happened at the governors' sessions by buttonholding his friends on the Council and was not permitted to see the minutes of the meeting pertaining to him until two and a half years later.

As extracted from the minutes of October 29, 1955, the record—which might reasonably have been made available to him the next day—read as follows in total:

The Relationship between Dr. Clarence J. Gamble and the IPPF.

Dr. Blacker recalled that this matter had been discussed at some length by the Executive Committee at Rome in September, 1954. But since at that time neither the President nor the Chairman of the IPPF was present, the Governing Body had avoided taking decisions which might have run contrary to the wishes of either. In the meantime further selections and appointments of field workers had been made by Dr. Gamble and fresh surveys had been initiated and financed by him. Hence it was essential that the Governing Body should clarify the position of the IPPF for the benefit of those national groups and others directly concerned.

Starting with the President and the Chairman, each member of the Governing Body was asked in turn to state their views on what should be the future relationship between Dr. Gamble and the IPPF. Dr. Blacker read a letter dated 27th July 1955 from himself to Dr. Gamble in which, in the hope of finding a basis for harmonious co-operation, he had put the three following proposals to Dr. Gamble. (These, a few days previously, he had submitted to Mrs. Sanger, Lady Rama Rau and Mr. [Rufus] Day).

(1) Individuals selected and appointed by Dr. Gamble, and projects financed by him on his own initiative, and independently of the regional and national organisations of the IPPF, should not be sponsored by the IPPF, and the financial subsidies involved should not be channeled through the IPPF.

(2) If, after appropriate consultations, Dr. Gamble found himself able to provide and subsidise an individual or a project recommended to him by a regional or national organisation of the IPPF (the approval of the regional organisation being essential), then the work could be made the

responsibility of the national or regional organisation, and the person concerned could be given out as representing it. The financial transaction could then be channeled through the IPPF.

(3) Funds relating to experiments in contraceptive methods or in other fields could be channeled through the IPPF only if these experiments were conducted under the auspices and control of the regional and national organisations of the IPPF.

In a letter to Dr. Blacker dated 17th August 1955 Dr. Gamble had accepted these three proposals.

On it being put to the vote whether these three proposals could form the basis of an understanding with Dr. Gamble, 20 members voted in favour and 14 against; there was one abstention.

Gamble had adopted the practice of writing his three field-workers "Dear Collaborators" letters and signing them "Your teammate, Clarence." From Taipei, following the Tokyo conference, he wrote in November 1955:

I came away from the conference with a sense of utter failure so far as building real cooperation with the corps of the IPPF. I am told that on the last day of the conference the governing body spent an hour and a half discussing me. Mrs. Sanger said she spoke in my favor but that she had had a heart attack the night before and was under the influence of sedatives so she couldn't "really fight." Dr. Stone was also quoted as being in my favor. Another quotation, however, was that many of them, one after another, said, "I agree with Lady Rama Rau." Just what she said wasn't revealed but past experience makes me think it is unfavorable. The organization eventually passed a motion which hasn't been clearly defined but apparently was approval of Dr. Blacker's letter. That would seem to be complete independence, but Mrs. Houghton says it was a resolution of cooperation. As I remember them, they said merely that the IPPF would accept money if it was approved by their regions and the projects came up to their standards.

So, I appear to be a very heavy handicap to your relationships with the IPPF and I am very sorry for that.

Gamble did not change, and he did not break off the relationship. In a letter to Mrs. Houghton not long after the conference, he administered one of the stiff, little pats on the back for which he was famous: "Let me tell you once again how much all that you are doing means to the planned parenthood movement and, therefore, to the world. Without your pushing and guidance the International Federation would make little progress. . . . Please don't let your enthusiasm lead you to overwork that would interfere with the Federation's progress. I'll try to reduce the correspondence needing your attention to a minimum."

The IPPF headquarters demonstrated that it was quite ready to work with Gamble on its own terms. At the time of the Tokyo meeting, Gamble support through the IPPF to FPA's in Pakistan, Malaya, and Borneo was at stake. The Executive Committee renewed these arrangements. In April 1956, Mrs. Houghton reported to Gamble: "With the engagement of an assistant secretary . . . we are now able to get down to following up the contacts made by Miss Gates and the committees she got started in various parts of Africa."

Dr. and Mrs. Gamble, on the last leg of their 1955–1956 around-the-world trip starting in Tokyo, met in London in March with Dr. Blacker and Mrs. Houghton in the library of the Eugenics Society, which gave free rent to IPPF headquarters. Mrs. Houghton, in a written report of the meeting to Mrs. Sanger, said they had "reached a stalemate."

Gamble asked whether the IPPF was considering appointment of its own fieldworkers. Blacker told him that the Governing Body in Tokyo had recognized the need for fieldworkers and had made provision in its budget for the hiring of one in each region. It was news to Gamble. At last the organization had come around to this, but it was a hollow victory. The IPPF had not accepted *his* fieldworkers.

Gamble meanwhile had turned to a matter of greater interest to him. In the field of independent action, where he excelled, and where he had tried to inspire the IPPF without much success and with little approbation, he brought off another *tour de force*. If he could not mold IPPF policy in his image—that is, a tireless swift searching for openings and testing of alternatives in pursuit of the Great Cause—he could create an organization of his own.

What was a crucial issue for the International Planned Parenthood Federation—its recognition as the world birth control organization—now came into view. To be harassed by an eccentric philanthropist from Milton, Massachusetts, was one thing— it was not difficult to truss such a man up in red tape and protocol—but to see him transformed into a foundation roaming the world with substantial resources was cause for alarm among conservative IPPF officers.

The trouble was that, while the IPPF was putting Gamble down, it was being rebuffed by the United Nations in a manner that frustrated its long-range strategy. The IPPF mission of establishing the Federation as *the* international birth control organization and building member strength throughout the world had a special significance to the internationalists among its leaders, such as George W. Cadbury, who for nearly ten years was a director of the UN Technical Assistance Administration, before becoming a special field representative of the IPPF in 1960.

The UN's World Health Organization, lacking in power or large resources, had been for the most part conceived along classic public health lines and therefore without longtime commitment to family planning or population control. More important, the Catholic nations in its constituency then prevented WHO from even introducing birth control as a topic of discussion in its meetings. Tuberculosis, malnutrition, malaria, hookworm disease, cholera—fighting these was not against anyone's religion. But who wanted to fight the Catholic Church?

IPPF leaders saw it as their mission to fill this gap in world health and, particularly, in maternal health programs at least until that hoped-for day that family planning became a part of world health and of maternal health services in every major government's health program. Such considerations provided rationale for stressing organization over crusade, lines of authority rather than routes of attack, position ahead of opportunity. There were more subtle justifications for following this course, one being the impossibility of exhibiting a strength either in manpower or money.

In 1955, the year of the Gamble-IPPF "Tokyo decision," the UN Economic and Social Council unanimously rejected the IPPF's application to the accepted as a consultant agency. It was not until some years later that the United Nations agencies adopted a positive policy on population control and its Council formally recognized the IPPF as an ally in the voluntary field. With funding from AID, the IPPF vastly expanded its program, supported in 1972 by a $25 million budget (40 percent from AID) as contrasted to about $5,000 in 1952.

chapter 18   The Pathfinder Fund

In 1957, Gamble founded the Pathfinder Fund as a family foundation and became his own granting and operating agency. It was the suggestion of his son-in-law, Lionel Epstein, a Washington, D.C. attorney who specialized in tax law, that Gamble form his own nonprofit, tax-exempt foundation. Such an entity would eliminate Gamble's dependency on other channels including the Brush Foundation in making contributions to the IPPF, which did not have United States recognition as a recipient for tax-exempt gifts.

Clarence and Sarah Gamble discussed "Li's" idea with their five children and spouses, and it was agreed that the whole family would contribute to an organization that accepted as its primary purpose worldwide fieldwork in family planning.

What should it be called? Sarah, having shared in Clarence's trials and tribulations as an individualist who tended to run ahead of others in getting things started, thought of the American pioneers, the frontiersmen and scouts, the Daniel Boones and

Lewises and Clarks who went ahead of the settlers, exploring the land, blazing trails, and bringing back reconnaissance reports. She suggested it be called the Pathfinder Fund and it was chartered in the District of Columbia.

The first meeting of the Pathfinder board of directors, held on February 27, 1957, was of a preliminary nature. Two generations of Gambles and their spouses, ten in all, constituted the original board. These were Clarence J. and Sarah B. Gamble, Sarah G. (Sally) and Lionel C. Epstein, Richard B. and Frances P. Gamble, Walter J. and Anne C. Gamble, and Julia G. and Stanley J. Kahrl. The youngest son, Robert D. Gamble, became the eleventh director in 1958.

The purposes of Pathfinder were simple enough: To go right on doing what Gamble and his teammates had been doing without a hunting license from the International Planned Parenthood Federation, but, nevertheless, with a desire to communicate in a common objective.

Dr. and Mrs. Gamble with Pathfinders, Milton

By and large, the idea was to spread the word in the depressed areas of the world that mothers were not merely animals of reproduction and did not need to ruin their health and deny opportunity for health and education to their children through unregulated bearing of children from menarche to menopause. Specifically, the family made annual contributions to meet costs to employ field representatives to travel in all parts of the world, but particularly the underdeveloped parts of Asia, Africa, and South America; to talk to people about birth control; to encourage them to form family planning associations; to open clinics or start home visiting programs; to supply these programs with a variety of contraceptives mostly free of charge; and further to test and evaluate new methods. The emphasis would be on the inexpensive methods that doctors, nurses, and social workers could encourage people to use themselves without being dependent on personal examinations and instruction by physicians who, for the most part, were not available in the rural villages and out-back areas.

Gamble had notions of his own about the functions and potentialities of the outsider, agreeing that the indigenous peoples had to learn to do for themselves but refusing to be concerned about the rising tide of nationalism, the rebellion against racism, and the demand for self-determination. He was accustomed to going where he wanted to go, where he was uninvited and even perhaps not wanted, and had results to show for his efforts. And he was not persuaded by the refrain, "Give money for *us* to spend." He had not been this lavish with his own children. He used money to teach them responsibility and accountability. Money, to be useful, had to be managed. Gamble often said that he had something more than money to give in birth control, and that was knowledge and experience in how to use it. That came free of charge.

Writing about the philosophy and procedures of the Pathfinder Fund at home in Milton, the day after Christmas, 1962, Gamble was back on the subject of fieldworkers:

For the most part these have been English-speaking women over 50. While it would be advantageous to have a knowledge of the local language, experience has shown that English is widely known. Most doctors learn it to get access to medical textbooks, and British influence on colonies [is] widely distributed. An American, a Canadian, or a European is free of the jealousy which often attaches to neighboring countries. This jealousy is illustrated in the Family Planning Federation of Japan. Though funds have been available they have not been able to find a suitable person to travel to other countries. As one of them put it, "We would not accept a person coming from our neighbors, why then should we expect them to accept one of us?" A widely travelled person visiting many countries has the advantage that she can tell those she meets of procedures which have been found successful in the family planning groups she has visited.

While a physician can be useful in certain parts of the field work, a physician free to travel is difficult to find. Local physicians, also, often feel more comfortable with a non-medical person who is obviously not coming to instruct them.

In choosing the countries for the field workers to visit priority has been given to those in which family planning is either underdeveloped or has not progressed far. It has been found that favorable public opinion regarding family planning takes years to develop. A major objective has been to help local citizens to establish at least one group in each country and to assist them in opening services, especially for the under-privileged. Return visits are planned from time to time. . . .

On reaching any country, contact is made with the leading physicians to learn from them the status of family planning in their surroundings and to enlist their interest. . . . While physicians are indispensable as medical advisors of [a family planning association], they seldom have the time or interest to become the most active persons.

Visits are then made to community leaders, including government officers. The latter are often willing to give their sympathetic support but with such a new and possibly controversial subject, politicians are hesitant to give public support.

In helping a family planning committee to organize the inclusion of all local races is encouraged. Interested Europeans are included but the greatest support is sought from local leaders. . . .

The provision of clinical family planning services is encouraged, in as advanced a degree as possible. The simplest service is . . . the office of a sympathetic physician. Later the establishment of a clinic with regular monthly or weekly hours may be possible either in the physician's office or in some clinical center. In some cases governmental maternal or other clinics will allow representatives of the FPA to talk to patients in their waiting rooms, and it may in some cases be possible to add contraceptive instruction to the governmental clinics.

Where possible it is arranged to tell maternity patients in the hospital wards of the possibility of family planning and to give instruction there or at the follow-up visit to the clinic. Local associations are encouraged to arrange for follow-up visits to family planning patients in their homes and to enlist new users by visits to the homes and if the supervising physician approves to give supplies to those who wish them. In all cases it is recommended that technical procedures should be decided on by a physician's committee of the association.

. . . In discussing contraception for the under-privileged with the family planning association the contraceptive foam tablets are recommended.[1] In many cases these are supplied free to the new or growing association. The association is allowed to choose the brand it desires. The method of salt solution and sponge is described and suggested as an alternative if the foam tablets prove too expensive. In some places the sponge and directions for making the solution are given to new patients for use if the foam tablets are exhausted.

No objection is given to the use of diaphragm and jelly if the local groups wish them, but their intricacy and expense is pointed out together with the difficulty of making the necessary physical examination. Contributions are not made to the local associations for the purchase of diaphragm and jelly but they are not discouraged from providing their own funds for this purpose. . . .

In each place the importance of public education in family planning has been emphasized. The field worker often arranges for public meetings in local halls. . . . The local groups are assisted in the purchase and designing of literature. They are often helped with the preparation of leaflets in the local language or languages. Contact is made with newspapers, and in some places with the motion picture houses. . . .

In many places it has been found worthwhile to provide a subsidy for the early expenses of the association, for printing, for meetings, for clinical services and for nurses or midwives to follow up users and to enlist new ones. It is explained to the local group that this cannot be a permanent arrangement and they are encouraged to begin raising local funds for its continuation.

Gamble touched, briefly, on a sore subject:

When Pathfinder field workers were starting in Africa and for South America, the IPPF was informed of this and asked for suggestions as to contacts and procedures. These have not been received. . . .

As arranged by Mrs. [Edna] McKinnon, the expenses of half of the midwives and doctors from Indonesia attending a training session in

[1] The period recorded was prior to the availability of the IUD and pill.

2

rthfinder Overseas [PART 3

Singapore were provided by the Pathfinder Fund. To Mrs. McKinnon's disappointment, she was excluded from the clinical training sessions so that our knowledge of how these were conducted is scanty.

Family planning groups with whom we have been working have been encouraged to apply for membership in the IPPF and a number of them are now among their constituent organizations.

It is to be hoped that collaboration and free exchange of information can be arranged between the IPPF and the Pathfinder Fund for more efficient progress in the family planning field.

The Pathfinder Fund began activities on a small scale from an office over a grocery store at 73 Adams Street, in Milton, less than a mile down the street from the Gamble residence. At first, the president—Clarence Gamble—was allowed $10,000 a year for new projects over and above an ongoing annual budget of $50,000 to $60,000, mainly for salaries and expenses of fieldworkers. From year to year, the expenditures of the Pathfinder Fund progressively increased, until they reached approximately $250,000 for birth control activities in 1965, the year before Gamble died.

An information sheet on the Pathfinder Fund in October 1961 provides some idea of the extent of the field activities in the early years:

The work of the Pathfinder Fund was carried out by six workers experienced in medicine, public health, health education and nursing, with Dr. Clarence J. Gamble as coordinator. Dr. John E. Gordon worked in seven countries in Central and South America. Mrs. Margaret Roots, who had previously worked six years in Asia, was active in Spain, Malta, Jordan, and Israel. Mrs. Edna McKinnon assisted the family planning associations in Malaya and Indonesia. Ruth Martin, R.N., worked in five countries in West Africa and three in South America. Mrs. Sarah Lewis talked to delegates to the International Conference on Social Work in Rome, visited six countries in Europe and the Near East, and met with Asian and African visitors to London. Edith M. Gates, who had worked six years in Asia, Africa, South America, and the Near East, supervised the work of the home office in Milton, Massachusetts. Dr. and Mrs. Gamble met the family planning workers in Italy, Jordan, and Israel.

Like fieldwork, research and development remained a Gamble interest. Soon, Pathfinder moved on to the field testing of the new contraceptives, the oral pill and particularly the IUD. Meanwhile, foam tablets, as Gamble indicated, were the preferred method for contraception among less developed rural people. Progressively more and more studies attested to the effectiveness, safety, and comparative acceptability of approved brands of foam tablets.

Estimates from birth controllers on the value of Clarence Gamble's pathfinding depend to some extent on the existence of conflicts in personalities and objectives. George Cadbury, whom Gamble for several years urged to become an IPPF field representative and who later become IPPF chairman, was quoted as lamenting: "Wherever I go, that fellow Gamble has been there first and queered my pitch." There is ample documentation that Gamble's activities made life miserable for Cadbury in 1960 and 1961, during the latter's new efforts to negotiate a *modus vivendi* aimed at "dividing the turf" so that Pathfinder might stay out of the IPPF's way, and vice versa. In this abortive and somewhat anticlimatic episode, involving the usual barrage of letters as well as face-to-face discussions, Gamble exhibited his usual independence. In 1964, Gamble ran into Cadbury at an international conference in Singapore, and said: "Please sit down for a few minutes. I'd like to talk over with you some of the reasons you don't like the work I'm doing. Maybe we can smooth things out." Cadbury retorted: "We've wasted too much time on you already, Gamble," and walked away.

But there were others who admired Gamble in his services as a cutting edge. One was S. M. (Sam) Keeny, an old hand in international affairs including UNICEF, UNRRA, and IRO who in 1964 became Taiwan representative for the Population Council. Keeny in 1969 summed up Gamble's overseas contribution in this way:

I was impressed by the number of individual doctors he had got interested in family planning. . . . At first my impression of him was that he was a bit cranky, and was running a sort of one-man show. Then as I went around to the countries that were beginning to get something that looked like a national program I found that in innumerable instances he was the one that got the family planning groups started. . . . If you want to get something done, whether it be in family planning or elsewhere, one of the nicest ways is to start doing it . . . and that is what so many of them have failed to do.

part 4 the new contraceptives

chapter 19 The Pill—Margaret Sanger's Dream Come True

Clarence Gamble, always confident in the service of the Great Cause, nevertheless was realistic in contemplating the limitations of contraceptive methods available, and quite willing to play the game of trial and error with whatever cards were dealt him. Moreover, when the hands were running small in hoped-for results, he would divert himself with wild cards—that is, novel ideas about contraception. When oral contraception (the pill) and the intrauterine device (the IUD) burst upon the overpopulated scene in the late 1950s and early 1960s, he was among the first to seize upon these new techniques and subject them to field tests, and in fact had been eagerly awaiting such innovations.

Before then, he and Margaret Sanger exchanged many strange recipes for preventing conception, in the simple hope that folklore might reveal something that science had overlooked. Mrs. Sanger was an early prophet of the pill. In 1939, she wrote Gamble from her summer home in Fishkill, New York:

I've got herbs from Fiji which are said to be used to prevent conception. I'm hoping this may prove to be the "magic pill" I've been hoping for since 1912 when women used to say, "Do tell me the secret—can't I get some of the medicine, too?" I'm talking to one of the Squibb men and if they can analyze it for us we may find out "somefin."

Gamble was already talking to Hoffman LaRoche Company about an African root that an explorer claimed was a native contraceptive drug, and to Johnson & Johnson about some herbs from Ecuador. The potent kakaula tea from Fiji was, however, a good illustration of how widely birth controllers were casting their net for the ideal contraceptive.

A Mr. Charles Kellogg of Morgan Hill, California, who had travelled in the Pacific, told Mrs. Sanger about the marvelous bush in Fiji. He had the secret from a Fijian medical student whose mother had confided it to him. This occult potion—"I have brewed it and have drunk . . . it several times and I find it not at all unpleasant"—was supposed to be the explanation of how the Fiji islanders kept their birth rate down despite government pressure to multiply.

Gamble recommended that Kellogg's supply of scrapings from the kakaula bush be submitted to Merck & Company. Tests, made after a year's negotiation of a suitable contract, indicated that the Fijians must have had some surer method up their sleeves. As a matter of fact, they did make other claims. One was an herb that was supposed to produce abortion and another was a so-called "stop" drug and produced sterility—that is, it supposedly stopped reproduction altogether.

Gamble supported research in oral contraception in the early 1950s before the advent of the modern pill. From the oil of the common field pea in India, Dr. S. N. Sanyal of the Calcutta Bacteriological Institute developed a pill taken once or twice a month. Rats eating this cereal grain tended to become sterile; this was a systematic laboratory observation rather than vague folklore. Sanyal extracted the active ingredient in inhibiting conception, metaxylohydroquinone, and later snythesized it. Supported by Gamble with technical assistance, funds and encouragement, the Indian physician performed extensive human tests with this drug but was unable to achieve better than 50 to 75 percent effectiveness in his human subjects (in contrast to nearly 100 percent protection with the progestin-estrogen pills available a few years later). The pea pill, buttressed by competent research, was an unusually promising idea, but it, too, landed on the age-old dump-heap of contraceptive prescriptives.

Medical scientists in the late nineteenth century suspected the existence of an ovarian hormone that inhibits ovulation but the controlling ingredient, progesterone, was not isolated until 1934. After that, they demonstrated the power of this hormone to block the ovary's cyclical production of an egg-cell in rats, later in cattle, and finally in humans.

In mid-twentieth century, Gregory Pincus and biologist co-workers at the Worcester Foundation for Experimental Biology in Shrewsbury, Massachusetts, studied 200 synthetic substances related to progesterone and therefore classed as progestins. They found three that were particularly potent as inhibitors of ovulation. These were called 19-norsteroids because they lacked a carbon atom found at the nineteenth position in the molecular structure of the pure progesterone extracted from animals. Of the three, two were of continued interest in conception control. They were norethynodrel and norethindrone, later produced in oral pill form by the pharmaceutical industry under such names as Enovid, Norlutin, and Orthonovum.

Meanwhile, Dr. John Rock, head of the Fertility and Endocrine Clinic and Reproductive Study Center at the Free Hospital for Women in Brookline, Massachusetts, was developing the concept of pseudo-pregnancy. As a Catholic physician and Harvard obstetrician-gnyecologist, Rock for many years had pursued the problem of unexplained sterility in women who wanted children but could not have them. These women sometimes suffered from painful, difficult, or irregular menstruation, which indicated some underlying disturbance in ovulation. Rock gave them various combinations of estrogen and progesterone in oral pill form, suppressing both ovulation and menstruation for three-month periods. When he stopped treatment, regular menstrual cycles emerged and some hitherto barren women rather promptly became pregnant. It appeared that the hormones created a state simulating pregnancy and somehow, in a kind of pump-priming effect, the treatment restored the normal balance between sterile and fertile phases in these women.

Rock, as the clinician, and Pincus, as the basic scientist, exchanged information. Pincus suggested that the Rock treatment be improved through the administration of large doses of oral progesterone alone from day 5 to 25 of the menstrual cycle, producing inhibition of ovulation during the treated cycle and followed by cyclical bleeding within two or three days after treatment was stopped. Again, more than the usual number of expected pregnancies followed. In 1955, Rock, Pincus, and others began using the synthetic 19-norsteroids as a treatment for infertility. It was their report in *Science* on a clinical trial of these original discoveries that stimulated Gamble again to support field trials of an oral contraceptive. The eye-catching summary statement was as follows:

Despite adequate coitus, none of the 50 women became pregnant during the months of medication. Their long-standing infertility may make this zero figure of no import. Nevertheless, it seems of at least passing interest that within only 5 months of the last treated cycle, seven patients conceived.

The tantalizing fact was that these norsteroid synthetics were recognized and described as ovulation inhibitors—anything that prevents ovulation must prevent conception. Naturally, birth controllers seized on this point. Rock and Pincus were sure that they would, and welcomed their interest. The salient question to be answered was whether one would get a zero conception rate in fifty *normally fertile* women regularly treated with progestins. Rock and Pincus, with encouragement and support from the Planned Parenthood Federation of America and pharmaceutical companies, set out to answer the question as quickly as possible. It was ironic that the search for a treatment for sterility led to a break-through in contraceptive methodology, but such unexpected turns are familiar to scientific research. There was little further talk about antisterility treatment.

The first field test of norethynodrel as an oral contraceptive began in April 1956, in San Juan, Puerto Rico, among 265 women living in a housing development in a slum clearance area known as Rio Piedras. Pincus directed the study, made in cooperation with the Family Planning Association of Puerto Rico and under the immediate supervision of a woman gynecologist, Dr. Edris Rice-Wray, and later a Puerto Rican doctor, Manuel Paniagua. The G. D. Searle Company of Chicago furnished the pills, trademarked as Enovid—a combination of 10 milligrams of norethynodrel and 0.15 mg. of an estrogen, ethinyl estradiol, given every day for twenty days in each menstrual cycle. Some 141 women continued the treatment through August 1957, the rest dropping out for various reasons. Nineteen of the treated women became pregnant, five because they missed taking some of their pills and fourteen who stopped medication because of reactions or carelessness. This study produced a pregnancy rate of 13 per 100 marriage years at risk, as compared to an expected rate of 67 among Puerto Rican women not using contraceptives. The finding also compared to a pregnancy rate of 29 for diaphragm and jelly and 33 for foam powder and sponge in the old Beebe-Belaval studies sponsored by Gamble.

Clarence Gamble was slipping. Accustomed to being the first to stimulate and support field trials of contraceptive methods at various times and places, he could claim no better than second in the case of the progestin-estrogen pill. While he was well acquainted with Rock and Pincus, it was inevitable that in a world increasingly disturbed by the population explosion they, the originators, were in the best position to move ahead in clinical application. On the other hand, with their encouragement, Gamble got busy as sponsor, coauthor, and all-around ramrod on field studies conducted from the Ryder Memorial Hospital in Humacao, Puerto Rico. These, largely due to the competence and personality of Dr. Adaline Pendleton Satterthwaite, tended to dominate the clinical research interest of the *aficionados* of contraception until the mid-1960s. Pincus and his collaborators continued their field research in Puerto Rico, but became diverted in pursuit of his conviction that progestin contraception, far from increasing the danger of cervical cancer in women, operated as protection against it. This research did not pay off, due to experimental difficulties in long-term follow-up. Eventually others found no connection between oral contraceptives and cancer, except that estrogen stimulates (but does not cause) growth of breast cancer.

Ryder Memorial Hospital, operated by the American Missionary Association Division, Board of Home Missions of the Congregational Christian Churches (New York), was well-known to Dr. Gamble from his contraceptive field studies of 1937. In November 1956, he wrote Dr. John Smith, director of the hospital, mentioned Dr. Rice-Wray's tests of the pill among women in Rio Piedras, and offered to support similar testing in Humacao. Smith referred the letter to Dr. Satterthwaite who ran the obstetrics and gynecology service in the small hospital, which then had only sixty-six beds and five doctors.

Dr. Satterthwaite, then about forty years old, was a prototype mission doctor of striking vitality, strength, and competence, as interested in humanity as she was uninterested in money, as devoted to her patients as they were to her. A California Presbyterian, she in 1944 had married William Satterthwaite, a Quaker and conscientious objector from Bucks County, Pennsylvania, who became a maker of artificial limbs and vocational rehabilitation teacher. Under foreign mission sponsorship, they went to Puerto Rico and later to China, where Satterthwaite died in 1949 of a pulmonary embolism associated with an acute tuberculous pleurisy. They had one son, David, born in 1946.

Dr. Satterthwaite had been at Ryder for five years when Gamble got in touch with her. She was interested in family planning, and had been fitting diaphragms and doing tubal ligations for Puerto Rican mothers. This was not her main preoccupation, however. She was delivering 500 babies and doing 800 operations a year as well as running an out-patient service, an extremely heavy practice. In the crowded hospital, bed occupancy often ran 120 percent of approved capacity—as she said, "When someone is carried down a slippery, muddy mountain trail in a hammock in the middle of the night, you can't say, 'There are no beds;' you have to find space somewhere."

Gamble flew down to Puerto Rico in January 1957 to make plans. With the approval of the Home Missions Board in New York and the Hospital Board of Managers in Puerto Rico, he and Adaline Satterthwaite, two mavericks of the American medical profession, agreed on a joint project. The Hospital would furnish the working base for the fieldwork; and as its staff obstetrician-gynecologist, she would supply the medical supervision including initial and follow-up physical examinations as well as instruction or treatment as needed; Searle would donate the Enovid, Gamble would provide statistical supervision and pay all expenses except her hospital salary of $3,600 a year; the Population Studies Unit at the Harvard School of Public Health in Boston (mainly Gamble and Gordon) would analyze data from the medical and social service records.

The general aim of the study was to get as many women as possible to use the contraceptive to be tested for as long as possible, and meanwhile, make a careful medical and statistical record of what happened. Humacao is a Municipal District in the eastern part of Puerto Rico, thirty miles from San Juan; it then had a population of about 30,000. The fieldwork followed a familiar Gamble pattern dating back twenty years or more—to have a social worker regularly visit married women of child-bearing age in their homes and supply them a free contraceptive in return for their cooperation in the research. In this case, the contraceptive was Enovid in 10-milligram doses distributed in vials of twenty, or enough for one month.

As the study got underway in April 1957, recruitment of users was slow. Therefore, although he at first was against it, Gamble agreed with Dr. Satterthwaite that she should undertake a parallel series among her regular patients coming to the clinic for post-natal check-ups. These were identified as the P-series (for Pendleton or, as her friends called her, "Penny"). The others were R-series, for Mrs. Noemi Rodriguez, who became the home visitor.

Reading a well-conceived, well-written report of a piece of research, one is struck by how well the authors have mastered their subject, at the skill with which they have organized and interpreted their data. What one does not know is the troubles they went through to collect and analyze it, including wear and tear on the human psyche and soma. If the Humacao study was to become another classic, there was little indication of it in the correspondence extending from 1957 to 1966—indeed, human interest ran scientific interest a close second as a source of instruction.

Gamble was known to his long line of women fieldworkers as a taskmaster whom they could satisfy only by responding to his constant bombardment of letters with an even heavier barrage. It was hard for him to be anything but a frustrated taskmaster, however, in his effort to manipulate a Catholic social worker and a Presbyterian mission doctor as independent as Noemi Rodriguez and Adaline Satterthwaite.

The first problem was that Mrs. R., hearing that Pincus fieldworkers in San Juan were getting $200 a month, felt underpaid when Ryder—not Gamble—set a ceiling of $130 for her job. Gamble tried to appease her by paying an extra $20 a month through the Family Planning Association, but thereafter suspected her of dragging her feet because she felt underpaid. In June, he complained for the first of countless times to Dr. S that, judging from the number of *hojas de vistas*, or records of visits, mailed to him in Boston, Mrs. Rodriguez was falling behind in her recruitment. He asked that she send him a progress report every Friday. Dr. S, who at the time had her own hands full with abortions, premature labor, and rare cases of central placenta previa and hydatidiform mole, wrote back that the slowdown in R-cases was due to small-town gossip: one woman had a severe headache requiring hospitalization and blamed it on the pill. "I told Noemi that she should at least put the data of each visit on the revisit sheets so that when you finally received the sheet that you would know how many times she had to visit that patient in the month to keep her spirits up and to keep her from being convinced by the neighbors that she is . . . being poisoned." To make matters worse, Noemi herself was pregnant again, and had to be hospitalized a few days for hyperemesis (excess vomiting) and meanwhile her little boy had a circumcision and, because of complications, was also in the hospital.

Judging from Gamble's continual complaints in the next four years, Mrs. R never met her Friday deadline, but instead mailed her reports in batches, three or four weeks at a time, perhaps during remissions in her family problems. In October, Noemi went to the hospital with a severe influenza and in premature labor. Gamble wrote Dr. S that he was sorry to hear this, but "Won't you ask Mrs. Rodriguez to send me the carbon copies of her visits and census records? None has come since the 9th of September."

In November 1957, not long after Gamble asked Dr. S to hold up Mrs. R's November 1 paycheck until she got her September reports in, the multiparous social worker "surprised us," as Dr. S blandly put it, with a baby girl. It was no surprise when, in another year, she became pregnant again. In early 1959, she prematurely bore a boy baby who lived only a few hours. At that time, she was up to 130 R-cases, while her chief had 222 P-cases.

Mrs. R weaned her 1957 baby when it was two weeks old and hustled back to work, her substitute during her maternity leave having been unable to work, due to illness in *her* family. The beginning of 1958, found Gamble still hounding Mrs. R for *hojas de visitas* and trying to persuade Dr. S to hold back her pay. Dr. S, who steadfastly ignored these demands, now found herself on the carpet: "It will be helpful if you will write a little more carefully and with more push behind the pen. We find it difficult to guess some of the words." Dr. S apologized and said:

I shall try to do better. . . . Noemi seems to have the work well in hand. The ladies are getting their pills. I can't seem to fathom why you have so much difficulty receiving the reports. . . . One trouble is that you frequently ask her special information which involves revisiting many of the cases again and in order to collect this information she gets behind. . . . We are interested to note that the postmark on your last letter came from Arizona. We hope that you are having a fine vacation.

As an impersonal exchange between two-strong minded doctors, there was an unmistakable chill, if not bite, in these words, quite possibly lost on Dr. Gamble, who enjoyed having people talk back to him. Dr. S next heard from him in London and, later, in Maine. At one point, he revealed his primary need for many, long letters:

> Mrs. Rodriguez seems unable to write. I will be glad to receive Spanish letters. I was in hopes that when Miss McDonald was added to the team she would be a corresponding secretary, but the news from her has been very scanty. Won't you use some of your authority (and as little time as possible) to improve the situation?

Dr. Satterthwaite was unable to oblige, being at the moment a patient herself in bed in bronchitis. Later, when Miss Elizabeth McDonald did write, she mentioned that Dr. S was seeing an average of forty-five patients a day in the clinic, plus deliveries, operations, emergencies, medical records, and taking her turn on night calls.

Meanwhile, as early as 1959, Gamble was putting all possible pressure on Dr. Satterthwaite to write, present, and publish reports about the study—he called it "our partnership." His insistance was well-founded. In a Planned Parenthood conference in India in February of that year, Pincus discussed "Field Trials with Norethynodrel as an Oral Contraceptive." Pincus combined his San Juan data with that from the Humacao study (his group had been receiving copies of the work sheets) and that of a third study begun in late 1957 in Haiti. In this report, soon to be published in *Science*, "Dr. Adaline Pendelton" was credited as one of nine authors. In his acknowledgments, Pincus explained that he was acting as spokesman for the collaborating investigators, but he did this without Gamble's knowledge and consent, a maneuver that Gamble accepted mildly, at least outwardly.

The news, of course, was good.

Pincus presented the 1956–1958 oral contraceptive experience of 830 subjects in 8,133 woman-months of pill-taking, including 126 Humacao-P and 117 Humacao-R cases. These women had a pregnancy rate of 61.2 per 100 woman-years of exposure before taking the pill and only 2.17 during the course of treatment. Interestingly, the pregnancy rates were 3.2 and 3.4 for San Juan and Haiti cases, and 2 for Humacao-P and only 0.9 for Humacao-R cases, indicating that Mrs. Rodriguez had done a very good job of shepherding her contraceptive flock, whatever her failings as a correspondent. Her women had the lowest rate of days missed in taking the pill. Curiously, Mrs. R's women also reported only one-third as many adverse reactions as Dr. S's cases (6 versus 18 percent), and about one-third less sexual intercourse (about 6.5 versus 9 times per month). Over all, one-third of the 830 women reported an increased sense of well-being "on the pill" and less than 10 percent, decreased well-being. Most noticed no change in libido.

In May 1959, Gamble wrote Dr. S that Dr. Hale H. Cook, an American Congregational missionary to India, had come to Harvard for a year's training in public health and was looking for a subject for a thesis. Would it be possible for him to use her cases? Dr. S wrote back that she would be happy to have Cook come down and help with the study. She was so busy there seemed little chance of her writing it up any time soon, and she would welcome the collaboration. This arrangement led in due course to her first joint publication with Gamble, covering the Humacao experience up to February 1960: "Oral Contraception by Norethynodrel."

As time went on, Dr. Satterthwaite found herself much sought after, not only by Gamble but by Pincus and doctors from the birth control organizations, pharmaceutical industry, and the Population Council, who were making Puerto Rico the leading testing center for the oral pill and, in due course, the IUD. Here was a doctor of medicine who was not only a true clinician and seeing more patients than John Rock himself but a woman—

calm, competent, and personable. Dr. Alan Guttmacher, a leading professor of obstetrics and gynecology at Columbia University, and later president of Planned Parenthood–World Population, for one, recognized her potentialities and invited her to New York in January 1961 to sit with some important men in a closed circuit television symposium on Enovid sponsored by Searle.

In 1961, Dr. Satterthwaite, now thoroughly bitten by the research bug, had second thoughts about her first love, clinical medicine for women. It was the old question of divided loyalties. Dr. Smith, the director of the hospital, wanted Dr. S to stay and continue her clinical service in obstetrics and gynecology. Dr. Gamble wanted her to stay and continue the research project— "You are much needed. Is there anything I can do to help?" he wrote in 1961. Dr. Christopher Tietze from the National Committee on Maternal Health and the Population Council convinced Dr. S that she should devote herself fulltime to contraceptive research. As a compromise, she was willing to stay at Ryder and do research if the Hospital would get someone to take over her clinical service, although she feared that, as long as she remained at Ryder, patients would make demands on her time. Always inclined to keep his eye on the main chance, Gamble at her request agreed to pay her salary to do fulltime research. "When will that start? I would say the sooner the better," he wrote. After she got established in her new program, he said that he'd like her to travel in South America to talk to doctors about family planning. Where else could he find a doctor like Adaline Satterthwaite? He happily approved of her budget of about $13,000 for her first year, exclusive of $7000 in one-time expenses, including a new Jeep. Gamble met the Satterthwaite budget as he had the previous smaller one; the project was often in a deficit position but Gamble readily made further advances as needed without fuss and, on occasion, with an apology.

From the standpoint of research, the new arrangement worked well, but Dr. Satterthwaite's relationship with the Hospital continued to deteriorate.

Her basic difference with Smith, was one of policy. She thought the Hospital should affiliate with the University of Puerto Rico School of Medicine, founded in 1949 at San Juan, and train and employ Puerto Rican medical graduates, instead of short-term American doctors. Her immediate concern was that the *government's* medical school was not training Puerto Rican doctors in birth control, and she wanted to do something about that.

Consistent with her original desire, Dr. S submitted her resignation from Ryder in January 1963, to take effect in June. She and Gamble remained on good terms, and her relationship with the Hospital improved, administratively and gynecologically. What she proposed to do, and what Gamble agreed to, was establish herself in San Juan and continue the study at Ryder two days a week, while undertaking new projects in Rio Piedras, Castaner, and Guacio, under the sponsorship of the Ortho Research Foundation, Population Council, and others. She accepted an appointment as research associate in the Department of Obstetrics and Gynecology at the University of Puerto Rico Medical School, collaborating with top Puerto Rican professors in pathological studies of tissue from the endometrium in pill-users, and became a consultant to the Population Council. Gamble continued to support the Humacao project until his death in 1966. That year, Dr. Satterthwaite joined the Council's technical assistance field staff first in Thailand, then Pakistan, and in 1971, Caracas, Venezuela. In addition to publishing several studies, she helped start a family planning training program for Puerto Rican doctors and nurses throughout the Island before she left.

Adaline Satterthwaite, a liberated medical woman as insistent on having things her way as Gamble was in having his, was one of his most unusual finds, as he himself came to appreciate. He wrote her enthusiastically in 1964 about her first IUD report and closed his letter, "Admiringly."

As a capstone, the Population Council chose Dr. Satterthwaite to give the report on "Oral Contraceptives" at its International Conference on Family Planning Programs in Geneva, August

1965. This report encompassed her Humacao experience, six different studies, seven years of work, and 1,771 women patients
who received various progestin-estrogen combinations, a pure
progestin, and sequential therapy of progestin and then estrogen
in more than 40,000 treatment cycles—in other words, about
3,333 woman years of pill-taking.

She emphasized the special advantage of the pill as a contraceptive: "Woman is now in a position to control procreation precisely and scientifically with the daily ingestion of a tablet at a
time unrelated to the sexual act." She recognized that the pill was
a money-maker for the pharmaceutical industry, that it produced
systemic effects, that it was publicly accepted or condemned with
equally violent emotion. But it had been provided free to Puerto
Rican women in the field studies and "We have fortunately not
observed the more serious sequelae reported by some investigators."

What mainly concerned her were reasons why many women
discontinued use of the pill. In every study, from 50 to 75 percent
stopped using the pill within a year or two, despite an obvious
need measured by the fact that many soon became pregnant
again.

Side effects (17 percent) were not the most numerous reason for
dropping out, although they were usually the first to emerge,
often during the first cycle of treatment. In general, the women
felt pregnant, the most common disturbances being nausea, vomiting, stomach pain, headache, dizziness, and nervousness, followed by weight gains and patchy discoloration of the facial skin.
Rarely there was breast engorgement, breakthrough bleeding, loss
of libido, vaginal discomfort, and possible thrombophlebitis (one
case).

Personal or nonmedical reasons for discontinuing exceeded the
medical ones. These included a simple failure to return for a
second month's supply of pills because of fears, the husband's
objection, or religious scruples, or because of a desire for another
baby, separation from the husband, menopause, sterilization, or

moving away. Competition from the IUD following its introduction in 1961 also had an effect on acceptability of the pill (reversing in this instance Gamble's observation that women accustomed to hearing about one method will reject a competing one). Pill users switching to IUDs outnumbered IUD users switching to pills about two to one over the four-year period on which Dr. Satterthwaite reported. "The only exception was in one small, largely Catholic town where the pills outnumber the IUD because the priest has given special dispensation for use of the pills in cycle regulation," said Dr. S.

"In summary," she concluded, "there is no ideal method for every couple. The oral contraceptives offer a useful and effective method of family planning in certain situations; but widespread application in public health programs seems to be of limited value. . . . The search for better methods of fertility inhibition must continue."

Clarence Gamble agreed. He was not impressed with the oral pill for mass contraception at that time among the poor, the objection that he most often voiced being that they "cost too much." This view was quickly reinforced by their quickly rising popularity among millions of American women, who could afford the three to five dollars a month the pills originally cost when purchased on a doctor's prescription at the nearest drug store (the retail cost per cycle now has decreased to a two-to-three-dollar range). Related to American purchasing power (as well as a higher level of sophistication in the daily use of a medicine) was the judgment of the birth control experts that the United States was the only country in the world where the pill accounted in part for a decrease in the national birth rate at a time when the increasing proportion of women in the child-bearing age was expected to produce another baby boom.

With the pill, it was not simply the initial but the continued cost that worked against its economic feasibility in the early years. Gamble did not live to see the outcome, but in the end the cost was not the overriding objection. In response to the demand created by massive government purchases (for example, by the United States Agency for International Development), the pharmaceutical industry brought the public service price down to as low as ten to twenty cents per cycle—usually twenty pills, but sometimes thirty when placebos or iron supplements were used to piece out an uninterrupted daily cycle. Overseas, the pills are distributed free to the needy; for the impoverished consumer, therefore, cost is no object. To governments who must ultimately finance such massive programs, cost is still a concern.

There are other objections to the pill. One of the more fundamental is that oral contraception constitutes a general manipulation of a complex hormonal system to achieve one specific effect and therefore requires continued medical management. But where does one find a good gynecologist in the rural villages of India, Africa, or South America? Also of critical importance was the problem that always has dogged contraception: motivation. The pill's capacity to produce 100 percent protection depends on 100 percent diligence in daily use. Even well-intentioned, educated people may forget to take their medicine. Experience showed that the continuation rate—that is, the number of women not only willing to start with this method but who continue its use—was essentially the same as with any other contraceptive.

A 100 percent method will be 100 percent effective in preventing unwanted pregnancies only if all women use the method all the time. Effectiveness is reduced to the extent that women will not try the method, or discontinue using it once they start. Field trials have often shown very high dropout rates with as many as 85 or 90 percent of women discontinuing within three to five years after starting to use the method.

What was the general outcome in Puerto Rico of Gamble's initiation of contraceptive field trials beginning as far back as 1938?

In twenty-five years, the annual birth rate in Puerto Rico gradually declined from 40 per 1,000 population to around 25, whereas in the United States the rate dropped from 25 to 15 or so. The decline in Puerto Rico matches the usual trend in a country accomplishing the demographic transition from agricultural and underdeveloped to industrial and developed. What part earlier or later methods of contraception have played in the reduction is difficult to measure. Many experts on population believe that sterilization—an irreversible procedure—may have had the greatest impact. An estimated one out of three women of child-bearing age with three or more children has been sterilized. In countries with modern infant mortality rates, such as Puerto Rico, however, first, second, and third births represent the bulk of population growth. Nonetheless, sterilization—in this case of the woman and not the male—may be an important factor. Although a controversial issue, it has been conjectured by some and denied by others that vasectomy in the Spanish-speaking male, like a woman who says no, may be a threat to his *machismo*.

chapter 20   The IUD and the New Frontier

The idea of placing a foreign body of some kind in the uterus to interfere with conception appears to be an ancient one. Both folk literature and medical literature contain mention of a wide variety of substances and objects that have been placed in the uterus to attempt the management of contraception and gynecological disorders. Hippocrates referred to a lead tube used to instill medication into the uterine cavity. Other materials mentioned elsewhere include pewter, silver, gold, platinum, glass, wood, wool and ivory. Several centuries ago many varieties of intracervical or partially intrauterine devices came into use, reaching a height of popularity in Europe and the United States of the Victorian era. Their inventors took great care, at least publically, to avoid mention of contraception as their purpose; these early devices were allegedly to correct structural and organic disorders of the female reproductive system.

The modern era of the IUD began with the Grafenberg ring, first reported in 1928, about the time that Clarence Gamble became interested in birth control. He manifested no interest in the IUD at the time. There were good and sufficient reasons. For one thing, the vaginal diaphragm was then enthroned as queen of contraceptive methods, among those few doctors who would have anything at all to do with birth control. Secondly, the medical profession itself shared the antagonism of the biological organism for foreign bodies; every medical student learns in bacteriology and immunology of the body's several reactions to intruding objects, whether animal, vegetable, or mineral. The primary reaction is an attempt to consume the foreign body, through the mobilization of "eater cells," called *phagocytes* or *macrophages*. What cannot be consumed may be expelled through irritability, inflammation, pus formation, ulceration, and muscular spasms. Or, if the foreign body is inert and relatively benign, the living organism may attempt to encapsulate it (as the oyster does with the grain of sand that becomes a pearl). Or, if the invader is a noncompatible protein, the host may produce specific antibodies that reduce the foreign protein to waste products.

Thirdly, another contraceptive device, the stem pessary, already had fallen into disrepute following its advent around the turn of the century. This pessary resembled a collar button or a wishbone, made of gold, silver, or other metal. When placed into the cervix, it extended upward into the uterine cavity and downward into the vagina, an effective stopper but one that often produced ill effects. Through dilation of the cervix, it furnished a pathway for bacteria to ascend from vagina to uterus and produce infection. Also, its presence was blamed for tissue erosion and cancer of the cervix or uterus; at times, the wishbone type perforated the uterine wall.

Despite a quite different design, the newer, strictly intrauterine device ran into a wall of prejudice among American and European gynecologists who had not seen or tried it. Ernst Grafenberg of Berlin was one of several German physicians who in the 1920s experimented with silkworm gut, a surgical suture material extracted in a single thread from a silkworm killed at the inception of its cocoon-spinning stage. Grafenberg first tied the threads in a star shape, but because of the tendency of the contracting womb to expel it, shifted to a ring of twisted threads bound with a thin silver wire to hold it in shape. He later substituted spiral rings of coiled silver or gold wire, and eventually added silkworm gut or metal wire to hold the ring together.

By 1930, he was able to report on 600 patients fitted with silver rings, of whom only 1.6 percent had become pregnant with the ring in place. To insert the ring, he dilated the cervical canal and pushed the ring into the uterus with a probe ending in a forked tip. At first, Grafenberg changed the rings once a year, but when he became more sure of himself he left the rings in place and simply examined his patients once a year to see if there was displacement or complication.

Grafenberg emphasized the need for a physician to make an examination before insertion of the ring, to exclude all cases of preexisting pelvic inflammation, acute or chronic. To avoid intrusion of the IUD on an unsuspected pregnancy, he recommended making insertions immediately following menstruation. He insisted on using a sterile technique to avoid inducing infection, and observed: "A certain amount of gynecological experience is absolutely necessary."

Grafenberg had few followers. Gynecologist opposition— essentially blind opposition—became so general that, when he emigrated to the United States in 1940, he made no attempt to promote his ring, and only rarely recommended it to a patient.

With a single exception, financed by Gamble, there were no published studies of IUD contraception from 1934 to 1959. Mary Halton, Robert L. Dickinson, and Christopher Tietze published a report, "Contraception with an Intrauterine Silk Coil," in 1948. Dr. Halton, a New York gynecologist, used her own modification of a Grafenberg ring for sixteen years, with the great Dickinson looking over her shoulder from time to time and Tietze doing the statistical analysis of case records and evaluation of results. "I frankly admit that I would not have dared to attach my name to so subversive a piece of medical literature had I not had the encouragement of the venerable Robert L. Dickinson," said Tietze.

Dr. Halton introduced a novel method of inserting her silk coil into the uterus: she placed it in a gelatin capsule and then pushed the capsule through the dilated cervix. Once in place, the gelatin dissolved and the coil rounded out to fit the contours of the cavity. The coil was made from a single twelve-inch strand of the coarsest silkworm gut, rolled tightly and sterilized in alcohol. To insure continuous medical supervision, she removed the coil every two months. As calculated by Tietze, 266 patients using the silk coil had 468 years of exposure to pregnancy with a failure rate of only 0.9 per 100 years of exposure. In all, four unwanted pregnancies occurred. Nearly two out of five patients had some uterine disturbance and one of five discontinued using the coil. There were only twenty-seven spontaneous expulsions. The main complaint was menstrual pain and cramps. But there was no evidence of permanent sterility or other damage.

At that time, there was little public concern about birth control for the masses. In 1959, a decade or so later, the outlook had changed, and the editors of the *American Journal of Obstetrics and Gynecology* deemed it time for another look at Grafenberg rings. They found that Dr. W. Oppenheimer, chief gynecologist and obstetrician at the Shaare Zedek Hospital in Jerusalem, Israel, had maintained his clinical enthusiasm for Grafenberg's contribution, and invited him to contribute a review of his own experience.

Between 1930 and 1957, Oppenheimer equipped 329 women with 866 rings. He first used silver wire spirals but turned to silkworm gut rings. He reported twenty pregnancies in 793 woman years of use, a failure rate of 2.5 per 100 years of exposure. Oppenheimer considered the method absolutely harmless.

Dr. Atsumi Ishihama, gynecologist and obstetrician at Iwate Medical College in Morioka, also published an article in 1959 on Japan's experience with the Ota ring. In 1934, the Japanese gynecologist, Dr. T. Ota, modified the Grafenberg ring, made of gold or silver, by placing a lentil-shaped capsule, suspended from three radial springs, in the center of the ring. Over the years, Japanese manufacturers produced many Ota rings, in some cases substituting nylon or polyethylene plastic for the metal ring and a flat disk for the hollow capsule. There was a considerable modern literature on the Ota ring, but, being all in Japanese, it was largely hidden from Western view. Ishihama's review, on the other hand, was soon translated into English. He reported on a personal experience with 973 cases and a less intensively studied series of 18,594 cases in 149 hospitals. Ishihama had a failure rate of 1.3 to 1.7 percent among his own patients, depending on whether he used a metal or polyethylene ring. The percentage of pregnancies in the larger hospital series was 2.3. He himself observed no serious side effects.

The two articles stimulated a worldwide discussion among birth-control-minded gynecologists who, in view of the population problem and the increasing availability of money for contraceptive research, exhibited a marked bandwagon effect in their rush to try out previously neglected IUD's of various types. Some were quick to add their own notions of what an intrauterine device should look like, what it should be made of, and how it should function. An important advance in the new IUD's was the development of plastic with a "memory" which could be changed in shape then would return to its original contours. For anyone disposed to manual dexterity, handicraft, and gadgeteering, the obstacles that presented themselves posed a rare opportunity. Within a year or two, a wide varity of shapes, sizes, and materials in IUDs became available—coils, double coils, S-loops, double-S loops, stainless steel rings, bows, shamrocks, IUDs with thread tails and beaded tails, triangles, Ms, Ts, and so on.

Not all experimenters were as successful as the Grafenbergs, Haltons, Oppenheimers, and Ishihamas. Some encountered sizable pregnancy rates, including ectopic (tubal) pregnancies and normal deliveries with the IUD still in place, some severe hemorrhages, inflammations, and infections of the pelvic area, and a few perforations of the uterus. It became apparent quite early that good results depended on unmeasured factors including the gynecologist's skill, and that, from the standpoint of medical competence alone, the IUD could not be regarded as a foolproof method. In 1962, Tietze compiled a composite table on accumulated experience, and found failure rates varied from less than 1.0

to almost 10 per 100 woman-years of use. Accumulated experience was limited, and reported data was rudimentary, but even the high failure rate compared favorably with other methods. The condom and the diaphragm, the most successfully used of the five common methods reported in a sample of 1,165 metropolitan U.S. couples in 1957 each had a failure rate of 14 per 100 woman-years of use.

At the same time, the advantages of the IUD were immediately apparent. Most of all, it disposed of the human tendency to "take a chance," by relieving the man and woman of any responsibility for contraceptive preparation immediately before intercourse (or, in the case of the pill, during the month before). At first the IUD appeared to reduce the need for strong motivation only to that required to bring about the original insertion (in contrast to the pill, which depends for success on the compulsion to take a pill twenty days a month, 240 days a year, without skips or stops). Later there would develop a body of opinion that substantial motivation is required to continue using the IUD. But what the more effective pill offered in protection when diligently used, the somewhat less effective IUD appeared to counterbalance through greater acceptibility. In the long run, the question of ultimate reliability became a matter of comparative statistics. Meanwhile, there was much to be learned about the biological nature of the IUD; at the outset, its mode of action was not known.

Birth control scientists were stimulated to move ahead in the use of the IUD as rapidly as possible for a variety of reasons. Obviously, from the economic standpoint, such a small plastic gadget could be made and sold for a few cents and, from an operational standpoint, was a one-time procedure. Quite surprisingly, also, it did not produce an obvious foreign-body reaction in most cases. Lastly, while pelvic inflammatory disease (P.I.D.) remained a danger that no doctor would knowingly impose on a woman, its threat to life had been substantially eliminated by the advent of antibiotics, offering a control of chance infection not available to Grafenberg and his cohorts.[1] Fear of causing cancer

[1] Today many doctors do not believe that IUD's cause any significant amounts of P.I.D.

was present, but neither Grafenberg nor his successors had seen a cancer in their patients which could logically be connected with use of the ring; cancer usually forms over a considerable period of time; it was possible, of course, for it to appear coincidentally.

Among several contenders for improvements on Grafenberg and Ota designs, the names of Margulies and Lippes came to the fore in the modern period. Paradoxically, it was Margulies who contributed the basic patentable features—the "breakthrough ideas" as he called them—in the new IUD era, but Lippes devised the loop that became most widely used.

Dr. Lazar C. Margulies was a gynecologist-obstetrician at the Mount Sinai Hospital in New York and an associate of Dr. Alan Guttmacher, then chief of OB-GYN at Mount Sinai. Stimulated by a lecture by John Rock on the perils of overpopulation, Margulies began work on a new device in January 1959, before the Oppenheimer and Ishihama articles were available. Mary Halton's idea of inserting a silk coil contained in a gelatin capsule appealed to him, but he saw that it was not suited to mass production and consumption, and, in any event, her method of insertion depended, as her predecessors', on dilation of the cervix. His first compelling idea was to achieve painless insertion without dilation, even in the nulliparous woman whose cervix never had been stretched by childbirth. His second idea, borrowing from Japanese experience with plastics, depended on the flexible capacity of a plastic strip in coil or loop form to spring back into shape after being stretched out straight.

By inserting a thin, straight plastic tube through the cervix from vagina to uterus, Margulies could feed a plastic coil through the tube and extrude it into the uterus by pushing a plastic plunger. Dilation was not necessary. For the IUD, he experimented with forty-six different plastics molded in a variety of forms, but settled on a flat coil (or spiral) with a thin, beaded tail. The purpose of the tail, extending through the cervix into the vagina, was to enable the woman or her doctor to feel with a finger whether the IUD was still in place. Whether this tail, reminiscent of the stem pessary but much thinner would provide a path for infection remained to be tested, but it is a matter of general gynecological philosophy that the nonpregnant uterus is a self-cleansing organ and usually difficult to contaminate, in contrast to the vagina.

Starting with a small-sized coil an inch across, Margulies encountered an expulsion rate of 22 percent among his first forty-nine cases. By increasing the size of the coil, he reduced this rate. Among his first 500 patients, 1960 to 1962, fifty-seven expelled the IUD. The pregnancy, or failure, rate was 4.3 per 100 years of exposure.

Margulies' report on his first two years of work provided a focus of attention at the first international conference on intrauterine contraceptive devices held in New York by the Population Council in May 1962.

Dr. Jack Lippes, professor of gynecology of the University of Buffalo School of Medicine, was at the conference, a watershed for intrauterine contraceptive action. Lippes reported on his experiments with IUDs at the Planned Parenthood Center in Buffalo, New York. He had a somewhat later start than Margulies, beginning in 1961 with modifications of the Japanese polyethylene and nylon rings. It was his idea that the IUD should conform to the shape of the uterus, an inverted triangle, or T, with the cervix at the lowest point and the two horns (fallopian tubes) at the upper corners. From a thin polyethylene rod, Lippes molded a double S, with the upper S about one inch wide and the lower S about one-half inch. Concerned about the difficulty in removing the older rings, Lippes attached a short, monofilament string to the smaller end. He used the Margulies tube method of insertion without dilation. Among his first 100 loop patients, he observed a pregnancy rate of 4.5; only two patients expelled the loop.

Clarence Gamble and his collaborator, Adaline Satterthwaite, attended the conference and made their own first report on IUD testing. Having elected to devote herself full time to contraceptive research at the Ryder Memorial Hospital, in Humacao, Puerto Rico, with Gamble's support, Dr. Satterthwaite began inserting Margulies coils in November 1961, later adding Lippes loops. This first report involved only five months' experience with 125 women coming to Ryder Hospital but Dr. Satterthwaite progressively extended her study to Castaner and Guacio, in the mountainous coffee country, with a staff of two doctors, three clinical attendants, and two fieldworkers jointly supported by the Population Council and the Pathfinder Fund.

The choice of methods and early results were to some extent influenced by the availability of coils and loops, both then in short supply even for experimental use, and also by Lippes' change in the size of his loop. Experience showed that a smaller loop was more easily expelled than a larger one.

Dr. Satterthwaite offered either coil or loop to any woman with one or more children, meaning to women from sixteen to forty-eight years of age some with as many as fifteen children. Not unmindful of the cancer scare accompanying the earlier arrival of the oral pill in Puerto Rico, she performed Papanicolaou smears and endometrial biopsies on the first examination of each patient and repeated the smears every six months.

Insertions were made eight weeks or more following delivery or abortion, preferably immediately following menstruation. Combined with the snipping of uterine tissue for the biopsy, this approach was calculated to provoke spotting or bleeding in the first month after IUD insertion, and did so in nine of every ten cases, but severe bleeding was reported in only 4 percent. (Routine biopsy is no longer practiced, but heavy bleeding still frequently occurs in the first months following IUD insertion.)

The Satterthwaite team made 590 insertions in 522 women in the fourteen months ending December 1962. Prior to the team postponing insertions until at least eight weeks following delivery or abortion, one case developed acute pelvic inflammatory disease six weeks after childbirth and eight days after insertion of a Margulies coil. Her fever, pain, and purulent discharge were controlled with antibiotics. Among others, there was an occasional case of infection with such bacteria as *gonococcus* or *trichomonas vaginalis*, but these are common female diseases and could not be blamed on IUDs.

Seventy-two of 522 women expelled their coils or loops ninety-two times, a few as many as two or three times, with the small Lippes loop as the greatest offender (there was only two calendar months' use of the larger Lippes loop during this period). The Margulies pregnancy rate was zero, compared to 7.5 for the Lippes loop in this series, with failure defined as any unintended pregnancy, irrespective of whether the IUD was or was not *in situ* at conception.

In June 1964, Satterthwaite and Gamble compiled a report covering their first two years of IUD experience, from November 1961 through November 1963, and reflecting a more extensive experience with the testing of the IUD under rural conditions among people with high birth rates and limited medical care facilities. Some 1,160 women had been accepted for coils, loops, or other IUD's. The insertion procedure had been reduced to five minutes per patient, or ten IUDs an hour, provided the attending physician had adequate assistance. The women had been observed from one month to twelve months after insertion, those failing to report back having been visited in their homes.

By now the large Lippes loop (No. 2) had the best combined record. True, among the forty accidental pregnancies in the entire series, the large Margulies coil had a smaller failure rate—0.4 per 100 cases—than the large Lippes loop—1.5 per 100. However, from the standpoint of acceptability, the large loop was clearly superior. The number of expulsions for the large loop was 8.5 per 100 in contrast to 23.2 for the large coil. Again, in the matter of removal for medical and personal reasons, the large loop was somewhat better than the large coil, 3.6 against 5.6 per 100. The large loop was far ahead in the percentage of women who continued to use the device following first insertion, 83 against 50.

One woman was found to have cancer of the cervix at the time her IUD was inserted, and was subsequently treated by total hysterectomy, but none developed a cancer while wearing the IUD.

It was customary in the study to offer contraception "cafeteria style"—the woman could choose any method she wanted. Most chose either IUDs or progestin pills, and showed a slight preference for the IUD over the pill.

Satterthwaite and Gamble were explicit that the intrauterine devices offered "no promise of being the ideal contraceptive." About one out of five women experienced severe bleeding with various types of IUDs, and slightly more than that suffered cramps, abdominal pain, or stomach discomfort, most often in the first month. On the other hand, one of five reported no side effects whatsoever. In sum, complaints were frequent but, for the most part, not sufficient to discourage use.

The gain was immense; compared to an overall pregnancy rate of 2.6 pcr 100 woman years of exposure among all IUD users the pregnancy rate among women living in the study area who were observed but not contracepted was 74—an average of one child every sixteen months.

chapter 21 Margaret Roots in Korea

Gamble's role in promoting the intrauterine contraceptive device (IUD) provided an exciting climax for more than thirty years of effort to put over the elementary but revolutionary idea that people can reduce poverty and suffering by tailoring the size of the family to fit their income. There was much complex reality still to be faced; an almost interminable number of sizes and shapes of IUDs have been introduced, each determined by the individual doctor designer's notions of how the IUD ought to pass through the cervix and fit the uterus, and by trial-and-error effort to overcome various discovered drawbacks. Yet intrauterine loops and coils appeared to Gamble to come closer than the oral pill, the condom, or anything else in meeting the criteria for mass contraception of the poor—simple, harmless, reliable, acceptable, inexpensive.

Gamble seized on every opportunity to plunge ahead following the Puerto Rican trials of the Lippes loop and Margulies coil. Now, however, he had the Population Council and the American pharmaceutical industry to reckon with; this was quite a different matter than the unproductive jousting with the International Planned Parenthood Federation or the old American Birth Control League. The drug industry, with its natural interest in patents and profits, was for the most part an off-stage presence, but his interactions with the Population Council were direct and abrasive, albeit superficially cordial. As Gamble remarked following a conference in 1964 with Dr. Frank W. Notestein, longtime director of the Office of Population Research at Princeton, who became president of the "Pop Council" in 1959: "We parted with friendliness unusual among [birth] controllers." All in all, they provided an interesting comparative study in pace, prudence, and propriety. In its first five years, the Population Council had been criticized for "a slow start," just as John D. Rockefeller III had in effect rebuked the Rockefeller Foundation for foot-dragging on population problems when he formed the Population Council in 1952. In contrast, Clarence Gamble had a well-grounded reputation for action.

The correspondence between Gamble and the Population Council began in 1956 with his letters to Mr. Rockefeller, board chairman, and Frederick Osborn, first president, expressing his admiration for the Council's population control work centered on research, training, and technical assistance. Gamble seemed especially pleased with the quality of the Council's leadership, drawn as it was from the leading private foundations, universities, and research institutes of the United States and including some respected demographers, medical scientists, and administrators. From 1962 to 1965, Gamble frequently visited the Pop Council's headquarters on Park Avenue in New York City to consult with Dr. Warren O. Nelson, medical director, Dr. Notestein, Dr. Christopher Tietze, and others.

A series of informal exchanges buttressed by a substantial correspondence was triggered when, in October 1962, Gamble wrote Nelson that he was supporting an American missionary doctor, Ralph Ten Have, in a study of Lippes loops in Korea, and wrote Tietze for copies of his standard record forms for contraceptive research. This information came less than a month before Dr. Marshall Balfour, who had been Far Eastern representative for the

Rockefeller Foundation and now held the same position in the Population Council staff, planned to make a team survey of the family planning program in South Korea for the Ministry of Health and Social Affairs. Clearly, in Pop Council eyes, Gamble was a fly in the ointment.

South Korea, with American and Allied help, from 1950 to 1953 had defended itself against invasion by North Korea and the Chinese communists. Meanwhile, it was dawning on the Korean government that it also was being attacked from within, by one of the world's highest population growth rates—about 3 percent per year, a population-doubling rate of 24 years. This had been satisfactory to Dr. Syngman Rhee, elected president of the constitutional republic following the World War II eviction of the Japanese; Rhee is alleged to have had the vision of conquering 8 million North Koreans and 700 million Chinese with 25 million South Koreans. At any rate, his regime had laws prohibiting the manufacture or importation of contraceptives and a generally negative attitude toward family planning, despite the interest of some South Koreans and Christian missionaries in birth control.

A student revolt in 1960 forced Rhee to resign and leave the country. The constitutional government survived briefly. A year later military leaders overthrew it and set up a Supreme Council of National Reconstruction with Lieutenant-General Chung Kee Park as its head. As an interesting reversal of the usual military outlook, the Korean junta was alert to the disastrous impact of overpopulation on economic development and national well-being. In due course, the Supreme Council approved of the importation and manufacture of contraceptives and adopted a friendly posture toward family planning. When, before the ouster of Rhee, it had been "a crime and a sin" to talk birth control, the military dictatorship permitted free discussion.

George Cadbury, special field representative of the IPPF, visited South Korea in late 1960. Cadbury recommended the organization of the Planned Parenthood Federation of Korea (PPFK), as an affiliate of the International. The new Federation was an outgrowth of the earlier National Mothers Club—a doctor-patient organization in which 1,000 mothers paid fifty cents each to obtain contraceptive advice from twelve participating doctor groups. The PPFK was largely financed by the IPPF, under an $18,000, three-year grant. When the first IPPF money was a bit slow in coming, the Pathfinder Fund helped out with a $300 unrestricted grant. Subsequently, Pathfinder contributed the salary of the PPFK's field director, Dr. Kang Joon Sang, for six years, as well as paid for a nurse doing family planning in a tuberculosis clinic (all told, something in the order of $20,000).

In the choice of Dr. Yang Jae Mo as chairman of the PPFK Board of Trustees, the Pathfinder Fund, International Planned Parenthood Federation, and Population Council all counted themselves as fortunate. Yang juggled these three groups and his own with a rare combination of frankness, good will, and adroit diplomacy. Professor of preventive medicine and public health at Yonsei University Medical College in Seoul, then forty-one and father of five, the son of a farmer and a man who had worked in farm cooperatives, Yang was interested in rural health. Following his graduation from Severance Union Medical College in 1948, he had gone on to graduate work in public health at the University of Michigan. "We are lucky to have the Yangs of this world," Margaret Roots wrote Gamble when she visited Korea in the summer of 1962. "He is really an outstanding person . . . and I myself firmly believe that the lack of 'internal politics' (which is the bane of all welfare work) in the family planning of Korea is due to his foresight and guiding." In an interview in 1969, the remarkable Dr. Yang said that the IPPF, of which he became an officer, warned him against getting heavily involved with the Pathfinder Fund, claiming that in some countries it had supported persons obstructive to government cooperation and sound national planning. But the Pathfinder Fund was quick and the IPPF was slow to act, he said, and each, plus the Population Council, had something to offer, and it was his policy to pursue the advantages and avoid the disadvantages: "I may be too opportunistic . . . My objective is to take advantage from every source available for the benefit of Korea."

For example, Mrs. Roots came to Korea with samples of the Lippes loop, and suggested she could get more for Korean doctors who would like to try them and report their results. Yang said he would be glad to have loops, and requested that equal numbers of any IUD allocation be distributed to the leading university hospitals. Intrauterine devices were not unfamiliar to Korean gynecologists who, like the private practitioners of Japan and Taiwan, had known of and often used the Ota ring. Yang and Margaret Roots got on famously; in 1966, the PPFK gave her an official citation "in grateful appreciation of your outstanding contributions to many aspects in the field of family planning in Korea and to the development of this Federation. . . . Furthermore, the fact that you are the first to have introduced to us the IUD which is widely used now among the Korean wives will be remembered to be an epoch in the history of our movement."

On the same trip, Mrs. Roots met an unusual young physician, Ralph Ten Have. Ten Have was a Dutch-American, born in Grand Haven, Michigan, and graduated from the University of Michigan Medical School in 1955. Following his two-year residency in radiology at a Public Health Service Hospital in Winnebago, Nebraska, the Christian Reformed Church and the Holt Adoption Program persuaded Ten Have to take a job providing medical care in the transportation of several thousand Korean infants to the United States for adoption. Some of the babies had been dying en route for want of medical attention . Recognizing that a preventive approach to the problem would be to cut down on the source of babies, who were being abandoned in Seoul daily, as many as 1000 to 2000 a year, Ten Have had become interested in doing family planning in PPFK branch offices and government health centers. He told Mrs. Roots, "My purpose is to provide vasectomies free to any poor man whose wife agrees that their family is large enough." Mrs. Roots told Gamble that he, Ten Have, already had done many sterilization operations.

Now, Ten Have was helping the Christian Reformed Korea Mission develop a Mobile Mission Clinic to work in various city slums and rural areas at certain times each week. Assisting him in this work were Dr. Peter Boelens, a University of Illinois medical graduate who had trained at Cook County Hospital; Dr. Kim Ok Soon, a woman gynecologist well trained in Korea; a nurse who lived in the slums close to her patients, and an administrative clerk. Ten Have, who might well be judged as hyperactive, also flew his own light airplane about South Korea, making use of the 150 air bases built by the American armed forces and the fact that these bases would sell aviation gasoline at fifteen cents a gallon.

When Mrs. Roots showed Ten Have the Lippes loop and suggested that the Pathfinder Fund would make them available without charge to doctors who would undertake carefully controlled studies, he became excited and said that he could insert 500 a month. Ten Have wrote Gamble, pointing out that the usual delays in importing foreign goods through customs inspection could be avoided by mailing IUDs and inserters to the Mobile Mission Clinic, 8th Army Chaplain's Welfare Service Section, APO 301, San Francisco, California, whence they would be flown by military air transport without further postage. This appealed to Gamble.

The loops were being produced by the small firm of Hohabe, Inc., Buffalo, owned by Dr. Jack Lippes and directed by Paul Bronnenkant, a plastics manufacturer. By the end of August, Ten Have had received his first 100 loops together with inserters and instructions from Lippes. He made his first insertion on Mrs. Ten Have, who was then a few months postpartum. He wrote Gamble for 1,000 more loops, and expressed the need for consultation on technique—necessarily by correspondence with Lippes and Gamble. Inserting his first fourteen loops in the poor women of Seoul, Ten Have exclaimed to Margaret Roots in September 1962: "You never saw such happy faces in your life. They have just NO money at all, but babies START without money."

Back in Boston scrounging for more Lippes loops, Gamble put an economic damper on their soaring enthusiasm: "The opportunities in Korea are so great and the need for money to use them that I feel they are beyond PF's capabilities, and want to take all possible steps to get help from other sources."

Meanwhile, Ten Have talked to Yang and they agreed on a cooperative plan under the sponsorship of the PPFK. By mid-

October, Gamble had placed 2,735 more Lippes loops at the disposal of Dr. Ten Have and Mrs. Roots. Of these, Mrs. Roots turned over 650 to Yang for the clinics of the Seoul National and Yonsei University Hospitals. The Mobile Mission Clinic study now went into high gear.

It was at this point that Gamble wrote to Nelson and Tietze in New York about the IUD study that he was supporting in Korea. In reply, they questioned whether Ten Have was qualified to undertake such research.

Tietze wrote: "I feel obliged to state once more that I am deeply perturbed by your willingness to initiate this large-scale study without adequate information." Before there was any United States participation, he said, Gamble should have evidence of the gynecological experience of the doctors inserting loops, of the stability of the sponsoring organization, and of the availability of nurses for follow-up and careful supervision of patients. Nelson wrote: "I am sure that you have had nothing but the best of motives in mind in encouraging a project in Korea, but circumstances there are delicate enough that it is important to be sure that a mistake that might jeopardize the entire program is avoided." On the same day, Gamble had called Buffalo to place a new order for 5,000 loops. The usually friendly and helpful Lippes said he would first need Pop Council approval. Gamble called Nelson and asked him the requirements for approval. Nelson wrote him, discussing in general some of the elements involved:

It is our firm opinion that these devices presently are very much in the category of experimentation and that it is highly essential that the studies that are undertaken be properly organized and thoroughly controlled with faithful attention to the matter of record keeping. Although we receive many inquiries for small numbers of coils and loops which very obviously would be used in casual studies only, we have consistently rejected such requests except for providing single examples of the devices. We have informed the people making inquiries and submitting requests ... that we would be quite pleased to receive properly documented proposals for sound investigations.

From this time in 1962 until 1965, the Population Council denied the Pathfinder Fund direct access to the various models of

Lippes loops made by Hohabe, Inc., while authorizing their use in increasing numbers by grantees who were accepted as participants in the Cooperative Statistical Analysis directed by Tietze.

The Pop Council staff enjoyed high professional prestige and progressively established itself as an international control organization in IUD work. From 1952 to 1964 its annual program commitments increased from less than $200,000 to $4.5 million a year.

Its superior resources notwithstanding, the Population Council could make an excellent case for the elements that shaped its policy. In the first place, the perils are real in placing a new drug or technique in the hands of enthusiastic therapists, whether they are lacking in a background in the specialty, specific training in the procedure, or a wise physician's conservative approach to treatment. Medical history contains many examples where uninformed treatment or overtreatment has led to disaster and the treatment so eagerly embraced at the outset ultimately has been rejected as yet another source of iatrogenic (doctor-induced) disease.

The Medical Advisory Committee of the Population Council was made up of men known to Gamble—Dr. George W. Corner of the Rockefeller Institute, Dr. Alan F. Guttmacher of Mt. Sinai Hospital, and Dr. Howard C. Taylor, Jr., of Columbia-Presbyterian Medical Center. They did not arrive at an IUD research policy all in one piece, but proceeded cautiously.

A second element shaping policy was that the United States Food and Drug Administration had not approved IUDs for general use. It was presumed that would be possible when safety and effectiveness had been thoroughly demonstrated. To introduce experimental drugs in other countries before they were accepted in the United States was to invite the old ethnic charges of the white race experimenting on browns, yellows, or blacks. Such an approach would encourage opposition rather than cooperation. Notestein was able to furnish an example of how this worked when Gamble came to see him and Balfour in June 1963. Gamble, who made it his habit to type up notes on these encounters, remarked as follows:

Notestein said he thought the loops had great promise, and that the Council was ready to back it with large funds as soon as the medical committee . . . thought the time was ripe. It should be made, as far as possible, to seem the idea and the request of the country, and should not be made to appear as forced by US or PC. The value of local pushing was shown by the history of Sushila Mayer, Health Minister of India. Guttmacher took his movie to San Francisco to show her, but found her against IU. On the way home on a train in India, she met a scientist, Indian, who had been putting spirals into monkeys, financed by PC. He convinced her it was good, and she has been in favor ever since. . . .

I presented the usefulness of planting a good IU doctor in each country to save time needed for him to insert, observe, tabulate, and get ready to report to his countrymen. Notestein recognized the value, but thought we should wait "six months to a year." "I'm afraid something might happen to give the method a black eye. Perhaps you are more adventure-some than I am. Aren't you afraid?" "No, I've seen no serious difficulties with Margulies, or Lippes, or our 700 in Puerto Rico, or Ten Have's 1,000 in Seoul, or anywhere else. I think we're ready to plant national seeds, as soon as you'll give us the loops."

The story of legal complications extended over a three-year period, and during this time, it will be seen, the IUD supply was in flux, with Clarence Gamble forced to live by his wits, a cir-cumstance he at times seemed to enjoy.

Never fazed by previous rebuff and consistent with his warning to Margaret Roots that Pathfinder did not have the money to exploit all the opportunities in Korea, Gamble went to Notestein to ask that the Pop Council finance Ten Have's study and do so through the Pathfinder Fund, because the Dutch Reformed Mis-sion was not incorporated as a tax-exempt agency. The Mobile Mission Clinic project cost him around $3,000 in 1963 and was headed for a $4,000 budget in 1964. Gamble wanted to start IUD projects elsewhere. This was not the only time that Gamble attempted to make use of the Council's greater resources, nor was it the only time he was refused. Notestein and Balfour rejected his request on the ground that it was against policy to give to a

Christian mission, since again it smacked of a foreign power imposing something on the indigenous people.

What the Population Council wanted to do, and was setting up a technical assistance program to do, was work through the governments of the underdeveloped countries, their health ministries, national family planning associations, and the gynecologists in their leading universities to carry out evaluation projects. The Council operated in this fashion in Korea, Taiwan, and Pakistan, where by the end of 1964 150,000 loops had been placed in women, officially on the responsibility of their countrymen. In Korea, for example, the Council recognized Yang and his PPFK medical committee as IUD controllers and placed all loops for Korea at their disposal. In 1963, these totaled 5,000 and rose to 30,000 in 1964.

Meanwhile, the Pop Council carried out a definitive evaluation of the IUD in about fifty projects, mostly in the United States and all under the direction of professors of gynecology in approved medical schools. These investigators sent their data to Tietze, still with the National Committee on Maternal Health but supported by the Pop Council, for compilation and analysis and reports to, among others, the Food and Drug Administration. Tietze thought it would take two to three years to complete this evaluation. In one of their friendly talks in 1965, Notestein gave Gamble his opinion of the difference in the Pathfinder and Pop Council theories. "They felt IU must be established with professors of gynecology before it is extended to practitioners, while PF is ready to distribute to doctors," noted Gamble. The danger of the latter approach Notestein illustrated with charges that one doctor in South America whom Gamble was supplying with IUDs was an abortionist (the unstated implications could have referred to the unsavory reputation of abortionists at that time, or that this doctor at best had a conflict of interest or, at worst, a good thing, since he could turn a profit on every treatment failure by aborting the pregnancy). "Perhaps if it comes out right you will have accomplished a great stroke, but it is a chancy gamble," Notestein said.

Gamble and Notestein had several confrontations on operations theory over a three-year period. Notestein had stated the Pop Council's objectives clearly in its 1959 annual report, the year he became president: "The purpose of the Population Council is to help develop the scientific and technical information which will assist the world's people in understanding and coping with their own population problems." What was not said was conspicuous to the *cognoscenti*—the Council was not financing the organization and delivery of contraceptive services as such. Its interest was "action research."

Gamble explained the Pathfinder policy to Notestein in 1962: "The objectives of the Pathfinder team may be defined as helping spread the availability and use of contraception especially in the overcrowded parts of the world and the countries in which the development of this part of medicine has yet been slight."

For the time being in October 1962, the question of qualifications hung heavily over the head of young Dr. Ten Have. When Nelson and Tietze raised the question, Gamble immediately made inquiry. He wrote Ten Have:

> Some of the doctors in New York with whom I have discussed your work have asked whether you have had training in gynecology. Won't you tell me what your experience has been? . . .
>
> I hope when you give our inserters or twists to other doctors you will make sure that they are competent to do intrauterine procedures either from previous experience or training under your direction. The reputation of the procedure will be seriously damaged if there are infections or other accidents resulting.

Ten Have was embarrassed. In his first reply, he described his own experience and then deleted these passages. It took Gamble a little more digging to assemble what health professionals normally pass around in a routine, mimeographed *curriculum vitae*. In a separate note, Ten Have tended to low-rate himself by stating he had no surgical training; while at the Public Health Service Hospital in Nebraska, he had done about fifteen dilatation and curettages, one female sterilization, and a few other operations, he said. "I don't think I'm well trained and I'm not real bright and I make many mistakes." These remarks did not necessarily distinguish him from many other practicing physicians, but, on the other hand, did not qualify him in the eyes of the Population Council for the work at hand. Actually, as he later disclosed, he had obtained a good amount of experience as an intern in delivering babies, handling problem cases in consultation with a certified OB-GYN man. His unfinished residency in radiology, of course, did not count for much in his present mission.

Ten Have wrote Gamble in November 1962 that he was concerned about the supply of loops, in view of the Pop Council's reaction. "So am I," Gamble replied. He now had found out what Nelson and Tietze had meant by "qualified." The Council required that the doctor receiving loops should have gynecological training, have a substitute doctor in case of the senior's illness or other absence, preferably, have medical school backing, use approved record forms, do careful follow-up on all cases, and provide full reporting and analysis of results to the Pop Council. One thing that had alarmed the New Yorkers, Gamble indicated, was Ten Have's request for 500 loops a month. They "feel it utterly impossible" for him to record and follow up 500 new insertions a month. Gamble now asked a long list of questions about available doctors, nurses, and social workers, as well as the problem of translating the Tietze form from English to Korean and back again. By this time, Ten Have had sent Gamble records of his first fifty-five cases. On the whole, they looked good.

These records were the first in what became the Pathfinder Fund's International IUD Program, but Gamble was not yet thinking of it in this way and, indeed, prospects for such a program looked dim.

The problem was to convince the Population Council that it should allow Lippes to continue to supply the Mobile Mission Clinic and other Gamble projects with loops. Lippes suggested that Dr. Ten Have talk to Dr. Balfour when the latter was in Seoul on his November survey, but unfortunately Balfour was forced to bed with influenza and nothing occurred to change the Population Council's judgment. On the contrary, at a time when Balfour was preparing a report advising the Korean Ministry of Health and Social Affairs that "the potential value of intrauterine devices . . . should be investigated in one or more small-scale pilot projects to determine acceptability, effectiveness, and safety"—all within a government and Population Council-supported format—it could not but irk Balfour to know that the Pathfinder people already had such unapproved projects in progress.

At the outset, the Mobile Mission Clinic project appeared ill-fated. Ten Have's wife became ill, and he was forced to return with her in November to Grand Haven, Michigan. This left Dr. Boelens in immediate charge, but in 1963 Boelens contracted infectious hepatitis and also returned to the United States. The Americans, however, still had an ace in the hole. Ten Have had written Gamble: "I've a rather aggressive Korean woman doctor working with me. She is bright and keen and not afraid to work nor to see this thing through." This was Dr. Kim Ok Soon. Furthermore, she was a trained gynecologist, and she did see the study through. Gamble went to Korea in March 1963 and helped assemble the results of her insertions from the accumulated records.

After a six-month experience, Dr. Kim and her associates published a report that gave full credit to Mrs. Roots and Dr. Gamble for furnishing the loops and to Dr. Han Shu Shin, chairman of the medical advisory committee of the Planned Parenthood Federation of Korea, for sponsoring the study. Through March 1963, loops had been inserted in 1,027 women living in or near Seoul. In 2,477 months of exposure among 887 users who had follow-up examinations, there was one pregnancy following an unnoticed expulsion, producing a pregnancy rate of 0.5 per 100 women per year. Some 3.8 percent of the women expelled the loop and 4.5 percent had it removed for physical reasons. "The remaining 771 observed women continued to use the loop satisfactorily. . . . Acceptability by the women was excellent. . . . We found that the neighborhood clinics visited weekly by the medical team rapidly became popular because of the convenience of the clinic, modest cost of service, and the easy, simple, and inexpensive methods of contraception."

At the Population Council's second international conference on intrauterine contraception in New York in October 1964, Dr. Shin rounded out the experience of the three study groups designated by Yang—the Mobile Mission Clinic and Seoul National and Yonsei University Hospitals. Through July 1964, 3,658 women were fitted with Lippes loops, including later models. They had more than 12,000 months of exposure. Depending on the loop model, pregnancy rates varied between 2.3 and 6.2 per 100 woman-years of exposure. Expulsions and removals varied with the model but were consistent with previous experience. Major reasons for removal were pain and bleeding. As Shin stated, the purpose of these studies was to determine safety and effectiveness of the IUD's prior to their nationwise use. He concluded: "The results of these studies, so far, indicate that the Lippes loop provides a safe, reliable, and acceptable means of contraception in this country."

If the proof of the pudding is in the eating, then Gamble was vindicated. Notestein had told Gamble, he wanted to wait six months or a year before taking the IUD overseas on any major scale, and Tietze had estimated it would take two to three years to complete the American evaluation. On this basis, Gamble estimated that he had saved Korea a year or two in getting started on an IUD program. Further, on a second look, Ten Have no longer raised eyebrows at the Pop Council. Back in Michigan and training in public health at the University of Michigan, he convinced the Council it should support him in an IUD project in Wayne, Michigan.

There was no doubt in Gamble's mind that his impatience was rewarded. Through widely scattered distribution of small numbers of loops he was able to proceed in helping family planning programs, by increasing the availability of persons with actual experience in using loops. He moved ahead of the Population Council in distributing IUD's in Korea and elsewhere overseas in 1962 and at least part of 1963, but the Population Council program of free distribution of IUDs in the underdeveloped countries soon leaped ahead. In 1964, the Pop Council supplied 70,000

IUDs; in 1965, 1,720,000, and in 1966, 820,000. The nine-year total, 1964–1971, was 7,130,000. In the long run, birth controllers have been dismayed to find, people's interest in using the IUD declined, following early enthusiasm, rather than continuously accelerated.

No figures on total consumption of loops exist. No complete records are available on distribution of loops manufactured in the underdeveloped countries, such as Hong Kong, Taiwan, India, Pakistan, and Korea, under Pop Council sponsorship. Nor does the Pop Council total include Ortho overseas sales.

It is impossible, therefore, to either evaluate the effect of the loop, or to assess how much of continuing overseas interest in population-impacted countries was stimulated by Clarence Gamble, acting as advance man of the Great Cause. But he did his best to spread the word.

chapter 22   The Population Council: Gamble vs. Notestein

Clarence Gamble gave Frank Notestein many uneasy moments. These accumulated and reached the point of near crisis in 1965. At a time when Notestein, as president of the Population Council, was engaged in some ticklish negotiations with the Ortho Pharmaceutical Corporation concerning national and international patent rights to the Lippes loop, Gamble, as Notestein put it, was "flying like a bird over countries dropping loops." A great deal was involved, including the fact that Gamble, when he could not buy American-made Lippes loops, had them made in Hong Kong and shipped to the Pathfinder Fund in Boston for distribution free of charge to individual doctors all over the world who wanted to try them. By the end of 1963, Gamble was sending IUDs to, and receiving reports from, doctors in twenty countries, and this number rapidly grew until by early 1965 he was serving 340 doctors in sixty-nine countries. Meanwhile, from 1962 until

1964, the Population Council restricted its overseas program to Korea, Taiwan, and Pakistan. In 1964, it expanded to thirty countries.

The Population Council carefully dissociated itself from what it specified as the "separate" and "independent" efforts of Gamble to introduce the IUD wherever the opportunity presented itself. From Notestein's viewpoint, Gamble might have undermined an international IUD program in several different ways—through inadequate planning, incompetent research, bad publicity if there was any slip-up, or violation of patent and licensing agreements.

From Gamble's standpoint, the Population Council was frustrating his urge to push ahead with IUDs, trusting to Gamble intuition and Gamble luck, nonquantifiable but identifiable elements in his success as a family planner. As matters stood, the Pop Council had cut him off from Lippes loops except for those made available to his Mobile Mission Clinic project through the medical committee of the Planned Parenthood Federation of

Edna McKinnon, Indonesia, 1964

Korea. He could get Margulies coils. In 1963, the Ortho Pharmaceutical Corporation of Raritan, New Jersey, offered the Margulies Spiral (Gynekoil) for sale to private physicians at fifteen for $6.00, or forty cents each, and later, for sixty-five cents. Gamble became a regular customer, although he begrudged the price and bought limited amounts. He had been able to buy loops from Lippes for five cents each the year before.

From 1963 on, before patent and licensing questions were finally resolved, the Population Council encouraged national family planning associations and governments, in underdeveloped countries to consider making local arrangements for the manufacture of the loop for home consumption, for example in Korea, Taiwan, and Pakistan. This suggested to Gamble a much-needed avenue of supply and he moved to develop it in Hong Kong.

As in Korea, Margaret Roots was the first to bring samples of the Lippes loop into Hong Kong. In the spring of 1963, she received an enthusiastic reception from Dr. Daphne Chun, professor of obstetrics and gynecology at the University of Hong Kong and Queen Mary Hospital, who was president of the Family Planning Association of Hong Kong, and from Dr. S. Y. Cheng, head of the FPAHK's fifty clinics.

Nowhere in the world did population pressure project itself more dramatically than in this isolated city, where 3.75 million persons lived on eighty square miles of habitable land and even drinking water had to be imported. While the British Crown Colony covered nearly 400 square miles, most of it was wasteland; in the inner city of Kowloon, a matter of twelve square miles, population density was 250,000 persons per square mile. The city's growth rate was 3.1 percent per year, due to a high birth rate and the influx of refugees from mainland China. The Hong Kong population was only 600,000 in 1945; in 1970, it was 4.3 million.

One of the most striking features of Hong Kong is its sampan people, who lived out their lives on boats moored in the many bays and inlets of the island. These were mainly cargo boats that lightered cargo from ocean-going freighters anchored offshore, or carried goods to various smaller islands. The larger were motor-powered junks from thirty to sixty feet long, with high poop decks at the stern. The small sampan boats, from twelve to twenty-five feet long, were maneuvered through the crowded waterways by a long stern sweep.

Mrs. Roots reported that 30,000 families usually of seven to nine persons each lived in Yaumati Harbor on the Kowloon waterfront—an estimated quarter of a million persons living on boats.

The husband-and-wife doctor team of Phillip and Amelia Cheung described a typical sampan family as a coolie, forty years old, with a wife, thirty-eight, having twelve children from one month to sixteen years old. She had miscarried three times, was in poor health, and her children were malnourished. Their boat home was twelve feet long and five feet wide. The husband also had to support his aged parents. The whole family was illiterate. They were superstitious and worshipped idols.

The Cheungs, advisers to the FPAHK, were just beginning work on the Floating Clinic, a house on a barge, sponsored by Project Concern, Inc., founded by Dr. James W. Turpin. They worked in the clinic during the day and visited families by sampan two hours every evening, five nights a week. In the clinic, they saw an average of 150 patients a day, the high being 250.

Mrs. Roots, when she came to Hong Kong, first looked over the sampan people as candidates for IUDs, but Turpin felt that the Floating Clinic's patients did not meet the research requirements laid down by Gamble. Follow-up would be difficult because a sampan family often sculled off and moored elsewhere, so it would be difficult for a woman to reach the doctor in case of bleeding. Turpin preferred to wait until the IUDs had proved their practicality—"We will use the foam tablets until then." He and the Cheungs were eager to introduce family planning and, supplied by the Pathfinder, provided foam tablets and condoms to 1,100 boat families living in the Yaumati Typhoon Shelter, plus ninety-seven IUDs for selected patients, in six months.

Meanwhile, Mrs. Roots promoted a coil and loop study in the FPAHK clinical program under the direction of Dr. Cheng. Pathfinder provided support covering part-time salaries of doctor, nurse, and clerk starting June 1, 1963. Gamble, foreseeing additional expenses, granted HK$5,124.56 for one year—$900 U.S. dollars. First supplied by Gamble with 600 coils, Cheng inserted nearly all of them in the next seven months. Dr. Chun started work in a second FPA clinic at Kowloon Centre; together, Cheng and Chun reported 2,000 IUD coil and loop cases in 1963 and nearly 10,000 in 1964. In his first 446 insertions, mostly Margulies, Cheng was amazed to find a zero pregnancy rate among users. Expulsions were 9.4 percent and other removals, mainly through lack of confidence or fear, were 6.2 percent. Of some significance for loop size, it was observed that the Asian uterus is generally smaller than the American.

The two doctors Cheung wrote Gamble in 1963: "The boat people thank you for giving them the instruction and contraceptives free of charge. They are most grateful if you would go on providing them the contraceptives and continue the work in family planning."

Clarence Gamble had cause to feel good that summer. From Kennebec Point in Maine, he wrote Margaret Roots in Hong Kong: "I am sitting in the comfortable sunshine on the edge of the water with the delightful view unobstructed by microphone and the tape recorder." He asked Mrs. Roots to make a report on Hong Kong that he could pass on to the IPPF, where he said that he was still trying to "open satisfactory communication." "To show you what I have in mind (not to write your report for you), I am enclosing an imaginary edition for you to correct, improve and approve." He then dictated two double-spaced pages. Mrs. Roots, who had been reporting on her activities for ten years with outstanding vitality and color, reciprocated with a report of three pages single spaced entirely in her own words, and sent it to him without reference to his. He accepted hers.

Among others in Hong Kong, Mrs. Roots met an energetic Californian, Robert H. Gillespie, a volunteer worker in his early

twenties who had gone to the Far East to do publicity for the
Meals for Millions program and, as some others, recognized that
success or failure in feeding hungry children depended as much
on the number of mouths to feed as on the availability of food.
Would it not, in the long run, be more economical to limit the
supply of children than to attempt to feed unlimited numbers
with a limited supply of food?

Mrs. Roots told Gamble about Gillespie. Gamble wrote Gillespie in May:

> Can you take time to explore the possibility of getting Lippes loops
> manufactured in Hong Kong? I hope there are some good plastic man-
> ufacturers in the Colony. . . . Samples of his No. 2 loop and inserter are
> enclosed. Dr. Lippes tells me that construction of the steel mold is
> expensive, costing, in this country, $800 U.S. or more. He is ready to
> provide a detailed mechanical drawing of the loop. . . . There is no hurry
> about getting the loop produced, since we have the Margulies spiral to
> work with.

But Gillespie was in a hurry; among other things, he wished to
return to his home in Bel Air in August to get married to
Katherine Deuel, who in 1958 had made her debut from the
Valley Hunt Club, a Pasadena social institution well-known to
Gamble. Gamble was much taken with Gillespie, a college dropout who otherwise seemed to be a young man of discriminating
judgment.

Gillespie talked to twenty-five plastic manufacturers. Yu Un
Ek of Ekder Plastic Works was interested, and directed Gillespie
to a mold maker, Mr. Kohn. The FPAHK gladly accepted the role
of sponsoring organization. Gamble obtained the drawings from
Lippes, sent them along, and ordered raw materials from DuPont.
The letters flew back and forth in late May and early June as the
collaborators worked out details. Gillespie took the time to quote
Machiavelli's *The Prince*:

> There is nothing more difficult to take in hand, more perilous to
> conduct, or more uncertain in its success, than to produce a new order of
> things, because the innovator has for enemies all those who have done

fair under the old conditions, and lukewarm defenders in those who may do well under the new.

Whatever the case, Gillespie was able to send Gamble a "Gamble sample loop" on July 4, 1963, remarking that "Mr. Kohn, the mold maker, seemed to understand the mechanical drawing but this loop is far from perfect." On July 22, thanks to the enterprise of Yu, Gillespie sent Gamble 1,000 Hong Kong manufactured Lippes loops, complete with suture-thread tails, in a box labeled: "Made in Hong Kong—plastic loops." Three days later, Gillespie was on his way back to California.

It wasn't a bad summer's work for a college dropout, and indeed Gillespie (who some years later worked for the Population Council in Taiwan and then became their representative in Iran) demonstrated promotional and managerial initiative and skill above that of some professionals well beyond him in years. Gamble wrote Gillespie: "It was thrilling to get the finished and threaded loops. To me they look completely satisfactory. . . . I'm going to ask Dr. Boelens in Seoul to test them immediately."

At one point Gamble had found it necessary to caution Gillespie, who wanted to come back and talk to Lippes, Margulies, and the Population Council about the loop situation in Hong Kong:

> The Population Council has asked Lippes to give loops only with their permission, to people approved by their committee. I have told no one in this country about plans for manufacture and do not want them to know of these until the appropriate time comes. Please do not tell anyone, except the manufacturers, that I, or the Pathfinder Fund, are considering the manufacture. Margulies has applied for a patent, and believes that he can prevent Lippes from manufacture when the patent is granted. Probably he will do what he can to prevent manufacture in Hong Kong.

A shared secret, alas, does not keep. Too many persons knew what was going on in Hong Kong, where by September the FPAHK had a large-scale research project in progress, using Hong Kong-made loops. Every IPPFer and Pop Councillor passing through this mixing bowl of the Far East heard about the Pathfinder Fund's latest finesse. Thus, it was not surprising that when

Gamble went to see Notestein in New York in October he was able to record this comment: "Notestein told me he understood I was manufacturing loops in Hong Kong."

Dr. Notestein's understanding was correct. He also understood the implications of this new source of supply of Lippes-like loops, inasmuch as Gamble cheerfully told him that the Pathfinder Fund was sending IUDs to doctors all over the world. Obviously, Gamble now had the opportunity to circumvent the Pop Council's refusal to let him have Buffalo-made Lippes loops. He could undertake an international IUD evaluation competitive with—and, for the time being, ahead of—the Council's program overseas.

Gamble contracted with Yu to sell his loops to the Pathfinder Fund for three cents each. They were mailed to Boston in packages first of 5,000 and later of 1,000 each, marked "Medical Samples" and addressed either to Dr. Clarence Gamble or to Dr. David Burleson, a young anthropologist who became Pathfinder director of field services in 1964 (and more recently a senior research associate in the Carolina Population Center). The Pathfinder Fund distributed the loops in small lots to participating physicians, making it a practice to send 100 and then wait for the doctor's first set of case reports before mailing him more.

The Pathfinder's international IUD program was carried on by a staff of three or four persons working in the office on the second floor of Sparr's Drug Store, Huntington and Longwood Avenues, hard by the Harvard Medical School Quadrangle. They corresponded with birth controllers all over the world. Both Burleson and Mrs. June Weiss, who was Gamble's executive secretary, spontaneously commented: "It was fun to work for Dr. Gamble." He obviously was able to inspire a strong personal loyalty among his workers. "He had a quick mind, and was creative in service projects," recalled Mrs. Weiss. "He had a talent for getting people involved and excited."

In those days, the Pathfinder Fund operated in three places—in an office over a grocery store in Milton, where Mrs. Grace Putney dealt with Pathfinder affairs; in Cambridge, where Miss Edith Gates handled educational matters from her apartment, and over Sparr's drugstore, where the IUD and other contraceptive studies had replaced Dr. Gamble's earlier laboratory research. No members of his staff had a comprehensive view of Gamble's activities, since he declined to delegate administrative authority, eschewing staff conferences and dealing with one employee at a time. When Mrs. Weiss remonstrated with him that he should keep her better informed on matters relevant to her duties, he replied, "If I told you everything I know, you would know as much as I do."

His curiosity about others was unrestrained. For example, he had the habit of going through the waste basket when he came into the Boston Pathfinder headquarters two or three times a week. (He did not have an office or a desk of his own there). It was not clear to Mrs. Weiss whether he was checking how much stationery was being wasted, or whether this was his way, in the manner of a detective, of informing himself what went on in his absence. Howbeit, his persistence annoyed her enough to make her empty her waste basket every day in the lady's washroom, presumably beyond his reach.

When they first moved in, he was upset to find a bar of Palmolive soap in the men's room. He told her to go down and see Landlord Sparr and demand a bar of Ivory. This was Mrs. Weiss's first inkling that her boss was related to Procter & Gamble.

From Gamble's notes on interviews with Dr. Notestein in 1963 and 1964, it is easy to conclude that (1) Gamble must have made Notestein nervous but (2) Notestein was nice about it. In fact, there is no hint that either man lost patience with the other. Notestein explained to Gamble why the Population Council was restricting overseas expansion of IUD testing. While "the medical committee has become convinced that there is less danger to the woman in intrauterine contraception than in no contraception at all," the Council was accumulating evidence on safety and effectiveness sufficient to win the approval of the Food and Drug Administration. Until such data were available, the Council "feared political repercussions," in the countries involved because of racial and nationalistic prejudices. Notestein was resistant to what Gamble was doing from both scientific and political standpoints, but not these alone. Control of the manufacture, sale, and distribution of the Margulies and Lippes IUDs was still unsettled and fascinatingly complex.

The Population Council supported the research and development of both the Margulies coil and the Lippes loop, but its financial stake became greater in the loop. Over a five-year period, 1961-1965, it made grants totalling $20,300 to Margulies; in a ten-year period, 1962-1972, it financed Lippes's work to the extent of $236,331.

Margulies applied for a United States patent on his coil in November 1960, assigning the application to his institution, Mount Sinai Hospital. He did not obtain a patent until August 1965, long after he had, in turn for a small royalty, made Ortho the exclusive licensee to make, sell, and distribute the coil under the foreign, as well as American, patent applications filed.

Lippes applied for a patent on his loop in April 1963 and obtained it in 1966. Notestein told Gamble that the Margulies patent, sold to Ortho, "covered everything with two ends which could be straightened out to put in a tube and which would recover its shape after insertion." This was a patent on a principle, as opposed to Lippes' patent on the shape of his loop. Lippes admitted from the first that he was using the Margulies principle; thus, when the coil and loop reached the patent stage, it was evident to all concerned that the loop was an infringement on the coil. Because of greater acceptability, however, the loop was far more marketable. To avoid litigation—nobody wanted it—Ortho sought to acquire control of the Lippes as well as the Margulies patent.

By 1965, all parties were eager for a settlement. There then began a protracted period of negotiations between Lippes and Ortho, concerning the transfer of commercial rights, and between the Population Council and Ortho, involving the control of IUD-LDC public service rights in underdeveloped countries. These negotiations were conducted in a friendly manner and, according to all sources, Ortho, Population Council, and Lippes (Hohabe, Inc.) all behaved in an enlightened manner. There never was a suit or threat of one.

All parties agreed that control of overpopulation was of the utmost importance to economic development as well as personal health in less developed countries, and that the IUD was the instrument best suited to mass contraception among the uneducated. These were people who could ill afford to buy food, much less contraceptives, and therefore whatever contraception was offered would have to be free. On this basis, Ortho said it would give the Population Council royalty-free rights to control the loop for nonprofit use (oral agreement, August 3, 1965 and letter of agreement, September 7, 1965). A feature of this agreement was that the council could license governments or voluntary agencies in developing countries to manufacture loops for domestic use but not for profit. The first such license went to the Family Planning Association of Hong Kong in 1965.

The Hong Kong license permitted the FPA and Mr. Yu to manufacture and distribute loops for nonprofit use in Hong Kong, but not to export them to their old friend, Dr. Gamble, in the United States, or to other countries. Nor could Yu make loops commercially without Ortho approval, for Ortho's controlling patent application in Great Britain also applied in Hong Kong. As for Gamble, the Council once more had cut off his source of loops. The first time it was from Buffalo. Now it was from Hong Kong. The reasons for the stoppages were different but the effect was the same—no loops for Pathfinder. He faced a crisis in his ad hoc commitment to supply loops to hundreds of doctors.

Where was Pathfinder to obtain loops now? Gamble put the question to Notestein in New York in May 1965. According to Gamble's notes on this meeting, Notestein was sympathetic and suggested that Gamble buy 100,000 loops from Hohabe (Lippes). The earlier fear that starting IUD evaluation programs in foreign countries would produce negative reactions because the device was not approved by the United States government had pretty well disappeared. As it turned out, the Food and Drug Administration refused jurisdiction over the IUD, on the basis that it was a device and not a drug (the law made the FDA responsible for investigating the safety and effectiveness of drugs). There had been no significant nationalist or ethnic opposition to IUDs.

As Lippes remembered in an interview in 1972, Notestein called him and asked if he could sell Gamble some loops. Lippes could not see why not, if the Population Council had no objections. He had always been friendly to Gamble, and appreciated the man's habit of cutting red tape. Gamble at various times had come to Buffalo to see Lippes's work, and had given him $700 when he needed it quickly to perfect an inserter different in design from Margulies. Most important, while he was negotiating with Ortho to take over his patent application, Lippes still controlled American and foreign rights to make and sell his loop for profit (he sold these rights to Ortho in 1966 for a modest sum).

Gamble in the summer of 1965 placed an order with Lippes for 100,000 loops at eight cents a loop, and later repeated the order. The Pathfinder IUD program was able to continue without interruption. Except for the doubling in cost, the shift to the Hohabe Lippes loop was advantageous, because it later became evident that Mr. Yu at times had trouble with quality control. Due to tiny cracks in the plastic, some of the Hong Kong loops broke while in use, as doctors in various parts of the world reported. Sometimes, Lippes loops got the blame.

While all this was going on, Clarence Gamble was, in his determined way, breaking another bottleneck. This was the general conviction, from Grafenberg on, that the insertion of an IUD had to be done by a physician with gynecological training and experience. Certainly this was an ideal difficult to refute, based as it was on a good doctor-patient relationship as well as technical competence, but in mass use of IUDs the requirement posed a major obstacle because of the shortage of gynecologists in the less-advanced nations and, most of all, in rural areas where there might be no physician at all.

Gamble wrote Ten Have, who was back in Korea in 1964, he had learned that in Santiago, Chile, where Pathfinder was supporting an IUD project, midwives had performed 4,000 insertions without serious difficulty. Was this something Korea might want to try? Ten Have replied that Dr. Yang Jae Mo and others involved favored such a "pioneer study." Pathfinder than made a small grant to Yonsei Medical School to pay the traveling expenses of Dr. Sang Whan Song as director and the salary of a midwife for a study in the village of Chang Kock, near Seoul. Beginning in January 1965, Dr. Sang trained the nurse midwife for five days in the technique, requiring her to insert thirty loops in his presence before permitting her to work alone. By May 1965, 144 women were wearing IUDs that she had inserted. The experience was sufficient to convince the PPFK that the nurse midwives in more than 200 government health and family planning centers should be so trained, as part of a large birth control training program supported by the Population Council.

The Pathfinder's IUD program continued to grow; at the time of Gamble's death in July 1966, it was sending loops to 504 doctors in 74 countries. When extensively reviewed a year later by Roger P. Bernard, then Pathfinder director of research, the number had grown to 628 doctors in 82 countries. These doctors had reported on more than 71,000 insertions. The Pathfinder IUD program was most active in Africa and Latin America, followed by the Far East and Oceania, Europe, and the Middle East.

While achieving a higher acceptability than previous con-traceptives and therefore a greater impact in countries where it has been widely used, the IUD in recent years has encountered the phenomenon of a diminishing return that seems to be inher-ent in its nature as a foreign body tending to mobilize the body's defenses to reject it. The common side effects of pain and bleeding soon following insertion work against acceleration of the IUD's popularity.

A decline in birth rates and population growth rates has been observed in countries where in the last ten years government and voluntary forces have pushed large IUD programs, such as Korea, Taiwan, Hong Kong, Singapore, Costa Rica, and Chile. These efforts, which helped as one of several social phenomena in the claimed reductions in birth rates by as much as one-third or one-half and cutbacks in population growth rates by as much as

20 to 30 percent, undoubtedly reflect the combined organizational efforts of many different agencies, public and private. These include the Pathfinder Fund, often acting by analogy as the hand planter of the first seed, and the Population Council, cast in its technical assistance program more in the role of the mechanized farmer, as well as many other organizations of all sizes, notably the United States Agency for International Development, the International Planned Parenthood Federation and its national affiliates, United Nations, Church World Service, Brush Foundation, and others.

Gains in population control, however, cannot be credited wholly to the IUD, oral pill, or any single method, for all countries have employed a combination of old and new methods, typically offering the wife and husband a choice. In addition, there is much disagreement among demographers as to the specific effect of family planning action programs as compared to the impact of the well-established general phenomenon of declining birth rates in countries in transition from the peasant-farming to an industrial stage of economic and social development. Then, too, there are questions regarding the reliability of statistical data on births, deaths, and population growth. It is axiomatic that underdeveloped countries underreport their vital statistics due to defects in systematic and uniform data collection. Even studies within the same country may yield contradictory results. For example, one study in South Korea covering an eight-year period showed a drop in the net growth rate from 2.6 to 2.1 percent, whereas another calculated it to be from 2.8 to 1.9. There was agreement in direction, but not in magnitude.

Gamble had been able to show in early field tests that the pregnancy rate could be reduced among women practicing birth control irrespective of the contraceptive used. But before the advent of the oral pill and the IUD, no agency found it possible to make an impact on the population growth rate through a planned, organized, and delivered effort. In certain European countries where the population growth rate has fallen to 0.5 percent or less, it was not a matter of government policy or public service but self-determination—the collective will of husbands and wives to reduce their number of offspring. Japan, too, might be taken as an exception, but again it was mainly a matter of strong individual motivation with induced abortion furnishing the main instrument, establishing a life style reinforced and to a great extent replaced by organized efforts to introduce modern contraception.

chapter 23   The DeMarchis and the Pope's

Children

"The Italian people are too prolific. I am glad of it. I will never countenance birth control propaganda. . . . Births exceed deaths by 440,000 yearly in this small peninsula, with 40,000,000 inhabitants. . . . As the country grows, only three roads are open to it: To addict itself to voluntary sterility—Italians are too intelligent to do that—to make war, or to seek outlets for overpopulation."

Thus Benito Mussolini, the Fascist *Il Duce,* in 1924 placed the longstanding pressure of numbers in the service of his ambition to build another Holy Roman Empire. He was speaking in Milan two years after becoming dictator over a land that in area is about the same size as the state of Arizona. The outcome of this political commitment to strength in numbers, reinforced by the Pope's holy decree of uncontrolled procreation, is now a matter of history. Misdirected by Mussolini, the Italians made war in North and East Africa and a half million migrated there, only to return to the homeland as war refugees. In time, Italy lost its war abroad and at home, assassinated its dictator, and founded a Republic, a 95 percent Catholic populace whose constitution recognized no separation of church and state and accepted compulsory teaching of Catholicism in public schools. Among these religious teachings was the doctrine that sexual intercourse is carnal sin unless its purpose is conception; ergo, any attempt to interfere with this outcome in intercourse is immoral. It seemed an excellent way of guaranteeing a large flock of sinners.

The DeMarchis

Like Japan, another nation whose dream of empire metamorphosed in a nightmare of destruction and misery, Italy emerged from World War II in a state of chaos, following eight years of war in Africa, enemy bombardment of Italian cities, civil war, Allied invasion of Italy, loss of territory, and deportation of prisoners of war. At the end of this tragic failure, the population had risen to 45 million (by 1972, it was up to 55 million). One out of four lived in total poverty, and 50 percent of the poor consisted of families of five or more, many of them living four to a room. More than 300,000 families dwelt in cellars, caves, or shacks. With overcrowding and unemployment came attendant problems of increasing promiscuity and illiteracy. Children were hired out to professional beggars and farmers for six or seven dollars a year. Many became vagabonds and thieves, rich material for postwar novelists and film-makers. One small boy, asked by the judge why he stole a motor scooter, explained: "Because I am not big enough to steal an automobile."

Even so, it was not true, as commonly observed, that "Italians are multiplying at the speed of rabbits." Unlike Japan, Italy had witnessed a long, steady decline in its birth rate, the same as had other advanced countries of Western Europe. Mussolini, with his policy of *il numero e forza*, failed to stop this downward trend, even with salary raises and promotions for high fertility and with harsh laws, such as Article 553 of the 1930 Fascist penal code: "Whoever publicly incites to practices against procreation or makes propaganda in their favor is punishable by detention of one year."

When *Il Duce* marched into Rome in 1922, Italy's annual birth rate was 30.8 per 1,000 population. It continued steadily downward to 23.5 in 1940 and 17.6 in 1952, largely the result of an estimated 600,000 to three million illegal abortions per year but also assisted by the forbidden method of withdrawal before ejaculation and use of condoms among the more affluent. The typical village abortionist in rural South Italy, where the birth rates were the highest, was a medically untrained woman called *La Mama*. In brief, with as many as two abortions for every live birth, it appeared that a majority of Italian mothers did not agree with their priests or their politicians.

The fundamental cause of population growth in Italy was neither a predilection for "la dolce vita" nor the alleged national characteristic of easily aroused passions, as some foreigners like to remark, but a death rate that dropped well ahead of the birth rate, maintaining a substantial excess of births over deaths. Mortality sank still lower after the war, when the Rockefeller Foundation and the United Nations Relief and Rehabilitation Administration (UNRRA) joined with the Italian government in the DDT eradication of mosquitoes, thus effectively controlling endemic malaria, an ancient and modern Roman plague.

Italy's population growth rate in the postwar years dropped lower than that of the United States, but the demographic damage had been done over the previous one hundred years. The country had filled up with people and overflowed in the mass emigations of 1876 to 1930. The problem was complicated after World War II by socioeconomic disorganization and depression, hitting harder in the toe-and-instep farm areas of the Italian boot than the more prosperous industrial north, but nonetheless manifest in the *borgate* (slums) of Rome and other large cities.

The Remarkable DeMarchis

Against this backdrop, on this stage, and with a dependable Italian capacity for high drama, a young husband-and-wife team, Luigi and Maria Luisa DeMarchi, neither one a physician, became national heroes in Italy's contraceptive revolution. The DeMarchis are the inspirational and operational leaders of the *Associazione Italiana per l'Educazione Demografica* (AIED), founded in 1953. The Italian Association for Demographic Education is a family planning association, or planned parenthood federation; its name was designed to skirt the prohibition on public education in birth control existing when it began. The AIED had two purposes from the outset: to publicize birth control and to abolish Mussolini's law prohibiting such publicity. It took eighteen years to accomplish the latter goal, against the chronic opposition of the Church, police, government, and—with bitter irony—the International Planned Parenthood Federation. The goal of publicizing birth control has not yet been achieved.

The DeMarchis are a striking couple. *The Christian Science Monitor* once described DeMarchi as a "slim, wispy-bearded journalist." One feels in his presence a formidable and facile intellect. His spirited redhaired wife is contrastingly tall; she wears her clothes with a grace and style found only among certain Roman women. Both are socially agreeable persons, but in matters of sex reform and contraception they are outspoken, aggressive, militant. Typical Roman intellectual radicals, they are frugal in their personal tastes. They do not smoke, drink only small amounts of table wines, and have limited themselves to two children, a girl and a boy.

DeMarchi was born in 1927 at Brescia, near Milan, the son of a minor social security officer but descendant of a considerable line of university professors; a grand-uncle was Emilio DeMarchi, the novelist. Luigi graduated *cum laude* from Rome University in 1951, with a doctoral degree in psychology. His dissertation was "Psychogenesis of D. H. Lawrence's Conception of Sex." Later, he wrote several scholarly works, including *Sex and Civilization* (1959), *Sociology of Sex* (1963), *Psycho-politics* (1965), and *Wilhelm Reich, Biography of an Idea* (1970). The Italian Socialist newspaper *Avanti!* wrote: "DeMarchi unquestionably has the historical merit of being the first Italian author to try to apply depth psychology to the great social, political, economic, and cultural problems of our times."

From his academic start, DeMarchi was interested, as he said, "in a moral revolution giving back to sexual love the poetic, religious, and ethical potential which naturally belongs to it." He saw no future as a university professor inasmuch as the Italian academic world was largely stifled by Catholic and Marxist dogmatism. Of all the effects of what he called "sex-negative morality," he concluded that the population explosion was the most disastrous, and this view united him with the small group of liberal dissenters who formed the AIED. For a living, he had his experience and skill as a reporter on various Rome newspapers, including the Social Democratic daily, *L'Umanita*, beginning when he was eighteen.

He met Maria Luisa Zardini while vacationing in Cortina d'Ampezzo, the Italian mountain resort in the Dolomites, near Austria. She was the local telephone operator. Her father, a shopkeeper, had died four years after her birth in 1925, and she went to work at the telephone office when she was fourteen. When she was twenty-five, she moved to Rome. She and Luigi defied the Church by undertaking a trial marriage of a year or so and then married, in 1951, in a civil ceremony—a rare thing in Italy. It is noteworthy that they do not regard themselves as atheists, but hold radical opposition to the Church to be a basic component of true religiousness.

The young birth controllers saw Catholicism, Fascism, and Communism as their three ideological enemies. Carlo Matteotti, Social Democrat member of the Chamber of Deputies and founder and first president of AIED, was their close friend. The Fascists had murdered his father, a Socialist hero, in 1924—many avenues and squares now bore the name of Matteotti. The AIED attracted much press attention when it began, including the Vatican's *L'Osservatore Romano*; the newspaper called on the police to suppress this subversive propaganda. The Communist daily *Unita* attacked the new organization as "a provocation of international capitalism, aimed at destroying the proletariat with contraceptives, after the failure of MacArthur's atomic plots."

During these early years, the DeMarchis meanwhile worked in the American Embassy in Rome, he as a cultural editor for the United States Information Service, and she as a telephone operator. The ambassador was Clare Boothe Luce, a Catholic convert. An Embassy official, learning of the "unbecoming activity" of the DeMarchis in birth control, summoned them both to the personnel office in 1955 and warned them of Mrs. Luce's possible reaction to their behavior. They declared they had no intention of changing. If Mrs. Luce wanted to accept the consequences of firing them, that was up to her. DeMarchi continued working at the Embassy until a budget cut overtook him in 1957; Mrs. DeMarchi resigned in 1958 when she became pregnant.

Matteotti was unable to get a hearing on the bill he had introduced in Parliament to abolish the Mussolini anti–birth-control laws. The AIED made small progress in its first three years. It did establish headquarters in Milan and a country-wide membership of men and women, both professional and working classes, but their fund-raising capacity was negligible. Birth control had only one philanthropist in Italy; he was Adriano Olivetti, the typewriter industrialist, who was deeply interested in community development. Olivetti gave modest but dependable sums for the support of AIED and *il controllo delle nascite* (birth control). The DeMarchis worked for the AIED as parttime volunteer workers in Rome, as did their friends.

In 1955 they yearned to start Italy's first birth control clinic, just as Margaret Sanger had opened America's first birth control clinic in New York forty years before. The advantages of such initiative, they saw, would be twofold: they could publicly challenge the law; they could give needy people some help. If the authorities prosecuted them they could appeal to the Constitutional Court, the Italian equivalent of the United States Supreme Court; if the authorities did not, the ban on public incitement to prevent procreation would be demonstrably obsolete.

They decided against taking the total leap into a conventional birth control clinic, however, mostly because they had no physician or nurse friends willing to take such a risk. Instead, the DeMarchis and their AIED supporters planned an intermediate step that would enable them to claim, as far as contraceptive advice and technique was concerned, that they were not engaging in public incitement. They would establish a Rome Consultation Office for Birth Control. No contraceptive advice *per se* would be offered on the premises. Persons coming to the office for this kind of information would be referred to one of the participating physicians for service in their private offices. No professor of gynecology in Italy was interested in contraception, but the DeMarchis had fifteen doctors in Rome who wanted to learn contraceptive techniques for use in private practice—mainly the vaginal diaphragm recommended by the IPPF, of which the AIED was then an associate member. Certain AIED officers from Milan, in a fit of caution, argued that the Association should not be involved in such circumvention of the law. DeMarchi resolved the problem by inviting from these opponents a written disclaimer, stating they did not approve of the Rome office and that it was promoted on the personal initiative of the DeMarchis and not the AIED.

DeMarchi was shrewd, and seldom missed a trick. He even thought to have four of his good friends in Parliament, including Matteotti, sign a letter assuming responsibility for the Rome office in case of police or court action. They had parliamentary immunity under Roman law.

Now all that was lacking was a few hundred thousand lire a year to pay for office expenses. Since there were 600-odd lire to a dollar, the expense was not great. The DeMarchis would give their own time free.

A Pathfinder Finds the Path

Edith Gates, field representative for Dr. Gamble and the National Committee on Maternal Health in 1955 made a one-day stop in Milan, where she talked to the young, beautiful, and intelligent Dr. Vittoria Olivetti Berla, vice-president and member of the AIED National Council. Like DeMarchi, Mrs. Olivetti (as friends usually called her) had a university degree in psychology. She was the daughter-in-law of Adriano Olivetti, and became interested in birth control about the time she married the industrialist's son, Roberto. This much Miss Gates reported by letter to Gamble, but did not mention that the young couple had separated only a few weeks after their marriage and, since Italy did not then recognize divorce, contemplated an annulment.

Mrs. Olivetti was interested in finding some kind of easy contraception for the poor people of South Italy, and Miss Gates told her about salt-and-sponge. Mrs. Olivetti described plans for a birth control center in Rome. Gamble promptly wrote her, in July 1955, and, as soon as he learned of the DeMarchis, began corre-

sponding with them. He offered the AIED financial help in starting the Rome office. He sent Mrs. Olivetti nine square feet of
sponge rubber, to be cut into two-inch squares and soaked in salt
water for vaginal contraception. He offered the DeMarchis free
vaginal diaphragms and jelly from the United States. In August,
Gamble sent DeMarchi 200,000 lire—$300 or so—to get started,
increasing this to $800 for the first year and later to $1,000
annually, paid to the AIED treasurer in Milan.

The Rome Consultation Office for Birth Control opened in
January 1956, as both Mrs. Olivetti and DeMarchi informed
Gamble: "We are organizing in these days a service in Rome with
the help of Mr. and Mrs. DeMarchi," she wrote, thanking him for
his help. "The first Italian service of contraceptive assistance is
born," DeMarchi wrote on his own behalf. "How long it will live
it is difficult to forecast, in view of the uncertain Italian political
situations. I was able to weave my cobweb in such a way that the
Catholic circles will be forced to choose between a government
crisis and a passive acceptance of our initiative." He referred to
the coalition government, dominated by the Christian Democrats
but dependent on Communist, Socialist, Social Democrat, Republican, and even Monarchist elements to appoint a Prime
Minister and form a Cabinet.

The consultation office consisted of one rented room in the
central city. DeMarchi said he wanted to start "with as much
noise as possible," and he welcomed the possibility of police
intervention and even his own arrest. The innovation did get
considerable attention in Italian newspapers; the police came to
take a look, but did not interfere. "It is quite thrilling to have the
Center opened in the shadow of the Vatican," Gamble wrote Mrs.
Dorothy Brush.

The office had 200 visitors and answered 600 letters in the first
eight months, but activity thereafter fell off and by 1957 DeMarchi called it a substantial failure. The press had publicized the
service as a heroic act of defiance; not many who needed contraception wanted to be heroes. Also, the diaphragm-and-jelly
method that the physicians offered discouraged them.

DeMarchi and Mrs. Olivetti meanwhile became good friends. "Naively enough," as he reflected later, he urged her to leave Milan and move to Rome and join forces with the birth control group there. She did so in June 1956. As indicated, angels were scarce in Italy, and Mrs. Olivetti still communicated with her father-in-law about his AIED contribution. Rome undoubtedly struck her as a more effective power base.

DeMarchi, during this early period, attracted the first two of fifteen denunciations by police or state's attorneys for violation of Article 553 of the penal code. Italy's criminal denunciation is equivalent to a charge or summons in the United States; it may or may not involve arrest and jailing prior to court arraignment and trial. The Attorney of Rome simply filed the first two denunciations without court action.

Following initial aid in the Rome Consultation Office for Birth Control, Gamble and the Pathfinder Fund, chartered in 1957, became progressively more involved in *procreazione cosciente* (conscious parenthood). The Italian language has no counterpart for "family planning."

While habitually outspoken and frank, DeMarchi was not above flattery when it suited him. "Maybe the 'Gamble aid' . . . will appear in historical perspective much more decisive than the Marshall aid in solving Italian problems!" he wrote Gamble.

During the next ten years, Dr. Gamble became an important off-stage presence in five significant episodes:

1. Highly successful field tests of contraceptive suppositories used by poor women in Rome and the small southern village of Vibo Valentia, with Mrs. DeMarchi showing her mettle as a field worker in a long-term study eventually published in a book subtly mocking the Pope, *Inumane Vite* (Sugar Editore, 1969).
2. A final, futile effort to prove the worth of the salt-and-sponge method.
3. A rousing newspaper and magazine information campaign conducted by DeMarchi.
4. A power struggle between Mrs. Olivetti and DeMarchi within the Italian Association for Demographic Education overlaid by the older conflict between Gamble and the International Planned Parenthood Federation, ending with Mrs. Olivetti's loss of membership in AIED and AIED's loss of membership in IPPF.

5. The eighteen-year fight of DeMarchi and his political friends to prove the Mussolini law a violation of the right of free speech, climaxed by victory with the 1971 ruling of the Italian supreme court that the law was unconstitutional.

These five episodes, while chronologically intermingled and occluded by various internal and external misunderstanding and alarms, will be treated separately and in the order shown.

Out of the Office into the Field

Mrs. DeMarchi began her field work in the *borgate*, on the outskirts of Rome, in response to Gamble's question when he visited the Rome Consultation Office in April 1958: "Why don't you get out of this office and do some house-to-house visiting? You are wasting your time here." He had been saying much the same thing in behalf of fieldwork ever since 1934.

As usual in making his point, Gamble cut through a certain amount of human relations undergrowth of no interest to him. Not long before he had agreed, at the suggestion of Mrs. Dorothy Brush, then acting as an IPPF field representative, to pay Mrs. DeMarchi a salary to work as parttime secretary to Mrs. Olivetti, beginning in March. Mrs. Olivetti had persuaded Mrs. Brush that she needed this help to run the affairs of the AIED in Rome.

Gamble began his discussions of a contraceptive field trial with Mrs. Olivetti and then extended them to the DeMarchis. He first suggested that the Italians try foam tablets, of the kind tested in Puerto Rico and India. Mrs. Olivetti pointed out that Italian laws prohibited the import or manufacture of anything identified as a contraceptive. It was possible, however, to make and distribute medicines for such vaginal infections as leucorrhea. Her father-in-law, she said, suggested starting a factory to make foam tablets for "medicinal purposes." Gamble was not persuaded.

He had heard of Rendell's gel, a vaginal suppository made in Great Britain. It already was being imported and sold in Italy's drug stores as a vaginal antiseptic. Its ingredients were mostly cocoa butter plus quinine bisulfate and nonylphenylethylene oxide. The suppository, inserted in the vagina five minutes before intercourse, melted due to body heat. Gamble wanted to build a home-visit program to test the suppository as a contraceptive. Again, this was the kind of thing he had done ever since he sent Lena Hillard into the hills of Kentucky with jelly and syringes in 1937.

Mrs. Olivetti looked into the availability of these suppositories in Italy. The Rendell agent told her his company would furnish the contraceptive free for such an experiment among the poor, a fact that Gamble confirmed in London on his way to Rome. She wanted to start the field project in Florence or the village of Vibo Valentia, south of Naples.

Gamble meanwhile wrote Mrs. DeMarchi about the possibility of her doing a home-visit program in Rome, and also to ask her to see if she could find an already established pharmaceutical factory that would add foam tablets to its products.

Gamble had no objections to a Vibo Valentia project, but liked the idea of starting in Rome in the shadow of the Vatican. Some AIED officers opposed starting in Rome for the same reason. They feared the wrath of the Church.

As usual, it was a complicated picture. One of the complications was the problem of finding a medical supervisor and field-worker to do the Rome project who had the nerve to risk police questioning and possible arrest. Gamble discussed this with Mrs. Olivetti and the DeMarchis repeatedly. The absence of an immediate solution was the main reason why, in the fall of 1958, they started the Rendell's suppository project in Vibo Valentia, where there was a strong AIED chapter president and an able midwife.

Another complication was that, from the start, two emancipated women, Vittoria Olivetti and Maria Luisa DeMarchi, did not hit it off in a boss-and-secretary relationship. The DeMarchis, previously established as birth control advocates in Rome, were of the view that Mrs. DeMarchi was working for the AIED and not Mrs. Olivetti, who was a national vice-president but not an officer of the Rome branch. In either case, Gamble was paying

Mrs. DeMarchi (Adriano Olivetti at the time was financing De-Marchi to do legislative and publicity work). It was the usual kind of administrative confusion that occurs in voluntary health organizations. Mrs. Olivetti complained to Mrs. Brush that Mrs. DeMarchi behaved as if she worked for Gamble. Mrs. DeMarchi denied this, but said that she refused to take orders from Mrs. Olivetti—"She treats me like a lady's maid." Mrs. DeMarchi wrote Gamble: "Since Mrs. Brush writes to me that I had been hired to help Mrs. Olivetti personally, in case you share her opinion, I would be forced to present my dismissal. . . . I cannot accept to become the personal attache of a person who has not right of control on the organization either in Rome or in Milan."

Conversely viewed, the dispute seemed to be emerging as a contest between the DeMarchis and Mrs. Olivetti as to who had the prior claim on Gamble. Whatever the case, when Dr. Gamble came to Rome it was definitely in the role of peacemaker. He told Mrs. DeMarchi he hoped that she should make concessions and cooperate with Mrs. Olivetti, whose "interest . . . and ability have been of great value." I hope you will do that for the future of Italy," he said, in one of his familiar pieces of rhetoric.

In any event, it was at this juncture that Gamble suggested Mrs. DeMarchi get out of the office and into the homes. He would pay her salary through AIED. Above all else, it had become obvious that the Rome Consultation Office for Birth Control could not reach the poor people with their large families. It was the American birth control clinic story all over again.

But there was still another obstacle familiar to birth control workers. After seven years of marriage, Mrs. DeMarchi became pregnant for the first time. In July, 1958, she bore Laura, a seven-month, three-pound baby who flourished in an incubator and developed normally.

The new mother was unable to begin her adventures in the *borgate*, a collection of high-rise tenements and tin shacks, until March 1959. From then, however, her devotion to this project, soon with the help of a beautiful, raven-haired social worker, Mrs. Marcella Finzi, was continuous for the next ten years.

Inhuman Life

Mrs. DeMarchi exploded a myth when she went into the slums. The notion was extant that the sex life of laborers was somehow healthier and less neurotic than that of the upper classes. But in talking to the women in the *borgate* she found many who lived brutalized lives, reduced to involuntary servitude by their husbands, who were mainly manual laborers, employed or unemployed: some of them, frustrated, angry men who insisted on sex on demand. This and wine were their habitual escapes. Mothers told her of fathers who forced wives to watch while they raped their daughters. She saw women whose arms were broken when they tried to protect their children from their husbands' blows. She saw the battered children. The women did not seek police protection, both from fear that their husbands would come home and beat them and that the family could not survive if the father was in jail.

The sex lives of these people were characterized by the clumsy savagery of the husbands and the defensive frigidity of the wives. Eighty percent of the women interviewed said they only occasionally experienced pleasure in sex; the other 20 percent said they never enjoyed it. Mrs. DeMarchi concluded that conventional morality, considering female masochism, male sadism, and dissociation of love and sex, was spiritually far more damaging to the proletariat than to the affluent class. Church and state did not intervene, but in their dogmatic defense of the force of numbers, fostered a social system that offered little but unhappiness and suffering for both parents and children. The typical slum child grew up shy, sly, distrustful, and often destined for a life of deprivation and crime.

One woman had dreams of castrating her husband. "I think I am going crazy," was a common refrain among these wretched women, trapped between their husbands and their children and angry at both.

The typical woman in the Rendell suppository experiment had quit school in the elementary grades, was about thirty years old, had been married ten years, had at least one pregnancy for every two years of marriage, had borne three to four babies alive, had two to three living children, and had had two induced abortions. Nine out of ten couples had tried two means of contraception, *coitus interruptus* and the condom. Men were prone to say, however, that they would not insult their wives with a condom; this they reserved for prostitutes, to protect themselves from venereal disease.

Maria Luisa DeMarchi, who has been called the unsung heroine of the Italian birth control revolution, manifested a remarkable skill, patience and sensitivity in befriending and instructing these oppressed women. She collected incredible case histories.

FELICETTA, FROM QUADRARO

Felicetta was born in Rome, is 28 years old, and has been married for fourteen years. She has eight living children, of whom two are tuberculous. Four of her children are dead. Her husband is an asphalt worker. They live in a humid basement full of mice. To keep away from the water which comes in from the street the mice have opened a series of holes in the opposite wall. The floor is slanted, so the water runs under the beds and comes out the other side. The living quarters consist of a single room, the walls of which are dark with moisture. Furnishings are a hotplate, a bureau, and a lot of beds. The two youngest children sleep in a burlap hammock hung from the ceiling beams.

After Felicetta had been on the list of assisted women for six months I found her husband at home one day.

"I wanted to have the same number of males and females," he said slyly, "so I stopped after eight."

He is a man who likes to chat, and it was clear that he liked wine. While Felicetta is a small, stunted woman and her children all look emaciated (they are very thin and shriveled, and the smallest one still could not walk at the age of two) her husband is fat and ruddy. Next to him his children seem even paler.

After having used the suppositories for five years, Felicetta stopped for several months. It is not unusual that after a few years of using a certain method the women is less regular, less careful. Sometimes she is induced to believe that she is no longer fertile, either because she has used the contraceptive for a long period of time or for some other reasons. In general a pregnancy results, but is rarely terminated in abortion. In fact, after a few years have passed between pregnancies the woman is no longer so oppressed by her offspring and she accepts the new pregnancy with a certain serenity.

FILOMENA, FROM QUARTICCOLO

Filomena is a thin, pallid woman, all bones and eyes. She is nervous but has a beautiful smile. She is 33, had been married for eleven years. She and her husband are both Pugliese. She completed 3rd grade. She has five living children, one dead, eight aborted. Her husband, who is illiterate, is a manual laborer when he can find work; otherwise he is a car attendant. They live in one of the huts in via Molfetta.

The door is a cloth curtain. One enters directly into the low-ceilinged kitchen; behind it is the bedroom. It is hard to understand how eight persons—including an old woman—can find room to sleep here.

"I'm sure my husband will say yes, too, because he doesn't want any more children either. We only wanted the first two. The others just came, even though he was careful. Maybe he has weak kidneys."

"Have these things been around long? They never tell us about these things. We have to have children and misery, that's how they, the rich, can use us the way they want to. *They* don't have children. I've seen so many times that rich ladies only have two or three at the most, and I always asked myself why. Is it possible that the rich can always be so careful? They just have a few babies, so they can always stay rich and we get poorer. And the priests are on their side, because they tell us it's a sin if we don't have babies. Meanwhile the rich people go out to eat with the priests. On television you always see priests around when they're inaugurating something new. They get along with the people who have money."

"No, don't worry about my religious beliefs. I'm not afraid of hell and here's why: I have hell right here, summer and winter, always. Forty days ago I had a bad time with an abortion. How many have I had? I don't really remember. Maybe seven or eight. You want to know exactly. But I don't remember. I only know I need something that makes me sure. I need it so much, something that takes away this worry. I think God must have sent you to me. God, He knows how much I've suffered, he knows I needed this."

Filomena used contraceptives for five years, from 10 to 12 suppositories a month. I talked to her about the pill.

"A thousand lire ($1.60) a month," she said. "I couldn't afford that every month. I'd like to work a few hours, but my husband doesn't want me to. In the meantime we'll make do with what we have. Really, sometimes my husband wants to do it without, because these things are a little slippery. So he says he'll be careful, but even so I put one in right afterward. Leave some for me. As soon as I get a little money I'll try to go to the doctor for the pills, but I don't have any welfare clinic to go to."

One evening while I was talking to Filomena her husband arrived. He looked at me for a moment and then recognized me. He had seen me other times.

"Good evening," he murmured, and slipped into the bedroom.

"He doesn't talk much," Filomena said smiling. "He's happy we found a way to stop having children. Sure, if I could get the pill I'd be happier for him. You know, he says these are matters for *women* to talk about, but that women should do something before they put so many children into the world. You know, he also said that you were a woman and I'm just a bag of bones."

Gamble instructed Mrs. DeMarchi in statistical survey methods, and she, with writing guidance from her husband, proved to be a brilliant student. Periodically, she made progress reports to the Pathfinder Fund and the Medical Committee of IPPF. She prepared a two-year report on the first 200 cases in 1962, signed by Dr. Teresita S. Scelba, a physician, together with Mrs. DeMarchi and Mrs. Finzi. Dr. Scelba was well-known as a pioneer for women's rights in Italy, had been president of the AIED Rome Committee, and was the new national AIED president.

From London, Dr. Margaret Jackson, IPPF Medical Committee chairman, wrote that the two-year report was "most impressive." Dr. Christopher Tietze of New York, at Gamble's urging, visited the DeMarchis and reviewed their data. He told them their study was excellent. Tietze, director of the Population Council's contraceptive research program, was by common consent the leading biostatistician in birth control.

Gamble was eager to publish the report. DeMarchi, however, was in this instance reluctant to have publicity, even in a medical journal. He feared that publication might lead to police and court action stopping the experiment. In 1963, he changed his mind and called a press conference that made page-one news in several newspapers. It was the first that Italy had heard of the suppository experiments in the *borgate*, and it brought indignant attacks from the Catholic press, including statements that the "AIED offends God and damages Italy" and demands that the DeMarchis be jailed.

Mrs. DeMarchi in 1969 published her findings in her arresting book, *Inumane Vite*. By then, she and Mrs. Finzi had made 7,708 home visits to 558 couples, and supplied 499 women with vaginal suppositories for from one month to nine years ten months. They had 10,492 months of cumulative use. Stretching over ten years, it was one of the longest field experiments of this kind, if not the longest, ever conducted.

The suppository method proved to be highly acceptable and surpassed everything except the oral pill and IUD in effectiveness. Two-thirds of the woman approached accepted suppositories and used them. Subtracting those who quit the method because their husbands disapproved or stopped for other reasons, only 13 percent rejected contraception.

Rendell's gel was impressive from the start, even with the number of errors in use that arise early in such a study. When Mrs. DeMarchi reported to Gamble in 1960 that the pregnancy rate among users was 12 per 100 couples per year in the first 120 cases, he replied: "This is as good as Dr. Koya gets with the condom in Japan."

In the end, the result was much better. The pregnancy rate dropped from 65 to 6.4 per 100 couples per year, or from one pregnancy per woman every two years before use to one in every sixteen years during use. Meanwhile abortions fell from one per woman every six to one every fifty years. In some women, Mrs. DeMarchi saw "a gradual emancipation from misery" during the course of the study.

She derived the title, *Inumane Vite*, from the encyclical published by Pope Paul VI in 1968, *Humanae Vitae*. In it, Paul reaffirmed the 1930 encyclical of Pope Pius XI. All popes held that, aside from total abstinence from sexual intercourse, the only acceptable method of avoiding births was temporary abstinence during the woman's fertile period (the rhythm method), and then only for "serious motives."

Artificial contraception might still be an offense against God and Italy, but some poor Catholic women who could not read Latin knew where the sin really lay. They felt that these were the Pope's children, as implied by one who said, "Who's going to feed them? The Pope?"

Salt-and-Sponge

In the DeMarchis, the man from Milton found someone who took him seriously on the salt-and-sponge method of contraception. In May 1961, Gamble sent the new AIED Executive Committee $1,500 to test the acceptability and effectiveness of this homely method, which so offended Dr. Helena Wright and other IPPFers. The AIED, well aware that the International Federation disapproved, deferred for six months and then decided in November to take the plunge.

Tests would be made on from 50 to 100 women in Rome. Gamble had confidence that the DeMarchis would be systematic and conscientious. Mrs. DeMarchi and Mrs. Finzi said they wanted to experiment with the vaginal sponge on themselves before offering it to their friends in the *borgate*. They first tried natural sponges. DeMarchi reported to Notestein: "To this end, they had tried to insert and use the sponges . . . but had found them (and I, too, can testify it on the Bible) utterly discomfortable: too big, too encumbering, too rough and draining unpleasantly all vaginal secretions."

Gamble replied that artificial sponges were better—either foam rubber or plastic—and sent sheets of these materials. Maria Luisa and Marcella and some of their patients tried squares cut from these sheets and likewise found them uncomfortable. There was much correspondence across the Atlantic about the correct size, finally determined to be two by two by one inch. The experimenters went back to natural sponges of these dimensions.

There was equally detailed consideration of several other matters. Rather than ask the women to make their own salt solution, the researchers decided to furnish them a 20 percent solution of salt in water artificially colored orange, and not tell them that it was only saltwater.

Each woman was given a glass jar with a screw top in which the sponge would be kept in the solution, always at the ready. Some women had difficulty getting the sponge out of a 100-cubic centimeter jar, so this was changed to one of 350-cc. (seven-tenths of a pint).

Mrs. DeMarchi and Mrs. Finzi expressed "good reasons for concern," because their preliminary survey of women's attitudes showed "a much deeper distrust and fear about the sponge method than, two years ago, about suppositories."

DeMarchi prepared a well-thought-out research plan and Gamble complimented him: "It will have both scientific and political value." The two fieldworkers started with women who knew them, often those who had stopped using Rendell suppositories, and then moved on to friends of these women. They planned to continue the study two years, following each patient to see that she used the method and to refer to a cooperating physician all who complained of burning or discomfort. "Once again let me say how glad I am that this important test has begun," wrote Gamble. "It will mean much to many parts of the world."

The trial got underway in May 1962. Three months later, in July, the fieldworkers reported having approached thirty-nine women. Seven refused to try it, seven tried and then rejected it, one became pregnant in the first month. Twenty were still using it, but only five said they were satisfied. Mrs. DeMarchi commented: "We feel that the rest of them are using it but fighting a tremendous disgust together with fear." One woman used the method in daily intercourse with her husband for fourteen days, but the liquid in the jar became turbid and smelled badly. "It appears that the salt is not strong enough to prevent the growth of bacteria," commented Gamble. Instead of storing the sponge in the jar, the fieldworkers now told the women to rinse the sponge out after use and wrap it in a clean handkerchief.

Some women found it difficult to remove the sponge after intercourse. Gamble recommended attaching a string, but Mrs. DeMarchi found none willing to use a sponge with a string on it. Gamble suggested that when they got used to manipulating the sponge, they would cut the string off.

Toward the end of the year, Mrs. Finzi complained to him: "Our work in the *borgate* is very hard with the sponge because there are many resistances and in this last month two women became pregnant and the others are now afraid. But we don't feel discouraged and are going on with the work."

Mrs. DeMarchi reported results to the end of November 1962. "As you will see, we met with a remarkable number of refusals (31 out of 71 patients interviewed) and a preoccupying rate of failures (3 in 102 months of use). There were also 14 objecting discontinuers and eight non-objecting discontinuers. So . . . out of 71 patients . . . only 18 are active users. We feel that this is a not very brilliant result and would like to know both your opinion and some *reliable* information about similar experiments in other regions." Unfortunately, there was no scientifically reliable information elsewhere.

"Your letter about salt-solution-and-sponge is discouraging," Gamble replied. "I hope you will continue your attempts to find those who want to use it."

In the spring of 1963 the AIED National Council debated the salt issue with mounting skepticism. "This trial is not meeting the same success as the Rendell one," Mrs. DeMarchi wrote. DeMarchi agreed with his wife: "Maria Luisa and Marcella Finzi are meeting severe difficulties with the sponge. There have been many failures and many patients react negatively to the procedures of introduction and removal involved (as they do, after all, with the diaphragm)."

This was the last of it, as far as the correspondence shows. Again, the salt-and-sponge method succumbed to low acceptability. There was no scientific publication. The DeMarchis, who had won their spurs in the suppository trials, stopped writing to Gamble about the sponge method, while the tempo of their correspondence about other matters increased. His final word, in 1963, in addition to another admonition to keep trying, was "It is my belief that it [salt and sponge] is as effective as the suppository if used."

If salt ever had a place in the contraceptive armamentarium, it was doomed to much the same fate as other earlier contraceptives. The oral pill and the intrauterine device were now occupying the attention of birth controllers. In the late 1960s, the pill became more popular in Italy—with Catholic women, if not with the Catholic Church. In 1975 only 2 percent of Italian women using contraception are on the pill.

Free Press and Free Love

Italy has well over a hundred newspapers, many of them with political or church affiliation, and many, like the American tabloid, leaning heavily on graphic art and sensational headlines to

win readers. Luigi DeMarchi wrote provocative articles for sixteen or more of these newspapers. Except for those influenced by
the Church or by the extreme right-wing party loosely called
Neo-Fascists, the press happily fanned the flames of controversy
about contraception, despite its immoral and illegal implications,
or perhaps because of them. The Constitution of the Republic
entitled the mass media to a free press.

DeMarchi, in his letters to Gamble, almost invariably described
his writings as "propaganda;" he used the word not in the American, odious sense but with due regard to its original ecclesiastical
denotation as propagation of a doctrine or faith.

When DeMarchi's arrangement with Adriano Olivetti for
financial support of his journalistic efforts ended, he turned to
Gamble. The latter believed in publicity as an effective means of
public education; he was glad to support DeMarchi in parttime
writing of newspaper and magazine articles. He paid DeMarchi
$160 a month, beginning in November 1959, and did so from then
on, raising the amount to $190 in 1963. They considered this an
agreement between two individuals, separate from DeMarchi's
voluntary leadership of the AIED Committee in Rome and his
seat on the AIED National Council. It was also separate from
Gamble's contributions to the AIED, including $80 a month for
Mrs. DeMarchi and $16 a month for Mrs. Finzi. The new ar-
rangement was a bargain. DeMarchi was prolific. From time to
time, he sent Gamble a batch of clippings of articles that he had
placed.

In January 1960, DeMarchi published his first book, *Sesso e
civilta* (Sex and Civilization). Unable to read Italian, Gamble
perforce accepted the content on faith.

On the basis of the book, Mrs. Olivetti charged DeMarchi was
advocating "free love" and as such was a menace to the Italian
birth control movement. The AIED certainly had no policy favoring extramarital sex relations, if that was what free love meant.

DeMarchi encompassed more than that. Gamble wrote him
and asked for a short summary of the views he had expressed in
his book. DeMarchi explained that his program of sexual reform

included sexual and contraceptive education, recognition of divorce, abolition of discrimination against illegitimate children, and abolition of censorship, among other things. He wrote:

> I take a more radical attitude on certain points (advocating, for instance, freedom of love, and not only to know, for youngsters, or sustaining the principle that freedom of love is one of the "inalienable rights" nobody can be deprived of or renounce, even in marriage). . . . I claim that the methods followed up to now by sex reformers have proved largely ineffective. My thesis is that sex reformers must try their best in order to make sex reform a major sociopolitical issue, integrated in the political message and program of progressive parties. Ideological propaganda, organizational activity, legislative revision, and above all the influence of mass media . . . must become the aims and methods of sex reform. I am sorry that you cannot read Italian and were unable to take a direct look at the book.

So DeMarchi did believe in freedom to love, in a sexual context, but, as he and other officials of the AIED later were to point out, he did not let his personal philosophy intrude on official policy. All this did not seem to bother Gamble even though, except for contraception, he himself was a conventional, conservative, monogamous, American Protestant Republican. He renewed his financial arrangement with DeMarchi and frequently complimented the Italian on his good work. In birth control, they were going in the same direction.

The Struggle for Control

It was William Congreve, in *The Mourning Bride*, who claimed that hell has no fury like a women scorned. The rising popularity of Luigi and Maria Luisa DeMarchi occurred during a time when the personal life of Mrs. Vittoria Olivetti, nee Berla, was in turmoil. Following their early separation, her husband sought an annulment of their marriage, but she refused to consent. When, after a few years, she bore twins to another man, Roberto Olivetti sued her for adultery. She was forced to grant him an annulment in 1963; he eventually remarried. Meanwhile, her wealthy father-in-law died, depriving her of this financial power base in birth control.

Mrs. Olivetti, finding the DeMarchis unresponsive to her demands, resigned as vice-president of the AIED National Council as 1960 began. She wrote the Governing Body of the International Planned Parenthood Federation in February 1960 that she was resigning because of "internal dissension among members of the Executive Committee resulting from assignments received by members personally from foreign donors—namely, Dr. Gamble. . . . This problem has arisen because the assignments and contributions are made directly to individual members without consulting or informing the responsible officials of the organization."

She sent Gamble a copy of this letter and he replied in the mild way in which he approached heated conflict: "Your letter . . . puzzles me greatly." His collaboration in the Rome and Vibo Valentia studies had been arranged with the *Associazione Italiana per L'Educazione Demografica* and he had sent his contributions to the AIED treasurer in Milan, he said. More recently, he had provided DeMarchi some money for newspaper and magazine writing, but "This has not involved the *Associazone* in any way nor had any connection with it. . . . We have considered it an entirely separate project. Consequently I do not see how our partnership can disturb you."

DeMarchi's problem of dual personality was not a new one in leadership of an organization. When can a man speak for himself and when does he speak as an official, or can he truly differentiate between the two positions? It is difficult to do when his private opinion and organization policy differ but relate to the same field of interest—in this instance, birth control. It is even more difficult when someone of actual or presumed authority within the organization challenges his right to express a private opinion differing from that of the organization.

Mrs. Olivetti had a case only if the AIED agreed she was responsible for the Rome office. Replying to Gamble, she said that, after making the arrangement for direct Gamble support, DeMarchi had told the Executive Committee that he wished to work under AIED sponsorship, and accordingly expected to use its name, office, and secretary. "A condition of his proposal was that he be allowed to work independently, and specifically—as he stated—not to be answerable to myself." The Committee approved; Mrs. Olivetti was not present. She found her position untenable, she said, and therefore resigned, taking four other members of the Council with her (but one, a vice-president like herself, reconsidered and stayed on).

Milan was one thing; Rome, another. DeMarchi called for a new election of Roman AIED Committee members. Mrs. Olivetti and two others were dropped. Mrs. Olivetti called the election rigged and said that the Committee had violated a by-law stating that paid staff members cannot be members of the Committee. "I trust that I have made our difficulties clear," she told Gamble.

Once more, as he had been back in the days of the American Birth Control League, Gamble by implication stood accused of treating the cause as more important than the organization. He promptly disassociated himself from the Olivetti-DeMarchi conflict: "As we are not Italians we have no part in the operation of the AIED, and have no responsibility for the difficulties in the organization."

Gamble and Mrs. Olivetti corresponded sporadically but unproductively the rest of the year. In December, she signed herself "Vittoria Olivetti Berla," causing him to ask, "Does this new name mean that you have married again?" It is conceivable that he was teasing, but it is more likely that, in his detachment, he was merely unaware of what was going on off-stage. The Gamble papers say nothing of the Olivetti scandal.

Certainly it was beneath IPPF notice. But the DeMarchi-Olivetti conflict soon became merged with older Gamble-IPPF hostilities. Gamble wrote DeMarchi in October 1960: "In a recent talk with Mr. George Cadbury, the special representative of the President and Governing Body of the International Planned Parenthood Federation, who is now circling the world in their interest, he presented the view that I had wrecked the Italian organization by an arrangement with you. I pointed out that it was entirely separate from the organization, but he said that it gave you time and opportunity to work with the organization in a manner which he implied was injurious. I disagreed."

In January 1961, the AIED National Council met in Milan and elected new officers. DeMarchi's friend, Dr. Teresita S. Scelba, became president and he, national secretary, by a vote of 12 to 2. Only one other voter shared Mrs. Olivetti's opposition to DeMarchi. The new Executive Committee included DeMarchi but not Mrs. Olivetti, who remained on the National Council. As it turned out, all five new Executive Committee members were from Rome. It was decided to move headquarters there, the capital being a more suitable place for parliamentary and international contacts. It was, all in all, a complete victory for DeMarchi.

Mrs. Olivetti did not accept defeat, however. She complained bitterly to anyone who would listen. At one time, toward the end of 1962, the AIED National Council threatened her with expulsion if she did not stop defaming the organization in Italy and abroad. She promised to stop, according to Dr. Scelba, but continued at the IPPF conference in Singapore in early 1963. Mrs. Olivetti accused DeMarchi of not accounting for funds that he had received, packing the Rome AIED Committee with his family and friends, doing nothing to promote family planning, and most of all, of advocating free love; that it was gossiped in Singapore that he had set himself up as an expert in sexology and, in lectures, was advising university students to engage in "unrepressed and promiscuous sexual activity."

Sarah Gamble, attending the conference, wrote to Dr. Scelba for information in February 1963. Dr. Scelba denied all but one allegation. She said that "The only correct statement made by Mrs. Berla is that Mr. DeMarchi has indeed written and is writing on sexology," but his two books on the subject had been published as serious, scholarly works, and his lectures were personal talks and not part of his activities as AIED national secretary. However, since the distinction was subtle and might lead to confusion, he had been asked and agreed to step down as national secretary at the next board meeting. "It cannot be said therefore that the work of the Pathfinder Fund, as carried out by the DeMarchis, has been harmful to the AIED; what has been very harmful to the AIED are the constant allegations by Mrs. Berla, who has succeeded in arousing suspicion among our foreign donors as to our correctness.... Unfortunately, her resentment against Mr. DeMarchi is such that there can be no appeasement."

In the spring, the AIED held an election. With 800 members voting, Mrs. Olivetti was dropped from membership. The National Council met in April and, with fifteen of twenty-one members present, unanimously rejected DeMarchi's offer to resign. The Council announced "new, more daring policies," particularly in seeking abolition of the Mussolini law. Carlo Matteotti, now Under-Secretary of State, was elected president again. Matteotti wrote Gamble: "I am convinced that nobody else in Italy has done as much as Mr. DeMarchi for the development and expansion of the birth control movement."

Mrs. Olivetti remained unconvinced. In 1964, she gave a taped interview to a reporter from the leading Italian extreme right weekly, *Il Borghese* (The Bourgeoise). The newspaper quoted her as saying of the AIED:

> In the past, it was financed by the late Adriano Olivetti, my father-in-law at that time ... We have been able (or at least I had been able) to obtain strong financial help also from America ... The IPPF is giving something—one or two thousand dollars per year. DeMarchi is paid by an American, whose name is X, who owns a large chemical industry. Do you know the X soap? They are paying DeMarchi in order that he operates this office and goes around distributing their products."

It was not difficult to recognize the newspaper's Mr. X as Dr. Gamble. Thus, Mrs. Olivetti managed to revive an old canard first heard in the early 1930s—that Gamble was a contraceptive manufacturer who supported birth control clinics using his product. Or did she mean that DeMarchi was a soap salesman? A month later, *Il Borghese* attacked DeMarchi and the AIED in a series of seven articles charging that they were distributing contraceptives that had killed an "incalculable" number of women.

DeMarchi wrote Gamble that he was suing Mrs. Olivetti for libel. Gamble replied that he did not think her remarks worthy of attention. DeMarchi disagreed: "In Italy, I cannot afford this magnanimity without being personally disqualified and without ruining the whole Association and the planned parenthood movement." When DeMarchi brought suit, Mrs. Olivetti's attorney offered a retraction, but DeMarchi insisted on a court decision. He was unable to prove damage, and the court granted her amnesty, in Italian law a sort of cross between clemency and pardon, but with the right to appeal.

Through all this, the officers of the International Planned Parenthood Federation, despite several visits to Italy, seemed incapable of objectively appraising the birth control movement there. By the one-plus-one method, they appeared to conclude that they had two troublemakers in the same basket, Gamble and DeMarchi, and the best thing to do was abandon them both on Italy's doorstep.

On October 19, 1965, DeMarchi wrote Gamble: "Astonishment, incredulity, humiliation, rage, and utter discouragement are mixing in my mind." He had just received from Mrs. Joan Rettie, IPPF regional secretary in London, a note transmitting a letter from Sir Colville Deverell, Secretary-General of the IPPF. It read:

Subject: A. I. E. D. Membership
At the meeting of the Governing Body of the International Planned Parenthood Federation held in London on the 17th September, the status of all Associate Members was reviewed.

I have to inform you that as a result of this review the Governing Body decided not to confirm the associate membership of the Associazione Italian per L'Educazione Demografica.

I am to request you to be good enough to convey this decision to the President and Secretary of the A.I.E.D. so that they may be aware that the A.I.E.D. is no longer an associate member of this Federation.

Neither Sir Colville nor Mrs. Rettie gave any explanation for this arbitrary action. It was an interesting way of handling a national organization that had grown from a small beginning twelve years before to a membership of 2,000 with six birth control centers—Rome, Milan, Genoa, Florence, Vibo Valentia, and Palermo—and had done it in defiance of the moral code of the Vatican and the penal code of Mussolini.

Actually, there had been forewarnings of the action best appreciated in hindsight. The IPPF had given the AIED general financial aid in one year, $2,000 in 1963, and then discontinued it because of "lack of funds." Mrs. Olivetti had formed a competing organization, called The Marriage Education Association, ostensibly for marriage counseling but mainly for family planning. The thing that presumably bothered the British the most about supporting the AIED, as Mrs. Edna McKinnon sensed on a visit to London in July 1965, was that its national secretary undermined family planning by favoring sexual relations outside of marriage—or so Mrs. Olivetti had led the IPPF to believe. As repudiation, Virginio Bertinelli, now the AIED president and Social Democrat leader in Parliament, sent Sir Colville a complete collection of AIED publications showing that "neither a line nor a word can be found in this collection which directly or indirectly advocates or approves extramarital relations." If the AIED favored free love, he would not be its president, Bertinelli said.

The IPPF rebuffed AIED efforts to ascertain why it had been dropped from membership. Gamble suggested to DeMarchi that "the step was taken partly because of Pathfinder's contributing to AIED. As you know, IPPF has been unfriendly to me, though I had hoped things were improving." In January 1966, Gamble visited Rome, where Bertinelli told him, "I do not find anything wrong with Mr. DeMarchi." In London, Gamble saw Sir Colville and pointed out that AIED had received no explanation of its rejection. Gamble wrote Bertinelli in January 1966 that Deverell told him that a requirement for IPPF membership is that an association should represent the whole country, whereas AIED did not represent all of Italy as there were other family planning associations in Italy. Pressed for elaboration, Deverell said, "We have told them all we are prepared to tell them."

The IPPF's action against the AIED did no tangible damage. DeMarchi reported that "the Olivetti group . . . sent in October a circular letter to all our members informing them triumphantly of the 'good news' about the exclusion. But not one of the 2,000 AIED members resigned."

All in all, however, it had to be scored as a very personal victory for Mrs. Olivetti to have the British look down their nose at the Italian birth control movement—although now, thanks to De-Marchi's willingness to fight the Mussolini law through the courts, it was on its way to a larger victory for family and motherhood.

"Luigi DeMarchi Has Made It!"

Politics, in Italy above all, makes strange bedfellows. At the time the Italian Association for Demographic Education came into being in 1953, the two leading political parties, the Catholic Church-dominated Christian Democrats, with a plurality of about 40 percent, and the Communists, who commanded the second largest number of seats in Parliament, were united on at least one issue—their opposition to birth control. Their condemnation of contraception stemmed from quite different roots. The Church held interference with the generation of human life to be a sin against God and nature. Marxist philosophy, as interpreted by Italian Communists, advocated uncontrolled proliferation as a means of increasing mass oppression and hence the will to revolt against a capitalistic system. Neither doctrine showed much compassion for the overburdened or oppressed individual mother.

Against these formidable forces, it was not surprising that a bill first introduced in the Chamber of Deputies in 1951 to abolish the old Fascist anti–birth-control law got nowhere. Carlo Matteotti introduced similar legislation in 1953 and 1958. In 1966, Virginio Bertinelli offered a fourth bill. None of these came to a vote, due to "Catholic obstructionism and lay apathy," as DeMarchi put it.

Meanwhile, in 1963, the National Council of the AIED decided to broaden its strategy. Perhaps it would have better luck in court than in Parliament. From time to time the police or prosecuting attorney charged one nervy liberal or another with inciting the public to limit procreation by publishing an article or delivering a lecture. Sometimes the denunciation was stimulated by a complaint from a priest.

While it was possible to jail a man a year for violating Article 553, no one went to jail. Some judges were secular-minded and inclined to be lenient. Sometimes, innocence was determined by the court's hair-splitting on whether the offending matter *incited* the reader to do something he would not otherwise have done or merely *instructed* him in something he already wanted to do. Simply a prefatory disclaimer that the publication was intended not for public but private use might be enough to take the defendant off the hook. If found guilty, he might receive amnesty; or, he might be fined several thousand lire, entitling him to appeal. An occasional friendly judge might acknowledge that a constitutional question was involved, requiring appeal to a higher court, in the hope that the old Mussolini law would be declared unconstitutional.

Luigi DeMarchi found his first opportunity to face trial for his convictions in December 1962. The state attorney in Novara, in North Italy, "denounced" DeMarchi for a magazine statement favoring birth control. As DeMarchi wrote Gamble: "Personally I an very happy because I hope that—if the Tribunal will accept the denunciation and start a trial—we shall be able to make a case of it. Anyway, this fact can explain to you why so many people are still afraid of cooperating with us. The Italian situation is such that everybody can still risk jail if his words or acts are heard of by a pro-Fascist or pro-Catholic justice."

DeMarchi was not happy with the outcome. In March 1963, the Tribunal (district court) in Novara granted him amnesty. There being no appeal, his plan to take his case to the Constitutional Court was forestalled.

In February 1964, Carlo Matteotti was denounced on a similar charge in another district court in North Italy. The court obligingly convicted him, for the purpose of sending the case on up to the Constitutional Court. The issue was free speech, guaranteed by the Italian Constitution.

Then, in March, DeMarchi had a bit of luck. The public attorney of Florence happened to be present at a lecture DeMarchi gave upon the occasion of opening a new AIED center in that city. Charged with another Article 553 violation, DeMarchi was found guilty by a Florence judge who fined him 20,000 lire (a little over $30). He promptly appealed, requesting a trial. He wrote Gamble that he was happy—now both the president and the secretary of the AIED were on trial!

DeMarchi, tried in May, reported to Gamble "at least some good, heartening news." The higher Florence tribunal, he said, accepted his thesis that the Fascist law forbidding birth control propaganda might be unconstitutional, in particular agreeing that birth control has nothing to do with sexual morality and accepting the fact that use of contraceptive measures was already widespread in Italy. It was an important admission because the Constitution guaranteed free speech as long as it did not infringe on good manners and morals. The court transmitted the case to the Constitutional Court in Rome for an opinion.

DeMarchi was delighted with the widespread publicity the trial received. "The bomb exploded with unprecedented noise throughout Italy," he wrote. Meanwhile: "We would not be surprised . . . if a trial against Maria Luisa will be started." He based this hope on the fact that, for two days, a photographer had hidden in an automobile in front of their Rome office, taking pictures of all women entering and leaving, and she was kept under surveillance at her home. Also, persons representing themselves as physicians and social workers were showing the photographs to women in the *borgate* and asking, "Have you ever seen one of these women?" They identified Mrs. DeMarchi and were warned, "that this lady is a fanatic English Protestant who is trying to experiment on you with dangerous pills." Some of the women answered that the "pills" were harmless—they had been using suppositories for five years. When the interrogators tried to get them to accuse Mrs. DeMarchi of giving them oral contraceptive pills, as yet an unregistered drug in Italy, the women said that they did not know about these. The interrogators turned out to be from the Pope's Office of Assistance, the Vatican's charity organization.

The Constitutional Court heard the Matteotti and DeMarchi appeals in December and ruled on them in February 1965. Since the state's attorney claimed that contraceptives were bad for women's health, DeMarchi presented statements from international authorities—Dr. Alan Guttmacher, Dr. Christopher Tietze, and Dr. Clarence Gamble—stressing the harmlessness of scientifically recognized contraceptives.

The Court ruled that Article 553, banning contraceptive propaganda, was constitutional, interpreting its purpose as defense of public morals, a permissible qualification of free speech. This was a setback for the AIED; yet DeMarchi found some cause for happiness and, in fact, held a press conference, pointing out "an important step forward." The Court also ruled that "propaganda of the necessity of birth control in certain social and historic conditions" was legal. It further declared, "The existing laws should not be interpreted as a veto on scientific information and teaching." What was forbidden was "propaganda in public places of contraceptive techniques."

Thus, Italian judicial opinion on dissemination of information about birth control advanced to a point approximately equivalent to that in the United States in the early 1930s. The press could talk about birth control, but could not tell its readers how to do it. Unfortunately for the movement, Italian jurisprudence is built on civil law rather than the common law of the Anglo-American type, meaning that in Italy a lower court could disagree with the interpretation of a higher court in the application of the law. This proved to be the case in the 1965 decision. Having lost his appeal, DeMarchi was again brought to trial in Florence in October 1965, convicted, and fined $100. Matteotti likewise lost and paid a fine.

In March 1969, DeMarchi and his National Council, frustrated in an eighteen-year effort to change the law, but responsive to prevalent disappointment in the unyielding position of Pope Paul VI in his encyclical of 1968 and confident that they had the support of the majority of the people and the press, decided to offer Church and State an ultimate challenge. The AIED opened a public birth control clinic in Rome, with the cooperation of four physicians. Italy's first, the clinic on the Via Toscana offered a range of conventional family planning services—gynecological, psychiatric, and contraceptive counseling. Among other methods, the clinic provided free samples of vaginal diaphragms and prescriptions for oral contraceptives.

The Solicitor's Office of the Republic was quick to take offense. The clinic opened on March 14 and on March 25 the Attorney of the Republic issued a denunciation of DeMarchi for violation of Article 553 and called on the Pretore (judge) of Rome for a ruling. The Pretore proved to be sympathetic to the question of whether the Mussolini law was constitutional and suspended prosecution of DeMarchi in May 1970, asking the Constitutional Court for a new decision.

The high court joined DeMarchi's case with one pending against Virginio Bertinelli, former AIED president and former deputy. He had been charged in Viterbo in April 1969, with inciting the public to prevent procreation by publishing an Italian translation of a University of Chicago study, *Responsible Parenthood*. This was a scientific publication, and was permissible under the Constitutional Court's 1965 decision.

DeMarchi and his young Socialist attorney, Giorgio Moscon, prepared their case well, basing it on a whole series of rights guaranteed by the Constitution of the Republic. They had the assistance of Luke Lee, professor of law at Tufts University in Medford, Massachusetts, who provided a brief showing that the Republic of Italy had incorporated in its constitution certain international conventions, stating that planned parenthood is a basic human right. Likewise, the AIED marshaled documentation of the population explosion, illegal abortion, increased unemployment, increase of pollution, and other adverse factors related to overpopulation.

DeMarchi and Bertinelli presented their case before the fifteen judges making up the high court on February 24, 1971. Justice now moved more swiftly; on March 18, the Constitutional Court handed down its decision.

The *Corriere Della Sera*, Italy's largest daily newspaper, summed up the result in the first sentence of its page-one story the same day: "Luigi DeMarchi has made it!"

The Court declared the infamous Mussolini law to be a violation of the Constitution's guarantee of free expression of thought. The decree covered other issues, but that was the nub of the matter. Article 553 was abolished; null and void!

The Court reasoned this way: the original purpose of the law was to support the Fascist policy of population expansion— "numbers mean power." This purpose had "ceased to be valid." ". . . The problem of limiting births has, at the present time in history, taken on such importance . . . it is impossible to consider that . . . publicity on behalf of birth-control practices is to be looked upon as an offense against public morals."

As for the protection of public morals, which the Court had interpreted before as the purpose of Article 553, other provisions of the Penal Code adequately provided for this, as for example in the laws against obscene acts, publications, and performances.

As for constitutional guarantees of the protection of maternal and child health, the Court held that Article 553 violated, rather than supported, these purposes, in view of the damage to health brought about by too-frequent births and frequent illegal abortions. In fact, public information on birth control contributed to healthy motherhood, it ruled.

In the case of DeMarchi, involving the organization of the birth control clinic, the court ruled that Article 553 violated the constitutional guarantee of freedom of association. In the case of Bertinelli, science had a right to do research and communicate its findings.

The Foreign Press Club in Rome, the day after the court's announcement, invited DeMarchi to hold a press conference dealing with the significance of the decision. Most Italian newspapers published his opening statement that "the Court's decision, seen in an historical and scientific perspective, appears the most important legislative reform made in Italy during this century. It eliminates unwanted prolificity and removes a prohibitive obstacle to the solution of all major national and international problems—from war to hunger, from mass abortion to illegitimate birth, from chronic unemployment to mass emigration, from the social degradation of women to pollution, from the forced labor of children to the multiplication of parasitic bureaucracy."

In broad outline, including the frequent encounters with police, courts, and Church, as well as rivalry and contention within the birth control organization, the DeMarchi story repeated that of Margaret Sanger. Her crusade had reached its climax in the United States Circuit Court of Appeals decision overturning the Comstock law (the case of the United States versus One Package of Japanese Pessaries, 1936). The judicial issues were somewhat different, since the American case was based on the right of physicians to disseminate contraceptive devices and information, implying the reciprocal right of patients to receive advice and treatment.

There was an extralegal exception: the IPPF did not invite the AIED back into its high, international realm, although the relationship of individual officers did become friendly. The IPPF had recognized Mrs. Olivetti's organization.

The Italian birth controllers, other than Mrs. Olivetti, fully recognized the catalytic action of Clarence Gamble in his modest support, continuing through the Pathfinder Fund after his death in 1966. As DeMarchi said:

Pathfinder support and solidarity were a decisive factor in this great Italian victory. It was Dr. Clarence Gamble who first helped us in 1956 in our initial efforts to challenge the law by opening the first Italian center of planned parenthood assistance, and it was still Pathfinder which, over the years, maintained its friendly confidence in the DeMarchis and AIED in their darkest and loneliest moments.

DeMarchi, a realist, appraised the judicial victory as but the first step toward real success. The medical profession in Italy was, and still is, backward in *il controllo delle nascite*. Following the decision, he said, it was now up to the Ministry of Health to undertake a birth control information program, up to universities and medical schools to teach birth control to their students, and up to Parliament to legislate free contraception for the entire population. And beyond all this lay the need to motivate that population, both men and women, to keep procreation within the bounds of the two-child, zero-population-growth family.

To save Italian male pride, DeMarchi suggested pursuit of a new strategy emphasizing sexual prowess and not high fertility as the true expression of *machismo*, and including responsibility toward the woman as part of the "good" male. The new slogan would be "Full man, full father, full dinner pail." But the only free love Dr. DeMarchi officially promoted was married love free of unwanted pregnancies.

part 5 "there isn't time... in one lifetime"

chapter 24   Ebb Tide

Clarence Gamble enjoyed life but not good health. Blessed with a stupendous flow of energy and a compulsive need to master the situation at hand, Gamble was destined to live beyond his constitutional means much of his life, sustained by his determination to prevail over extrinsic circumstances and events quite beyond his control.

The Gambles' family doctor in Pasadena was one of the first to suggest that Clarence was not robust, when he advised the youth to drop out of track at Occidental, on the basis that running the mile was too much of a strain on his heart.

Gamble, while occasionally tempted, found tobacco and alcohol too potent for him. He was forced to recognize that coffee, tea, and even cocoa and chocolate were overstimulating to his nerves or irritating to his gastro-intestinal tract. Balancing these inadequacies against the man's astonishing capacity for activity, mental and physical, indoors and out, the biographer senses an inner struggle to achieve equilibrium necessarily waged at some cost to the organism. He seemed to be continually testing himself up to, and sometimes beyond, his breaking point. Simply to catalogue the less commonplace of Gamble's medical diagnoses is to set him apart from ordinary individuals, most of whom expect or, at any rate, encounter their share of illnesses; angina pectoris; catarrhal jaundice; chronic lymphocytic leukemia, deafness (requiring a hearing aid); fever of unknown origin; seven fractures, including suspected skull fracture; gallstones; hiatus hernia; kidney stone; mental depression; peptic ulcer; pneumonia; pulmonary embolism; thrombophlebitis; typhoid fever; urinary tract infection.

It is remarkable that a man carrying such a heavy burden of pathology and disability including all the complications of leukemia should not only impress others with his vigor and enthusiasm, but survive beyond the normal life expectancy for American males, to the age of seventy-two and a half years, and remain active until four months before his death.

In the face of all this, Gamble maintained a determined optimism, the more remarkable because his medical training prevented him from indulging in self-deception about his health. Gamble was hospitalized twenty or more times and in many different places—San Francisco, Colorado Springs, Stockbridge (Massachusetts), Philadelphia, Boston, North Conway (New Hampshire), and the Virgin Islands. However, Massachusetts General Hospital, where he had trained as a physician, provided the principal stage for his various patient roles. From 1922 to 1966, he was hospitalized fifteen times in this great teaching hospital of Harvard.

As recounted earlier, Gamble's first twenty-nine days as a patient in M.G.H. were in 1922, the result of his airplane accident. The accident became a reference point in attempts to explain the energy deficit he suffered for years to come; some observers were inclined to blame a brain concussion as the primary source of his difficulty in maintaining a regular work and social life, but the considered judgment of some who knew him before and after the

accident was that whatever central nervous system damage occurred simply served to aggravate a pre-existing tendency toward
nervous fatigue.

The record shows that Gamble was vulnerable to stress during
his first year in Harvard Medical School and thereafter. Among
other things, he experienced end-of-the-winter episodes of
"epigastric discomfort." In retrospect, his doctors identified these
as peptic ulcer, but no diagnosis was made at the time. Typical of
ulcer, his stomach pains came two or three hours after meals, and
were relieved by food. Notwithstanding its gross physical man-
ifestations, peptic ulcer is often closely identified in psychosomatic medicine with emotional stress.

Following the airplane accident, Gamble avoided hospitalization until, at the University of Pennsylvania, Dr. A. N. Richards
recommended that he go to the Austen Riggs Center in
Stockbridge for psychiatric evaluation in 1928. The attending
psychiatrist apparently associated Gamble's fatigue syndrome
with his head injury and meanwhile put him down as a perfec-
tionist. Nothing of clinical interest emerged in Gamble's happy
marriage and family life. In the spring of 1932, he contracted
infectious hepatitis. Some three or four months later, his epigastric distress became more severe, and he was admitted to the
Hospital of the University of Pennsylvania with "severe upper
right quadrant pain made worse by respiration." His gallbladder,
containing stones, was removed and a prophylactic appendec-
tomy performed. At the time, the surgeon noted a bump, or
deformity, on the duodenum, suggestive evidence of a healed
peptic ulcer just beyond the stomach. It was during these years
that Clarence Gamble began living from time to time on milk, a
diet rigidly followed during the usual recurrences of his symptoms in the spring and also, thanks to Thermos jugs, during his
many travels.

In 1937 the Gambles moved from Philadelphia to Milton during
one of the most active periods in the development of fieldwork in
birth control, a time when he repeatedly locked horns with officials of the American Birth Control League. In 1939, Dr. Edward

D. Churchill, Harvard surgeon and an old medical school classmate, admitted Clarence Gamble to Massachusetts General Hospital with a suspected "penetrating, leaking duodenal ulcer." Gamble remained in the hospital twenty-one days and was discharged as "improved and recovered."

Hearing that Gamble was in the hospital, Mrs. Cecil Damon of the Birth Control Clinical Research Bureau in New York wrote his secretary, Miss Sue Search:

Somehow or other none of us can imagine Doctor Gamble lying quietly in bed being a good patient so we are all prepared for that agile mind of his to be checking back on the things he has asked us to be thinking of or doing in the past year and finding ourselves on the carpet for our sins of omission. Please take his little black book away from him during this period!

The following spring, in 1943, Gamble returned to M.G.H. for nine days, this time in the hands of an internist, who appraised Gamble:

. . . He is a terribly tense person with a curious superficial outer calm. His arguments are serious and facile. The fact remains that he has a bad and frequently recurrent ulcer. It should be operated on by election once this episode is over.

The doctor discussed the desirability of surgery with Gamble, but the latter, in view of the possibility of recurrence, was not persuaded. The discharge note read: "Result and disposal: Poor—practically against medical advice."

Gamble enjoyed his wartime period of teaching physical diagnosis at Harvard, and managed to put three and a half years between himself and M.G.H., until late 1946. The admission note read: "This is the fifth Phillips House admission of a 52-year-old physician who is sent in with a diagnosis of a penetrating duodenal ulcer."

It was in this period that Gamble gave himself, and also taught some of the children to give him, injections of demerol. This new synthetic drug had been advocated as a substitute for morphine on the claim that it was a non-habit forming narcotic, as Paul de

Kruif reported in one of Gamble's favorite magazines, *The Reader's Digest*. Demerol, however, ultimately proved to be habit-forming. Looking back, Dr. Walter Gamble was amazed that his father did not become addicted.

The internist noted of Gamble:

> He still continued to have several flare-ups a year, generally precipitated by traveling, over-work, and emotional strain. These are generally controlled by one or two weeks' bed rest and copious milk. . . . Three weeks ago (he was on a trip, under heavy work load, and under much pressure) . . . he started having epigastric pains necessitating consumption of quart of milk at night. After several days this increased to a three-quart pain a night. . . . Pain usually worse at night, occurring at fifteen minutes. During the daytime it occurs every two or three hours. . . . Uses no coffee or tea. Two or three cigarets a year. Very little alcohol.

Gamble's rare cigarette-smoking was a matter of family amusement, as Walter recalled. In tense situations, while traveling and maneuvering the children and baggage, Gamble would take out a pack, light a cigarette, puff it for a few moments, snuff it out, carefully remove the ash, and restore it to the pack for later use. He explained to Walter that it helped him think. In this way, he carried around a little-used but very stale pack of recycled cigarettes.

A radiologist confirmed the diagnosis: "The duodenal cap is deformed. In the lesser curvature there is a fairly well defined crater."

Gamble's physical examination again contained mention of inner anxiety: "A well-developed white man, quite normal, highly apprehensive person who disguises his apprehension about 95 percent."

The internist's discharge note, after ten days, stated: "Symptoms have subsided and patient is going home. I have advised vagotomy. I am sure this would be refused. I am also sure there will be ulcer recurrences."

Gamble did refuse an operation and was back in the spring, five months later. This time, he was given no choice. There had been a severe flare-up when he became fatigued by preparations for a trip to California and another when he went without food for several hours while preparing for a fluoroscopic examination of his G.I. tract. On a steady diet of up to five quarts of milk a day, he was gaining weight.

The admission history observed, "He speaks in a bland and unconcerned manner." But the operation, performed on April 18, 1947, was a big one, requiring transfusion of two pints of blood and necessitating twenty-six days in the hospital.

The ulcer operation was a success, as Gamble acknowledged. Rather promptly, however, he ran into difficulty from a new quarter. It was in 1947 that he first suffered from angina pectoris.

He apparently received his first treatment for this affliction from his family physician in Milton, in the early 1950s. The main source of information about Gamble's angina pectoris is his own summary written in 1962. He first noticed a feeling of pressure in his chest when he was fifty-three, while playing tennis, a sport he casually pursued as a family game. "Tennis became impossible," he said and noted:

> Chief complaint. A sense of pressure and discomfort in the chest appearing with exercise especially after meals and relieved by nitroglycerin. It was not a sharp pain and has not radiated to arm, shoulder, or back. It resembles the sensation after a 100-yard dash in youth.

His electrocardiograms and blood pressure were normal, but the chest pains became more frequent as the years passed.

Between the ulcer operation of 1947 and the next hospitalization of major consequence, in 1964, Gamble was an M.G.H. patient on five difference occasions, three of them only one-day stays. One of these, in August 1949, was due to a "pain of unknown etiology."

The next three hospital admissions resulted from Gamble's established capacity for overdoing outdoor sports, angina pectoris not withstanding. He broke the tibia and fibia in his right leg while skiing at Jackson, New Hampshire, in 1952. After two weeks in the North Conway Memorial Hospital, he received follow-up treatment at M.G.H. on three different occasions the following summer—a season of dragging a cast about, before going to Asia in November. He completed two trips to India, in the next two years without any mishap of note.

For the next seven years he avoided the M.G.H. wards, but did manage to get in several days in a hospital at St. Thomas, the Virgin Islands, in 1958, when he was sixty-four and on a winter vacation with Sarah Gamble and Dr. Stuart and Emily Mudd. On the beach, a scuba diver approached them and asked if they would like to try diving on the coral beds, not far from shore. He would rent them the mask and air tank. Mudd said no, he had no experience. Neither did Gamble, but he said he would try it. His small mustache proved his undoing. The mask leaked around it, he breathed in water, panicked, breathed in more water, thrashed about, and sank. "He was cyanotic by the time we got him on the shore," said Mudd, who took Gamble back to his hotel room. In the middle of the night Mrs. Gamble called Mudd to tell him that Clarence had a bad cough and pain in his chest. Mudd took him to the local hospital with an acute pneumonia, and, fearing Gamble might have a heart attack, stayed with him in the hospital until he recovered. It always mystified the Mudds, they said, that Gamble could be so conservative in some ways—for example, in his financial affairs—and take such physical risks in sports.

Four and a half years passed. Then, at 2 a.m. on January 22, 1964, Gamble woke up at home in Milton with a sharp pain in his upper right abdomen. Sarah was in New York, to attend a board meeting of the Experiment for International Living. Gamble had no gallbladder or appendix, and it was not the typical ulcer pain. It gradually diffused through the entire right flank. The pain was dull but steady and intense, waxing and waning every ten minutes or so. He relieved it some by taking codeine and keeping his right hip flexed. When it was time to get up, he called his son, Walter, and said he thought he might have a kidney stone and was going into Massachusetts General.

Gamble came into the emergency ward at 9:10 o'clock that morning. To a urologist, he complained of "a post-operative problem." His presenting symptoms did not seem to relate, though, to past problems. In spite of his many surgical scars, much X-rayed abdomen and chest, and history of different sources of pain, he and his doctors would quite promptly identify the cause of his pain as a kidney stone.

Far more arresting was the finding, in the course of the physical examination, of "large juicy nodes," or swollen lymph glands, in Gamble's neck, armpits, and left groin, as well as above the collarbone. They were soft and painless. To the mind of the clinician, such a finding immediately suggests leukemia. On the other hand, palpation disclosed no enlargement of the liver or spleen.

Laboratory tests confirmed the diagnosis of chronic lymphocytic (or lymphatic) leukemia.

Leukemia—in lay terms, a "blood cancer"—occurs in several different forms, acute and chronic, all involving a progressive weakness, fatigue, pallor, lack of appetite, and weight loss. Chronic lymphocytic leukemia occurs mainly between the ages of fifty and seventy, and is three times more common in males. In the long run, the proliferation of lymph cells is considered irreversible and fatal, but there may be remissions, arising spontaneously or as the result of treatment and lasting for months or years. The average life expectancy from the onset of symptoms was then usually given as 3.5 years, but one out of four C.L.L. patients lived from five to ten years. During the next two years, Gamble was treated as an M.G.H. out-patient, with the antileukemic drugs, prednisone and cytoxan, and an occasional blood transfusion. He attempted to take his poor prognosis in stride and, for the most part, did rather well until early 1966. He discussed his condition with Walter and Sarah, but said little or nothing about it to others. At one time, he told David Burleson, Pathfinder Fund director of field services, when discussing what he wanted to do: "There isn't time . . . not enough time in one lifetime." Not one prone to misgivings, all he seemed to ask was more cooperation from the world around him in his will to go on.

The years 1964 and 1965 were intensely busy ones for him in the promotion of his IUD program and his scrambling for Lippes loops. Nor did he lose the puckish sense of humor that he reserved mainly for members of the family and friends. When gasoline rationing was enforced during World War II, he had bought a motorcycle with a side car to commute from Milton to Harvard. When it came time to go to Maine in the summer of 1965, he told Sarah he was going to ride a motorcycle to Kennebec Point, a one-hundred-seventy-five-mile trip, and she could follow along behind him. Concerned for her husband's life, Mrs. Gamble called their family physician and said, "I have a motorcycle problem."

"Tell your son to sell it, or chain it up in the attic," said the doctor. "As a coroner, I've seen too much of what happens to motorcyclists."

"It isn't my son, it's my husband!"

Dr. Tudor said he would come over and talk to Dr. Gamble.

"The next day," Sarah recalled, "as we started for Maine, Clarence mounted the motorcycle and told me to follow him. We were stunned but didn't know what to do but comply. He drove to a motorcycle sales garage in Brookline and emerged on foot, saying not one word. Nor did I, and we continued to Maine."

He found another opportunity to demonstrate his determination to do as he pleased in 1965, at the International Conference on Family Planning programs in Geneva cosponsored by the Population Council and Ford Foundation. All recognized birth control agencies were invited, and the Pathfinder received an invitation to send one person. Gamble gave it to Burleson, who deferred to his employer, suggesting it would be more appropriate for him to be present. Gamble insisted Burleson use the invitation and himself elected to go without one. Pacing up and down the corridors of the Intercontinental Hotel, outside of the meeting room but not trying to go in, Gamble made secretarial staff members of the Pop Council so uneasy they spoke about it to Dr. Notestein, Council president. "Let him come in," said Notestein. Later, in a discussion of the increasing financial resources available for international birth control, the chairman called on each of the many birth control organizations represented to give the group an estimate of its annual expenditures. Asked to state the Pathfinder Fund budget, Gamble replied: "I haven't added it up lately."

Clarence and Sarah decided to spend Christmas of 1965 with Dick, his wife Frances, and their children in Lagos, Nigeria, where Dick was establishing needed industries and management training programs in Nigeria, as part of his interest in economic development in underdeveloped countries. Gamble said it would give him a chance to see some people at the University of Ibadan about family planning. On the way back, they could talk to the DeMarchis in Rome and visit birth controllers in London.

It was a difficult trip, more so for Sarah than for Clarence. In the first place, she said, in view of his health, that they should fly first class "for the extra bit of comfort." Not until they boarded the plane did she discover Clarence had booked her first class and himself tourist. This meant sitting apart throughout the trip, except on the Lagos-Rome flight, where a perceptive stewardess ordered him to go forward and occupy the empty seat beside his wife.

On the way out to Lagos, angina seized him in the airport at Paris. With no attendant in sight, Sarah found a baggage cart and pushed him into the terminal. This was something she secretly feared—that someplace, sometime, he would overtax his heart. They had arrived from the United States at the Orly Airport and were settling down to await their flight for Lagos with the help of his nitroglycerin pills, when an attendant, checking their tickets, told them the Lagos flight left from LeBourget Airport, on the other side of the city and more than an hour and a half away by bus, or a good hour by taxi. The attendant hustled them, bag and baggage, into a cab and they made the connection with only minutes to spare.

The visit with Dick and his family did Clarence good, hot weather notwithstanding, Sarah noted. The trip home, via Rome and London, went smoothly until they arrived in New York. The first-class and tourist passengers deplaned by separate exits. When Sarah got off the plane and went to the gate, there was no Clarence. Alarmed after a few minutes, she spoke to an attendant, who went into the airplane and found Gamble reclining in his seat, taking a tourist-class nap.

While Gamble was obviously aging and had lost weight, he struck the family as in relatively good shape, considering his insidious disease. In February, he and Sarah went to St. Croix in the Virgin Islands with the Mudds, and then on to Puerto Rico for another look-see at family planning. The trip did not go well—at St. Croix he was upset that he did not have a room with a view of the harbor and he was able to get in only one good sail.

In mid-March, Gamble had a little chill and came home from the Pathfinder office with a fever. He felt weak and depressed. The fever, of a type known as "saw tooth," continued during the next ten days, with temperature normal in the morning but spiking to 102 or 103 degrees in the evenings. Antibiotics did not help. His hematologist brought Gamble into the hospital for more intensive study of this "fever of unknown origin." The kinds of diseases one might pick up in the tropics, such as malaria, hepatitis, and amebiasis, had to be considered, although Gamble had used powdered milk and boiled water, ate only cooked foods, was not exposed to insect bites, and had no fever or diarrhea in his recent travels.

The hospital work-up continued for five days, revealing nothing to pinpoint the fever. The X-ray examination showed his spleen to be enlarged. Such an enlargement could have been caused by malaria, but more probably was due to his leukemia. A urinary tract infection was suspected, but there was no confirming test. After two days of normal temperature, Gamble felt better and he was discharged.

He was back in the hospital in April, hardly three weeks later for bone marrow aspiration. "He has had daily spiking fever now for over a month," said the admission note. The hematologist doubted that it was a manifestation of leukemia. He had taken the patient off the anti-leukemic drug, cytoxan, thinking it might be the culprit, but the fever persisted and this treatment was renewed. The white blood cell count was elevated to 65,000. The liver, enlarged, now came under suspicion. Did it harbor the infection? A bacteriologist was called in consultation. Gamble told the doctors that he had typhoid fever twice in his childhood, and had been inoculated for typhus, typhoid, and cholera just before going to Nigeria.

Physical examination showed his weight to be 122, down from 135 a year before and from a high of 165 in previous years.

Gamble told the house officer who examined him that he had taken the anti-malaria drug, chloroquin, while in Nigeria and it was noted: "Patient trying desperately to believe he has malaria."

Not because there was any chance of malaria, but to please the patient, it was recommended that chloroquin be given should Gamble run a fever again. On April 21, Gamble's temperature rose abruptly and he insisted on having the anti-malaria drug. The bacteriologist reported no malaria parasites were seen in bone marrow tests. The doctors agreed on doing a lumbar puncture to obtain spinal fluid to determine whether there was an infection of the central nervous system; none was found: "Nothing has turned up to find a cause for his fever other than CLL . . . In the meantime, Dr. Gamble is taking one gram of chloroquin on his own. He is treating himself for possible malaria and amebiasis."

His fever definitely dropped on April 24, following three days of chloroquin. The hematologist now was more disposed to continue this drug, not because it was curing Gamble of malaria but because it apparently did have some subtle effect. The drug is beneficial not only in malaria but in amebic dysentery.

On April 25, the results of a blood test were disturbing. The white cell count had fallen to 42,000—that was to the good—but the red cells were down to 8.2 grams—this was dangerously low. The doctor ordered 200 milligrams of Delastestrol to help stimulate hemoglobin synthesis, cut back on the dosage of cytoxan, and continued the chloroquin—the patient was still without fever.

Relief of the fever did not, however, improve Gamble's mental depression. He complained of not being able to use his mind, to think and do his work. A psychiatrist was called in consultation.

The psychiatrist interviewed Gamble the next day: "Tears from time to time, but he says that he is somewhat less depressed than a few days ago. He ascribes it to lack of fever. At this point then it appears that he is emerging from depression and therefore antidepressant is not needed. Also possibility of induction of hyperactivity by antidepressant, since there is a previous history. . . . Important meeting on Sunday. He and the wife would like a tranquilizer for the night before; when he might become keyed up. Denies suicidal thought. Determined to go home now. Would let him go today."

The recommendation was carried out on the eleventh day of his fourteenth admission to M.G.H. Gamble went home, without fever and still taking chloroquin.

It did him good to get home from the hospital. In fact, he did well for three days, or until the day after the meeting. The purpose of the meeting at the Gamble home in Milton, on Sunday, April 28, was to introduce Dr. Elton Kessel, who was soon to become the new executive director of the Pathfinder Fund, to the Board of Directors and the Advisory Council. Although he had told Edna McKinnon it was the happiest day of his life when his children had started arranging the continuation of Pathfinder, the meeting could hardly have been anything but depressing to Clarence Gamble. The frontiersman, with his independence of action, his control over decision making, is seldom at ease or even interested in the more formalized consequences of his trail blazing. The more active interest and participation of Sarah, his children and their spouses, who made up the Board of Directors, had led Pathfinder into new policy directions not altogether compatible with Clarence's "one man band" mode of achieving his successes. He had surrendered to the often-recommended formation of a committee of experts to advise them. He also had acceded to the need of establishing a consolidated headquarters for the Pathfinder Fund but deplored the expense of furniture and carpeting. He had submitted to pressure to find someone who would become administrative head of the Pathfinder staff, after telling Mrs. June Weiss: "Why get somebody else when we have you?" Repeatedly, he talked to members of his small staff in terms of what his children thought should be done, to a point where Mrs. Weiss asked him: "What do *you* want to happen?" "I have to be happy with what *they* want," he replied.

Gamble sat on the sofa in his living room during the April 28 meeting. To the Mudds, who had seen him in February, he never had looked more frail. Physicians present, such as Drs. John Meier and Alan Guttmacher, had not been informed he had leukemia but guessed it. When the Mudds privately asked him pointed questions about his health, Gamble said, "I'd just rather not talk about it." They realized then, the last time they saw "Jim," that he was "no longer his own boss." It is hard for any man to surrender the hero's role for the sick role: it is equally difficult for the physician to become the patient. Sarah Gamble noticed that at lunch he smoked cigarettes and ate chocolate, in a desperate effort to keep himself stimulated until the meeting was over.

Stuart Mudd provided the keynote in this meeting. He thought the principal task of a new director would be to improve communications with other family planning and population control agencies. Gamble had never been able to do this, he said. The Agency for International Development now had Congressional authorization and appropriations to help underdeveloped countries reduce their birth rates, including the purchase of contraceptives for free distribution. The mission of the Pathfinder Fund was finding paths—"What we from the Middle West would call bird-dogging," said Mudd. "You find where the birds are; that's fine, but now AID is in the business of doing something about the birds once you have found them. AID seems to me to be your natural ally."

In the days following the meeting, Gamble's spiking fever returned, his condition worsened. His angina troubled him and he had no appetite. Chloroquin did not help, nor did cytoxan. Four nights later, he rose to go to the bathroom, lost his balance, and fell, breaking a rib on his left side. The family doctor strapped up his chest, but it remained painful and he stayed in bed, suffering from repeated chills and sweating. Consulting the hematologist, he returned on May 1 by ambulance to Massachusetts General Hospital for the fifteenth and last time.

Again, his presenting complaint was "fever of unknown origin, associated with chronic lymphatic leukemia." The note on the physical examination followed the ritualistic clinical first-impression pattern: "A thin, white, gray-haired man lying flat in bed, appears chronically ill." The patient was quite dehydrated; his weight had dropped to 116. His hemoglobin was 8.6 grams and white cell count was up to 74,000. His lymph nodes were large and moveable. His liver was three fingers down. "Depression continues severe and now pain from fractured rib brings an additional burden." There were consultations with the bacteriologist, psychiatrist, and chest physiotherapist. To the latter, the attending physician wrote: "Please help patient breathe properly to avoid atelectasis and pneumonia within the limits of a reasonable amount of discomfort." Then the next day: "I have decided to treat more vigorously with intravenous cytoxan, as well as following temperature, blood, liver size, and uric acid closely. His CCL with rising WBC despite oral cytoxan is clearly out of control."

Yet on May 10, the doctor noted that Gamble's mood had improved. He smiled, laughed, and volunteered a little joke. On May 11, however, his appetite declined and he again became depressed. These fluctuations continued from day to day. At times, rales could be heard in the base of his right lung and an x-ray film showed "a very poorly defined area of increased density in the right mid-lung field . . . suggests the possibility of a pulmonary infarct." Despite the rib fracture, his left chest was clear.

The hematologist decided to start his patient on Vancristine, a new drug with some effect on chronic lymphocytic leukemia. After three days of this treatment the lymph nodes, production site of the runaway lymphocytes, were considerably diminished in size. On May 14, Gamble was able to walk the length of the corridor without staggering or feeling weak. Also, his fever subsided, and he was in better spirits.

Then, on May 16, the bacteriologist reported finding *Staphylococcus albus* in a urine culture. This is one of the lesser pathogens among the large and virulent family of staph bacteria, but it occasionally causes urinary tract infections. At last, it appeared, a source of infection and an explanation of the fever was at hand.

"Another problem has arisen," read the report. A repeat chest film showed the hazy density of six days ago in the right lung had become smaller and denser, "quite suggestive of a pulmonary infarct." On physical examination that night, "there is a little edema of the lower left leg and fullness of the veins not matched by the right leg. This certainly could represent phlebitis. I am not sure what to do at the moment. Anti-coagulant therapy is fraught with danger in a patient with CLL and a low platelet count. On the other hand, I doubt that he could tolerate a venous ligation. Will seek advice." Meanwhile Gamble was suffering a pleuritic pain in his left chest! "What do we do here with an elderly man with CLL, low platelets, and very debilitated?"

Another consultant on May 19 agreed both with the findings and the judgment, and added: "The outlook seems grim. . . ." The hematologist added on May 20: "We have agreed to do nothing further at the moment. The prognosis . . . is . . . poor."

On May 24, he recorded: "Patient has been doing a little better with less fever and an improvement in morale over the past two days. Then this morning at 5 AM he was found lying down in the doorway of his room bleeding from the nose and lip. He was conscious but a bit confused apparently and admitted falling after getting out of bed to go to the bathroom across the corridor. Evidently vital signs have been unchanged. He went back to sleep."

This last hospitalization dragged on for fifty-four days as various Gamble organs made their concessions to the indignities of age, disease, and disability. Following the fall, his angina returned. Sarah, visiting him, noticed his memory was poor. At night, he had a dry, hacking cough and felt short of breath, with a continual pain in his chest, probably from the pulmonary infarction. His wife and family had tried to buoy Clarence up by making him, while in the hospital, a pivotal point in Gamble activities. Richard had returned from Nigeria and coincidentally entered M.G.H. for the surgical repair of a hernia; he was still in the hospital when his father left. Robert, having just graduated from the Episcopal Theological Seminary in Cambridge, arranged to have his ordination in the Protestant Episcopal Church in the M.G.H. chapel, so his father could look on from his wheelchair.

Walter had come over from the Children's Hospital regularly to see his father and consult with the doctors, well aware that his father's care was taxing some of the best clinical brains of Boston. The psychiatrist, called in from time to time to consider Gamble's mental depression, told Walter: "There is no psychiatric problem. The man faces reality. Reality is his problem."

In June, the Vancristine therapy seemed to be taking hold, and Gamble showed some improvement, but his white cells were up to 160,000 with 97 percent lymphocytes. It was now proposed to try anti-lymphocytic serum, a rabbit serum, if the sensitivity tests were negative. They were, "There is some risk here of increasing angina as the result of the serum injection but he knows this and is willing to go through with it in the hope of a later general improvement." Gamble received injections in right and left thighs on June 14. Promptly, his temperature rose, both thighs pained him, and the doctor found him in tears. Demerol comforted him, but the next day his white cells were up to 175,000, and he had a pleuritic pain in his right chest. On June 16, it was noted: "We have achieved no effect with the preparation of anti-lymphocytic serum." The serum fever subsided on one day and returned the second. The third day, there were signs of a new pulmonary embolism. Regularly, in this period Gamble's pulse was 120, abnormally fast. But fortunately his platelet count was up. The hematologist wanted to give another injection of the rabbit serum before the patient developed antibodies to it, but held back.

On June 24, the doctor recorded: "He wants to go home soon. More depressed and teary this morning. Decrease in his intellectual activity is what depressed him the most. . . . Anticipating discharge this week with joy. . . . Nursing care and hospital bed will be provided." The discharge sheet, on June 29, listed the principal and associated diagnoses—chronic lymphatic leukemia, urinary tract infection, pulmonary infarcts. It recommended continued treatment with seven different drugs, for his leukemia, his heart, his infection, and his anxiety. The patient's condition: "Improved."

On the way home from the hospital to Milton, he asked to be taken for a visit to the new Pathfinder office. Gamble sat in an aluminum chaise lounge. The main topic, Bob remembers, was a discussion of how to insure effective spending of the forthcoming federal funds soon to be invested in birth control. The pioneer days were over, the era of massive government spending had begun, something which he had always hoped would occur.

It is difficult to say when Gamble concluded that he was going to die. Before he left the hospital in June, he told Sarah that leukemia was "an easy way to go out." Not long after he got home, he said to Walter: "I don't have more than three months to live."

It was on this occasion, next to the last time that Walter saw his father alive, that Gamble asked him to make arrangements to give his body to Harvard Medical School, for use by the students in gross anatomy: "He said—well, he did not say it, he wrote it—he wanted to make one last contribution to science," Walter later recalled. Gamble was choked, tearful—"I never had seen him do that"—and could not control his voice. He wrote Walter a letter explaining what he wanted him to do. His body could go to Harvard. There would be no funeral. There could be a memorial service anywhere, anytime. He did not care what happened to his remains following dissection.

"It is actually a very fine thing and I recommend it," Walter said. "At the time of the loss of someone, all the decisions about casket and burial are out the window—It completely pulls the rug out from under excessive undertaker expenses—You are not swayed by grief, and so on—I wouldn't be surprised if he thought of all this, but he was not expressing it to me. He was a quiet person, and he was condemned for this sometimes—I suppose not completely unjustly."

Caring for a terminally ill patient at home and in bed is not an easy task, but as Judy said, "Mummy was magnificent." One thing Sarah did was order a sort of one-man escalator, actually a motorized chair lift that runs along the wall of the staircase, so that her husband could ride effortlessly between his second-floor bedroom and the first floor. It was a gadget that he would have loved, but it did not arrive in time.

Gamble's decision to go to Maine took Sarah by surprise. She was unaware that he had it in his mind until one night the nurse came to her and said that Dr. Gamble wanted to make a long-distance telephone call. At two o'clock in the morning, it struck the nurse that her patient must be out of his mind. But it was only eleven o'clock in California, and he wanted to talk to Edna McKinnon, who was in Carmel. "Do you know the telephone number?" Sarah asked. "Of course, I do, " he said. "It's an elephant with a pink rose behind its ear." The nurse now was sure that he was crazy; but his system for remembering phone numbers was familiar to Sarah. In a precise manner he associated each number with a consonant. He then added vowels to make a word or group of words which could then represent the number he wanted to remember. Such words often yielded absurd images, easily recalled, which could be decoded into the original number. He had Mrs. McKinnon's number, and Sarah overheard him tell her: "I am going to Maine."

Sarah knew her husband too well to dismiss his yearning for their cottage at Kennebec Point. She now began two or three days of hectic preparations. They would need a hospital bed, at least two nurses, and a small drug store of medicines and medical equipment, as well as a communicating link between M.G.H. and a local doctor in Bath, the nearest town. Clarence requested that Walter build a ramp for him to be wheeled down to the beach. At first, Gamble wanted to go in an ordinary station wagon, but Sarah overruled him. They would hire an ambulance. At one moment, before plans were complete, he told her: "Call the ambulance." She thought he was in a crisis, and wanted to return to M.G.H., but found he was merely impatient to head north.

At last, on Monday, July 11, twelve days after he had left M.G.H., they began the trek to Maine. Sara, Robert, and one nurse rode in the ambulance with Clarence and the driver. The nurse's twelve-year-old son and a volunteer state policeman followed in Sarah's car. Walter and his wife Anne had gone up earlier that weekend with medical equipment and medicines, and to construct the ramp, and ready the house.

The three-hour trip went smoothly. The ambulance driver, when he returned to Milton, told Mrs. Helen Davidson that he never had seen anyone look so relieved as Dr. Gamble did when he arrived at the cottage. Contentment replaced anxiety in his thin, tired face.

Few individuals find it within their power to control the circumstances of their death, in a place and at a time of their own choosing, with people they know and love around them. The majority simply disappear into hospitals and nursing homes, in a vast, impersonal, system for disposal of the terminally ill; and many when death comes, face it alone, meeting social death before biological death, rejected by members of their family and put aside as technical failures by doctors and nurses. But not Clarence Gamble. Stubbornly insistent on mastering his environment, if not his destiny, he managed to control his dying while surrendering to death.

One could hardly imagine a more peaceful place to come to rest. Kennebec Point, on Georgetown Island, is a typically rugged slice of the Maine coast, bounded by the deep estuaries of the Kennebec and Sheepscot rivers, a shoreline that is by turns rocky, wooded, marshy, and sandy. The Gambles began coming there after Judy married Stanley Kahrl—the Kahrls had summered there for many years. The family bought two cottages not far away across the marsh from the Kahrl house. Bob shared his parent's house.

The gray-shingled and white-trimmed cottage, where Sarah continues to summer, has a modesty becoming the Gambles. It was of a kind any upper middle-class family could, and indeed many New England academic families do, afford. It had a living room, sunroom, bedroom, two small, old-fashioned bathrooms, and a small kitchen downstairs, with two tiny bedrooms upstairs.

The south, or front, side of the house overlooks Little Harbor, a shallow cove with a sandy beach bordered by rock ledges and dark green spruce trees. Farther out, Stage and Salter Islands bracket the seascape, crossed at a still greater distance by Seguin Island. Two lighthouses, on Seguin and Pond Island, complete the picture that, on any summer day and certainly in the course of any summer week, may range through bright sunlight and blue skies, dense fog down to the water, a wind-blown yellow haze, or dark squall clouds rolling over still darker currents and sharply contrasting white caps below. Maine waters and winds delight the sailor who does not mind the taste or the gritty feeling of salt water spray, or the visceral tension of navigating in tricky tidal currents through deep but rocky and often narrow channels. Transplanted from Lake Michigan, Clarence had loved sailing here with Stanley, and, when he was not sailing, simply sitting and gazing out to sea.

Gamble asked to have his hospital bed placed where he could command a view of the cove. But this meant that, lying in bed with head raised, he could not see what was going on in the living room behind him. He asked for a hemispherical mirror to be placed above the window, so he might have something approaching a 180-degree range of vision either fore or aft. One does not see a hemispherical mirror on every shopping trip in Maine, but Anne, Walter's wife went to Bath and returned with one.

Bob said that he would sit up with his father at night—a task of peculiar significance to him because, as the youngest, he had not come to understand his father, and "Daddy and I did not communicate very well." The two nurses split the daylight hours into two shifts. Sarah, quietly competent as always, saw that everything that had to be done was done. Sally was in Washington, planning to come up the next weekend. Dick was in Woods Hole

The cove at Kennebec Point, Maine

recuperating from his surgery. Walter had come and gone, promising to return the following Friday night. Stan was doing research in England, but Judy and the children and Anne and her children were there. Edna McKinnon was coming the next weekend.

The stage was set. No one thought of it as a death watch. Sarah had no sense of the end being close at hand, she said. The Maine air and his grandchildren seemed to have refreshed Clarence. It was a busy, active week, with grandchildren running in and out, cranking Granddaddy's hospital bed up and down at his suggestion, laughing, and chattering. Clarence watched them in the mirror, smiling; his voice was weak and he did not talk much. On Tuesday, the family wheeled him on a chaise lounge down to the water's edge on Walter's ramp, and he lay there content.

When his children were small, Gamble read to them. "He read aloud to us a great deal—I can still hear him," recalled Judy. "He would read *Microbe Hunters* and Mummy would read *Lorna Doone*." Now it was his turn to be read to. Sarah offered poetry and prose, mainly from the classics, even a bit of Chaucer. Jenny Kahrl, who was in the second grade and proud of her reading, sat beside her grandfather's bed reading some of her favorites, *Ferdinand the Bull*, and *Blueberries for Sal*.

Thursday was his last good day, and a memorable one in the minds of Judy and Bob, both of whom felt the drama of the event. "He really let go. He decided to let go. He hadn't done everything he wanted to do. There would never be enough time for that. . . . There was a surprising retention of his sense of humor until his physical state overtook him, and that was really, I guess, only in the last eighteen hours."

Judy described their last evening together:

"Then, at one point—he wasn't always very clear and I couldn't understand him—but he said something—he looked out at the ocean—and I heard him say something like, 'My ship is going out to sea,' or 'That is where I'll sail away.'

"Sailing was almost a religious experience for him . . . You put him in a boat and a sense of peace would come over him. It was extraordinary. It wouldn't always come over my mother when it was too windy.

"And that last evening we had with him, he was scarcely talking at all then, and we were talking about something particularly heartening. I can't remember what it was, but it was really quite exciting. Mainly Mummy, Bob, and I were talking and Daddy just listened, and he said very little, but it was a beautiful evening—that wonderful cove, it was full of water, the tide was very high, and I think the moon was full at that time, and the terns had come in chasing little herring, and all around they were circling . . . and then you hear them go plop in the water. They were feeding there, and we wheeled him out on the ramp Walter had made, toward the top of the dune. He always sat there in the evenings, and it was absolutely still in the lovely rosy sunset, with the terns flying around there."

What Bob heard his father say, when he had wheeled him out—*thought* he heard him say, for he, too, found Clarence's voice barely audible—and they paused to watch the black-capped terns diving into the minnow boil, was "Survival of the fittest."

There were unanswered questions here, but they did not matter. The next day, Friday, July 15, 1966, Clarence Gamble sank rapidly; he was not in pain; he was unconscious much of the time. At his request, they wheeled him out on the porch to take the sun, but when it grew windy, they brought him back in. In the late afternoon, Sarah was walking on the beach when the nurse called her in. Clarence again was unconscious.

Later, he roused himself and said, "I want to see Walter."

"He will be here at nine o'clock," Sarah told him. She had called Walter, and Bob, who had returned to Boston, to come at once. Sally and Dick were coming the next morning.

"I want it to be nine o'clock now," he said.

When nine o'clock and Walter and Bob did come, Clarence Gamble had gone. Impatient in death, his last whim denied him, still a little secretive, he had drifted away an hour or two before while Sarah read from their favorite poems. She did not think he was listening, but thought perhaps the sound of her voice might help him.

Index